In August 1966, The Black Monk of Pontefract began his reign of terror over the Pritchards, an ordinary English family. For three years the Pritchards were plagued by unidentifiable banging noises in the night. An inexplicable force overturned beds in which family members slept. And then there were the more and more frequent appearances of the huge black-robed figure throughout the house. Many objective witnesses testified to these bizarre events, but all attempts to exorcise the presence met with defeat. In May 1969, the "haunting" ceased as suddenly as it began.

Read this, and hundreds of other poltergeist cases in *Poltergeist!*

✦ The case on which William Blatty based *The Exorcist*

✦ Uri Geller and his poltergeist effects

✦ The poltergeist that claimed to be a kidnapped girl

✦ Frederick Bligh Bond and the Glastonbury Scripts

✦ Fodor's investigation of the talking mongoose

✦ The dracu that bit and scratched

✦ Robert Monroe and his "out-of-the-body" experiences

✦ Maria Ferreira, the girl who was driven to suicide

✦ The Scottish TV interviewer who saw a gnome

✦ David St. Clair's experience of a black magic curse

✦ Pilney's case of the haunted house of Athens

✦ The phantom drummer of Tedworth

About the Author

Colin Wilson, who lives in Cornwall, England, has written over fifty books on crime, philosophy and the occult, including the best-selling *The Outsider*, *The Occult* and *Mysteries*.

To Write to the Author

If you wish to contact the author or would like more information about this book, please write to the author in care of Llewellyn Worldwide, and we will forward your request. Both the author and publisher appreciate hearing from you and learning of your enjoyment of this book and how it has helped you. Llewellyn Worldwide cannot guarantee that every letter written to the author can be answered, but all will be forwarded. Please write to:

Colin Wilson
c/o Llewellyn Worldwide
P.O. Box 64383-883, St. Paul, MN 55164-0383, U.S.A.
Please enclose a self-addressed, stamped envelope for reply, or $1.00 to cover costs. If outside U.S.A., enclose international postal reply coupon.

Free Catalog from Llewellyn

For more than 90 years Llewellyn has brought its readers knowledge in the fields of metaphysics and human potential. Learn about the newest books in spiritual guidance, natural healing, astrology, occult philosophy and more. Enjoy book reviews, new age articles, a calendar of events, plus current advertised products and services. To get your free copy of the New Times, send your name and address to:

The Llewellyn New Worlds
P.O. Box 64383-883, St. Paul, MN 55164-0383, U.S.A.

Fate Presents

Poltergeist

A STUDY IN DESTRUCTIVE HAUNTING

COLIN WILSON

1993
Llewellyn Publications
St. Paul, Minnesota, 55164-0383, U.S.A.

FIRST LLEWELLYN EDITION, 1993

Cover Painting by N. Taylor Blanchard

Library of Congress Cataloging in Publication Data
Wilson, Colin, 1931–
    Poltergeist : a study in destructive haunting /
Colin Wilson.
        p.   cm. — (Fate presents)
    ISBN 0-87542-883-5 : $5.95
        1. Poltergeists. 2. Haunted houses. 3. Ghosts.
I. Title. II. Series.
BF1483.W54   1993   92-38152
133.1'4—dc20   CIP

Reprinted with minor revisions.
Originally published: New York: Putnam, 1981.
First Perigee printing, 1983

Llewellyn Publications
A Division of Llewellyn Worldwide, Ltd.
St. Paul, Minnesota 55164-0383, U.S.A.

ABOUT THE FATE PRESENTS SERIES

Since 1948, FATE magazine has brought true, documented reports of the strange and unusual to readers around the world. For more than four decades, FATE has reported on such subjects as UFOs and space aliens, Bigfoot, the Loch Ness monster, ESP, psychic powers, divination, ghosts and poltergeists, startling new scientific theories and breakthroughs, real magic, near-death and out-of-body experiences, survival after death, Witches and Witchcraft and many other topics that will astound your imagination.

FATE has revealed the fakers and the frauds and examined the events and people with powers that defy explanation. When you read it in FATE, you can be sure that the information is certified and factual.

One of the things that makes FATE special is the wide variety of authors who write for it. Some of them have numerous books to their credit and are highly respected in their fields of speciality. Others are plain folks—whose lives have crossed over into the world of the paranormal.

Now Llewellyn is publishing a series of books bearing the FATE name. You hold one such book in your hands. The topic of this book may be one of any of the subjects we've described or a variety of them. It may be a collection of authenticated articles by unknown writers or a book by an author of world-renown.

There is one thing of which you can be assured: the occurrences described in this book are absolutely accurate and took place as reported. Now even more people will be able to marvel at, be shocked by, and enjoy true reports of the strange and unknown.

ACKNOWLEDGEMENTS

Many people have provided me with invaluable assistance and information for this book. Nick Clark-Lowes, the librarian of the Society for Psychical Research, went to immense trouble to find for me information about the Bingen poltergeist, contacting Michael Goss on my behalf; he in turn went to considerable inconvenience to find the relevant passage in Fulda's *Annales* and to have it translated for me by Mrs. M. Duffield. Fr. Brocard Sewell, O. Carm, also translated for me some relevant passages from Grimm's *German Mythology*. Guy Playfair provided me with dozens of invaluable references. Joe Cooper kindly lent me the typescript of his book on the Cottingley fairies and has given me permission to quote from it. Dennis Stacey and Stephen Spickard have sent me quantities of interesting material from America, including the Chua case. Tony Britton pointed out to me the relevance of *A True Fairy Story* by Daphne Charters. Robert Cracknell provided me with invaluable assistance and advice in looking into the Croydon case, and Maurice Grosse's speculations and suggestions were most helpful. Leonard Boucher and Harold Phelps wrote down, at my request, personal experiences that I have used in the book. Stephen Jenkins always responded promptly and generously to queries about ley lines. My sister Susan provided me with material on the Billingham case and the Humber Stone. Mr. Thomas Cunniff provided invaluable material and advice during the compilation of this book. Finally, my thanks to Brian Marriner, an invaluable research assistant.

CONTENTS

ANALYTICAL LIST OF CONTENTS

"benevolent possession"? The riddle of multiple personality. Sally Beauchamp. The Teresita Basa murder case. The Louis Vivé case. Lurancy Vennum—the Watseka Wonder. Was Mary Roff a spirit or a secondary personality? The problem of reincarnation. The case of Jasbir. The case of Shanti Devi. The reincarnation of Kitty Jay. Cyril Burt's case of May Naylor. Jung's case of "Ivenes." The "higher personality." The "ladder of selves." Does the human mind have an attic as well as a cellar?

Chapter Three: Cases Ancient and Modern.

The haunted house on Cape Cod. The "Grand Piano smash." Why no disturbed adolescent? Do poltergeist cases need a "focus"? Sacred sites and the "earth force." Guy Underwood and his "Holy Lines." Alfred Watkins and leys. Phantom battles. The invisible elves of Pevensey Castle. The Ardachie Lodge haunting. Are ghosts and poltergeists the same thing? Pliny's case of the haunted house of Athens. The earliest poltergeist case on record. The Dagg poltergeist. Are poltergeists juvenile delinquents? The indiscreet poltergeist of Giraldus Cambrensis. The haunting of Anthoinette de Grolée. The case of Johannes Jetzer. The case of the "Bell Witch." The Grottendieck case. The talkative poltergeist of Mâcon. The phantom drummer of Tedworth. The Rambouillet case. The Epworth poltergeist. The "Cock Lane ghost." The Stockwell ghost. Angelique Cottin. Do poltergeists use electricity? The Phelps case.

Chapter Four: The Black Monk of Pontefract.

Chapter Five: Fairies, Elementals and Dead Monks.

The case of the Cottingley Fairies. Conan Doyle investigates. Do fairies really exist? The Scottish TV interviewer who saw a gnome. Marc Alexander's story of the pixie. Lethbridge's "elemental" on Skellig

Chapter Eight: Speculations and Conclusions.

This Book is Dedicated to
GUY PLAYFAIR

PREFATORY NOTE

In 1978, I was asked by Professor Richard Gregory (of the Brain and Perception Laboratory at Bristol University) to write an article for *The Oxford Companion to the Mind* on "Paranormal Phenomena and the Unconscious." I began the article by citing the case of "Philip, the invented ghost" (which is discussed in Chapter 6 of the present book), and then went on to argue that poltergeists are probably a creation of the unconscious mind. When Professor Gregory asked me where I thought they got their energy and how they used it, I had to admit I had no idea.

At the time I write this, *The Oxford Companion* has still not appeared in print. Which places me in the embarrassing position of having to admit that I now no longer agree with what I wrote there. I suspect I *do* now know where poltergeists get their energy, and even have some ideas about how they use it. This I owe largely to Guy Playfair (and I have explained how it came about in the chapter on the Black Monk of Pontefract). That is why I have dedicated this book to him.

Other Books by the Author
(Not Available from Llewellyn Publications)

Non-Fiction

The Outsider

Religion and the Rebel

The Age of Defeat

Encyclopaedia of Murder
  (with Pat Pitman)

The Strength to Dream

Origins of the Sexual Impulse

*Rasputin and the Fall of the
  Romanovs*

Brandy of the Damned
  (Essays on Music)

Beyond the Outsider

Eagle and Earwig (Essays on
  Books and Writers)

*Sex and the Intelligent
  Teenager*

*Introduction to the New
  Existentialism*

Poetry and Mysticism

A Casebook of Murder

*Bernard Shaw –
  A Reassessment*

New Pathways in Psychology

*Order of Assassins
  Mysteries*

A Book of Booze

The Occult

Strange Powers

The Geller Phenomenon

Starseekers

The War Against Sleep

The Craft of the Novel

The Genius of David Lindsay
  (with E. H. Visiak)

Men of Strange Powers

Frankenstein's Castle

The Quest for Wilhelm Reich

Fiction

Ritual in the Dark

Adrift in Soho

The Schoolgirl Murder Case

The Philosopher's Stone

The Mind Parasites

The Killer

God of the Labyrinth

The Glass Cage

The World of Violence

Necessary Doubt

Man Without a Shadow

The Black Room

The Space Vampires

Rasputin: a novel

Autobiography

Voyage to a Beginning

Introduction

Writing this book on the poltergeist was a turning point in my life. It was the point at which, to my own astonishment, I became convinced—as far as any human being can be convinced—of the reality of life after death.

Although people who are familiar with my books now associate me with "the occult," my interest in the subject was a fairly late development. As a child I had taken an interest in Spiritualism because my grandmother was a Spiritualist, but at the age of ten I began to read books on astronomy and atomic physics, and suddenly had a feeling that I had achieved a kind of sheet-anchor: *this*, I felt, gave me a glimpse of what life was really about. Suddenly, human existence seemed far more serious and exciting, and I could see clearly that my task was to spend my life acquiring knowledge and trying to understand the riddle of why we are here and what we are supposed to do now that we *are* here.

So I read voraciously and planned to become an atomic physicist. But at sixteen, when I left school, not having the means to attend college or a university, I found that work in a factory plunged me into depression about my future, and the prospect of becoming another Einstein seemed an absurd daydream. I began reading a great deal of poetry, which would induce gradual relaxation, then a feeling of relief and catharsis. The result was that when I was offered a job as a laboratory assistant at my old school, I realized with embarrassment that I no longer cared all that much about science. What I really wanted was to become a writer, and to explore—like Dostoevsky and Nietzsche and Shaw—the confusing problem of what life was all about.

Even at the age of thirteen I had been preoccupied with this riddle of the meaning of human life. It seemed to me then that it was all probably quite pointless: that the truth lay in the scientific picture of the evolution of the universe, and that the kind of emotional stupidities that human beings spend their lives worrying about are merely a sign that we are, after all, earthbound animals. It was a bleak picture, and gave me a frightening feeling of loneliness, as if I had ceased to be part of the human race. I had always been a detached, cheerful kind of person, not at all given to misery or self-pity, so this sense of alienation was not as bad as it might have been. Yet, although I was inclined to accept that most of human life is based on illusions, there was a part of me that deeply wanted to believe that the universe *does* have a meaning, and that the ultimate truth is not lumps of dead planetary matter revolving in endless space.

This is how I came to be preoccupied with the problems of "the Outsider," the alienated man, who *does* suspect that life is meaningless. And it began to seem to me that there is, in fact, a basic answer that can be grasped by human beings, if only we were not so dull and mechanical. It could be found, for example, in Dostoevsky's *Crime and Punishment* when Raskolnikov—who fears that he may be arrested and executed for murdering an old woman—suddenly thinks: "If I had to stand on a narrow ledge for ever and ever, in eternal darkness and eternal tempest, I would still rather do that than die at once." We all *know* exactly what he means. We all feel that we want to live more than anything else, and that faced with the question: "Narrow ledge, or shall I blow your brains out?" we would all instantly cry: "Narrow ledge." Yet what would we *do* on that narrow ledge? Probably jump off.

Our problem seems to be that we cannot *focus* that vision of "seriousness" that we grasp in moments of great crisis, or facing death. Within hours, or even minutes, we return to this superficial, mechanical level of consciousness from which we find it so difficult to escape. Triviality entraps us, even though we struggle and protest like a fly stuck in flypaper. Auden once said: "Even war cannot frighten us enough."

How could we somehow transcend that triviality? One way is obviously to concentrate the mind on things that wake us up to "the vibration of seiousness." I used to read and re-read that passage from Hemingway's *For Whom the Bell Tolls*, in which El Sordo and his fighters are bombed to pieces as they make their last stand on a hilltop. "Now and at the hour of our death, amen, now and at the hour of our death . . . "

This was obviously a kind of answer. If only human beings could learn how to *focus* this seriousness and keep it in the forefront of their minds, they would obviously be saved from the sheer pointlessness of most human existence. Our problem is that we are constantly *distracted* by everyday problems, so we waste our lives.

This is how, at the age of 23, I came to write a book about "Outsiders," about men who are tormented by this sense of "the triviality of everydayness," and who have fought to live on a deeper level—to see visions, to strive with a sense of purpose. We are obviously *capable* of a more purposeful and powerful form of existence than this silly everyday charade, yet do not know how to achieve it.

Dostoevsky also said that surely the question of whether there is life after death is the most serious problem in the world—the most important question we can ask. I was inclined to feel that he was incorrect. After all, the Spiritualists have decided that there *is* life after death; so have the adherents of most religions. But it does not seem to save them from wasting their lives in the act of living them. So it seemed to me that the problem of life after death is of minimal importance compared with the problem of how we can escape triviality and live more deeply. Whether we live after death is fairly unimportant compared with what we can do—and mostly fail to do—in *this* life.

My book about these questions, *The Outsider*, was an unexpected success. Suddenly I was "famous," and the problem of how to afford food and lodgings—which I had solved by working at laboring jobs and in coffee bars—was behind me for good. I moved to a quiet cottage in the country with my girlfriend, Joy, and began work on my second book. Yet once again, I became aware that I had failed to solve the *basic* problem. When I walked up to the farm to collect my letters every morning, in warm spring sunshine, I felt that same sense of being trapped in a world of mere appearances. I had still not learned how to tune in the "vibration of seriousness."

But at least I was a step closer, for I could now devote my life to its pursuit, since this was precisely the subject of the books I wanted to write. When I worked in factories or offices, I felt bored and resentful at having to devote my life to a task that prevented me from even trying to focus "the vibration of seriousness." Now, at least, I was free. But free for what? How did you go about escaping that sense of being trapped in triviality?

One thing was clear: it involved working *alone*. I had never much enjoyed socializing; a few days back in London was enough to give me a dose of what I called "people poisoning," and I rushed back to the country like a man gasping for a breath of air. I realized that, in a sense, my salvation lay in writing. When my second book was slaughtered by the critics, in reaction to the success of the first (*Religion and the Rebel* still seems to me as good, in its way, as *The Outsider*), it only deepened my conviction that my destiny involved being something of a hermit.

The one thing that seemed clear to me is that we are living in an absurdly pessimistic culture, and that the authors usually singled out for admiration—like Graham Greene, Samuel Beckett, Eugene Tonesco—are sick pessimists who are really poisoners of our culture. With their superficial and empty-headed pessimism, they prevent us from pursuing the problem of an intenser form of consciousness. The six books of my "Outsider cycle," with their postscript *The New Existentialism*, were an attempt to create an existential philosophy based on moments of vision and insight—Maslow's "peak experiences."

In the late 1960s I was presented with a new challenge when Random House asked me to write a book on "the occult." I had not taken the subject seriously since I was eleven, although I often bought books with titles like *The Unknown* at airport bookstalls. Now I settled down to serious study of the evidence produced by a century of psychical research, and was startled to find it deeply convincing. This evidence for telepathy, clairvoyance, precognition, shamanistic magic, "second sight," apparitions of the living and of the dead was impressively consistent. If anything proved that the human mind was a vast repository of unconscious powers, this was it. And this, on the whole, was my approach to the problem in my book *The Occult* (1972). It sold so well that I was asked to write a sequel; *Mysteries* followed six years later. In both these books, my point of view was consistent: that "the paranormal" was a manifestation of man's extraordinary subconscious powers, a proof that he is a god rather than a worm.

Then, in 1980, I received a letter describing the case of "the black monk of Pontefract," and suggesting that I write about it. The full story is told in the chapter of that title: how, on my way to Yorkshire to investigate the case, I stopped at a weekend conference in Derbyshire and met Guy Playfair, with whom I had corresponded. His view—that poltergeists are "spirits," struck me at first as absurd, since I had been totally committed to the usual idea that poltergeists are some strange manifestation of the unconscious minds of disturbed children or adolescents. In the same chapter I describe how my subsequent investigations in Pontefract changed my mind and convinced me that Guy Playfair was correct. Poltergeists are, for the most part, spirits of the dead.

This obviously entailed the view that human beings survive death. Although I could see that this followed logically, my basic "existentialism" (which means skepticism) made me disinclined to leap into Spiritualism. Besides, it still seemed more important to unlock the hidden secrets of the unconscious mind than to bother about whether we survive death. It was not until the mid-eighties, when, asked to write a book called *Afterlife*, that I realized that the evidence for life after death is overwhelming. In a later volume called *Beyond the Occult*, I tried to unite the result of twenty-five years of study of "the occult" with forty years of obsession with the mysteries of human consciousness; this is, in my opinion, my most important book.

An hour before starting this introduction, I recalled that I had forgotten to switch on a radio program that my mother enjoys at Sunday midday, and went upstairs from my workroom to do it. I was vaguely surprised that my mother was not up yet—she is, at 81, a late riser, but is usually around by midday. I told Joy to check to see if she needed any help getting dressed. Moments later, Joy called me; my mother was lying, half-dressed, on the bedroom floor, and it was fairly clear that she was dead.

This is why I began this introduction by saying that writing *Poltergeist* was a turning point in my life. Oddly enough, we had switched on an American television program called "Mysteries" the night before, and two items had been about "Near Death Experiences"; a schoolgirl who had almost drowned, and a man who had been crushed under a car. Both told of finding themselves travelling down a tunnel with a light at the end, and how the experience had been so convincing that they would never again fear death. After this, an "expert" expressed his view that the Near Death Experience is merely a defense mechanism of the human mind against its fear of death. This struck me as illogical. I can see why other people might choose to *believe* people who have had Near Death Experiences. But I find it hard to believe that so many people, many of them children, could have "dreamed" the experience as a "defense against fear of death."

Watching the program, it had seemed appropriate to me that my mother should be watching (or rather, listening, for her sight was poor). She accepted the idea of "survival," but it can never do harm to reinforce a belief. Now, as I looked down at her body, I felt that it was a fortunate synchronicity that this had been the last television program she had seen.

Alone in the bedroom, as my wife telephoned the doctor, I felt a deep sadness that she was dead, yet suspected that her spirit might still be there in the room—as in so many cases I cite in *Afterlife*. I found myself saying aloud: "I love you, Mum," and then knelt down on all fours and kissed her cold face.

Of course, I knew my mother had to die; she had had two strokes, and was obviously failing. Yet I felt guilty that she had died while I was not there. And I have to admit that the thought that, after all, her spirit might be there in the room, made the guilt more acceptable.

Besides, consider this. I have spent my whole life combatting the notion that life is a "tale told by an idiot" or a malevolent joke on the part of fate. It seems clear to me that these are the purely *subjective* views of bewildered human beings, and have no objective validity whatever. In spite of the appalling things we do to one another, and that nature occasionally does to us, I feel that life is decent, sensible, and meaningful. The sense of purpose, the sense that meaning lies hidden behind a thin veil, and that if we were a little less stupid we could pull the veil aside, is the basic reality. That means that my job—and yours—is to try to establish order and decency, and to convince our children that there *is* meaning, and that all the talk about meaninglessness is the chatter of idiots who are not capable of putting two thoughts together, or are so blinkered by their immature emotions that they cannot see beyond the ends of their noses.

And *if* there is some kind of continuation of "this life" elsewhere, then my mother is merely waking up on a new Monday morning, facing a new reality. I can see that to feel sorrow about her is as illogical as feeling sorrow for anyone who has to go to work on a Monday morning. When I experience a pang of misery as I realize why she isn't in her usual place on the settee, this is merely my selfish response to the feeling that my routine has suddenly been changed, making me feel uncomfortable. *I* may wish that she was back here; but I'm pretty sure that she doesn't.

So do I believe in life after death? No. Not in the same pragmatic way that I know that my publisher is waiting for this introduction. Yet I *am* convinced of the reality of poltergeists, and that they are "spirits"; not "recurrent spontaneous psychokinesis." Logically speaking, life after death seems to me to be as certain as anything can be. And that, while I still feel oddly bewildered that my mother is not upstairs, gives me a sense of comfort.

ONE

Professor Lombroso Investigates

At the age of forty-seven Professor Cesare Lombroso was one of the most celebrated scientists in Italy. His book, *Criminal Man (L'Uomo Delinquente)* had made him an object of discussion throughout the world. What made it so controversial was Lombroso's theory that the criminal is a degenerate "throw-back" to our cave-man forebears—a kind of human ape. According to this view, a man born with these tendencies can no more help committing crime than a born cripple can help limping. It gave violent offense to the Catholic Church, which has always felt that "sin" is a matter of choice; but it also upset psychologists who liked to feel that man possesses at least an atom of free will. Lombroso regarded free will as something of a myth. In 1876, when *Criminal Man* was published, he looked upon himself as a thorough-going materialist.

Six years later, his skepticism received a severe setback. He was asked to investigate the case of a girl who had developed peculiar powers. In fact, it sounded too silly to be taken seriously. According to her parents, she could see through her ear and smell through her chin. When Lombroso went to see her, he expected to find some absurd deception.

She was a tall, thin girl of fourteen, and the trouble had begun when she started to menstruate. She began sleep-walking, and developed hysterical blindness. Yet she was still able to see through the tip of her nose, and through her left ear. Lombroso tried binding her eyes with a bandage, then took a letter out of his pocket and

1

held it a few inches away from her nose; she read it as if her eyes were uncovered. To make sure she was not peeping under the bandages, Lombroso held another page near her left ear; again, she read it aloud without difficulty. And even without the bandage, she would not have been able to read a letter held at the side of her head.

Next he tried holding a bottle of strong smelling salts under her nose; it did not make the slightest impression. But when it was held under her chin, she winced and gasped. He tried substances with only the slightest trace of odor—substances he could not smell if he held them two inches away from his own nose. When they were under her chin, she could identify every one of them.

If he still had any doubts, they vanished during the next few weeks when her sense of smell suddenly transferred itself to the back of her foot. If disagreeable smells were brought close to her heel, she writhed in agony; pleasant ones made her sigh with delight.

This was not all. The girl also developed the power of prediction. She was able to predict weeks ahead precisely when she would have fits, and exactly how they could be cured. Lombroso, naturally, did not accept this as genuine prediction, since she might have been inducing the fits—consciously or otherwise—to make her predictions come true. But she then began to predict things that would happen to other members of the family; and these came about just as she had foretold.

In medical journals, Lombroso found many similar cases. One girl who developed hysterical symptoms at puberty could accurately distinguish colors with her hands. An eleven-year-old girl who suffered a back wound was able to hear through her elbow. Another pubescent girl could read a book with her stomach when her eyes were bandaged. Another hysterical woman developed X-ray eyes, and said she could see worms in her intestines—she actually counted them and said there were thirty-three; in due course she excreted precisely this number of worms. A young man suffering from hysteria could read people's minds, and reproduce drawings and words written on a sheet of paper when his eyes were tightly bandaged.

Lombroso may have been a determined materialist; but he was willing to study the facts. And the facts led him into stranger and stranger regions of speculation. To begin with, he developed a simple and ingenious theory of the human faculties, pointing out that seeing, hearing, smelling and feeling all take place through the nerves, and that if one of these faculties becomes paralyzed there is no scientific reason why another should not take over. When he attended a seance with the famous "medium" Eusapia Palladino, and saw a table floating up into the air, he simply extended his theory, and argued that there is no reason why "psychological force" should not change into "motor force." But when he began to study other cases of prediction and "second sight," he had to admit that it became increasingly difficult to keep the explanations within the bounds of materialistic science. There was the case of a woman who refused to stay in a theater because she suddenly had a conviction that her father was dying; she got home and found a telegram to that effect. A doctor who suffered from hysterical symptoms foresaw the great fire of 1894 at the Como Exposition, and persuaded his family to sell their shares in a fire insurance company which had to meet the claims; when the fire occurred, his family was glad they took his advice. A woman whose daughter was playing near a railway line heard a voice telling her the child was in danger; she fetched her indoors half an hour before a train jumped the rails and ploughed through the spot where her daughter had been playing.

Slowly, and with painful reluctance, the skeptical scientist was converted to the view that the world was a far more complex place than his theories allowed. His colleagues were outraged. His biographer and translator, Hans Kurella, came to the conclusion that this was all a painful aberration due to the decay of his faculties—an argument difficult to sustain, since Lombroso was only forty-seven when he became interested in these matters, and he lived for more than a quarter of a century longer. Kurella can only bring himself to mention "Lombroso's Spiritualistic Researches" in a short afterword to his biography, and his comments are scathing. Talking about Eusapia Palladino, whose seances he had attended, he agreed that she was indeed a "miracle"—"a miracle of adroitness, false bonhomie, well-simulated candor, naivete, and artistic command of all the symptoms of hysterico-epilepsy." Which may well be true, but still does not explain how she was able to make a table rise up into the air when Lombroso and other scientists were holding her hands and feet.

Lombroso struggled manfully to stay within the bounds of science; he devised all kinds of ingenious instruments for testing mediums during seances. But, little by little, he found himself sucked into that ambiguous, twilight world of the "paranormal." Having studied mediums in civilized society, he turned his attention to tribal witch-doctors and shamans, and found that they could produce the same phenomena. But they always insisted that they did this with the help of the "spirit world"—the world of the dead. And the more he looked into this, the more convincing it began to appear. And so, finally, he turned his attention to the topic that every good scientist dismisses as an old wives' tale: haunted houses. Here again, personal experience soon convinced him of their reality.

His most celebrated case concerned a wine shop in the Via Bava in Turin. In November 1900, he heard interesting rumors about how a destructive ghost was making life very difficult for the family of the proprietor, a Signor Fumero. Bottles smashed, tables and chairs danced about, kitchen utensils flew across the room. So Lombroso went along to the wine shop, and asked the proprietor if there was any truth in the stories. Indeed there was, said Fumero, but the disturbances had now stopped. Professor Lombroso had visited the house, and the ghost had now gone away. "You interest me extremely," replied Lombroso. "Allow me to introduce myself." And he presented his card. Fumero looked deeply embarrassed, and admitted that the story about Lombroso was an invention, intended to discourage the curious. For it seemed that the Italian police had been called in, and that they had witnessed the strange disturbances and told Signor Fumero that, unless this stopped at once, he would find himself in serious trouble. So Fumero had invented this story of how the famous Professor Lombroso had visited the house, and the ghost had taken his departure.

In fact, the proprietor admitted, the ghost was as active as ever; and if the professor would care to see with his own eyes, he only had to step down to the cellar.

Down below the house was a deep wine cellar, approached by a flight of stairs and a long passageway. The proprietor led the way. The cellar was in complete darkness; but as they entered there was a noise of smashing glass, and some bottles struck Lombroso's foot. A lighted candle revealed rows of shelves with bottles of wine. And as Lombroso stood there, three empty bottles began to spin across the floor, and shattered against the leg of a table that stood in the middle of the cellar. On the floor, below the shelves, were the remains of broken bottles and wine. Lombroso took the candle over to the shelves, and examined them closely to see if there could be invisible wires to cause the movement. There were none; but as he looked, half a dozen bottles gently rose from the shelves, as if someone had lifted them, and exploded on the floor. Finally, as they left the cellar and closed the door behind them, they heard the smashing of another bottle.

The cellar was not the only place in the house where these things occurred. Chairs and plates flew around the kitchen. In the servants' room, a brass grinding machine flew across the room so violently that it was flattened out of shape; Lombroso examined it with amazement. The force to flatten it must have been considerable; if it had struck someone's head, it would surely have killed him. The odd thing was that the ghost seemed to do no one any harm. On one occasion, as the proprietor was bending down in the cellar, a large bottle of wine had burst beside his head; if it had struck him it would have done him a severe injury. Moreover, the "entity" seemed to have the power to make bottles "explode" without dropping them. They would hear a distinct cracking sound; then a bottle would fly into splinters.

Now Lombroso knew enough about hauntings to know that this was not an ordinary ghost. The ordinary ghost stays around in a house for many years, perhaps for centuries, and manifests itself to many people. But this bottle-smashing ghost was of the kind that the Germans call a poltergeist—or noisy spirit. Such "hauntings" usually last only a short period—seldom more than six months—and they often seem to be associated with a "medium"—that is, with some particular person who "causes" them, in exactly the same way that Eusapia Palladino caused a table to rise into the air.

In this case, Lombroso suspected the wife of Signor Fumero, a skinny little woman of fifty, who seemed to him to be distinctly neurotic. She admitted that ever since infancy she had been subject to neuralgia, nervous tremors and hallucinations; she had also had an operation to remove her ovaries. Ever since the case of the girl who could see with her ear, Lombroso had noticed that these people with peculiar "powers" seemed to be nervously unstable. He therefore advised Signor Fumero to try sending his wife for a holiday. She went back to her native town for three days, and during that period, the wine shop was blessedly quiet—although Signora Fumero suffered from hallucinations while she was away, believing she could see people who were invisible to everyone else.

It looked as if Lombroso had stumbled on the correct solution. But it was not so simple. On Signora Fumero's return, all the disturbances began again; so, to make doubly sure, Lombroso again suggested that she should go home for a few days. The poor woman was understandably irritated at being banished from her home on account of the spirits; and before she left, she cursed them vigorously. That apparently annoyed them, for this time the disturbances went on while she was away. On the day she left, a pair of her shoes came floating out of her bedroom and down the stairs, and landed at the feet of some customers who were drinking in the bar. The following day the shoes vanished completely, to reappear under the bed a week later. Worse still, plates and bottles in the kitchen exploded or fell on the floor. But Signor Fumero noticed an interesting fact. It was only the plates and bottles *that had been touched by his wife* that smashed. If another woman set the table—preferably in another place—nothing happened. It was almost as if the objects she had touched had picked up some form of *energy* from her . . .

So his wife came back from her home town, and the disturbances continued as before. A bottle of soda water rose up gently in the bar, floated across the room as if someone were carrying it, and smashed on the floor.

It seemed, then, that Signora Fumero was not to blame; at least, not entirely. So who was? There were only three other suspects. Signor Fumero could be dismissed—he was a "brave old soldier," and not at all the hysterical type. There was a head waiter, who seemed to be an ordinary, typical Italian. But there was also a young waiter—a lad of thirteen, who was unusually tall. Lombroso may have recalled that the girl who could see through her ear was also unusually tall, and that she had grown about six inches in a year immediately before her problems began. This boy had also reached puberty.

Accordingly, he was dismissed, and the "haunting" of number 6 Via Bava immediately ceased.

As a scientist, Lombroso's problem was to find an explanation that would cover the facts. At a fairly early stage, he was convinced that they were facts, and not delusions. He wrote to a friend in 1891:

> I am ashamed and sorrowful that with so much obstinacy I have contested the possibility of the so-called spiritualistic facts. I say the facts, for I am inclined to reject the spiritualistic theory; but the facts exist, and as regards facts I glory in saying that I am their slave.

By "spiritualistic theory" he meant belief in life after death. At this stage he was inclined to believe that he was dealing with some kind of purely mental force.

> I see nothing inadmissible in the supposition that in hysterical and hypnotized persons the stimulation of certain centers, which become powerful

owing to the paralyzing of all the others, and thus give rise to a transposition and transmission of psychical forces, may also result in a transformation into luminous or motor force.

He compared it to the action of a magnet in deflecting a compass needle.

But ten years later he had come to recognize that this theory failed to cover "the facts." It might be stretched to cover the case of the wine shop poltergeist, if the young waiter was an "unconscious" medium, and was using his magnetic powers without realizing it. But by that time, Lombroso had also studied many cases of haunted houses, and he concluded that there are basically two types: those like the Via Bava, in which there is a "medium" (and which usually last only a few weeks or months), and the more traditional haunting, which may last for centuries. Lombroso apparently never had a chance to study this second type directly, but he went about collecting evidence from witnesses he judged reliable. When he heard about Glenlee, a haunted house in Scotland, he asked a friend named Professor Scott Elliott to investigate. Elliott went to see a girl who had lived in the house, and sent Lombroso the following story. Glenlee was owned by a family called Maxwell, and was supposed to be haunted by the ghost of a lady who had poisoned her husband. A visitor named Mrs. Stamford Raffles was lying in bed beside her husband when she saw in the firelight a cloud of mist, which gradually turned into the shape of an old woman. The room became icy cold. The old woman seemed to be looking at the clock on the mantelpiece. Another visitor, Mrs. Robert Gladstone, had the same experience—but during the day, with the sun shining; the same cloud of mist, the same old woman looking at the clock.

Since the stories cited by Lombroso are second-hand, and lacking in the kind of precise detail that is to be found in that of the wine shop, let me offer here a case of haunting that provides a better comparison. It is to be found in *Lord Halifax's Ghost Book.*

In the 1890s, the Reverend Sabine Baring-Gould published in the *Cornhill Magazine* a "true ghost story" about a house in Lille. A Mrs. Pennyman, who had been involved in the case, wrote a long letter in which she corrected the inaccuracies of Baring-Gould's account. Her own is as follows:

In 1865, when she was a girl, Mrs. Pennyman's family had gone to France so that the children could learn French; and they rented a house in Lille, where they had a number of introductions. The rent of the house—in the Place du Lion d'Or—struck them as remarkably low. When they went to the bank to cash a letter of credit, they found out why. The place was reputed to have a *revenant*—a ghost. In fact, the girl and her mother *had* been awakened by footsteps overhead, but had assumed it was a servant moving about. After the visit to the bank, they enquired who was sleeping overhead, and were told that it was an empty garret.

Their maid soon heard the story of the *revenant* from the French servants. A young man who was heir to the house had disappeared under mysterious circumstances. The story had it that he had been confined in an iron cage in the attic by his uncle, who later killed him. The uncle sold the house, but it had never been occupied for long because of the ghost.

The family went to look in the garret, and found that there *was* a cage. It was eight feet high and four feet square, and was attached to the wall. Inside there was an iron collar on a rusty chain.

Ten days later, the maidservant asked if she could change rooms. She and another maid slept in a room between the main stairs and the back staircase, and which therefore had two doors. They had seen a tall, thin man walking through the room, and had buried their faces under the bedclothes. The mother told the maids to move into another bedroom.

Soon after this, the girl and her brother went upstairs to fetch something from their mother's room, and saw "a thin figure in a powdering gown and wearing hair down the back" going up the stairs in front of them. They thought it was a servant called Hannah, and called after her, "You can't frighten us." But when they got back to their mother, she told them that Hannah had gone to bed with a headache; they checked and found her fast asleep. When they described the figure, the maids said that it was the one which they had seen.

Another brother came from the university to stay. He was awakened by a noise, and looked out of the door to see a man on the stairs. He assumed his mother had sent a servant to see if he had put out his candle, and was angry about it. His mother told him she had not sent anyone.

By now, the family had found themselves another house. Some English friends named Atkyns called a few days before they left, and were interested to hear about the ghost. Mrs. Atkyns volunteered to sleep in the room with her dog. The next morning, Mrs. Atkyns looked tired and distraught. She had also seen the man wandering through the bedroom. The dog seems to have refused to attack it.

Just before they left the house, the girl herself saw the ghost. By this time they were so accustomed to the footsteps that they ignored them; but they kept a candle burning in their room. She woke up to see a tall, thin figure in a long gown, its arm resting on a chest of drawers. She could clearly see the face, which was that of a young man with a melancholy expression. When she looked again, he had disappeared. The bedroom door was locked.

This was the story as told by Mrs. Pennyman. Lord Halifax sent it to the Reverend Baring-Gould, who later sent him a letter he received from a reader of his account in the *Cornhill Magazine*. From this letter, it appeared that the haunted house had been transformed into a hotel in the 1880s. The reader—a lady—described how she and two friends had stayed at the Hotel du Lion d'Or in May 1887, and it is clear that one of the bedrooms they were given was the room in which the two servant girls had seen the ghost. The lady herself slept in the next room, and settled down after dinner to write letters. The hotel was very quiet—they were apparently the only guests—but toward midnight she heard footsteps on the landing outside the door. Then one of the ladies in the next bedroom—which was connected to her own— tapped on the door and asked if she was all right; she had been awakened by footsteps walking up and down. The two ladies unlocked the door and peered out on to the landing; but there was no one there, and no sound either. So they went back to bed. As she fell asleep, the lady continued to hear the slow, dragging steps which seemed to come from outside her door. They left Lille the next morning, and she thought no more about the experience until she read Baring-Gould's account in the *Cornhill* and realized that she had probably heard the ghost of the Place du Lion d'Or.

Stories of this type inevitably raise suspicions in the mind of the scientific investigator; they sound just a little too dramatic to be true—the young man confined in an iron cage, and so on. Yet since the foundation of the Society for Psychical Research in 1882, thousands of well-authenticated cases have been recorded. Sir Ernest Bennett's *Apparitions and Haunted Houses*, for example, contains more than a hundred carefully documented cases, and many of these have the same suspiciously dramatic air that suggests an active imagination. Case five will serve as an illustration: a General Barter of County Cork describes seeing the ghost of a certain Lieutenant B. in India—riding on a pony in the moonlight, complete with two Hindu servants. The general said: "Hello, what the devil do you want?" The ghost came to a halt and looked down at him; and the general noticed that he now had a beard, and that his face was fatter than when he knew him some years before. Another officer who had known Lieutenant B. immediately before his death later verified that he had grown a beard and become stout, and that the pony he was riding had been purchased at Peshawur (where he died of some sickness) and killed through reckless riding.

It certainly sounds a highly unlikely story. Yet it is confirmed (in writing) by an officer to whom the general told it immediately afterwards, by the general's wife, and by a major. The wife also states that they heard a horse galloping at breakneck speed around their house at night on several occasions, and adds that the house was built by Lieutenant B. Finally, Bennett himself confirmed with the war office that Lieutenant B. had died at Peshawur in January 1854. So although only General Barter saw the ghost, the evidence for the truth of his story seems strong. Other ghosts cited by Bennett were witnessed by many people—for example, the ghost of a chimney sweep who died of cancer, and who returned to his cottage every night for two months, until the whole family (including five children) began to take it for granted.

It is worth noting that nearly all ghosts mentioned in the records of the Society for Psychical Research look like ordinary solid human beings; so it seems probable that most people have at some time seen a ghost without realizing it. The late T. C. Lethbridge has described in his book *Ghost and Ghoul* how, when he was about to leave a friend's room at Cambridge in 1922, he saw a man in a top hat come into the room—he presumed it was a college porter who had to give a message. The next day he asked his friend what the porter wanted, and the friend flatly denied that anyone had come into the room as Lethbridge went out. It then struck Lethbridge that the man had been wearing hunting kit. If he had not happened to mention it to his friend, he would never have known that he had seen a ghost.

Now Lombroso, who died in 1909, gradually abandoned his skepticism, and came to accept the spiritualistic hypothesis that ghosts are, quite simply, spirits of the dead, and that the same probably applies to poltergeists, even though these can only manifest themselves when there is a "medium" present. The title of his book about his researches, which was published posthumously, was *After Death—What?* (This question would have struck him as regrettably sensational twenty years earlier.) In other words, Lombroso made no clear distinction between poltergeists and "apparitions." But even in 1909, this assumption would have been widely questioned. One of the most obvious things that emerged from the thousands of cases recorded by the SPR was that the majority of ghosts do not seem to notice the onlookers. (In this respect, General Barter's case was an exception. In fact, they behave exactly as if they are a kind of film projection. They wander across a room looking anxious—like the ghost of the Lion d'Or—as if re-enacting some event from the past. This led a number of eminent investigators—among them Sir Oliver Lodge—to suggest that *some* ghosts, at any rate, may be no more than a kind of "recording." In *Man and the Universe*, Lodge writes:

Occasionally a person appears able to respond to stimuli embedded . . . among psycho-physical surroundings in a manner at present ill-understood and almost incredible:—*as if strong emotions could be unconsciously recorded in matter* [my italics], so that the deposit shall thereafter affect a sufficiently sensitive organism and cause similar emotions to reproduce themselves in the sub-consciousness, in a manner analogous to the customary conscious interpretation of photographic or phonographic records, and indeed of pictures or music and artistic embodiment generally.

Take, for example, a haunted house . . . wherein some one room is the scene of a ghostly representation of some long past tragedy. On a psychometric hypothesis the original tragedy has been literally *photographed* on its material surroundings, nay, even on the ether itself, by reason of the intensity of emotion felt by those who enacted it; and thenceforth in certain persons an hallucinatory effect is experienced corresponding to such an impression. It is this theory that is made to account for the feeling one has on entering certain rooms, that there is an alien presence therein, though it is invisible and inaudible to mortal sense . . .

But why should this "hallucinatory effect" be produced only on "certain persons"? Why not everybody? To answer this, we need to understand what Lodge meant by the "psychometric hypothesis." Psychometry means the ability to "read" the history of objects by touching them. The word seems to have been coined by a professor of medicine called Joseph Rodes Buchanan around the middle of the nineteenth century. In 1842, Buchanan was intrigued when Bishop Leonidas Polk (who would become a civil war general) told him that if he touched brass in the dark, it produced a distinct taste in his mouth. Buchanan tested him and found this to be true. Then he tried experimenting with his students at the Cincinnati medical school, wrapping various metals and chemicals in brown paper parcels, and asking students to see if they could identify them by holding them in their hands. An amazing number were successful. Buchanan concluded that our nerves give off some kind of "aura"—like an electric field—which can penetrate the brown paper, and somehow convey the taste of the substance to the mouth.

What surprised him even more was that "good psychometers" could take a letter in the hand, and describe the character and the emotions of the person who wrote it. Presumably, then, the character of the writer had somehow been "recorded" on the letter, and could be "picked up" by a sensitive person.

William Denton, a professor of geology at Boston, was interested by Buchanan's account of his experiments, and tried repeating them. He used geological samples wrapped in paper. Once again, the success rate was remarkable. A good "psychometer" sensed a volcanic explosion when handed a piece of Hawaiian lava, vast depths of empty space with stars when handed a meteor fragment, and immense depths of ice when handed a pebble from a glacier.

Now obviously, there is no "powerful emotion" involved when a meteor flies through space or a pebble is frozen in ice. So Denton concluded that *all* events in nature are somehow "recorded," and that the human mind possesses a faculty for playing-back the recording—an extra sense that enables us to see into the remote past.

Unfortunately for Buchanan and Denton, the birth of "spiritualism" in the late 1840s—when strange rapping noises were heard in the home of the Fox Sisters of

Hydesville, New York—made scientists deeply suspicious of anything that seemed connected with this new craze. So instead of being taken seriously, psychometry and its theories were dismissed as a delusion. But Lodge and other psychical researchers revived the idea to explain haunted houses.

Half a century after Lodge, T. C. Lethbridge—who was Keeper of Anglo-Saxon Antiquities at Cambridge—stumbled on the "psychometric" theory as a result of his own observations. When he saw the "ghost" of the man in a hunting kit, he was at first inclined to wonder whether it had been purely a mental picture, perhaps "picked up" from somebody else's mind. Perhaps the huntsman had been a former occupant of the rooms, and was sitting in his armchair at home sipping a whisky as he thought about the good old days at Cambridge; and perhaps somehow the image had got itself transferred into Lethbridge's mind . . .

But other experiences led him to revise this notion. One day, after he had retired to Devon, Lethbridge and his wife Mina went to collect seaweed from Ladram beach. It was a dull, damp day, and as they walked on to the beach near a stream that ran down the cliff, both suddenly experienced a profound depression. Lethbridge noticed that this vanished as soon as he stepped a few feet away from the stream. His wife, Mina, went to the cliff top to make a sketch, and suddenly had the odd feeling that someone was urging her to jump. (Again, Lethbridge was inclined to think that she could have been picking up someone's thoughts—perhaps someone had stood on that spot, contemplating suicide, then had a change of mind and gone home—but later investigation revealed that a man *had* committed suicide from exactly that spot.)

Thinking about it all later, Lethbridge reflected that dampness can cause radio transmitters to short-circuit.

Could it have been the dampness on the beach that was somehow responsible for the feeling of depression? He had also been struck by the fact that it seemed to end so abruptly, as if it formed a kind of invisible wall. He had noticed the same kind of thing around the cottage of an old woman reputed to be a witch—who had died under circumstances suggesting murder. There was the same "nasty feeling" around the place just after her death, and he had noticed that he could step in and out of it, as if it ended quite sharply. Could it, Lethbridge wondered, be some kind of "field," like the field that surrounds a magnet?

Lethbridge was also an excellent dowser, and it struck him that the "nasty feeling" on the beach (he used the term "ghoul" to describe it) had been around the stream. This led him to the theory that the "field" of water can "tape record" strong emotions, and that people who can dowse are probably able to "pick up" these recordings. In short, a water-diviner would be far more likely to see a ghost than most people.

This, then, was Lethbridge's theory about "ghosts" and "ghouls," which he developed in a number of books written in the last ten years of his life (he died in 1972). It is a natural and logical extension of Buchanan's "psychometry"' and of Lodge's theory about "recordings." But Lethbridge has also placed it on a more scientific basis by suggesting that what does the "recording" is some kind of magnetic field associated with water. The principle sounds very much like that of a tape recorder, where a magnetic field "imprints" the sounds on an iron-oxide tape. In Lethbridge's theory, the magnetic field of water records emotions and prints them on its surroundings—in the case of the "old witch," on the walls of her damp cottage.

All this helps to explain why Lombroso's theory about haunted houses struck many contemporary researchers as "unscientific." The "psychometric hypothesis" seems to explain the majority of hauntings. For example, the ghost of the young man in the Place du Lion d'Or gave no sign of being aware of the presence of the various people who saw him, and that is what you would expect if a ghost is some kind of "film" or recording of a long-past event.

As to the poltergeist, the "mischievous spirit" theory found little acceptance among investigators, even in the earliest days of psychical research. The reason was simply that a scientific investigator prefers natural explanations. And where poltergeists were concerned, there were a number of plausible ones. Eusapia Palladino could cause tables to rise into the air. The famous Victorian medium Daniel Dunglas Home frequently caused heavy objects of furniture to float right up to the ceiling, while he himself floated out of third-story windows and came back by the window on the other side of the room. Home and Palladino claimed that their powers came from spirits; but they might have been deceiving themselves. One of the first thing that struck the early scientific investigators of poltergeists is that there usually seemed to be a disturbed adolescent in the house—usually a girl. Lombroso himself had noticed how often teenage girls seemed to be involved in his paranormal cases—like the girl who could see with her ear. And his original "nervous force" theory struck most investigators as far more plausible than his later belief in mischievous spirits.

This younger generation of investigators had another reason for dismissing the spirit theory. By 1909, Freud had made most psychologists aware that the unconscious mind is a far more powerful force than Lombroso had recognized. Lombroso has a section on the unconscious in *After Death—What?*, and it reveals that he thought of it as little more than another name for absent-mindedness or poetic inspiration. Freud had made people aware that the unconscious is a kind of ocean, full of dangerous currents and strange monsters. Moreover, Freud emphasized that the most powerful of these unconscious forces is the sex drive. Could it be coincidence that most poltergeist cases involve adolescents at the age of puberty?

This, of course, still fails to explain how the unconscious mind of a disturbed adolescent can make bottles fly through the air. But again, science had some plausible theories. In Basle, a university student named Carl Jung was intrigued by a female cousin who began to go into trances at the age of puberty, and spoke with strange voices. And at about the time this started, the dining-room table suddenly split apart with a loud report. There was also a sudden explosion from a sideboard, and when they looked inside, they found that a bread knife had shattered into several pieces. Jung suspected that his cousin's "illness" was responsible for these events, and he coined the term "exteriorization phenomenon" to explain them—meaning more or less what Lombroso meant by "nerve force." Jung had no doubt that it was caused by the unconscious mind, and a personal experience confirmed him in this view. One day he was arguing with Freud about "exteriorization" and Freud was highly skeptical. Jung's rising irritation caused a burning sensation in his chest "as if my diaphragm was becoming red hot!" Suddenly, there was a loud explosion in the bookcase. "There," said Jung, "*that* was an exteriorization phenomenon " "Bosh," said Freud, to which Jung replied: "It is not bosh, and to prove it, there will be another explosion in a moment." And a second explosion occurred. Jung had no doubt that he had somehow caused the explosions by getting angry.

Most modern investigators of poltergeist phenomena would agree with Jung. One of the rare exceptions was the late Harry Price, who wrote in *Poltergeist Over England:* "My own view is that they are invisible, intangible, malicious and noisy entities . . ." He adds: "Poltergeists are able, by laws yet unknown to our physicists, to extract energy from living persons, often from the young, and usually from girl adolescents, especially if they suffer from some mental disorder." Unfortunately, Price's reputation has declined steadily since his death in 1948, with accusations of lying, cheating, publicity seeking, and fraud; so most psychical researchers would dismiss his views on poltergeists as a deliberate attempt at sensationalism. Besides, Price himself admitted that poltergeists seem to be connected with sexual energies; and he described how the husband of the Austrian medium Frieda Weisl told him that, during their early married life, ornaments jumped off the mantel shelf when she had a sexual orgasm. This certainly sounds like Jung's "exteriorization phenomenon."

We may say, then, that the modern consensus of opinion is that a poltergeist is a person, not a spirit. The view is summed up by Richard Cavendish*:

> Because poltergeist incidents usually occur in close proximity to a living person, parapsychologists tend to regard them as instances of psychokinesis or PK. Since poltergeist incidents are recurrent and arise unexpectedly and spontaneously, they are commonly referred to as instances of "recurrent spontaneous psychokinesis" or RSPK. They appear to be unconscious cases of PK since the person who seems to bring them about is usually unaware of his involvement. Some persons remain convinced that RSPK phenomena are due to the agency of an incorpo-

---

* *Encyclopedia of the Unexplained,* p. 197.

real entity, such as the spirit of a deceased person or a "demon" which has attached itself to some living person and which causes the incidents by PK. However, since there is no evidence for such spirits apart from the phenomena themselves, most parapsychologists are of the opinion that poltergeist phenomena are examples of unconscious PK exercised by the person around whom they occur.

"Psychokinesis" means, of course, "mind over matter." And it has been widely accepted by investigators since the mid-1930s, when Dr. J. B. Rhine, of Duke University, conducted a series of experiments with a gambler who claimed that he could influence the fall of the dice by concentrating on them. Rhine's experiments showed that the gambler was correct; he could, to some extent, influence the dice to make it turn up sixes. Since then, there have been thousands of similar experiments, and the evidence for PK is regarded as overwhelming.

Yet it has to be admitted that even its "star performers"—Nina Kulagina, Felicia Parise, Ingo Swann, Uri Geller—cannot make objects fly around the room as poltergeists seem to be able to. The Russian Kulagina first came to the attention of scientists when she was in hospital after a nervous breakdown; her doctors were fascinated to see that she could reach into her sewing basket and take out any color of thread she wanted without looking at it. They tested her and found that she could, beyond all doubt, "see" colors with her fingertips. Her healing powers were also remarkable—for example, she could make wounds heal up in a very short time simply by holding her hand above them. But it was when they tested her for PK that they discovered her outstanding abilities. She could sit at a table, stare at a small object—like a matchbox or a wineglass—and make it move without touching it. She told investigators that when her concentration "worked," she felt a sharp pain in her spine, and her eyesight blurred. Her blood pressure would rise abruptly.

But then, Nina Kulagina's most spectacular feat was to make an apple fall off a table. Ingo Swann, an American, is able to deflect compass needles by PK; Felicia Parise, who was inspired to try "mind over matter" after seeing a film about Kulagina, can move small objects like matchsticks and pieces of paper. Uri Geller, the world's best-known "psychic," can bend spoons by gently rubbing them with his finger, and snap metal rings by simply holding his hand above them.

Now Geller has, in fact, produced certain "poltergeist effects." In 1976, I spent some time with Geller in Barcelona, interviewing him for a book I subsequently wrote about him. A number of objects fell out of the air when I was with him, and these seemed to be typical examples of "teleportation." Another friend, Jesse Lasky, has described to me how, when Uri was having dinner at their flat, there was a pinging noise like a bullet, and a silver button flew across the kitchen; it had come out of the bedroom drawer of Jesse's wife, Pat: Geller was standing by the refrigerator with a bottle of milk in one hand and a tin of Coca Cola in the other when it happened. Another odd feature of this incident is that the button—if it came from the bedroom drawer—must have somehow traveled through three walls to reach the kitchen. "Interpenetration of matter" is another curious feature in many poltergeist cases.

But then, Geller was not trying to make this happen. As I discovered when getting to know him, odd events seem to happen when he is around. On the morning I went to meet him, at an office in the West End of London, he asked me, "Do you have any connection with Spain?" I said that I didn't. A moment before I walked into the office, a Spanish coin had risen out of the ashtray on the desk, and floated across to the other side of the room, where Geller and a public relations officer were standing. I subsequently came to know the PRO well enough to accept her word that this really took place. When Geller left the Lasky's flat in central London, he buzzed them from the intercom at the front door and explained with embarrassment that he had damaged the door. A wrought-iron dragon which decorated the center of the door had been twisted—fortunately they were able to force it back without breaking it. Geller explained that he is never sure when such things will happen, or even whether the razor with which he shaves is likely to buckle in his hand.

In short, it seems that even the most talented practitioners of psychokinesis cannot produce real "poltergeist effects" *at will*. But this is not necessarily a proof that they themselves are not responsible. For we now come to the oddest part of this story: the recent discovery that human beings appear to have two different people living inside their heads.

In a sense, of course, this discovery was made by Freud, who called it the unconscious. Jung went further, and accepted that the unconscious is a kind of great psychic ocean, to which all living creatures are somehow connected. Yet it was not until the early 1960s that scientists began to suspect that the two different "selves" live in different parts of the brain.

If you could lift off the top of the skull and look at the brain, you would see something resembling a walnut, with two wrinkled halves. Joining the halves is a bridge of nerve fibers called the *corpus callosum*. In the 1930s, scientists wondered whether they could prevent epilepsy by severing this bridge—to prevent the "electrical storm" from spreading from one half of the brain to the other. In fact, it seemed to work. And, oddly enough, the severing of the "bridge" seemed to make no real difference to the patient.

In the 1950s Roger Sperry of the University of Chicago (and later Cal. Tech.*) began studying these "split-brain" patients, and made the interesting discovery that they had, in effect, turned into two people. For example, one split-brain patient tried to button up his flies with one hand, while the other hand tried to undo them. Another tried to embrace his wife with one arm, while his other hand pushed her violently away. In fact, it looked rather as if his conscious love for his wife was being opposed by an unconscious dislike. The split-brain experiment had given its unconscious mind the power to control one of his arms.

Now this upper part of the brain—the cerebrum or cerebral hemispheres—is our specifically human part. It has developed at an incredible pace over the past half million years—so swiftly (in evolutionary terms) that some scientists talk about the "brain explosion." And, like the rest of the brain, it seems to consist of two identical parts, which are a mirror-image of one another. (No one has yet discovered why the brain has these two halves—the obvious theory is that we have two of everything in case one is damaged.)

In the middle of the nineteenth century, doctors noticed that the two halves of the brain seem to have two different functions. A man whose left hemisphere is damaged finds it hard to express himself in words; yet he can still recognize faces, appreciate art or enjoy music. A man whose right hemisphere is damaged can speak perfectly clearly and logically; yet he cannot draw the sim-

---

* California Institute of Technology.

plest patterns or whistle a tune. The left cerebral hemisphere deals with language and logic; the right deals with recognition and intuition. You could say that the left is a scientist and the right is an artist.

Oddly enough, the right side of the brain controls the left side of the body—the left arm and leg—and vice versa. The same applies to our eyes, though in a slightly more complicated fashion. Each of our eyes is connected to both halves of the brain, the left side of each eye to the right brain, the right side of each eye to the left brain. (We say that the left visual field is connected to the right brain and vice versa.) If a scientist wishes to investigate the eyes of a split-brain patient, he has to make the patient look to the right or left, or hold the gaze fixed in front, so that different objects can be "shown" to the right or left visual fields. It will simplify matters if we say that the left eye is connected to the right brain and vice versa.

Sperry made his most interesting discovery about the eyes of split-brain patients. If the patient was shown an apple with his left eye and an orange with his right, and asked what he had just seen, he would reply "Orange." Asked to write with his left hand what he had just seen, he would write "Apple." Asked what he had just written, he would reply "Orange."

A patient who was shown a "dirty" picture with the left eye blushed; asked why she was blushing she replied, "I don't know."

It seems, then, that we have two different people living in the two halves of the brain, and that the person you call "you" lives in the left. A few centimeters away there is another person who is virtually a stranger—yet who also believes he is the rightful occupant of the head.

Now, at least, we can begin to see a possible reason why the "medium" in poltergeist cases is quite unaware that he or she is causing the effects. We have only to assume that the effects are caused by the person living in the right half of the brain, and we can see that the "you" in the left would be unconscious of what was happening.

But this would still leave the question: how does the right brain *do* it? In fact, is there any evidence whatsoever that the right brain possesses paranormal powers?

And the answer to this is a qualified yes. We can begin with one of the simplest and best authenticated of all "paranormal powers," water divining. The water diviner, or dowser, holds a forked hazel twig (or even a forked rod made from two strips out of a whalebone corset, tied at the end) in both hands, so there is a certain tension—a certain "springiness"—in the rod. And when they walk over an underground stream or spring, the rod twists either upwards or downwards in their hands.

In fact, dowsers can dowse for almost anything, from oil and minerals to a coin hidden under the carpet. It seems that they merely have to decide what they're looking for, and the unconscious mind—or the "other self"—does the rest.

I have described elsewhere* how I discovered, to my own astonishment, that I could dowse. I was visiting a circle of standing stones called the Merry Maidens, in Cornwall—a circle that probably dates back to the same period as Stonehenge. When I held the rod—made of two strips of plastic tied at the end—so as to give it a certain tension, it responded powerfully when I approached the stones. It would twist upward as I came close to the stone, and then dip again as I stepped back or walked past it. What surprised me was that I felt nothing, no tingling in the hands, no sense of expectancy. It seemed to happen as automatically as the response of a voltmeter in an electric circuit. Since then I have shown dozens of

---

* In *Mysteries*, p. 116.

people how to dowse. It is my own experience that nine out of ten people can dowse, and that all young children can do it. Some adults have to "tune in"—to learn to allow the mind and muscles to relax—but this can usually be done in a few minutes.

Scientific tests have shown that what happens in dowsing is that the muscles convulse—or tighten—of their own accord. And if the dowser holds a pendulum—made of a wooden bob on a short length of string—then the pendulum goes into a circular swing over standing stones or underground water—once again, through some unconscious action of the muscles.

Another experiment performed by Roger Sperry throws an interesting light on dowsing. He tried flashing green or red lights at random into the "blind" eye of split-brain patients (into the left visual field, connected to the right cerebral hemisphere). The patients were then asked what color had just been seen. Naturally, they had no idea, and the guesses showed a random score. But if they were allowed a second guess, they would always get it right. They might say: "Red—oh no, green . . ." The right side of the brain had overheard the wrong guess, and communicated by *causing the patient's muscles to twitch.* It was the equivalent of a kick under the table.

Unable to communicate in any other way, the right brain did it by contracting the muscles.

It seems, therefore a reasonable guess that this is also what happens in dowsing. The right brain knows there is water down there, or some peculiar magnetic force in the standing stones; it communicates this knowledge by causing the muscles to tense, which makes the rod jerk upwards.

Most "psychics" observe that deliberate effort inhibits their powers. One psychic, Lois Bourne, has written:

> One of the greatest barriers to mediumship is the intellect, and the most serious problem I had to learn in my early psychic career was the suspension of my intellect. If, during the practice of extra-sensory perception, I allowed logic to prevail, and permitted myself to rationalize the impressions I received, and the things I said, I would be hopelessly lost within a conflict. It is necessary that I totally by-pass my conscious mind ...

Similarly, Felicia Parise found that she was at first totally unable to cause "PK effects," no matter how hard she tried. But one day, when she had received an emotional shock—the news that her grandmother was dying—she reached out for a small plastic bottle and it moved away from her hand. From then on, she had the "trick" of causing PK.

All this underlines something that should be quite clear in any case: that in a sense, we are *all* "split-brain patients." The logical self interferes with the natural operations of the right brain. This is why the artist has to wait for "inspiration"—for the left brain to relax and allow the right to take over. Mozart was an example of an artist who was born with an unusual harmony between the two halves of his brain, and he commented once that tunes were always "walking into his head"— meaning into his left brain. In most of us, a certain self-mistrust, a tendency to ask questions, sits like a bad-tempered door-keeper between the two halves of the brain. When we become subject to increasing tension and worry, this has the effect of increasing the door-keeper's mistrustfulness. He thinks he is performing a useful service in keeping out the impulses from the "other half." In fact, he is simply isolating the left-brain self and making it more tense and miserable. Nervous breakdown is due to the increasingly desperate attempts of this door-keeper to cope with problems in what he considers to be the right way, and which is, in fact, the worst possible way.

What Lois Bourne has said about suspending the rational intellect seems to apply to most forms of "extra-sensory perception" and paranormal abilities. Most people have had the experience of reaching out to pick up the telephone and *knowing* who is on the other end. Everyone has had the experience of thinking about someone they haven't heard from in years, and receiving a letter from them the same day. "Extra-sensory perception" (ESP) seems to operate when we are relaxed, and thinking about something else.

All this, then, *seems* to offer a basis for an explanation of the poltergeist. It is true that human powers of psychokinesis seem rather feeble—it would be far more convincing if we could point to some medium or psychic who could cause objects to fly around the room at will. But then, perhaps the explanation is that the "door-keeper" inhibits the natural powers of the right brain. Even good "mediums" cannot put themselves into a "sensitive" state at will; some of them need to go into a trance; others need to be in the right frame of mind. Trance mediums who try to "work normally" (i.e., when wide awake) often find it exhausting and frustrating, because the "censor" keeps getting in the way. So if the poltergeist *is* some peculiar power or force residing in the right brain, perhaps this explains why it cannot be called upon at will, even by gifted psychics such as Uri Geller.

Dowsing also provides us with a possible explanation of the origin of that force. In some dowsers, the presence of underground water produces such a powerful effect that they go into violent convulsions. One of the most famous of French dowsers, Barthelemy Bléton, discovered his powers accidentally at the age of seven;

he was taking his father's meal out to the fields when he sat down on a certain spot, and felt sick and faint. Digging at this spot revealed a powerful underground stream. Again, an old lady who is a member of the British Society of Dowsers described at a conference a few years ago how she could pick up a large branch from the ground, and it would swing around in her hand like a pointer until it indicated water.

If the dowsing rod is responding to some magnetic force, either in water or standing stones, it seems possible that this same force, channeled through the right brain, could provide the energy for poltergeist effects.

It looks, then, as if the modern psychical investigator is in a far better position than his predecessor of a century ago when it comes to constructing theories about the paranormal. The recognition of the "two people" inside our heads may be the most important step ever taken in this direction.

Having said this, it is necessary to admit that most of the mystery remains unexplained. Lodge's "psychometric hypothesis" and Lethbridge's theory of "ghouls" may provide an explanation for the majority of ghosts— but what about all those cases in which the witnesses insist that the ghost behaved as if it saw them? Again, it would certainly be convenient if we could explain the poltergeist in terms of "unconscious psychokinesis." But why has no psychic been able to duplicate poltergeist effects? It is not really an answer to say that they have not learned to switch the power on and off. Many psychics can switch other powers on and off—telepathy, psychokinesis, second sight. So why not poltergeist effects?

These awkward questions remind us that there are others we have failed to answer. In the case of Lombroso's bottle-smashing poltergeist in the Via Bava, why did it stop smashing bottles when the wife went away for the first time? If Lombroso is correct, and the poltergeist was a "spirit" that drew its energy from people, then we have our explanation. The spirit needed energy from both the wife and the young waiter to smash bottles and crockery. When the wife went away for the first time, it lost half its energy supply and decided to take a rest. But the second time she went away, she cursed it, and it made a special effort to be disagreeable. In order to do this, it had to make use of the "vestigial energy" she had left on dishes and other objects she had touched. When the young waiter was eventually dismissed, the wife alone could not provide sufficient energy for its needs and it went elsewhere . . .

Modern psychical research has a way of ignoring such questions. It prefers straightforward distinctions. If there is a "medium" present (or, as we now say, a "focus"), then it is a poltergeist; if not, then it is a ghost.

But even this pleasantly simple distinction proves to be less useful than it looks. The "spirits" themselves seem to dislike being type-cast, and often decline to stick to their proper role. A case that starts as an ordinary haunting may develop into a poltergeist haunting, and vice versa. And then, just to confuse the issue, the spirits occasionally identify themselves as devils and demons, and manifest themselves in the highly disturbing form known as "possession." This subject is so complex that it deserves a chapter to itself.

Two

Possession is Nine Points of the Law

Paris has always led the rest of the world in new fads and crazes—from the can-can in the 1830s, to existentialism in the 1940s. In 1850, the newest and most exciting craze was "table turning." The rules were simple. A group of people sat around a table, resting their fingertips lightly on the surface, their fingers spread wide so that everyone's hands touched those of the neighbor on either side. When conditions were favorable, the table would begin to vibrate, then to move of its own accord. It might twist around at an angle of ninety degrees, or rise up into the air, or simply balance on two legs.

This entertainment had, of course, originated in America, the home of modern "spiritualism." In March 1848 the Fox family, who lived in a farmhouse in the village of Hydesville, New York, were kept awake at night by loud rapping noises, which defied all attempts to track them down. One of the two younger Fox sisters—Margaret was fifteen and Kate twelve—started snapping her fingers, and the raps imitated the sounds she made. A neighbor who came in to hear the raps tried asking questions, with one rap for "yes" and two for "no." The obliging spirit was able to give the age of various people who were present and to answer various other numerical questions.

At this point, the neighbor had the idea of devising an alphabetical code, and asking the spirit to answer questions about itself. It identified itself as a peddler named Charles B. Rosma, who had died in the house five years earlier. Asked for details, it said that it had been murdered in the east bedroom by having its throat cut, and had subsequently been buried in the cellar. Police investigation failed to locate a missing peddler named Rosma, and the murder inquiry was not pursued.* Soon afterward, the poltergeist rappings turned into a normal "haunting," with sounds of a death struggle, horrible gurglings (presumably as the man's throat was cut) and the sounds of a body being dragged across the floor. (Mr. Fox's hair turned white as a result.)

Meanwhile, the rapping noises followed the girls around from house to house. Various committees were set up to try and detect the girls in trickery—entirely without success. When Kate and Margaret separated to avoid the furor, the rappings broke out in both houses they stayed in. A man named Calvin Brown, who lived in the same house as the eldest Fox sister, Leah, seemed to arouse the spirit's dislike because of his hostile attitude, and it began to persecute him. Various objects were thrown at him—but without ever causing injury. Then the "spirit'" began snatching off Mrs. Fox's cap, pulling the comb out of her hair, as well as jabbing pins into members of the family when they knelt down to pray. The rappings turned into deafening bangs like cannon, which could be heard a mile away.

The household was in despair until someone decided to try and communicate with the spirit by using the alphabetical code. The result was a message beginning: "Dear friends, you must proclaim this truth to the world. This is the dawning of a new era . . . " It proved to be correct. The first "spiritualist" meeting took place on November 14, 1849, and within months this new "religion" had spread across America, then across the sea to Europe.

---

* But in 1904, a collapsing wall in the other cellar revealed a male skeleton; a peddler's box was found nearby.

All three sisters—including Leah—developed into "mediums," and gave seances. The simplest method of holding a seance is for everyone to sit around the tables and call upon the spirits. And at a very early stage, the spirits began indicating their presence by causing the table to vibrate, or even making it give raps by raising one leg in the air and banging it on the floor. It seemed astonishingly easy to make a table move (as, indeed, it still is). It was discovered that the best method was to take a fairly light table—a card table for preference— and place it on a smooth polished floor. The "sisters" then had to join their fingers in a "chain" and concentrate. And usually, within minutes, the table was sliding around the room, sometimes even rising into the air, in spite of all efforts to hold it down.

The Parisians were thrilled with this new game; there had been nothing like it since the days when Mesmer had "magnetized" groups of half-naked men and women and sent them into ecstatic convulsions. What astonished everyone was how easy it was to get results. If the phenomena were really due to spirits, then they seemed to be permanently on duty.

One of Paris's best-known intellectuals at this time was an educationalist called Leon Dénizarth-Hippolyte Rivail. Rivail was to Paris what John Ruskin and Herbert Spencer would become to London: a kind of universal educator, willing to dispense knowledge on any and every topic. His public lectures on such subjects as chemistry and astronomy were attended by huge audiences.

Rivail was one of the few people who still believed in the discoveries of Mesmer, that remarkable physician who had been driven out of Paris seventy years earlier by the hostility of the medical profession. Mesmer believed that illnesses can be cured by magnets, and one of his disciples made the discovery with which Mesmer's name is often identified—hypnotism. But when the doctors succeeded in driving Mesmer out of France, they also succeeded in convincing most people that hypnotism was a fraud. Rivail was sufficiently independent to test it for himself, and discovered that it worked. He also discovered that, contrary to what the doctors insisted, magnets *could* produce remarkable effects on sick people, as could various metals such as gold and copper. (This interesting notion still awaits rediscovery by the medical profession.) So Rivail was prepared to be open-minded on the subject of table-turning. He did not permit himself to be prejudiced by the fact that every empty-headed society woman in Paris was organizing seances, and that even the much despised emperor Napoleon the Third (whom Victor Hugo denounced as Napoleon the Little) held sessions at Versailles. He looked into the matter with his usual intense curiosity and scientific detachment.

Now it so happened that a friend of Rivail's named Becquet had two daughters who had begun to experiment with the new craze, and had discovered that they seemed to be excellent "mediums." It seemed to Rivail that this was not an opportunity to be missed. If the spirits really had anything sensible to communicate, then presumably they would be willing to answer questions put by a man of science. Accordingly, the Becquet girls were asked to devote a few hours every week to automatic writing; and to ask the "spirits" a number of specific questions written down by Rivail.

The results surpassed his most optimistic expectations. The spirits, it seemed, were anxious to explain themselves at length. Rivail was excited to find that what they said seemed to make sense, and constituted a remarkable and consistent philosophy about life and death. Interestingly enough, they seemed to agree with Mesmer, who said that the universe is pervaded by a vital or magnetic "fluid." When this fluid is able to flow through living beings, the result is health; when it is blocked, the result is illness.

According to Rivail's informants, the universe is pervaded by spirits of incorporeal intelligences. Human beings are simply "incarnate spirits," spirits united with a material body. They advance toward perfection by undergoing trials during their lifetime, and after one body dies, they are reincarnated in another one. In between reincarnations, they may wander around without a body. It is these "discarnate spirits" that are responsible for various forms of mischief, such as poltergeist effects.

In due course, the spirits instructed Rivail to publish the results of his questions. They gave him a title— *The Spirits' Book*—and even told him the pseudonym he should use: Allan Kardec—both names he had borne in a previous existence, they told him.

The Spirits' Book appeared in 1856, and created a sensation. Kardec became the founder-figure of the French spiritualist movement, and his works attained immense influence. But he died of a heart attack only thirteen years after the book was published, at the age of sixty-five, and his influence was soon being widely questioned by the French spiritualist movement. Rivail was totally committed to the doctrine of reincarnation, the slow perfection of the spirit through a series of rebirths, which can be traced back to ancient India. But most of the "spirits" who spoke through mediums at seances had nothing to say about reincarnation. So Rivail was inclined to be critical about trance mediums, while the trance mediums and their followers denounced Rivail as a dogmatic old man. After Rivail's death, his influence waned, and within a few years he was half-forgotten. Oddly enough, his works received immediate and widespread acceptance in South America, particularly in Brazil, and became the foundation of a religion—which calls itself Spiritism—which still flourishes there. We shall examine this at length in Chapter Six.

Now in Paris, in 1860, there was a particularly violent poltergeist in the Rue des Noyers; it smashed every window in the place, hurled all kinds of objects around the house (including many which the occupants had never seen before), and finally drove the unfortunate people out of the house. Rivail decided to try to find out what exactly had happened. His medium's "control" (i.e., the spirit who acts as Master of Ceremonies) explained that the disturbances were the work of a mischievous spirit. And, at the request of the control (a spirit called Saint Louis), the poltergeist of the Rue des Noyers was summoned. He appeared to be in a bad temper, and asked irritably: "Why do you call me? Do you want to have some stones thrown at you?" Rivail now asked the spirit: "Was there anyone in the Rue des Noyers who helped you play tricks on the inmates?" Certainly, replied the spirit, it had had an excellent "instrument." It added, "For I am merry and like to amuse myself sometimes." Who was it, Rivail asked. "A maidservant."

"Was she unaware you were making use of her?"

"Oh yes, poor girl—she was the most frightened of them all."

Rivail asked how the spirit managed to throw various objects about the place, and received the interesting answer: "I helped myself through the electric nature of the girl, joined to my own . . . thus we were able to transport the objects between us."

Rivail asked the spirit who it was. It replied that it had been dead about fifty years, and had been a rag and bone man. People used to make fun of him because he drank too much, and this was why he decided to play tricks on the inhabitants of the Rue des Noyers. He indignantly denied that he had done these things out of malice; it was merely his way of amusing himself.

This spirit seemed to belong to a class described in *The Spirits' Book:* "They are ignorant, mischievous, unreasonable, and addicted to mockery. They meddle with everything and reply to every question without paying attention to the truth." This latter remark brings to mind a comment by G. K. Chesterton, who describes in his autobiography how he once experimented with a planchette—a device for automatic writing. The sitters asked one of the "spirits" the name of a distant relative, and the board answered "Manning." When they said this was untrue, it wrote: "Married before." "To whom?" "Cardinal Manning." Chesterton remarks:

> I saw quite enough of the thing to be able to tes-
> tify, with complete certainty, that something hap-
> pens which is not in the ordinary sense natural . . .
> Whether it is produced by some subconscious but
> still human force, or by some powers, good, bad
> or indifferent, which are external to humanity, I
> would not myself attempt to decide. The only
> thing I will say with complete confidence about
> that mystic and invisible power is that it tells lies.

Elsewhere, Rivail asked the spirits about the sub-
ject of "demoniacal possession," and how far human beings can be unconsciously influenced by spirits. The answer to the latter question was that the influence of spirits is far greater than most people suppose—that they often influence our thoughts *and* actions. This is a theme that is often repeated in the books of "Allan Kardec." Asked about possession, the spirit replied: "A spirit does not enter into a body as you enter into a house. He assimilates himself to an incarnate spirit who has the same defects and the same qualities as himself, in order that

they may act conjointly." But, it added, the spirit cannot actually "take over" the body of the person it is "possessing." This is united indissolubly to the physical body.

In that case, asked Rivail, can a person be dominated and subjugated by a spirit until its own will is paralyzed? Yes, came the reply, this is precisely what is meant by possession. But the domination is established through the *cooperation* of the "possessed," either out of weakness or of their own free will. It added sensibly that many people who seem to be possessed are really cases of epilepsy or madness, and demand a doctor rather than an exorcist. Rivail asked whether exorcism actually has any power over such spirits, and got the answer: "No. When bad spirits see anyone trying to influence them by such means, they laugh." In fact, any investigator who has had anything to do with poltergeists knows that they cannot be exorcised.

The modern revival of interest in the subject of "demoniacal possession" was largely the result of Aldous Huxley's book *The Devils of Loudun*, published in 1952 and, later, of William Blatty's novel *The Exorcist*. Huxley takes a skeptical view of the possession of a convent full of Ursuline nuns:

> Bogus demoniac possession, artfully faked by a whole convent of hysterical Ursulines, under the coaching of their spiritual directors; monks plotting with lawyers to bear false witness against a hated professional and sexual rival; a fornicating priest, enmeshed in the toils of his own lust and vanity and at last judicially murdered on a false charge and with every refinement of cruelty—it is a story that takes a high place in the annals of human beastliness in general and religious beastliness in particular . . .*

---

* *Grey Eminence*, p.208.

Father Urbain Grandier, the parish priest of the small town of Loudun, was charged in 1633 of "bewitching" the nuns of the local convent, who had been going into convulsions and howling blasphemies in hoarse voices. When Grandier was finally taken in to perform an exorcism ceremony, the nuns began to accuse him of being responsible. Convinced of the absurdity of the charge, Grandier made no real attempt to defend himself until it was too late. Then he was tortured and publicly burnt.

Huxley is undoubtedly correct when he speaks of the plots against Grandier, and about Grandier's own fornications—he seduced at least two young girls in the confessional and made one of them pregnant. There also seems to be no doubt that the "plot" against Grandier began as a practical joke, with some of the novices frightening the others by dressing up in white sheets and pretending to be ghosts. But when we come to examine the actual "possession," the skeptical explanation no longer seems adequate. Four of the priests who came to exorcise the "devils" were themselves possessed, and two of them died of it. Father Surin, a remarkable mystic, became more or less insane for twenty-five years. The unfortunate Father Tranquille, a famous Capuchin preacher, went along to Loudun convinced that the authority of the Church would protect him from the "devils"; he proved to be mistaken. He found himself in the horrifying position of writhing around on the ground, listening to his mouth uttering blasphemies, while his mind remained a detached spectator. This continued until he died in a state of exhaustion. In a famous study of psychological possession, the German philosopher T. K. Oesterreich observes accurately: "This death is one of the most frightful which can be imagined, the patient being sick in mind while fully conscious, and a prey to excitement so violent that finally the organism breaks down under it." The same thing happened to Father Lactance, who had "expelled three demons" from the prioress of the convent, Sister Jeanne des Anges.

Surin came to Loudun after Grandier had been burnt. His death did not put an end to the possession of the nuns. Father Lactance was already dead. And fairly soon, Surin was writing to a friend:

> God has . . . permitted the devils to pass out of the possessed person's body and, entering into mine, to assault me, to throw me down, to torment me . . . I find it almost impossible to explain what happens to me during this time, how this alien spirit is united to mine, without depriving me of consciousness or of inner freedom, and yet constituting a second "me," as though I had two souls, of which one is dispossessed of my body and the use of its organs, and keeps its quarters, watching the other, the intruder, doing whatever it likes . . . The very soul is as though divided . . . At one and the same time I feel great peace, as being under God's good pleasure, and on the other hand (without knowing how) an overpowering rage and loathing of God, expressing itself in frantic struggles (astonishing to those who watch them) to separate myself from Him.

Now it is by no means impossible to explain all this in purely psychological terms. Poe has written about it in a story called "The Imp of the Perverse," in which he discusses the way in which we can feel a sudden urge to do something that horrifies us; the narrator of his story has succeeded in committing a "perfect murder," and cannot resist a compulsion to go and shout about it in the street.

There is nothing very strange in this. It is simply the operation of what the psychiatrist Viktor Frankl calls "the law of reverse effort." The more a stutterer wants to stop stuttering, the worse he stutters. On the other hand, Frankl mentions a stutterer who was asked to play a stutterer in the school play, and was then unable to stutter. All this is explained by the recognition that "you" live in the left half of the brain, and that another "you" lives a few centimeters away in the other half. As soon as the left begins to interfere too much, it has the effect of "throttling" the right, just as if a man had grabbed himself by the throat. We are all of us "divided selves."

But it is one thing to stutter and stammer, and quite another to die of exhaustion in the belief that you are tormented by a devil. Looking detachedly at the case of the Loudun demons, it is difficult not to feel that *The Spirits' Book* of Kardec explains it rather better than Huxley does. If we assume that the whole thing began as a plot against Grandier, and a sexual obsession on the part of the nuns—particularly Sister Jeanne des Anges—then we can begin to understand what Kardec's "St. Louis" meant when he explained: "A spirit does not enter into a body as you enter into a house. He assimilates himself to a [person] who has the same defects and the same qualities as himself . . ." Fathers Lactance and Tranquille behaved with a frightful vengefulness—Lactance superintended the torture of Grandier—and therefore laid themselves open to "possession." As to Sister Jeanne, she later wrote an autobiography in which it is made perfectly clear that she never much enjoyed being a nun; she was a dominant woman, and dominant women are usually "highly sexed." She admits that she made no real effort to push aside the indecent thoughts that came into her head when she was praying or taking communion. "This accursed spirit insinuated himself into me so subtly that I in no way recognized his workings . . . " She may have started out with a more or less conscious desire to cause trouble for Father Grandier; but a point came where, like Tranquille and Lactance, she found her body being used by demons. Unlike Tranquille and Lactance, she rather enjoyed being possessed.

The case on which William Blatty based *The Exorcist* took place in a Washington suburb, Mount Rainier, in 1949. Thirteen-year-old Douglass Deen was the "focus" of the occurrences, which began with a scratching noise in the walls. A rat extermination company was able to find no sign of rats or mice. The sounds occurred only when Douglass was near by. Then more usual poltergeist phenomena began to occur: dishes flew through the air, fruit was hurled against the wall. A picture floated off the wall, hovered in the air, then went back to its old position. After this, Douglass' bed began to shake and quiver when he was in it.

The family asked the local minister, the Reverend M. Winston, for help, and on February 17, 1949, Douglass spent the night in his home. The two retired to a room with twin beds. Douglass' bed soon began to vibrate, and there were scratching noises in the walls. Winston asked Douglass to sleep in an armchair. The chair slid over to the wall, then slowly tilted until it threw the boy on the floor. The minister improvised a bed on the floor; as soon as Douglass was in it, the bed slid across the room.

As these events continued, the boy was taken to two hospitals, Georgetown and St. Louis University, both Jesuit institutions. All attempts to treat him medically and psychiatrically were unsuccessful. Finally, a Jesuit priest undertook the exorcism. He fasted for two and a half months on bread and water, and repeated the ritual of exorcism no fewer than thirty times. The "spirit" showed its objection to these rituals—or perhaps its contempt—by sending the boy into convulsions, making him scream obscenities and blasphemies in a shrill voice, and sometimes making him reply to the exorcism in Latin—a language he had never studied. Finally, in May 1949, the phenomena ceased; the thirtieth exorcism was apparently successful. But then, as we shall see, most poltergeist phenomena last only a month or so; it may have gone away of its own accord.

Here, then, we have a case of poltergeist disturbances that turned into "demoniacal possession," with all the phenomena that occurred in the Loudun case. The "psychological" explanation would be that Douglass Deen's "other self" began by producing poltergeist disturbances, then took up the game of demonic possession suggested by the Jesuit fathers. (His ability to speak Latin is not as surprising as it sounds; he must have heard a great deal of Latin during his life—at mass—and may have picked it up unconsciously.) But Kardec's explanation about a mischievous spirit fits equally well. If Kardec is correct, then the physical changes that occur during puberty cause a "leakage" of a certain type of energy that can be used by a poltergeist; this energy is probably some form of nerve-force. When the physical adjustments of puberty have been made, the leak stops, and the poltergeist can no longer manifest itself.

In the Deen case, the two explanations seem equally plausible. But there are other cases where the balance of probability seems to rest closer to the Kardec explanation. One of the best known of these has become known as "the Amherst mystery." It took place in Amherst, Nova Scotia, in 1878. A shoe worker, Daniel Teed, lived in a two-story house with his wife and two sons, his wife's two unmarried sisters, Jane and Esther Cox, who were aged twenty-two and eighteen, his wife's brother William, and his own brother, John. (The house must have been grossly overcrowded.) All were

Methodists. Jane, the elder sister, was pretty; Esther was short and rather stout. Nevertheless, Esther had a boyfriend, a local factory worker named Bob MacNeal.

In late August, Daniel Teed complained that someone had been milking the cow; Esther was a suspect as she was unusually fond of milk. Esther was suffering from nervous tensions, and ran up from the cellar one night screaming that a rat had run over her leg. Her troubles were probably sexual in origin, as seems to be revealed by a dream she had at the time: hundreds of black bulls with bright blue eyes and blood dripping from their mouths tried to break into the house, while Esther frantically locked the doors . . .

The following evening, Esther and Bob MacNeal went out for a drive. Bob, who had a bad reputation locally, tried to persuade Esther to go into the woods with him, but she refused. He pulled out a gun and ordered her to get down from the buggy; he looked as if he might fire when the sound of an approaching vehicle distracted him. He leapt on to the buggy, drove back at a dangerous speed, let Esther off, then left Amherst for good. Esther cried herself to sleep, and for the next few days had red eyes.

On September 4, a damp, misty evening, Jane heard Esther sobbing in bed. Then Esther screamed that there was a mouse in bed with her. They searched, but no mouse was found. The following night, both heard a rustling noise, and made a search. It seemed to be coming from a cardboard box containing patchwork, so Jane stood it in the middle of the room, expecting a mouse to run out. Instead the box jumped into the air and fell over. She stood it up, and it jumped again.

Daniel Teed came in to see what the noise was about, pushed the box under the bed, and told them to go to sleep.

The next night, Esther went to bed early. Soon after the light went out, she leapt out of bed shouting: "Jane, I'm dying." Jane lit the lamp and saw that Esther's face was bright red, and her hair was standing on end. Daniel Teed came in, together with the other two men. Esther got back into bed, but began to scream. Her body appeared to be swelling like a balloon. Suddenly, there was a loud report like a clap of thunder. The men rushed out to search the house, but found nothing. When they came back, Esther was back to normal and fast asleep.

Two days later, as Esther was getting into bed, she began to feel ill again. All the bedclothes flew off the bed, and landed in the far corner of the room. Jane fainted. Esther began to swell again. The men rushed in, and someone replaced the bedclothes; they promptly flew off again, and a pillow hit John Teed on the head; he left the house never to return. Again, there were some loud explosions. Esther stopped swelling, and fell asleep.

The following day, a doctor came to see Esther. As she lay in bed, the pillow under her head inflated, as if filled up with air, then collapsed, then re-inflated itself. Raps sounded around the room. The bedclothes flew off. There was a scratching noise above Esther's bed and, as they all watched, they saw writing appearing on the wall. It said: "Esther, you are mine to kill." A lump of plaster detached itself from elsewhere on the wall and flew across the room to the doctor's feet. Then rappings and bangs continued for the next two hours, while Esther lay, terrified, on her bed.

The following day, Esther complained of an "electric" feeling running through her body. The doctor gave her morphine; instantly, there was a series of bangs and crashes that seemed to go up to the roof.

These disturbances continued for another three weeks. Then, one night, Esther fell into a trance, became rigid, and told the story of what had happened with Bob MacNeal. When she recovered consciousness, she admitted it was true. When Jane said that Bob must be responsible for Esther's problems, loud knocks suggested that the "spirit" agreed completely. Jane remarked that it seemed to understand what she said, whereupon there were three distinct raps. The doctor tried asking the "spirit" simple questions, with one rap for no, two for "no answer," three for yes. But the doctor's attempts to get it to explain itself were a total failure.

Esther became a subject of controversy; the house was permanently full of people. When a minister called to see her, a bucket of cold water on the kitchen table began to bubble as if it was boiling.

In December, Esther developed a severe sore throat which turned to diphtheria. While she was ill, the manifestations ceased. Then she went away to convalesce. When she returned, the manifestations started immediately. Esther said she heard a voice telling her that the house was going to be set on fire. As she told the others about this, a lighted match fell from the air on to the bed, and the sheets caught fire. Jane quickly put it out. More lighted matches fell around the room, most of them going out immediately. The rapping noises started later, and when the family asked the "spirit" whether the house would be set alight, it replied that it would not be. At that moment there was smoke from under Esther's bed; they found that a dress had somehow transferred itself from the bedroom door, and had been set on fire.

Three days later, Mrs. Teed smelled smoke coming from the cellar. They found a barrel of wood shavings burning vigorously and had some trouble putting it out.

The villagers were alarmed about this; if the Teeds' house caught fire, half the village would probably be burned down. They suggested that Esther ought to be sent away. A neighbor named John White offered to take her in if she would do some housework. For two weeks, all went well; then a scrubbing brush flew out of Esther's hand, went up to the ceiling, and came down and hit her on the head.

White owned a restaurant, and Esther went to work there. An oven door refused to stay closed, and jumped off its hinges. Metal objects began flying at Esther as if she were a magnet, and a boy's clasp knife made her back bleed. When iron spikes were laid in her lap, they quickly became too hot to touch.

All this seemed to support the suspicion that Esther was somehow "electrified." They tried making her wear a special pair of shoes with glass soles; but these gave her headaches and made her nose bleed.

When furniture began to move around the restaurant, John White decided it was time for Esther to go home. Again, she left Amherst for a few months; first to stay with a man and his wife in New Brunswick, then to a farm three miles from Amherst. She told various visitors about the "voices" that spoke to her—voices which claimed to be the spirits that were causing the mischief. One of these spirits, "Bob Nickle," threatened her with fire and stabbing.

In June, 1879, a stage magician named Walter Hubbell moved into the Teeds' cottage as a paying guest; he had heard about the "haunting" and thought it might make the subject of a book. Within a few minutes of arriving, he had no doubt that this was no fraud. His umbrella sailed through the air, then a carving knife landed at his feet, then his bag was "thrown," then a chair shot across the room and hit his own so hard that he nearly fell on the floor. From then on, the chairs in every room he entered performed a dance. Esther told him he was unpopular with the spirits. Undeterred, Hubbell tried asking them questions by means of raps, and the spirits were able to tell him the number engraved on his watch, and the dates of coins in his pockets. Later, Hubbell lay down on the settee and closed his eyes; Esther came into the room, and Hubbell cautiously peeped at her, perhaps hoping that she would give herself away as a cheat. Instead, he saw a large glass paperweight float up across the room and rebound off the arm of the settee.

During the next few days the poltergeist put on a special show for Hubbell. Objects floated around, strange noises were heard—like sawing wood and drumming on a washboard—and Esther was attacked by "six spirits" who stuck no fewer than thirty pins in her. Small fires broke out—on one day there were forty-five of them—and the sound of a trumpet echoed through the house; they later found a small silver trumpet which no one had ever seen before. When Esther went to the local minister to pray, "Bob Nickle" attacked her viciously on her return, cutting her head open with a bone and stabbing her in the face with a fork.

Hubbell thought he saw a way of making money. He hired a hall and persuaded Esther to put on a "show" or the people of Amherst. Inevitably, the spirits declined to operate, and the audience demanded their money back.

Tired of the non-stop disturbances, Daniel Teed sent Esther off to stay with some obliging friends; Hubbell, who now had enough material for his book, went to St. John to write it. It appeared in due course and went through several editions.

During Esther's stay with her friends, the spirits let her alone. She then took a job on a farm owned by people called Davidson. Her friends found that various arti-

cles were missing, and these were located in the David-
sons' barn. Esther was suspected of theft, but before the
case could be investigated the barn caught fire and
burned to the ground. Esther was accused of arson, and
was sentenced to four months in jail. After this, the manifestations came suddenly to an end.

This abrupt termination of the "haunting" seems to
favor the view that Esther's own unconscious mind was
responsible. This is, in fact, the view I favored when I
described the case briefly in a book called *Mysteries*.
Esther was sexually frustrated, and if Bob MacNeal had
adopted a more gentlemanly way of seducing her, there
would have been no *Great Amherst Mystery* (the title of
Hubbell's book). Esther was a classic case of "the
divided self": a part of her longing to give herself to her
lover, while the inhibitions induced by her background
and training made this impossible. So when she rejected
his advances, and he vanished into the night, her unconscious mind said, in effect: "Now see what you've done,
stupid!" and set out to punish her. As to the effects themselves, many of them fit the hypothesis I have suggested:
that the "energy" comes from the earth. When Esther
wore shoes with glass soles, the manifestations stopped
but she developed headaches and nosebleeds. Her sensation of electric currents is also highly suggestive. There
have been dozens of well-authenticated cases of "human
electric batteries." Again, nearly all concern girls or boys
at the age of puberty. Caroline Clare of Bondon, Ontario,
began to lose weight at the age of seventeen (in 1877),
then developed such powerful electric currents that people who touched her received severe shocks; pieces of
metal stuck to her as if she were a magnet. Jennie Morgan of Sedalia, Missouri, became an electric battery at
fourteen; when she touched metal objects, sparks flew.
Frank McKinistry, also of Missouri, would develop an

electric charge during the night and slowly lose it during the day. When highly charged, his feet would stick to the ground so that he had difficulty in walking—which sounds again as if the electricity comes from the earth. (Good dowsers receive a "tingling" sensation when they touch standing stones.) The Amherst minister, the Reverend Edwin Clay, was convinced that the secret of Esther's manifestations was electricity, and even delivered a lecture to that effect.

But how did Esther's unconscious mind know the number of Hubbell's watch and the dates of coins in its pocket—which no doubt he did not know himself? How did her mind scratch "Esther, you are mine to kill" on the wall above her head? How did it blow a trumpet all over the house? The truth is that the unconscious mind theory needs to be stretched so much that it loses the chief virtue of a good theory—simplicity.

But perhaps the strongest argument against the unconscious mind theory is simply that Esther's torment went on for so long. To actually read the case in detail is to feel that no one could get so angry with herself that she would continue relentlessly for more than a year. We may say, "Oh, I could kick myself," when we do something stupid; but no one has ever *done* it.

The fraud hypothesis also fails to stand up to close examination. If Hubbell's book was the main piece of evidence, then we might well feel suspicious, since he went to Amherst with the hope of writing it, and eventually made a great deal of money from no fewer than ten editions. But there are accounts in the *Amherst Gazette* that confirm everything Hubbell says. Moreover, in 1907, more than a quarter of a century after the events, the researcher Hereward Carrington went to Amherst and took various depositions from people who had witnessed the manifestations. By this time, Esther was unhappily married, and had turned into a sullen middle-aged woman, who agreed to talk to Carrington only on the payment of a hundred dollars; Carrington felt that such testimony would be valueless. But there could be no doubt that most of the people involved believed that the manifestations were genuine, including the farmer, Davidson, whose barn had been destroyed—he said that he had often watched Esther as she came downstairs and had noticed that she seemed to fly or float. (In the Middle Ages, levitation used to be one of the criteria for demoniacal possession.)

In 1919, Walter Franklin Prince, another eminent investigator of paranormal phenomena, wrote his own account of the Amherst case in the *Proceedings of the American Society for Psychical Research*, heavily criticizing Hubbell for vagueness and inaccuracy. But Prince had to end by agreeing that there was no question of fraud. What Prince suggested was an interesting variant of the "unconscious mind" theory: the notion that Esther Cox was an example of a baffling psychological illness called "multiple personality," in which an individual splits into two or more completely different persons. One of the most famous cases of the twentieth century was that of a girl named Christine Sizemore, which became the basis of a book (and film), *The Three Faces of Eve*, by Thigpen and Cleckley. But similar cases have been observed and recorded in detail since the beginning of the nineteenth century. In 1811 a young woman named Mary Reynolds, described as being "dull and melancholy," fell into a deep sleep for twenty hours, and when she woke up had lost her memory. She was like a newborn baby. She recognized no one, and became lost in familiar places. She had to be taught to speak, then to read and write—but learned so quickly that it was clear that her buried memory was coming to her aid. Her brothers and sisters were astonished at the change in her disposition. Suddenly, she was cheerful and buoyant. But she worried her family by taking long walks in the Pennsylvania wilderness, and ignoring their warnings about bears and poisonous snakes. She insisted that the bears were actually black hogs. One day, she actually met one in the woods, when she was on horseback, and the horse refused to go on. When the "hog" ignored her orders to get out of the way, she took a stick and walked toward it; at the last moment the bear dropped on all fours and went away.

One morning about five weeks after losing her memory, it came back just as suddenly, and the old Mary Reynolds was back—a dull, cautious girl who had no fondness for nature. Then, a few weeks later, after an unusually deep sleep, the "new" Mary returned with no memory of the past days. And the two Marys continued to alternate for the next twenty years, both of them finally coming to accept that the periods of amnesia were due to the revival of the "other self." Finally, at the age of thirty-five, Mary stabilized, and settled down for the rest of her life in her second personality. She died of a brain embolism at the age of sixty-one.

The most obvious thing about the case is that the second Mary—the cheerful one—contained elements that were not present in the first Mary: high spirits, love of nature, courage and daring. It is as if Mary's unconscious mind got tired of her dullness and lack of enterprise, and decided to take over. But the "new Mary" was not, in all respects, an improvement; her insistence that bears were hogs makes it sound as if she was slightly deranged. Eventually, the second Mary became strong enough to control the personality, and keep her "alter ego" out.

Walter Prince suggested that Esther Cox was a kind of variant of Mary Reynolds—and it is certainly true that

Esther was, like "Mary One," a dull and irritable girl, trapped in a rigid personality structure. The obvious objection is that Prince's hypothesis about "dual personality" still fails to explain all the poltergeist occurrences.

Yet Prince's argument begins to look rather more plausible in the light of a case of which he had direct personal experience. In 1910, Prince's wife got to know a girl called Doris (in his account, Prince gives her the pseudonym Doris Fischer). She was an easygoing, sweet-natured girl who lived with her drunken father, and who suffered periodic fits of amnesia, during which she was "taken over" by no fewer than three other personalities. Prince was so fascinated by the case that he invited Doris to come and live in his home, and ended by completely curing her.

Doris' problems had started when she was three years old; her father came in drunk one night, snatched her from her mother's arms, and hurled her on the floor. This had the effect of causing instant amnesia. Doris remembered nothing more until the following morning, when she suddenly found herself at the foot of the stairs. There had been a slight snap of the neck, as if an electric current had been switched on. Yet her mother had seen her walk upstairs in the normal way.

What Doris did not realize was that while she was in a state of amnesia, another personality had taken over her body, a mischievous little girl called Margaret. Like Mary Reynolds' "second personality," Margaret was a good-natured madcap, a bright, vivacious child who was generally liked. While Doris was serious and studious, Margaret was empty-headed and a born truant. Doris would promise her parents not to go swimming in the river; Margaret would go swimming, then slip out of the body and leave Doris to take the punishment. On one occasion, when Doris reached for a piece of cake, she "blanked out," and Margaret snatched the cake and ate it.

Oddly enough, Margaret knew all about Doris, but Doris knew nothing about Margaret until, one day, Margaret decided to tell her. So, leaving Doris's consciousness fully awake, she told Doris the whole story, using Doris's mouth to speak the words. This sounds very much like the "demoniacal possession" of Father Surin, watching his body convulse while unable to do anything about it.

When Doris was in her mid-teens, she graduated at the top of her class and decided to go on to high school. Margaret, who hated studying, refused; and, since she was the stronger personality, Doris left school and went to work as a seamstress.

At seventeen, another personality "appeared." One day at work, Doris had a visual hallucination of her mother; she rushed home and found her mother dying of sudden acute pneumonia. In the early hours of the morning, her mother died. Then her father staggered in, dead drunk, and, without noticing that his wife was dead, fell into bed and began to snore. Doris experienced a pain in her head, and again lost her memory. This new "Doris" was—like the second Mary Reynolds—virtually a new-born baby, entirely without memory. It was Margaret who had to teach her to speak. This new personality was nervous and rather stupid, a thoroughly dull, conventional girl with a monotonous voice.

When Doris was eighteen, she slipped and fell on the back of her head; as a result, yet another personality began to take over the body. This one was even less complex than the previous invader; she seemed to be little more than a memory, and could repeat word for word long conversations that Doris had had in childhood.

When Prince began to study Doris, in 1911, he realized that she seemed to be an incredibly complex series of persons, like Chinese boxes. First, there was Doris herself, a good-natured sensible girl, who unfortunately never seemed to be able to spend more than a few hours at a time in charge of her own body. She was likely to be taken over by Margaret, who was a delightful and mischievous ten-year-old—she had stopped developing at that age—who loved playing with dolls, and kept everybody in fits of laughter. Then there was the dull girl who had taken over when Doris's mother died, and whom Prince called Sick Doris—she was also rather childlike. The "tape recorder" personality also made brief appearances—Prince called her "Sleeping Real Doris." He also discovered that there was yet another personality, more mature and complex than any of the others, whom he called "Sleeping Margaret" because she put in an appearance when Margaret fell asleep. This personality seemed to be able to see into the minds of all the others. She also claimed to be a spirit or guardian angel who had come in reply to the prayers of Doris's mother for someone to protect her daughter.

So the personalities in Doris's body seemed to form a kind of hierarchy or "ladder." At the top was "Sleeping Margaret," the "guardian angel." Next came the mischievous and childish Margaret. Then Doris, then "Sick Doris," then the "tape recorder," Sleeping Real Doris.

Margaret could "eject" Doris at a moment's notice. Sometimes, Doris would be half-way through a sentence when suddenly her expression would alter, and Margaret would take over, with her typical mischievous grin. But Margaret was unaware of the "guardian angel" and on one occasion when she had unceremoniously forced Doris out of the body, the guardian angel got angry and forced Margaret out. Later that day, Margaret reappeared and confided to Prince that there must be someone else in this body because someone had thrown *her* out.

In the security of Prince's household, Doris improved steadily. The personality called Sick Doris began to fade out; she became virtually an idiot, and she and Prince took a final walk together and had a touching leavetaking. Then she reverted to babyhood, and "died." As an experiment, Prince tried encouraging the "tape recorder," seeing if he could turn her into something more like a human being; she responded so well that Prince decided it would be unwise to carry on. She also faded away.

Margaret also began to "grow backwards" as Doris's confidence increased, becoming more and more child-like and using the German pronunciations of Doris's childhood. Her senses seemed to fade, and her visual field narrowed until she could only see directly in front of her—like a baby. Then she too faded away.

The "guardian angel" never faded away; she remained around, and sometimes emerged after Doris had fallen asleep, and had long and interesting talks with Prince. In 1916, when someone suggested that Doris should go to New York to sit with a medium, Prince was dubious until "Sleeping Margaret" assured him that Doris would be perfectly safe in her hands. She was as good as her word, and the result was a remarkable series of seances in which the spirit of Doris's mother—or someone who claimed to be—wrote out long messages that showed an intimate knowledge of Doris's background. Doris' "mother" also insisted that all that had happened to her daughter was simply a case of "benevolent possession." And it has to be admitted that this explanation fits the facts amazingly well. For, on the whole, Doris's experience of multiple personality was not unpleasant. Margaret, although mischievous, was a good-natured and happy child, and the other personalities seem to have been basically harmless. Prince was disposed to believe the assertion of "Sleeping Margaret" that she was a guardian spirit who had come in answer to the prayers of the mother.

It can now be seen why Prince thought it possible that the Amherst case involved dual personality. He was more than half convinced that the Doris case of multiple personality was actually one of benevolent possession, so in suggesting that Esther was a dual personality, he was, in effect, hinting that this could be a case of non-benevolent possession. At the same time, his position as a well-known psychiatrist meant that, for public consumption, he was bound to lay most of the emphasis on the purely psychological explanation—of both the Amherst and the Doris cases.

And what *is* the psychological explanation? It depends, basically, upon the recognition that we are all, to some extent, multiple personalities, divided selves. Part of Esther Cox wanted to be seduced by Bob Mac-Neal, but the personality structure induced by her upbringing made her resist his overtures. If he had been more subtle, and succeeded in persuading her to become his mistress, then the "old" Esther would have slipped into the background, and the new, sexually experienced Esther have taken her place.

We all spend our lives trying to get rid of our "old" selves and develop new—and less constricting—personality structures. This is why we all crave experience, why every boy wants to run away to sea and every girl wants to marry a millionaire with a yacht. But then, we also spend most of our lives reacting "automatically" to familiar circumstances, hardly aware of anything that is further than the end of our noses. So it is difficult to escape the "old self," which consists largely of a set of habits. It is easy to see how rather dull people—like Mary Reynolds and Esther Cox—become trapped to the point of suffocation in this mechanical, habit-bound personality structure, and how the unconscious life urges—perhaps working through the right brain—can plan to overthrow the dreary tyrant.

But before we allow ourselves to be persuaded by this explanation, there are still a few curious points about the Doris case to consider. One of these is how several personalities could apparently *reside* together in the same body. While Doris was "in" the body—i.e., in charge of its movements—Margaret might be also "in," aware of everything that Doris was watching and thinking, and having her own ideas and opinions. Doris could be fast asleep, while Margaret was awake, observing her dreams. Moreover, the "guardian angel," who explained all this to Walter Prince, was also able to be "in," observing both Doris *and* Margaret, unobserved by both.

It is difficult to see how this could take place inside the head of a normal person, even if she happened to be torn by self-division. What the "guardian angel" is explaining sounds like a number of independent spirits, or entities, making use of Doris' body. (Significantly, Doris herself was unable to be aware of any of her other "selves" and their activities.)

Again, there exist a number of photographs of Doris' different personalities. One photograph shows Doris herself, and the caption explains that "Sick Doris" had sat down for the picture, but Doris had "taken over" for a few moments as the camera clicked. Another photograph of "Sick Doris" reveals that she is, indeed, a quite different person from Doris—she looks wooden and stolid, quite unlike the gentle, sensitive Doris. Margaret looks so completely unlike both Dorises that it is hard to realize that she is using the same body. In the *Proceed-*

ings of the American Society for Psychical Research, Prince also describes another case of amnesia, a man he calls Heinrich Meyer. Again, the photographs of the primary and secondary personalities are incredibly different. Physically, they are very similar, yet a different *person* looks out through the eyes of each. It is tempting for the non-professional observer to say simply that the same body has been taken over by different spirits.

Let us consider again the assertion of the "guardian angel" (and of Doris' mother) that the Doris case is basically one of "benevolent possession." Prince tries to explain the coming and going of the personalities in terms of weariness and exhaustion. Doris was easily tired out, and when she grew tired, Margaret would take over. While Margaret was "in" the body, she would say that Doris was "resting." Prince's theory is that Doris became a dual personality as a three-year-old child—to save herself from total breakdown. The shock of being snatched from her mother's arms and hurled on the floor might have seriously damaged her, perhaps turned her into a timid, listless, miserable child. Instead, the "guardian angel" took over the body (she insisted to Prince that she came first, *before* Margaret), and was later assisted by Margaret.

We know that sudden shock can destroy the reason, perhaps turning the person into a "vegetable." It is, in effect, as if a ship had been torpedoed. Other kinds of stress and misery can cause something more like a "slow leak"; a draining of vital energy. This is what happened to the unfortunate Father Tranquille, who virtually died of "shock" after being "possessed" by the "spirits." He went into "exhaust status." Prince's theory is that dual (or multiple) personality occurs when severe shock threatens a person's mental stability. The "other personality" could be considered as the mind's own defense against destruction. And, in fact, the majority of cases of multiple personality begin with a bad shock that threatens to overwhelm the person with "discouragement." We can see how such a shock might turn Doris—at the age of three—into Margaret, who treated life as a joke. But it is almost impossible to understand how it could create "Sleeping Margaret," the "guardian angel."

In *The Devils of Loudun*, Aldous Huxley tries to explain the behavior of Sister Jeanne des Anges by appealing to the concept of multiple personality. He prefers to speak of the case of "Christine Beauchamp," recorded by another famous American professor of psychology, Morton Prince, around the turn of the century. (Her real name was Clara N. Fowler.) Huxley summarizes the case:

> Here is Miss Beauchamp, a blameless but rather sickly young woman, full of high principles, inhibitions and anxiety. From time to time she plays truant from herself and behaves like a very naughty and exuberantly healthy child of ten. Questioned under hypnosis, this *enfant terrible* insists that she is not Miss Beauchamp but someone else called Sally. After some hours or days Sally disappears and Miss Beauchamp returns to consciousness—but returns only to her own consciousness, not to Sally's; for she remembers nothing of what was done, in her name and through the agency of her body, while the latter was in control. Sally, on the contrary, knows all that goes on in Miss Beauchamp's mind and makes use of that knowledge to embarrass and torment the other tenant of their shared body. Because he could think of these odd facts in terms of a well-substantiated theory of subconscious mental activity, and because he was well acquainted with the techniques of hypnosis, Dr.

Morton Prince, the psychiatrist in charge of this case, was able to solve Miss Beauchamp's problems and to bring her for the first time in many years, to a state of physical and mental health.

All that need be added is that the case of Christine Beauchamp—who lived in Boston—bears many resemblances to that of Doris Fischer. Her father was also a drunkard, and Christine became "neurasthenic" (inclined to suffer from nerves) when her mother died in unpleasant circumstances (which Prince does not detail). She greatly admired a close friend of her father's named William Jones, who seemed to her to possess all the qualities her father lacked; when Jones got drunk one night, and made some kind of sexual advance to her, she became even more depressed and neurasthenic. Prince began to treat her for general depression and fatigue, and tried hypnotizing her. This proved to be a mistake, in that it released the secondary personality—who called herself Sally—like a genie out of a bottle. From then on, Sally behaved toward Christine rather as Margaret did toward Doris, but with more malice. Sally, who was as strong as a horse, would take a long walk into the countryside, then abandon the body to the feeble Christine, who had to walk home. (One of the strangest features of cases of multiple personality is that the body seems to be as weak—or as strong—as the personality occupying it; in the case of "Eve"—Christine Sizemore—the secondary personality even emerged when the primary one was unconscious under anaesthetic.) When Christine went to New York to get an office job, Sally got off the train at New Haven and took a job as a waitress.

The main point to note about the cases of Doris Fischer and Sally Beauchamp is that the primary personality could be "dispossessed" of the body by the secondary one—exactly as in the case of the devils of Loudun. And this is by no means a common feature of all such cases. Rather more typical is the case of the Reverend Ansel Bourne who, in January 1887, drew five hundred dollars from his bank and vanished. He then went to Norristown, Pennsylvania, rented a shop, and carried on a trade as a shopkeeper under the name of A. J. Brown. Then one day "Bourne" reappeared, completely oblivious of what he had been doing since he withdrew the money from the bank. Hypnotized by the psychologist William James, "Brown" came back—a completely different personality from Bourne. Brown knew nothing of Bourne, and vice versa, so there was no question of one displacing the other at will. The same seems to be true of the Mary Reynolds case.

Stranger still is the case of Mrs. Remibias Chua, a Philippino woman of Evanston, Illinois. On February 21, 1977, a forty-eight-year-old Filipino nurse named Teresita Basa was stabbed to death in her apartment in Chicago. An attempt had been made to burn the body, which was naked; the medical examination revealed that there had been no rape. The motive was robbery—Miss Basa apparently had a quantity of valuable jewelry.

Teresita had worked at the Edgewater Hospital, where one of her colleagues was another Filipino, a respiratory therapist named Remy Chua, who was married to a doctor. Two weeks after the murder, Jennie Prince, the technical director of the department, had said, "Teresita must be turning in her grave. Too bad she can't tell the police who did it." And Remy Chua replied seriously: "She can come to me in a dream. I'm not afraid." Later the same day, when she was dozing in a locker room, she had a feeling that someone was trying to communicate with her. She opened her eyes, and saw Teresita Basa standing in front of her. In a panic, Remy Chua ran out of the room, and told her fellow workers about the apparition.

Mrs. Chua began to dream about the murder. Again and again, she saw Teresita Basa's face, with the face of a man close behind it. One day, looking at the face of a hospital orderly named Allan Showery, a black, she realized that he was the man of her dream. Showery was a boastful sort of person, claiming that he owned a town house, and kept an airplane at a nearby airfield so that he could fly to New York for weekends to lecture. Now that she had come to believe he was Teresita Basa's killer, Remy Chua became increasingly afraid of him.

In early July, Mrs. Chua was dozing one evening while her husband talked on the phone to his attorney, a man named Al. As José Chua spoke the name "Al," Remy Chua began to scream. Then, in a kind of trance, she got up from the bed and walked across the room, speaking in Tagalog, the language of the Philippines. When she lay down on the bed, a voice began to speak through her mouth: "I am Teresita Basa. I would like to ask for help from you." Dr. Chua asked her what she wanted. "A man came into my apartment and killed me. I want you to tell the police." Mrs. Chua woke up a few minutes later, and remembered nothing of what had happened.

The Chuas did nothing about it—although Remy Chua left the Edgewater Hospital. A few weeks later, as she was making a phone call, Mrs. Chua agan went into a trance. Once again, Teresita Basa's voice spoke through her mouth: "Dr. Chua, did you talk to the police?" Dr. Chua said that he had no evidence to offer them. This time, she named her killer as a man called Allan.

A few days later, it happened again. Mrs. Chua went into a trance, and began to scream out in agony, "I'm burning!" Then the voice of Teresita Basa named Allan Showery as the man who had murdered her. She went on to say that he had stolen her jewelry, and given it to his girlfriend. She mentioned a number of people who could identify her jewelry, even giving the telephone number of one of them. She added, "Tell them that Al came to fix my television, and he killed me and burned me."

This time, José Chua decided to call the police. Understandably, they were unconvinced, and for several days made no attempt to question Showery. When they did, Showery admitted that he had promised to call and repair the television, but insisted that he had simply forgotten. When they questioned his common-law wife, she showed them a cocktail ring that Showery had given her. The police called the telephone number that Mrs. Chua had spoken in her trance. As a result, Teresita Basa's cousin was able to identify the ring as an item of Teresita's jewelry. Faced with this evidence, Showery broke down and admitted that he had murdered Teresita Basa.

In court, the defense attempted to have the case dismissed on the grounds that the evidence had been provided in such an unorthodox manner; they were unsuccessful. Showery was sentenced to fourteen years for murder and four years each for two counts of armed robbery and arson.

It is, of course, possible that Mrs. Chua suspected Showery, and that her unconscious mind chose this way of bringing her suspicions to the attention of the police—certainly, the case for "possession" would be far more convincing if Mrs. Chua had never heard of Teresita Basa or Allan Showery. Yet this still fails to explain how Mrs. Chua knew about the cocktail ring, and the people who would be able to identify it.

The Chua case is fundamentally one of "mediumship"—she went into a trance, like a medium at a seance, and was "used" by another personality. But this draws attention to a similar feature in many cases of multiple personality. Mary Reynolds went into a long and very deep sleep before she was "taken over" by the other personality; Christine Beauchamp was hypnotized; Doris Fischer was probably stunned by her fall on the floor. The psychologist Pierre Janet was hypnotizing a neurasthenic girl when he plunged her into a sleep so profound that she appeared to have stopped breathing; when she woke up, a secondary personality had taken over.

In 1877, a fourteen-year-old French boy named Louis Vivé was attacked by a viper and severely traumatized. He began having fits and was sent to an asylum at Benneval. One day, he had an exceptionally severe attack which lasted fifteen hours. When he recovered, he had become a totally different personality. The primary personality had been a gentle, well-behaved youth who was paralyzed down his right side and spoke with a bad stammer. The "new" Louis Vivé spoke normally, was unparalyzed, and was violent, dishonest and generally badly behaved. After a conviction for theft, Vivé was sent to an asylum where the doctors were fascinated by his case. They tried a technique for transferring his "sensibility" from one side to the other by means of powerful magnets, and this was astonishingly successful; the primary personality again became established.

Here it seems clear that the viper attack caused some basic personality upset—like Doris's violent fall. The long fit, accompanied by a period of deep unconsciousness, allowed the secondary personality to "take over." This secondary personality may have been connected with Vivé's right cerebral hemisphere, since the "primary" Louis was paralyzed down the right side and had a stutter suggesting that it was the left hemisphere that was affected.

In all these cases—with the obvious exception of Remy Chua—the secondary personality has been strikingly different from the primary one; almost as if the personalities had been created out of the same construction kit, and the secondary one could only be created out of the pieces left over from the first. Christine Beauchamp, Doris Fischer, Louis Vivé, were gentle and docile—perhaps too docile; their secondary personalities were aggressive and uninhibited.

But there are also cases that look far more like gentle "possession," where the secondary personality is anything but a mirror image of the primary one. One of the most striking cases on record is that of Lurancy Vennum, the "Watseka Wonder." On July 11, 1877, a thirteen-year old girl named Mary Lurancy Vennum, of Watseka, Illinois, had a fit and became unconscious. The unconsciousness seemed to pass into a kind of trance in which she was able to speak; she claimed she was in heaven, and talking to a little brother and sister who had died. From then on, Lurancy continued to have these trances, in some of which she was apparently "taken over" by various disagreeable entities, including a sullen old woman who called herself Katrina Hogan. The Vennum family was tempted to have her committed to an asylum, but some friends called Roff persuaded them to call in a doctor, E. W. Stevens.

When Stevens first saw Lurancy, the girl was in a bad mood—"possessed" by Katrina Hogan. Then she said she was a young man named Willie Canning. Stevens persuaded her to be hypnotized; whereupon Lurancy returned and explained that she had been possessed by evil spirits. Stevens said she ought to try and find a better "control" (a name mediums apply to the spirit who acts as master of ceremonies). Lurancy then mentioned that a girl named Mary Roff had offered to become her "control." Mr. and Mrs. Roff, who were present, said that this was their daughter, who had died at the age of eighteen when Lurancy was a baby, twelve years earlier.

The next day, Lurancy's personality had changed. She now declared herself to be Mary Roff, and said she wanted to go home. Lurancy's father contacted the Roffs, and Mrs. Roff and her daughter (Mary's sister) went to call at the Vennum's home. As they approached, Lurancy, who was looking out of the window, said excitedly: "Here comes my ma and sister Nervie!" She flung her arms around their necks and cried.

In February 1878, "Mary" went back home with the Roffs, and told them that "the angels" would allow her to stay until May 21. She knew everyone—neighbors as well as family—and showed an intimate acquaintance with the life of the dead Mary Roff, who had died of mysterious fits in July 1865.

The lengthy account of the case written by Dr. Stevens (and later expanded by the researcher Richard Hodgson) is full of details which show that "Mary" knew things that could not possibly have been known to Lurancy Vennum. Her parents tested her with a velvet headdress Mary used to wear; she recognized it immediately. For three months "Mary" lived with her "parents," and gave them instance after instance of her knowledge of Mary Roff's life. On one occasion she mentioned an incident when Mary had cut her arm during a fit, and she started to roll up her sleeve to show the cut; then she seemed to recollect herself and said: "Oh, this is not my arm—mine is under the ground." She claimed to have encountered two of Dr. Stevens' deceased children in heaven, accurately described them, and also described Stevens' own home in Janesville, Wisconsin.

The house where the Roffs lived in 1878 was not the one in which Mary had died in 1865. They passed this other house on the way to the Roffs, and "Mary" struggled hard to get into it; she correctly named it as the place in which she had died. (She also accurately described her own funeral and described where she was buried.)

On May 21, 1878, Mary went around taking her leave of relatives and friends, hugging and kissing them. Then she left and returned to the Vennums' house. By the time she arrived there, she had become Lurancy again. From then on, Lurancy remained more or less normal, marrying a farmer in 1882; but her mediumistic powers remained, and after her marriage, Mary Roff made periodic "visits."

Richard Hodgson—who was associated with Morton Prince in the Christine Beauchamp case—agrees that the explanation could be that Mary Roff was simply a secondary personality of Lurancy Vennum's; but in that case, the secondary personality would have had to possess paranormal powers—at the very least, of telepathy. Hodgson seems to feel that the "spiritualistic hypothesis" is preferable.

But whether or not we can accept the notion of life after death, there can be no doubt that all these cases seem to point in the same direction: to the notion that the personality—or "spirit"—uses the body in much the same way that a driver makes use of a car. This flatly contradicts one of the most widely accepted notions of psychology—and indeed, of philosophy—that "personality" is some kind of "emanation" of the brain, and therefore of the body. Professor John Taylor writes in *The Shape of Minds to Come:* "We recognize personality as a summation of the different contributions to behavior from the various control units of the brain." One of the most widely respected of modern philosophers, Gilbert Ryle, has devoted his most influential book, *The Concept of Mind*, to arguing that it is a mistake to think of "man" as a "ghost in a machine." Man *is* his body and brain. Yet the evidence we have examined so far in this chapter suggests unmistakably that personality and body are as distinct as tenants and the houses they live in. This, admittedly, sounds regrettably old-fashioned—after all, the position "Man is a spirit" belongs to religion rather than science—yet it is hard to see how this conclusion can be side-stepped. Whether or not we can accept Kardec's *Spirits' Book* as a contribution to our scientific knowledge, it is necessary to admit that its basic theories explain the mysteries of the human personality rather more convincingly than Professors Taylor and Ryle.

And what of Kardec's other basic assertion: that spiritual evolution involves reincarnation? Reincarnation—rebirth into another body—is, of course, closely related to the whole problem of "possession," as we can see in the case of Mary Roff, who was (temporarily) reincarnated in Lurancy Vennum's body. The case of a Hindu boy Jasbir Lal Jat, recorded by Dr. Ian Stevenson in *Twenty Cases Suggestive of Reincarnation*, is perhaps one of the most striking on record. When the son of Sri Girdhari Lal Jat of Rasulpur, Uttar Pradesh, "died" of smallpox in the spring of 1954, his father decided to leave the body unburied until the next day. But before morning the boy had recovered, although he was unable to speak. When he began to speak, he asserted that he was the son of Shankar, of a village called Vehedi, twenty or so miles away. He claimed that he was of Brahmin caste, and refused to eat food cooked by his "mother." Only when a local Brahmin lady agreed to cook for him did he consent to eat. Gradually, over two years, he abandoned this insistence and ate with the rest of the family.

According to Jasbir, he had attended a wedding and been given poisoned sweets; these led to a fall from a chariot, and a head injury from which he died. One day Jasbir recognized a woman who was visiting the village as his "aunt"—she was in fact from Vehedi, and her nephew Sobha Ram had died just as Jasbir described. But the strange thing was that Sobha Ram had died in 1954, shortly before the "death" of the three-year-old Jasbir from smallpox. Jasbir later claimed that after his death, he had met a Sadhu (holy man) who had advised him to take over the body of Jasbir, which he did.

Sobha Ram's father heard of the case, and went to Rasulpur to see Jasbir; Jasbir instantly recognized him and other members of the family. A few weeks later, Jasbir was taken to Vehedi and asked to lead the way from the railway station to the main square; he did this without difficulty, and then led the way to Sobha Ram's home. He stayed there for several days, demonstrating a detailed knowledge of the family and its affairs. Dr. Stevenson investigated the case thoroughly, interviewing many witnesses in both families, as well as the boy himself. The case of the poisoned sweets has never been satisfactorily cleared up.

The case of Jasbir is one of the most remarkable in Stevenson's records; yet most of them contain the same feature of recognition of the family and home of the alleged previous existence. (Stevenson's twenty cases cover Brazil, India, Alaska and Lebanon.) In fact, the earliest such case to excite widespread interest was that of Shanti Devi, a girl born in Delhi in 1926. At the age of seven she told her mother she had been alive before, in a town called Muttra. She talked about her previous home, her husband and her three children. When she was nine, she recognized a stranger who came to their house as her husband's cousin. The man was from Muttra, and confirmed that his cousin's wife, a girl called Ludgi, had died ten years earlier. When the husband came to the house, Shanti Devi flung herself into his arms. Taken to Muttra, she recognized friends and relatives, and showed detailed knowledge of Ludgi's life. But she failed to recognize Ludgi's youngest child, whose birth had cost Ludgi her life.

I have had the opportunity to investigate personally only two cases of alleged reincarnation. One of these I have described in some detail elsewhere*; the other is sufficiently typical to be worth describing here.

In 1978, a Liverpool hypnotist named Joe Keeton was studying "hypnotic regression"—the tendency of some people under hypnosis to recall "previous existences." Under hypnosis, a young nurse named Pauline McKay asserted that she was a girl called Kitty Jay, who had committed suicide near Chagford, in Devon. Joe Keeton made enquiries through librarians in the west country, and was startled to discover that Kitty Jay was a real person. "Jay's grave" lies on the edge of Dartmoor, not far from the village of Manaton. (Conan Doyle set his *Hound of the Baskervilles* in this area.) In the late eighteenth century—the exact date has not been preserved—an orphan named Kitty Jay went to work at Ford Farm, Manaton, as a milkmaid. She became pregnant, and committed suicide by hanging in the barn of the nearby farm of Canna. As a suicide, she was buried at a crossroad not far away—suicides were buried at crossroads to confuse the spirit with a choice of ways and prevent it from haunting the site of its death.

The case came to the attention of Westward Television, and I was asked if I would be present on a program with Joe Keeton and Pauline McKay.

Pauline proved to be a pretty, dark-haired girl in her early twenties; Joe Keeton is a big, bespectacled

---

* The case of Dr. Arthur Guirdham; see my *Strange Powers*.

north countryman in his fifties. In the studio, we were shown his letter to a local librarian and the librarian's reply about Kitty Jay. Then Pauline was settled in a reclining chair in front of the cameras, and Joe talked to her softly until her eyes closed. First of all, Joe regressed Pauline to her own childhood, asking her about her third birthday and what she had done; it was astonishing to see the nurse suddenly "become" a little girl. If she was faking, she must have been a first-class actress.

Joe then took her further back into the past, until she said her name was Kitty Jay. Questioned by the interviewer, Kay Avila, Kitty said she was ten years old and lived in a big house near "Chagiford" (the old local pronunciation of Chagford)—apparently the orphanage or local poor-house. Taken forward to her fifteenth birthday, she said she was now working on a farm near Manaton, for a master named Thomas. She mentioned a cook called Maudie and a man named Rob who worked at nearby Canna Farm. She told how she and Rob sometimes went for walks "to the stones" (the area has many standing stones), and to a bridge; pressed for the name of this bridge, she said Fingle, and named the river as the Teign—both identifications being correct.

Taken forward again, she said she had now run away from the farm—apparently at Rob's instigation— and was living in a remote cottage that seemed to have no furniture. She was very hungry—Rob had promised to stay with her, and to keep her supplied with food, but had not kept either promise. She said her stomach hurt, but it was not clear whether this was hunger, or pains connected with pregnancy. Asked to describe Rob's last visit to her, she made it clear that he had insisted on making her lie on the floor to have sex, and that she objected. Finally, Keeton took her forward to her suicide on Canna Farm—she had obviously gone there hoping to see Rob; it was late afternoon. Her misery and despair were painful to watch, as she described her decision to kill herself. As she began to choke and gasp, Joe soothed her, then woke her up.

The whole thing was astonishingly convincing—doubly so, since Pauline had never visited the west country before, and had only traveled down that morning. Admittedly, there were a few features that were unsatisfactory. She had no idea of the year—except that it was "seventeen something"—or whether there was a king or queen on the throne. But for an illiterate orphan, perhaps this is not surprising. She did not know the surname of her master, and she refused to name Ford Farm (although it seemed that her reason was fear in case the questioner wanted to go and talk to her master). When, later in the day, we took Pauline to Ford Farm and Canna Farm, she did not seem to reccognize either. On the other hand, Pauline was quite definite about never having heard of Chagford or Kitty Jay. And since the legend is not widely known outside the area, this seems plausible enough.

Joe Keeton, who has regressed many people into "previous lives" (some of which are described in his book *Encounters With the Past*), says that he is not necessarily convinced that this is reincarnation—that it could be some kind of persistent memory from a forebear, freakishly carried in the genes. But since Kitty died with her unborn child inside her, this theory hardly seems applicable to the present case.

So we must admit that, while Kardec's assertions about spirits and the spirit world would be totally unacceptable to a scientific investigator, they make a strong appeal to common sense, particularly in the light of the evidence about "possession" and reincarnation. Without being too dogmatic, we can say that there is a great deal of evidence that personality is more than a "summation of brain reflexes." (Most parents have noticed that their children seem to be born with the personalities they possess for the rest of their lives.)

This still leaves us confronted with the mystery of the nature of personality. While cases like Mary Roff and Jasbir Lal Jat suggest "possession" by another "spirit," Mary Reynolds and Louis Vivé seem altogether simpler: their "secondary personalities" seem to be merely undeveloped aspects of the "normal" personality. One more example will make this very clear.

In 1917, various acquaintances of a foreman named Naylor began receiving obscene letters signed "May Naylor," the name of his daughter. A typical letter addressed to a Mr. Thomas—at the electric company where Naylor and he both worked— stated: "This is to tell you that your Mrs. Thomas came to our house on Saturday. That pig Naylor took her up to the bedroom and then he . . ." The remainder of the letter described various perverted sexual practices in explicit detail and with obscene language. Two more men at the same company received a similar letter at the same time. All were scrawled in the same childish hand and signed "May Naylor."

But Naylor's daughter May was a sweet-tempered, inoffensive child of nine who seemed quite incapable of writing such letters.

The psychologist Cyril Burt investigated the case, and found May to be an intelligent little girl, her mental age more than a year beyond her actual age. Her teachers, both at day school and Sunday school, insisted that she would be incapable of writing the letters. But Burt was convinced otherwise. Naylor had been married twice, and May was the child of the first marriage. He had divorced his first wife for repeated sexual misconduct. May committed many of the same spelling mistakes that were revealed in the letters. She told Burt that her favorite flower was lily of the valley—because it was so "white and pure and clean," which aroused his suspicions.

May allowed herself to be placed under hypnosis, and was soon openly admitting writing the letters. She was able to describe to Burt the contents of a letter he had received from "May" but had not yet opened. Yet when awakened, she repudiated with horror the idea that she had written the letters, and burst into tears— unaware that her "alter ego" had confessed to writing them. Burt says:

> Behind the visible May was an invisible May; and their natures were exactly opposed. The one was frank, the other cunning; the one was affectionate, the other mean; the one was fastidiously correct and scrupulously pure, the other coarse, revengeful and foul-mouthed. The child was in truth the nearest approach that I have ever known at an age so young to a dual personality. She seemed to be the living counterpart in feminine miniature of Dr Jekyll and Mr Hyde.

The cause of the "split" lay in the father's remarriage. May had actually witnessed her mother having sexual intercourse with various men; yet she loved her so much that she refused to believe any ill of her. When her father remarried, she deeply resented her stepmother, and resented a new baby brother even more. While he was away during the war her father had asked her to write him a letter every week, so now it was natural for her to pour out her hatred and resentment on paper. Occasional meetings with her own mother may have fueled the vengefulness. One of the letters even accused her father of attempted incest—which may just conceivably be true (Burt describes the father as a neurotic type).

Burt's treatment was to try to talk the child out of her hypnotic states—instead of snapping his fingers—so that "May Jekyll" could actually hear "May Hyde" confessing to writing the letters. Gradually, says Burt, the barricade between the two contending personalities was broken down, and they were synthesized. "May Jekyll" became rather less prim and proper, but May Hyde, "the jealous and vindictive letter-writer, vanished like a ghost at daybreak . . . "

Here, we can see, there is no need to assume that the two personalities were different "persons." Burt's description—"one was frank, the other cunning" and so on—makes it clear that "May Jekyll" was simply suppressing a part of herself that frightened her.

What seems to have happened, then, was roughly this. May Naylor was a pleasant, affectionate little girl who, like all children, wanted love and security. Her father became a soldier when she was six, and temporarily vanished from her life; but her letters to him brought affectionate replies and—if she seemed unhappy—a visit. While her father was away, her mother slept with other men; and, since she was also an alcoholic, she made no attempt to prevent May from seeing precisely what happened (May's letters reveal that her knowledge of unusual sexual practices was comparable to Krafft-Ebing's). May herself was given to masturbation. Yet all this "impurity" was a severe shock to her; she refused to believe that her mother was "wicked" and blocked it out. She wanted to be a normal little girl with a loving mother and father; she hated being forced into the grimy world of adults. But fate refused to allow her the security she craved; her father divorced her mother and married again, and the birth of a baby intensified her misery. Her own intense love of her father had an incestuous element, which he may or may not have encouraged. May had been prematurely sexually awakened—probably she took after her mother—and imagined her father in bed with her new stepmother. It was all too much of a strain for a nine-year-old girl; part of her determinedly put up the shutters against any knowledge of sin and evil, and tried to be simply a loving and lovable child. Whatever strange mechanism produces "split personality" now came into operation—probably some specific event triggered it—and the repressed "May Hyde" let off steam, and tried to revenge herself, by writing obscene letters. Burt succeeded in turning May into a unified personality by allowing one May to overhear the confessions of the other. One of the first results was that May then insisted on being called May Lomax—her mother's unmarried name—and allowed her resentment to express itself openly. In due course, the two personalities united— aided, no doubt, by Burt's acceptance of her confessions, which enabled "May Jekyll" to come to terms with her own urges.

The problem here can be seen clearly: like Peter Pan, May Naylor refused to grow up; she wanted to remain fixed at a stage of development that was free of conflict. Her problems were all caused by her refusal to go forward—that is, by *fear*. The same thing seems to have been true of Christine Beauchamp. The shock of her mother's death, the misery of her life with her drunken father, made her want to retreat from life. But this desire to run away is one of the most dangerous things we can experience, as dangerous as a driver losing his nerve when travelling at full speed. Whether we like it or not, the only "safe" way to go is forward. In Christine's case, there was no doubt also a perfectly legitimate desire to escape her problems by finding a man to love and protect her—the kind of man her father should have been. Her father's friend William Jones seemed to be such a man—

until he got drunk and made some kind of sexual advance to Christine. It was after this, according to the alter ego Sally, that she became "all queer and moony."

What happened then? We can now take our choice of two hypotheses. All the qualities that Christine had repressed—mischief, vitality, outrageousness—united into a "personality complex" called Sally, who became, in effect, "Christine Hyde." Or we may take the view that with Christine now in such precarious possession of her own body, some "spirit" saw the opportunity to invade and take over—as when Jasbir or Lurancy Vennum were unconscious. We may reject the "possession" explanation as too fanciful; but it fits the facts just as well as the other.

There is, however, one further aspect of the Beauchamp case that I have not so far mentioned, and which affords a further clue. Christine and Sally were not the only two "occupants" of the body. Under hypnosis, Morton Prince discovered a third personality, who was more mature and self-possessed than either Christine or Sally; he calls her simply "B-4." "B-4" never claimed to be a "guardian angel," like Doris Fischer's "Sleeping Margaret." But in other respects, the resemblance seems remarkable.

Moreover, these two are not the only cases in which the patient exhibited a "higher" personality. Carl Jung's first paper, "On the Psychology and Pathology of So-Called Occult Phenomena," describes his cousin (whom he calls S.W.), a girl of fifteen who would go into a trance and then speak with various other voices. One of the figures she "became" in her trances was a mature and rather saintly personality called Ivenes, who claimed to be "the real S.W." S.W. herself was a girl of mediocre intelligence; Ivenes was highly intelligent. She explained that S.W. was only the latest of her many reincarnations, and that she had been a Christian martyr in the time of Nero, a French countess called de Valours (who had been burnt as a witch), a clergyman's wife who had borne Goethe an illegitimate child, and another famous psychic of the thirteenth century called Friederika Hauffe, known as the Seeress of Prevorst (and the subject of one of the most popular books of the nineteenth century).*

Jung's cousin died at twenty-six. Jung speculated that she had an unconscious knowledge of her early death, and that the personality of Ivenes was an attempt to compensate for this—to grow up before her time, as it were.

Jung also believed that the explanation for his cousin's many trance personalities might be "possession" by spirits; but the psychologist Krafft-Ebing convinced him that the answer lay in psychiatry, probably in sex. Certainly, this sounds plausible when applied to the sexual adventures of some of her previous incarnations, which Jung describes as sounding like a typical adolescent girl's fantasies. But it hardly seems to explain Ivenes, "the real S.W."

Whether we regard Ivenes as "the real S.W." or as a "spirit," the problem remains. The evidence of the present chapter suggests that the "spiritualistic explanation" was not as unlikely as Jung finally assumed. Jung's description of her trances makes it sound exactly like a medium at a seance. When the girl woke up, she used to assert that she had been moving in a realm of spirits. So Kardec's explanation would fit the facts. But even if we decide that Jung was probably correct to reject it, we are left with a mystery that cannot be reduced to terms of Freudian psychology. Jung was much impressed by the mystic-philosophic system about the universe pro-

---

See Chapter 6.

pounded by Ivenes; Jung later read widely in "occult" philosophy and found many parallels to the system—particularly in the gnostics; but his fifteen-year-old cousin had certainly never read the gnostics.

Of course, this phenomenon of a "higher" personality can be understood without recourse to "occult" philosophy. Our personalities tend to be a reflection of our environment and the people around us. A person of medium dominance, brought up by highly dominant parents or among dominant brothers and sisters, will probably never develop his natural degree of dominance, because it has no chance to exercise itself. A moderately pretty girl, brought up among dazzlingly pretty sisters, will think herself ugly. In these cases, it is easy to see that an area of the personality remains "latent," although it may need only a little encouragement to develop. Similarly, we all know stories of mothers sitting by the bedside of their sick children for days without sleep. The crisis calls on a higher level of the personality. Once the crisis is over, she will probably go back to worrying about trivialities; lack of stimulus allows the personality to revert to a lower level of *organization*.

So no one would be very surprised if an adult responded to a situation of crisis by becoming more masterful and nature; we would simply feel that he (or she) had been like it all the time "really," but had allowed the "triviality of everydayness" to conceal it from himself. But it seems rather more difficult to understand in a case like that of Jung's cousin, or Christine Beauchamp, and well-nigh impossible to understand in the case of Doris Fischer's "guardian angel."

The explanation could lie in the concept that I have labeled the "ladder of selves."* As we have seen,

---

* *Mysteries*, introduction.

the "selves" in cases of multiple personality often seem to fall into a distinct "hierarchy": in the case of Doris, the "guardian angel" was the topmost "self," then came Margaret, then Doris, then "Sick Doris," then "Real Sleeping Doris." In Christine Beauchamp there was Christine herself, then, above her, Sally, then, above her, B-4. Christine was so upset and depressed by the death of her mother and by other problems that her personality ceased its normal development in her early teens. Under pleasanter circumstances, she might have developed the high spirits of Sally and the maturity and balance of B-4. And it is easy to imagine that there may have been still higher possible levels of personality waiting for her to develop "into them."

This obviously applies to all human beings. As we grow up we pass through what is virtually a series of "selves"; everyone has known the surprise of meeting at, say, fifteen, a child one last saw at the age of eight; the change may make him or her unrecognizable. With luck, we encounter the experiences that allow us to develop our potentialities, and slowly advance up the "ladder" of selves.

This ladder seems to have one peculiarity. Unlike the ordinary ladder, its sides slope inward, so the rungs became shorter. Everyone who has been through some personal crisis knows that in order to develop a new level of being, we need to make an effort of compression—we even use the phrase "pulling ourselves together" to express what we do when we have to achieve a higher level of *organization*.

This raises the obvious question: what lies at the top of the ladder? Clearly, it is a question that no one can answer. But if this theory of a hierarchy of levels has any basis in fact, then it seems that these higher levels *already exist* in us, before we even come to suspect their existence. In a sense, the Beethoven who wrote the last quartets was already present in the new-born baby, as an oak is latent in the acorn. But there may have been a dozen other Beethovens waiting to be developed. The same applies to the rest of us. Few people develop their obvious potentialities; but even the men and women of genius may be little more than undisciplined children when judged by the standard of their latent potentialities.

This whole problem of the personality and its potential is considered at length in one of the classics of paranormal investigation, F. W. H. Myers' *Human Personality and Its Survival of Bodily Death*. Discussing such problems as multiple personality, hypnotism and "possession," Myers argues that if we are to dispense with the idea of "spirit guidance" or possession, then we have to posit the notion of an entire "unconscious personality," with its own thoughts and ideas. And in an introduction in a recent edition of the book, Aldous Huxley carries this one stage further.

> Is the house of the soul a mere bungalow with a cellar? Or does it have an upstairs above the ground floor of consciousness as well as a garbage-littered basement beneath, Freud inclined to the bungalow-with-basement view

In other words, if the mind has an "unconscious" basement, why should it not have a "super-conscious" attic as well—a level of the "self" above the everyday self, yet equally unknown?

And this notion can lead us to a further interesting speculation. Could this "superconscious" self explain some of the phenomena of paranormal research? The adult personality is more controlled and disciplined than that of the child, and therefore capable of greater achievements; even Mozart could not have written *The*

Magic Flute at the age of twelve. In that case, the "superconscious" self ought to be capable of still greater achievements. Could this, conceivably, explain telepathy, "second sight," psychokinesis, knowledge of the future? Is it conceivable that "psychics" have some kind of "short circuit" to this superconscious level? Psychic abilities often appear after shock or severe illness; the Dutch "clairvoyant," Peter Hurkos, developed his curious abilities by falling off a ladder and fracturing his skull; when he woke up in a hospital he found he could read other people's minds. Uri Geller dates the development of his odd powers from a severe electric shock caused by pushing his finger into the works of his mother's sewing machine when he was three years old.

But here again, there is another possible explanation. Did Hurkos's accident and Geller's shock simply turn them into "mediums"—open some inner gateway to allow them to be "invaded" by "spirits"?

It would, I think, be a mistake at this stage to commit ourselves to either view—or to regard them as mutually exclusive. Meanwhile, let us try to extend the field of investigation by looking at the history of the strange phenomenon known as the poltergeist.

THREE

Cases Ancient and Modern

There are probably over a thousand recorded instances of poltergeist haunting, and in nine cases out of ten there is a frustrating lack of detail and a dreary similarity. Objects fly through the air, furniture waltzes around the room, crockery is smashed, bangs and crashes keep everyone awake, stones fly through windows. Then everything stops as suddenly as it began. The only possible comment, except for those unfortunate enough to be involved, would seem to be "So what?" It is the one case in ten that throws up the curious incident and, occasionally, the interesting clue; and it is mainly upon these that we shall concentrate. It may be as well to start with one of those typical cases. This was published anonymously in *Harper's Magazine* in 1962. How, then, can we assume it is true? Because it is so completely pointless.

A middle-aged businessman and his wife rented a house on Cape Cod for the summer; although it had been built nine years earlier they were, for some reason, its first occupants. It was exceptionally isolated.

The man, from internal evidence, was a publisher, and on their first night in the house, he sat up late over a manuscript. His wife, Helen, had gone to bed early. Suddenly his wife called: "Was that you?"

She had heard a sound like someone tapping with a cane on the brick wall near the front door. Neither paid much attention to the incident. But the next night, as they sat in the living room, the sounds came again—exactly like a cane on the brick wall. The husband rushed outside with a torch. As he opened the door, the tapping stopped. There was nothing to be seen.

During the next few months, they heard the sound again and again—almost every night, and always at about ten o'clock. The husband tried standing by the door at ten; but the moment he opened it, the tapping stopped.

During the second week, the man was awakened three times by noises. The first was a sound like a box of matches falling on the floor. He switched on the light and looked around the room; nothing had fallen down. The second night, it was a distinct sound like a sheet of newspaper swishing the length of the room. Once again, there was nothing to account for it. The third night, it was a noise like a rolling pin which seemed to fall on the floor, roll across the room and come to rest against the wall. But there was no rolling pin or anything else.

Then the clicking noise began—just a clicking that came from the walls. It could happen in any room of the house at any time of the day or night. It happened several hundred times during their four months in the house.

The third week, the footsteps began. They were loud and clear, like a man in leather shoes with solid heels, tramping loudly over the wooden floor. When they were downstairs, they came from the room above; when they were upstairs, from below. These happened about forty times during their four months. Helen often heard sounds from another room and went to look, assuming someone had come into the house—they had made a few friends in the area. There was never anyone there.

Then, in midsummer, came the noise they called "the grand piano smash." One night there was a deafening crash from the garage, enough to set the house quivering. He describes it as sounding as if a grand piano had suddenly lost its legs and fallen to the floor. Naturally, the garage—which was used to store books—was empty.

In September, they had visitors—his lawyer, and his wife and daughter. The lawyer was completely skeptical about the "ghost." On the first evening, the three women went out to an amateur theatrical and the two men stayed behind to work on a contract. The lawyer remarked: "I wish to heaven I could hear from your precious ghost." As they sat working, there was a crisp little click from the wall behind their heads. "The Universal Click?" inquired the lawyer.

"Yes."

"Drying wood."

Twenty minutes later, footfalls sounded from overhead. The narrator, with a considerable effort of will, went on reading; the lawyer, shouted: "What on earth is that?"

"Only the ghost."

"Nonsense, there's a man upstairs." They rushed upstairs, and the lawyer's jaw dropped when they found the room empty. He insisted on ransacking the bedrooms and attics with a torch, but found nothing.

That night, the lawyer and his family slept in Helen's large bedroom, while Helen moved into her husband's single room; he slept on the settee downstairs. The next morning, the lawyer asked: "What was that awful crash?" They described the "grand piano smash." It had been so loud that they had thought the garage ceiling had fallen in. They had been so alarmed that they had taken their daughter into bed between them. Yet the husband and wife had heard nothing.

That is the end of the story; and it is, in all respects but one, a typical poltergeist story. If it had been recorded in Latin in the year 1200, it would no doubt read: "In a house on Cape Cod there sounded footsteps, tapping sounds and loud noises, all without apparent cause. The spirit gave no indication of its purpose or identity." And, in fact, this *is* about the amount of detail we find in the majority of recorded cases. It can be seen why a comprehensive history of the poltergeist would be unreadable.

The one non-typical detail is, of course, the lack of a focus or "medium." The author mentions nothing about having a child, or of any children ever being in the house. In fact, he never mentions the word "poltergeist." Yet this case clearly belongs to the type of poltergeist haunting rather than to the "spectral" kind. And this, in itself, is an important clue. In ninety-nine percent of poltergeist cases, there is a pubescent teenager—or a child—present, and it is therefore a valid assumption that what is happening is "spontaneous psychokinesis." One of the earliest psychical researchers, Professor Charles Richet, reached exactly that conclusion in his huge and comprehensive *Thirty Years of Psychical Research*. But if in even one percent of the cases there is no disturbed adolescent, then the assumption becomes questionable, and we find ourselves reconsidering Lombroso's view that a poltergeist is a mischievous spirit. But where, in that case, does it get the energy?

One clue may be found in a remark thrown off casually by a popular writer on true ghost stories, Elliott O'Donnell, who notes that Windsor Castle seems to have an unusual number of ghosts, although no tragedies are associated with it, "an argument," he adds, "in favor of the theory that hauntings do not necessarily originate in tragedies . . ." Then what *do* they originate in? T. C. Lethbridge has already offered a clue when he speculates that ghosts and "ghouls" may be *tape recordings*, somehow preserved on the "energy field" of water. For, as a dowser, Lethbridge also observed the same powerful energy fields in the area of standing stones. He describes how, when visiting the Merry Maidens in Cornwall, he placed one hand on a stone and held a pendulum in the other, and felt an electrical tingling in his fingers, while the pendulum began to revolve like an airplane propeller. Lethbridge also notes that most "sacred sites" seem to have been used continuously down the centuries—so that, for example, a pagan sacred site may later become the location for a monastery, and later perhaps of a modern church. (More often than not, such churches are named after Saint Michael, who seems to be the Christian equivalent of the pagan sun god, to whom most ancient sites were dedicated.) And he observed in such places a powerful force of earth magnetism.

This same conclusion was reached by a retired solicitor named Guy Underwood, who decided to devote his retirement to studying dowsing. Underwood was convinced that at the center of most sacred sites—such as Stonehenge or the Merry Maidens—there is an underground spring, which seems to create a pattern of spiral lines of force around it. He also found straight lines of force passing through these sites, and often continuing for miles; these lines of force he called "holy lines."

Now Underwood's "holy lines" had already been observed more than a quarter of a century before he began his investigations by another lover of the countryside, Alfred Watkins, a retired brewer. But Watkins did not discover them with a dowsing rod. He simply noticed that the English countryside seems to be covered with "long straight tracks" which pass through sacred sites; he began by assuming that they were ancient trade routes, and only later concluded—tentatively—that they might have had some religious significance for our remote ancestors. He called them "ley lines," from the word "lea"; meaning a meadow. As a result of Watkins's researches, documented in his book *The Old Straight Track* (1925), a club of enthusiasts began searching for these lines all over England. But after Underwood, it began to strike "ley hunters"—chief among whom was a young Englishman named John Michell—that ley lines are, in fact, lines of "earth force."

A new generation of "ley hunters" soon noticed another interesting thing about ley lines—that a remarkable number of reputed hauntings, poltergeist occurrences and sightings of "unidentified flying objects" seemed to happen on them, particularly at the crossing point of one or more "leys."

One of the oddest types of haunting sounds so preposterous that it is hard to take seriously; yet it has been convincingly documented: the repetition of historical events. At Edgehill, in Warwickshire, where one of the great battles of the Civil War was fought, local residents heard all the sounds of the battle some months later. It happened so often that King Charles the First sent a commission to investigate; they testified on oath to having witnessed the phantom battle. The sounds are still heard today, and have been documented by the Reverend John Dening. Near Wroxham, in the Norfolk Broads, a phantom army of Roman soldiers has been recorded by a number of witnesses over the years, and in a cellar in York, a Roman legion has been witnessed marching by modern workmen (one of whom described his experience on the BBCs "Spotlight" program). An investigator named Stephen Jenkins had a similar experience on a track near Mounts Bay in Cornwall—an optical illusion of a crowd of armed men among the bushes in the evening light. Many years later, when he had discovered the existence of ley lines, Jenkins realized that the track he had been following was a ley, and that he had been approaching a nodal point—a crossing with other leys.

The possibility that begins to emerge, then, is connected with our earlier speculation that "human electric batteries" and "poltergeist mediums" like Esther Cox may derive their power from the earth: it is that poltergeists may also, under certain conditions, obtain their energy from the earth; and these conditions may be fulfilled on the nodal points of ley lines.

In a book called *The Undiscovered Country*, Stephen Jenkins has cited a number of cases that seem to support this theory. (For example, he prints a photograph taken in Pevensey Castle in 1957 that shows three strange little men—like elves—on a heap of stones; the lady who took the photograph saw no little men; but Pevensey Castle is a nodal point of a number of ley lines.)

It was Stephen Jenkins who drew my own attention to the "ley solution" to a curious case of haunting that I had presented on BBC television—the Ardachie case. In 1952, Mr. and Mrs. Peter McEwan rented Ardachie Lodge, on the edge of Loch Ness, hoping to raise pigs there, and they hired a couple named Mac-Donald to act as housekeepers. The McEwans had two small children—too young to raise the suspicion that they may have been the "focus" of poltergeist phenomena. On the night of their arrival, the MacDonalds went to bed, but were awakened by footsteps that came up the stairs and went into the room opposite. A few minutes later, they again heard footsteps. They went and peeped into the room, which they had supposed to be unused, and found that, in fact, there was no one there. They went downstairs and asked the McEwans if the house was haunted; the McEwans said no, not as far as they knew. But back in the bedroom, Mrs. MacDonald was terrified to see an old woman beckoning to her—neither her husband nor Mr. McEwan saw it. Mrs. MacDonald flatly denied that she was "psychic." They moved into another room; half an hour or so later they were disturbed by loud rapping noises on the wall. They looked outside the door, and saw an old woman with a lighted candle crawling along the corridor. And it was this that convinced the McEwans that this was not mere hysteria; the previous owner of the house, a Mrs. Brewin, had been an arthritic old woman who thought the servants were stealing from her, so she used to crawl around on all fours at night with a candle—this was vouched for by various people who knew her well.

The Society for Psychical Research sent two investigators. They were present when there were loud knocks, after which, Mrs. MacDonald saw a woman in the doorway. Later, there were more knocks from the wall, Mrs. MacDonald entered a semi-trance, and suddenly declared that the trouble stemmed from a tree in the rose garden; this had been a favorite of Mrs. Brewin's, and it had been allowed to die. This, said Mrs. MacDonald, was why the old woman was now trying to "communicate." The gardener verified the tree story.

The McEwans felt they had had enough and returned to London; the MacDonalds also left. The house was later razed to the ground by the army.

Clearly, Mrs. MacDonald was, without knowing it, a "medium." As the "haunting" progressed, she became more and more aware of her powers, and at one point offered to go into a trance for the investigators. But why did she have to wait to go to Ardachie before discovering that she was a medium? Stephen Jenkins, who saw my presentation on television, looked at an ordnance survey map of the area, and concluded that Ardachie Lodge stood on the crossing point of four major ley lines.* If his theory—and that of other "ley hunters"—is correct, then Ardachie had an abundance of the kind of energy needed for "spirits" to manifest themselves, and only needed a medium to act as catalyst. The old woman, with her curious obsession, was what Kardec calls an "earth-

---

* I have given more precise details of these in my book *Mysteries*.

bound spirit," like the rag and bone man who caused the poltergeist disturbances in the Rue des Noyers. She had been an "obsessive" in life, and continued to be so after her death. Kardec would probably have made some attempt to help the "spirit" to evolve and escape its earth-bound existence.

What is being suggested, then, is that a poltergeist and a "ghost" are not basically dissimilar in nature. Both need energy to manifest themselves. (One of the commonest features of hauntings is a sudden feeling of coldness in the room, as if the "spirit" is using up energy.) Some of this energy is taken from the "medium" or focus; but some comes from the place itself, which may be why many houses remain haunted over many years.

The earliest records of hauntings are unfortunately lacking in detail, and so obviously "touched up" by their authors, that they can only be taken as evidence that *something* out of the ordinary occurred. Probably the earliest account of a ghost on record is to be found in a letter of the Roman orator Pliny the Younger (first century A.D.), who tells of a haunted house in Athens where the spirit rattled chains. As the years went past, the house fell into disrepair, until the philosopher Athenodorus noticed it and thought that he might be able to rent it cheaply. The owners asked a remarkably low price, and told him frankly that it was haunted. Athenodorus was not bothered. On his first evening in the house he became so absorbed in his work that he forgot all about the ghost. Then he heard rattling chains, and looked up to see the old man with a tangled beard and heavy fetters. The ghost was beckoning with its finger. The philosopher was too absorbed to pay much attention, but the noise of the chains finally forced him to get up and follow it. The ghost led him into the garden, and vanished in the midst of a clump of shrubs. Digging at this point revealed a skeleton with the shackles still on its wrists and ankles. When this was given proper burial rites, says Pliny, the haunting ceased.

It seems unlikely that even a Stoic philosopher would go on working when a ghost was trying to attract his attention; but—this obvious exaggeration apart—the story fits the pattern of many better documented hauntings; the old lady of Ardachie seems to have behaved in much the same manner.

One of the earliest poltergeist stories on record also has many typical features; it is to be found in a chronicle called the *Annales Fuldenses*, and the event it describes dates back to 858 B.C. It took place in a farmhouse near Bingen, on the Rhine, where the farmer lived with his wife and children (his name is not given). The chronicle says that the "evil spirit" made itself evident "at first by throwing stones; then it made the place dangerous by shaking the walls, as though the men of that place were striking them with hammers." Stone throwing is perhaps the most typical of all poltergeist antics, as we shall see; the shaking of the walls as if beaten with hammers sounds not unlike the "grand piano smash" of the Cape Cod haunting. In fact, in many poltergeist cases, the occupants of the house are convinced that the place must be severely damaged, from the violence of the blows; but this seldom happens.

In the Bingen case, it seems that the farmer himself was the object of the malice of the "spirit." Apparently it followed him around—an unusual feature except in cases (like that of Esther Cox) where the "focus" or medium moves elsewhere—until his neighbors were afraid to receive him into their homes. The spirit also caused fires, burning his crops (presumably of corn) soon after they were gathered. And the poltergeist developed a voice—another unusual feature—and denounced the man for various sins, including sleeping with the daughter of the foreman or overseer. Finally, the Bishop of Mainz sent priests with holy relics, who also heard the voice denouncing the man for adultery. In a version of the same case, quoted in the *Golden Legend*, it is recounted that when the priests sprinkled holy water and sang hymns, the spirit hurled stones at them—another highly convincing touch. But the version in the *Golden Legend* adds that the spirit proved to be the "familiar" of a priest, who had also committed adultery. Neither version mentions whether it was "exorcised"—a reliable indication that it was not, since ecclesiastical writers never failed to emphasize the successes of Holy Church against spirits and demons.

The most interesting thing about this story is its obvious authenticity, which has survived the usual exaggeration of the scribe. Stone throwing, deafening hammering noises, spontaneous fires, contempt for the exorcists—all these are typical of poltergeists, as can be seen if we compare it with a far better documented case of the late nineteenth century. This also occurred on a farm, in the province of Quebec in Canada; the owner was called Dagg.

The disturbances began quietly, which again seems typical—the poltergeist seems to begin by trying out its powers on a small scale. On the morning of September 15, 1889, a boy named Dean, who was working as a "chore boy" for the Daggs, came down early to light the fire, and saw a five-dollar bill on the floor; he took this up to the farmer, George Dagg, who recognized it as a bill he had given to his wife the day before, together with another two dollars. She had placed them in a bureau drawer, from which they were now found to be missing. When the boy was out milking, George Dagg searched his room, and found the two dollars in his bed. Later that day, Mrs. Dagg found a streak of filth—presumably ordure—across the floor of the house, which so enraged her that she ordered the boy to leave. He protested his innocence. George Dagg took him off to a nearby town to see the magistrate; but while they were away, more streaks of filth appeared around the house, effectively vindicating the boy.

From then on, poltergeist disturbances were continuous. Milk pans were overturned, windows smashed, small fires started, water poured on to the floor. The "focus" seemed to be an eleven-year-old Scots girl called Dinah McLean, an orphan who had been adopted by the Dagg family. One day soon after the disturbances began, her braid of hair was tugged so violently that she screamed. It was found to be partly cut, so that it had to be completely severed. The "spirit" made a habit of attacking Dinah. And she was soon reporting that she could hear its voice, although no one else seemed to be able to.

An artist named Woodcock came to the house in November, and asked Dinah questions about the "haunting." She said she had seen something in a woodshed, so Woodcock got her to take him there. In the woodshed, Dinah said: "Are you there mister?" and to Woodcock's amazement, a gruff voice replied with some violent obscenities (another characteristic of the rare examples of the "talking poltergeist"). Woodcock describes it as being like the voice of an old man which sounded from the air a few feet away from him. When Woodcock asked "Who are you?"' the answer came: "I am the devil. I'll have you in my clutches. Get out of this or I'll break your neck."

But Woodcock refused to be intimidated; so did George Dagg, who was called in. An immensely long conversation ensued, and the "devil" gradually became less foul-mouthed and abusive. When Dagg asked: "Why have you been bothering me and my family," it replied: "Just for fun."

Dagg responded that it wasn't much fun setting the place on fire, to which came the significant reply: "I didn't. The fires always came in the daytime and where you could see them." And again, when Dagg asked why it had thrown a stone which had hit his four-year-old child Mary, he got the answer: "Poor wee Mary. I didn't intend to hit her. I intended it for Dinah. But I didn't let it hurt her." Again and again poltergeists do things that could kill or cause severe damage; yet in ninety-nine cases out of a hundred, no one is actually harmed. People may even be beaten with what sound like terrible blows—yet they are hardly hurt.

After more conversation, the spirit declared that it would take its leave of the house the following day, a Sunday. When this news spread around the area, people began to crowd into the farmhouse. The poltergeist did not let them down; as soon as they began to arrive, it was there, making comments. Like the original Hydesville poltergeist in the home of the Fox sisters, it seemed to have intimate knowledge of the people who came in, and of their private affairs. The voice was still the same as on the previous day; but when someone remarked on the improvement in its language, it replied that it was not the same spirit, but an angel sent from God "to drive away that fellow." But this seems to have been untrue, for it ended by contradicting itself, then lost its temper, and used some of the old bad language.

Woodcock took the opportunity of many witnesses to draw up a lengthy report, stating that they had seen fires break out spontaneously, stones thrown by invisible hands, a mouth organ apparently playing itself, and all kinds of mischievous and generally upsetting phenomena. This statement goes on to say that the "entity" had claimed to be a discarnate spirit who had died twenty years previously; it actually gave its name, but asked that this should be kept a secret. The spirit was able to make itself visible to the children—two-year-old John, four-year-old Mary, and Dinah. It had appeared to them at various times as a tall, thin man with a cow's head, horns and cloven hoof, as a big black dog, and as a beautiful man dressed in white robes with a starry crown. This statement was signed by seventeen witnesses.

On Sunday evening, Woodcock left the house to go back to his own lodgings; but the crowd found the spook so interesting that they begged it to stay on until 3 a.m. By this time it had ceased to speak in a gruff voice and began to sing hymns in a pleasant, flute-like voice. In the early hours of Monday morning, the spirit took its leave, but said it would show itself again to the children before it left permanently.

The next morning the children rushed in in great excitement. They claimed that the beautiful man in white robes had appeared in the yard, and had picked up Mary and Johnny in his arms, declaring that Johnny was a fine little fellow. The man then remarked that "that fellow Woodcock" thought he was not an angel, but he would show that he was. Whereupon, he ascended into the air, and disappeared. The children all told the same story, and repeated it word for word many times.

Father Herbert Thurston, who has summarized the story in his book *Ghosts and Poltergeists**, comments that the ghost's ability to appear to the children must have been some form of telepathy, and mentions that this has happened in many other cases—that the poltergeist has been seen by children, though not by adults.

---

* *Light* for December 1889 contained a far longer account.

The Dagg case parallels the Bingen case of 858 A.D. with remarkable closeness, even to the attitude of the neighbors, who in both cases became hostile and suspicious, believing that witchcraft or magic was at the bottom of it. Both poltergeists set fires, both spoke and identified themselves. These parallels make it clear that, for all its amazing features, the report in the *Annules Fuldenses* is probably basically accurate.

It must also be acknowledged that the behavior of the poltergeist seems to support the assertions of Kardec. According to *The Spirits' Book*, the aim of all spirits is to evolve, and they may choose freely how they do this. The spirit in the Daggs' farmhouse sounds very much like an ordinary human being with destructive or criminal tendencies. He commits all kinds of mischief and generally torments people—although he never actually does physical damage to them; he uses filthy language and sounds thoroughly resentful. He tells Woodcock that he is the devil, and actually appears to the children with a cow's head and cloven hoof. Yet in the course of a long conversation, he moderates his language, pleads that he never meant to hurt anyone, and ends by promising to go. Having set himself up as an angel, he loses his temper and gives himself away; yet his last appearance seems to be an effort to leave behind a good impression of himself. All this makes him sound like a mischievous but fundamentally good-natured juvenile delinquent. Superior spirits do not, says Kardec,

> amuse themselves with playing ill-natured tricks, any more than grave and serious men do. We have often made spirits of this disorderly nature come to us, and have questioned them as to the motives of their misbehavior. The majority of them seem to have no other object than amusing themselves, and to be rather reckless than wicked . . .

This is an interesting and important point, which seems to offer an insight into "the mind of the poltergeist." Human beings who lack a sense of purpose may behave very badly; they may lie and steal, not out of real criminality, but out of a kind of boredom. Their lying is an attempt to impress people, and they want to impress because they lack a sense of purpose, a personal center of gravity. As soon as such a person achieves a sense of purpose, he or she ceases to be badly behaved. In that sense, poltergeists seem to be much like human beings.

This is all the more puzzling because in other respects they seem to have very unusual powers. For example, they seem to know a great deal about the people they are dealing with. There is a case recorded by the Welsh writer Giraldus Cambrensis in 1191 in which "foul spirits" performed all the usual poltergeist tricks—throwing lumps of dirt, tearing clothes, opening doors.

> But what was stranger still, in Stephen's house the spirit used to talk with men, and when people bandied words with it, as many did in mockery, it taxed them with all the things they had done in their lives which they were least willing should be known or spoken about.

It took pleasure in causing dismay and embarrassment. In many respects, poltergeists behave like the traditional mischievous elves or goblins, and (as we shall see in a later chapter), there is a distinct possibility that the goblins and fairies of folk lore may be more than the spirits of dead human beings. The earliest case of "mediumistic phenomena" dates back to 1524. Some time in the early 1520s, a pretty nun named Alix de Telieux became bored with the dull life of the convent of St. Pierre, in Lyon, and ran away with some stolen jewels. She seems to have found the world harder than she bargained for, and died in misery in 1524. It was in this year that another sister named Anthoinette de Grolée, a girl of eighteen, woke up with a vague impression that someone had kissed her on the lips and made the sign of the cross over her head. She sat up, and heard rapping noises that seemed to come from under the floor. As the disturbances continued, various people were called in to witness them, including Adrien de Montalembert, almoner to Francis I. By this time, someone had tried asking the spirit questions, and it replied by means of a code of raps. In this way, they had discovered that it was the dead Alix de Telieux, whose spirit was earth-bound as a result of her misdemeanors. She was able to tell them where she was buried; the body was brought back to the convent and buried there. This does not seem to have put an end to the "haunting." Anthoinette de Grolée was evidently able to provide it with the energy it needed to express itself. In death, the spirit of Alix was apparently as restless as in life, and made Anthoinette's life something of a misery. Montalembert himself spoke to the spirit, and had his questions answered by means of raps, and he adds that it was able to answer questions whose answer was not known to any other mortal creature. He also reports that Anthoinette de Grolée was made to levitate up into the air by the spirit. Finally, according to Montalembert, the dead girl actually appeared to Anthoinette and said she intended to depart. At matins that day there were loud rappings and other disturbances. But that was her final appearance.

All this sounds like an invention of superstitious nuns who believed in evil spirits. But at the end of the printed account of Montalembert, a nun of the following century has noted that in 1630 she had heard the story from an old nun of ninety-four, who had the story from her aunt, another nun. Montalembert gives an eye-witness account of the phenomena, and mentions that the case was studied by Cardinal Tencin, who found the manuscript in the Abbey of St. Pierre. Andrew Lang, who tells the story*, says that it has "an agreeable air of good faith." He also points out that Montalembert and the other investigators established communication with the spirit by rapping, about three hundred years before the case of the Fox sisters inaugurated the Spiritualist movement. Then why did the earlier case fail to arouse interest in this problem of spirits and "the other world"? Because the nuns took it for granted that there was "another world," and that the spirits were either devils or souls in purgatory—like Sister Alix. In fact, one nun suffered from hysterics as a result of the uproar at matins on that final morning, and it was automatically assumed that she was "possessed." Three centuries later, very few educated people believed in the devil or purgatory, so exactly the same phenomena started a world-wide movement.

Yet even in these earlier times, genuine psychical phenomena sometimes led to fraud: as in the curious case of Johannes Jetzer, which took place some twenty years earlier than the Alix de Telieux case. Jetzer was a poverty-stricken young man from Zurzach in Switzerland, who managed to get himself accepted into the monastery of the Dominicans at Berne in 1506. From the evidence, it is now clear that Jetzer was simply a natural "medium." He complained that his rest at night was disturbed by a ghost, dressed as a brother, which kept pulling the clothes off his bed—another favorite activity of poltergeists. This specter was able to speak, and declared that it was suffering because of its sins; it also had a black face and hands. (Talking poltergeists are

---

* *Cock Lane and Common Sense*, pp 110-113.

fairly rare, yet there are a number of cases on record, including the recent case of the Enfield poltergeist; the tape recordings of this spirit sound oddly hoarse and breathless, as if the voice is not being produced in the normal way by vocal cords and lungs.) The prior of the monastery seems to have assumed that Jetzer must be exceptionally holy if he was able to see spirits—an illogical assumption—and he was soon initiated into the Order. Nevertheless, the disturbances did not cease; on the contrary, they became more violent. Bangs and raps resounded through the priory, keeping everyone awake at night. Jetzer also lost a good deal of sleep, and became increasingly alarmed as the phantom appeared in a kind of sheet of flame, asking for masses to be said for its soul. They decided to place some holy relics in the cell next to Jetzer's. This seems to have provoked the spirit to violence: a huge stone fell out of the air, and doors opened and closed all over the monastery. While all this was happening, the spirit again appeared to Jetzer and announced itself as a former prior, Heinrich Kalpurg, who had died a hundred and sixty years earlier. He had been forced to leave the monastery because of inefficiency in managing its affairs, and had been murdered in Paris. The spirit allowed Jetzer to see its face at close quarters, and he saw that the ears and nose were missing—cut off when he was murdered. The spirit touched Jetzer's hand, and caused acute pain in his finger, which persisted for a long time afterwards.

Monks who had listened behind the doors verified all that Jetzer described. And the spirit continued to pay visits, heralded by various poltergeist phenomena—knocks, falling stones, objects moving through the air without being touched. Meanwhile, masses were said. And in due course, the spirit apparently succeeded in achieving some kind of peace.

So far, the story appears to be an accurate report of common poltergeist phenomena, which is described at length in three contemporary pamphlets.*

But at this point, the Dominicans seem to have decided that it would be a pity to allow the spirit to take its leave. So the ghost apparently continued to visit Jetzer in his cell. And Jetzer was requested to ask its opinion on a highly controversial matter: whether the Virgin Mary was conceived immaculately—that is, born free of original sin. The Franciscans believed she was; the Dominicans opposed this view. So Jetzer asked his ghostly visitor which was correct. The spirit said he wasn't sure, but would send St. Barbara along to settle the point. The following Friday, St. Barbara arrived, dressed in white, accompanied by two cherubim, and went off with a letter for the Virgin Mary, written by the lector of the priory. The Virgin Mary apparently accepted the invitation it contained, and visited Jetzer's cell, accompanied by St. Barbara and the two cherubim. She stated authoritatively that the Dominicans were right and the Franciscans were wrong; she was born like anybody else. After that, she returned to Jetzer's cell on a number of occasions, proving she was not a demon by worshipping the host, and tearing up a tract arguing the Immaculate Conception.

Presumably these events spread the fame of the monastery far and wide. But the authorities advised caution, and instructed Jetzer to ask the Virgin various questions, to make sure she was not an evil spirit in disguise. The Virgin seems to have been unoffended, commenting that it was the business of men to make sure they were not deceived.

Jetzer seems to have taken her at her word. The next time she appeared she sprinkled holy water on Jetzer, and

---

* The story is retold by E. J. Dingwall in *Very Peculiar People*, 1950.

then took up a holy wafer and declared she would transform it into the true flesh of her Son. When she dropped it back on the table it was pink. At this point, Jetzer leapt to his feet and grabbed her hand—whereupon the other holy wafer fell on to the table. And Jetzer realized, to his horror, that the Virgin was the lector, Stephan Boltzhurst, and the two angels were the prior and subprior.

This was far from the end of the matter. The next day, the lector assured Jetzer he had been trying to test his powers of observation, and Jetzer accepted the explanation. The Virgin came again and pierced Jetzer's feet and one of his hands. But soon afterwards Jetzer became suspicious about a bowl of soup; he gave it to some wolf cubs, which instantly died. When the Virgin visited his cell again, he grabbed her hand; and again recognized the subprior. When the statue of the Virgin in the chapel began to weep tears of blood, a neighboring priest climbed up and found they were paint.

The ecclesiastical authorities decided on an investigation, and Jetzer was taken in front of a painting of the Virgin, which began to tell him what to say in court. He saw the painting move, and experienced a sudden suspicion; pulling it aside, he found the lector there. Soon afterward St. Bernard of Clairvaux visited Jetzer in his cell to give him more instructions; but as he was floating out of the window, Jetzer gave him a shove, and he fell out into the courtyard—it was the prior again. One more attempt to deceive Jetzer so enraged him that he wounded St. Catherine of Siena in the leg with a knife, and discovered her to be the procurator of the monastery. Jetzer was struck in the face.

At the subsequent investigation, it looked at first as if Jetzer intended to protect his colleagues; then he asked the protection of the bishop and told the whole story. He was unfrocked. At a subsequent trial, the four miscreants—

the lector, prior, subprior and procurator—confessed in full, after torture, and were burned. Jetzer became a tailor and died in his native village about ten years later.

What is so interesting about the Jetzer case is the ease with which we can, with hindsight, see the distinction between genuine phenomena and invention. The lector decided to cash in on the "supernatural" happenings. But his notion of the supernatural was based on absurd misconceptions. We can see that Jetzer was simply a "medium," and that the spirit was glad to find someone through whom it could express its problems. It may or may not have been the person it claimed to be— we know spirits are liars more often than not (at least, those that seem to manifest at seances). The lector's head was full of ideas about souls in purgatory, saints who float through the air, cherubs with wings and so on. It looks as if he had considerable ingenuity in devising the various effects—even for a modern stage designer, it would not be easy to have a "saint" floating in and out of windows. But Jetzer's own ingenuity is perfectly obvious. E. J. Dingwall, an eminent member of the Society for Psychical Research, who discusses the case at length, concludes that Jetzer was as much a deceiver as the others, but this seems contrary to common sense. The "ghost" produced all the poltergeist phenomena with which we have become familiar in other cases—bangs and raps, falling stones, slamming doors. But we must bear in mind that they were *not* familiar in the sixteenth century, when very few poltergeist cases were on record, and when the few that were were generally confused with the activities of the devil. Shakespeare thought that ghosts go marching around the place, glowing with phosphorescent fires, and delivering long orations; that was the general opinion of his time. If Shakespeare's ghosts made rapping noises and threw stones, we would know that he had had some first-hand experience of poltergeists. The case of Jetzer, like that of the Bingen spook, has all the marks of authenticity.

So far we have spoken only of "mischievous" spirits that seem to intend no one any harm—as Giraldus Cambrensis says of the Pembrokeshire poltergeist, it seemed to intend "to deride rather than to do bodily injury." They may occasionally get angry if provoked or treated with contempt—a Mâcon poltergeist of 1612 became irritable when someone tried to exorcise it with the words "depart, thou cursed, into everlasting fire," and replied: "Thou liest—I am not cursed . . ." The poltergeist in the Enfield case (which will be described in Chapter 6) hit a photographer on the forehead with a Lego brick, and caused a bump that was still there a week later. But such damage is rare; more typical is the behavior of the Münchof poltergeist of 1818*:

> As the three stood conversing . . . a big iron spoon suddenly left the shelf on which it was lying and came straight at Koppbauer's head. Weighing about a pound and travelling with great velocity, it might have been expected to inflict a serious bruise, but the stricken man declared that he felt only a light touch and the spoon dropped perpendicularly at his feet.

Yet there have been cases where the poltergeist has shown a remarkable degree of malice, and caused injury as well as discomfort—Guy Playfair even mentions a Brazilian case in which the unfortunate girl who acted as the "focus" was driven to suicide.† And in one of the most astonishing cases on record, the poltergeist

---

* Thurston, Chapter III.
† See Chapter 6.

ill-treated its victim until he died, then proclaimed itself delighted at his death. This is the extraordinary case known as the Bell Witch.

The case, as Nandor Fodor* points out, took place at an interesting time when Americans had ceased to believe in witchcraft, and had not yet discovered Spiritualism. As a result, there was no proper investigation. It is fortunate that the records that have survived are so detailed.

In 1817, a farmer named John Bell lived with his family in Robertson County, Tennessee, with his wife Lucy and nine children. One of these, Betsy, was a girl of twelve.

At first, the disturbances were so slight that no one paid much attention. There were knocking and scraping noises, and sounds like rats gnawing inside the walls. As usual, nothing could be found to account for these sounds. They seemed to be mostly the kind of noises that might be made by animals, and so did not cause a great deal of excitement. An invisible dog seemed to be clawing at the floor, an invisible bird flapped against the ceiling, then two chained dogs sounded as if they were having a fight. When lamps were lit and people got out of bed to search, the noises stopped—poltergeists seem to have an odd dislike of being observed. Then the entity started pulling the clothes off the beds, and making various "human" noises—choking and gulping sounds followed by a gasping noise as if someone was being strangled. Next, stones were thrown and chairs turned upside down. Slowly, the poltergeist began to get into its stride. The girl Betsy—Elizabeth—seemed to be the focus; things only happened when she was around.

When the disturbances had been going on for roughly a year, the household was in permanent chaos.

---

* *The Poltergeist Down the Centuries.*

They seldom got a good night's sleep; the house often shook with the noises. The thing seemed to be able to be in several places at once—one night, Richard Williams Bell was awakened by something pulling his hair so hard that he thought the top of his head would come off; as he yelled with pain, Betsy, on the floor above, also began to scream as something pulled her hair.

Like the Fox family thirty years later, the Bells decided to ask the advice of neighbors. A friend named James Johnson came to the house. When the "ghost" made a sound like sucking air in through the teeth, he told it to be quiet, and it obeyed him. But poltergeists dislike being given orders (they seem to react best to a friendly approach), and this one redoubled its persecution of Betsy; there would be a sharp slapping noise and her cheek would go red from a blow, or her hair would be grabbed by an invisible hand and pulled. At least, Johnson had discovered that the entity understood English; so he advised Bell to invite in more neighbors. At this stage, he still seems to have entertained the obviously absurd idea that the children might be responsible. They tried sending Elizabeth to stay with a neighbor; the disturbances in the Bell household stopped, but Elizabeth continued to be persecuted with blows and scratches.

Poltergeist phenomena always work their way up from small effects to larger ones—from scratches or raps to flying stones and furniture; it never happens the other way around. The "Bell Witch" seemed to take pleasure in developing new ways of upsetting everybody. Strange lights flitted about the yard after dark. As the children came home from school, stones and chunks of wood were thrown at them. These were usually thrown from a particular thicket, and (as usual in such cases) never hurt anyone; if the children threw them back, they were promptly thrown again. But visitors to the house received stinging slaps—as did the children if they tried to resist when the covers were dragged off their beds.

The next stage was a whistling sound, which gradually changed to a voice. Poltergeist voices—as I have already remarked—do not sound at all like ordinary human voices; at least, not to begin with. It seems as if the entity is having to master a strange medium, to form sounds into words. (Even the rapping noises are probably "manufactured" sounds, not genuine raps made by hard objects.) Most talking ghosts and poltergeists begin in a guttural voice that sounds as if it is made up from grunts or groans; the Bell witch made gasping, whispering noises more like an asthmatic cough. Gradually, the voice developed until it was a low but audible whisper. It made such remarks as "I can't stand the smell of a nigger." And Betsy undoubtedly provided the energy for these demonstrations; she became fatigued and miserable, short of breath, and subject to fainting spells. Whenever she was unconscious, the voice ceased, which led some neighbors to suspect that she was a ventriloquist. But, as Nandor Fodor has pointed out, it sounds much more as if she slipped into mediumistic trance. At the same time, John Bell himself began to suffer. His tongue swelled, and his jaw felt stiff as if someone had pushed a stick inside his mouth, pushing on both sides of the jaw. It gradually became worse, until he was often unable to eat for a day at a time. The "witch" also seemed to direct more and more of its malice toward "old Jack Bell," declaring that he would be tormented for the rest of his life.

Meanwhile, the voice had graduated from a whisper to a normal voice; it used to repeat bits of the sermons of various local parsons. Then it began using bad language—again, a common characteristic of "talking ghosts." In fact, "it" talked in several voices. One of its earliest utterances in a normal voice was: "I am a spirit who was once very happy, but have been disturbed and am now unhappy." And it stated that it would torment John Bell and kill him in the end. It identified itself as an Indian whose bones had been scattered, then as a witch called Old Kate Batts. Then four more voices made their appearance—the "family" of the witch; they identified themselves as Blackdog, Mathematics, Cypocryphy and Jerusalem. Blackdog had a harsh, masculine voice, Jerusalem a boy's voice, while the other two sounded "delicate and feminine." They apparently indulged in debauches, talking drunkenly and filling the house with the smell of whisky.

As much as the witch detested John Bell, it seemed to have gentler feelings for the rest of the family, especially for John Bell's wife Lucy. When she fell ill the witch lamented "Luce, poor Luce," and showered hazel nuts on her. At Betsy's birthday party, it called "I have a surprise for you," and materialized a basket of fruit, including oranges and bananas, which it claimed to have brought from the West Indies.

A local "witch doctor" offered to cure Betsy with some revolting medicine which would make her vomit; when she duly retched, her vomit was found to be full of brass pins and needles. Meanwhile the witch screamed with laughter and said that if Betsy could be made to vomit again, she would have enough pins and needles to set up a shop.

One day in winter, as the children were sitting on a sledge, the witch called "Hold tight," and hauled the sledge at great speed round the house three times.

It was also able to spit; it had a particular aversion to a negro slave girl called Anky, and one day covered her head with a foam-like white spittle.

It also showed a tendency to interfere in the personal lives of the family. In due course, Betsy became engaged to a youth called Joshua Gardner. As soon as the witch found out, she began to whisper: "Please, Betsy Bell, don't have Joshua Gardner." Betsy finally gave in, and returned Joshua's ring.

Meanwhile, the persecution of John Bell became steadily worse. His sufferings sound like the torments of the possessed nuns and priests of Loudun; but they were of a more physical nature. When he was ill in bed, the witch cursed and raved, using foul language. When he went outside, it followed him and jerked off his shoes. Then he was struck in the face so hard that he was stunned and had to sit down on a log. His face began to jerk and contort—another of the witch's favorite methods of tormenting him—then his body convulsed. His shoes kept flying off, and every time his son Richard put them on they flew off again. The witch shrieked with laughter and sang derisive songs (many poltergeists have shown themselves to be musical, although their taste seldom rises above popular songs). Finally, the attacks ceased, and the unfortunate man sat there stunned, with the tears rolling down his cheeks. The witch had been tormenting him for more than three years. When they got him back indoors, he took to his bed. On December 19, 1820, he was found to be in a deep stupor. In the medicine cupboard, his son John found a dark bottle one-third full of a smokey-looking liquid. The witch began to exult: "It's useless for you to try to relieve old Jack—I've got him this time." Asked about the medicine the witch replied: "I put it there, and gave old Jack a dose last night while he was asleep, which fixed him." When the doctor arrived, they tested the "medicine" by dipping a straw into it and allowing a drop to fall on the cat's tongue; the cat jumped and whirled around, then died. John Bell himself died the next day, while the witch filled the house with shrieks of triumph, and sang "Row me up some brandy, O."

As Fodor points out, there is something very odd about this death. The witch had often revealed strength enough to strangle Bell, or kill him by hitting him with some object; yet she never made any such attempt— only, as it were, drove him to despair, then administered some powerful drug when he was probably dying anyway. In most poltergeist cases we may feel that the entity is not particularly malicious, and that this explains the lack of injury—bullying children often threaten their victims with physical damage, and may even seem to be on the point of carrying out their threat; but there is an abyss of difference between the threat—or, perhaps, lashing out with a stick and missing by a hair's breadth—and actually causing bodily harm. Yet the Bell Witch seems to have been more malicious than most. It leads to the speculation that these entities may not be "allowed" to do actual harm; they are allowed to torment, but not to damage. This, admittedly, explains nothing; but it is certainly an observation that has struck everyone who has studied the poltergeist.

After the death of John Bell, the witch seemed to lose interest. It apparently refused to help John Junior to speak to his dead father, declaring that the dead could not be brought back; but on one occasion, it told John to go to the window, on a snowy day, then made footprints appear in the snow, which it claimed to be identical with those made by his father's boots—John did not bother to test this claim.

In 1821, four years after the disturbances began (an unusually long period), the family was sitting at supper one evening when there was a tremendous noise in the chimney—as if a cannon ball had rolled down it and out into the room. It burst into a ball of smoke. The witch's voice called: "I am going, and will be gone for seven years—goodbye to all." And the disturbances ceased.

Seven years later, only Lucy Bell and two of her sons remained in the homestead; the rest, including Betsy, had married or left. Once again, the manifestations started from the beginning, with scratching noises, then the covers being pulled off the bed. But the family ignored all this, and after two weeks, the manifestations ceased. John Junior claimed that the witch paid him two visits in his new home, and promised to return to one of his descendants in a hundred and seven years; but 1935 passed without any direct descendant of the Bell family being "haunted."

The case of the Bell Witch was fully documented in a book written in 1846 by Richard Bell, who had been seven when the witch first appeared, and was later the subject of a full length book by M. V. Ingram (1894). Nandor Fodor, who has written extensively on the poltergeist, discusses it fully in his book *The Poltergeist Down the Centuries*. As well as being a student of the paranormal, Fodor was also a Freudian psychiatrist. and he takes the view that the poltergeist is sexual in origin. Undoubtedly, he is partly correct—the poltergeist seems to be at its best when it can draw on the energies of a girl (or, less often, a boy) who has just reached puberty. But Fodor goes further than this, and suggests that the explanation of the Bell Witch lies in an incestuous attack made on Betsy by her father. This caused Betsy to hate her father, and her repressed hatred expressed itself in the form of "recurrent spontaneous psychokinesis." He also believes that John Bell felt a deep guilt about the supposed attack, and cites an occasion when Bell went to dinner with neighbors named Dearden, yet said nothing all evening, seeming depressed and confused; the next day he rode over specially to explain, saying that his tongue had been affected as if his mouth had become filled with fungus. This, says Fodor, probably represents "self-aggression."

But this theory hardly stands up to examination. As we have seen, poltergeists often take a delight in embarrassing people by revealing their most intimate secrets in public—in the Bell Witch case, it hastened the break-up of Betsy and Joshua by embarrassing them with personal revelations. So it is hard to see why it should have failed to state publicly that John Bell had committed—or tried to commit—incest with Betsy. Even if it *had* said so, we would be justified in treating the accusation with caution: poltergeists are not noted for truthfulness. The fact that it failed to say so weighs heavily against the incest theory. As to the notion that Betsy's unconscious aggressions caused the disturbances, this fails to explain why Betsy herself was—at first—treated so badly. It also fails to explain how the witch managed to return when Betsy had left home and was married.

Rather more interesting are Fodor's speculations about the nature of the poltergeist. He thinks that its denial of communication with the dead proves that it was not the spirit of a dead person. He is inclined to feel that the witch was "a fragment of a living personality that has broken free in some mysterious way of some of the three-dimensional limitations of the mind of the main personality." In other words, poltergeists are explainable as fragments of the "split personality." But this leaves us exactly where we were before—in complete ignorance of how the split personality performs its paranormal feats.

The truth is that this explanation—about the unconscious mind—sounded far more convincing in the 1930s than it does today, when Freud is no longer regarded as infallible. Moreover, it simply fails to fit the facts of the "haunting." On the other hand, Kardec's views fit them like a glove. According to *The Spirits' Book*, only a small proportion of the spirits involved in poltergeist cases are those of dead people—there are many other kinds. Besides, it seems clear that in the Bell Witch case, there was not one spirit, but several. So Kardec's explanation would be that the haunting in the Bell household was the work of a group of rowdy and mischievous spirits or "elementals" of no particular intelligence—the other-worldly equivalent of a cageful of monkeys. A house with nine children, many of them teenagers, would provide plenty of the energy poltergeists find necessary to perform their antics. We must suppose that the Bell household was not a particularly happy one—this deduction arises from the fact that there is no record of a poltergeist haunting taking place in a happy family. No doubt John Bell was a typical nineteenth-century patriarch, dictatorial and bad-tempered; and on a farmstead in a remote rural area, there was no doubt plenty of reason for tension and frustration in the family.

As to why the witch disliked John Bell so much, the reason may lie in an event that took place very early in the case. Before the first scratching noises were heard, John Bell saw one day a strange, dog-like creature sitting between two corn rows, and shot at it. The "witch" stated on a number of occasions that she could assume the shape of an animal. Poltergeists dislike aggression against themselves, and if the strange animal *was* the witch, then it had a cause for feeling resentment about John Bell. Apart from that, he was the head of the household, the "tyrant." If the witch was capable of showing generosity and affection toward various members of the family—Lucy, Betsy, young John—then she (they?) would also dislike the bullying paterfamilias. This is, admittedly, speculation; but it fits better than Fodor's Freudian guesses.

It would also be interesting to have a "ley map" of Robertson Country, Tennessee, showing the Indian sacred sites, and to know whether the Bell farmstead was situated over a blind spring or underground stream. A combination of a house with nine children and powerful "telluric currents" would provide an ideal situation for a bored and mischievous "elemental."

It is important to realize that poltergeists are one of the most common of all "psychic" manifestations: as common, say, as plane crashes, or accidents in which people are struck by lightning. At any given moment, there are probably dozens of cases going on in different parts of the world. Nandor Fodor begins his study with brief summaries of about five hundred cases, starting in 355 A.D. and extending to the Douglass Deen case in 1949. Other books by researchers of other nationalities—Richet, Lombroso, Aksakov, Bender, Roll—make it clear that there are hundreds more that could be added to the list.

This wealth of material is actually something of an embarrassment, for most cases are so similar that they can teach us nothing new about the poltergeist. How does it help us to know that in 1170 A.D., the hermitage of St. Godric was bombarded with showers of stones, and that the poltergeist threw at him the box in which he kept his altar beads and poured the communion wine over his head? It merely suggests what we already suspect, that poltergeists are mischievous spirits who behave very much like "demons." More than seven hundred years later, in 1906, the poltergeist is still indulging in the same rather boring escapades on the other side of the world, in Sumatra, when a Mr. Grottendieck was awakened in the bedroom of a makeshift house by falling stones, which appeared to be penetrating the roof (made of dry leaves). When he fired his rifle into the jungle, the barrage of stones only increased (another example of a poltergeist resenting aggression). His "boy" (who was presumably the "focus") told him that the stones were being thrown by Satan. But in the Sumatra case, we at least have one interesting detail. Mr. Grottendieck tried catching the stones as they fell, but they seemed to avoid his hand. He says: "It seemed to me that they changed their direction in the air as soon as I tried to get hold of them." And from this we can make one solid inference. The stones were not "thrown." Whatever agency caused them to fly through the air was *still holding them* when Grottendieck tried to grab them. And this observation is confirmed by case after case in which "thrown" objects manage to perform right-angle turns in mid-air (which, interestingly enough, seems also to be a characteristic of "flying saucers").

So let us, in the remainder of this chapter, glance at a number of famous cases that offer some new feature or provide a clue, and ignore all the hundreds of others that provide no new information. All they can tell us is that the poltergeist is undoubtedly a reality, and that anyone who thinks otherwise—like the eminent investigator Frank Podmore, who concluded that naughty children are responsible—is being willfully blind or stupid.

The poltergeist that appeared in the home of a Huguenot minister, M. Francois Perrault, in September, 1612, is remarkable solely for being one of those rare cases in which the "spirit" developed a voice and became extremely talkative. When the minister came back to Mâcon after a five-day absence on September 1, 1612, he found his wife and her maid in a state of terror. The disturbances had started when something drew the curtains in the middle of the night. The following night, the poltergeist pulled the blankets off the bed. When the maid tried to go into a room, something pushed on the door from the other side; and when she finally got in, she found that everything had been thrown about. Every night after that, the poltergeist made loud bangs and crashes. On the night M. Perrault returned, the poltergeist hurled pots and pans around the kitchen, convincing him that he was dealing with an evil spirit. A week later, on September 20, it spoke for the first time, starting with a whistling noise—as did the Bell witch—then repeating the words "Minister, minister" in a shrill voice. Finally it began to sing a simple tune of five notes. Soon the spirit was holding lengthy conversations with various regular visitors to the house, singing French popular songs, saying prayers (to prove it was not a demon) and offering to transform itself into an angel—a promise it never carried out. It also declared that M. Perrault's father had been murdered, and named the man who did it. M. Perrault was inclined to disbelieve this tale, and his skepticism proved justified as the entity invented various other malicious stories about the townspeople of Mâcon. These strange conversations continued for two months— the spirit obviously enjoyed having an audience—and objects continued to be hurled about. Toward the end, huge stones weighing two or three pounds were thrown about the house—although, as usual, they caused no harm. M. Perrault states his opinion that this was because his household was protected by God; but it seems more likely that the spirit simply lacked destructive tendencies.

One day in November, the racket suddenly stopped. Twenty-four hours of blessed silence made it clear that the "demon" had departed. On a nail above the fireplace hung some bells that he had often thrown about the place. The day after his departure, a large viper—a rare snake in that part of France—was seen leaving M.

Perrault's house, and was caught; but it proved to be a perfectly normal snake, and presumably had nothing to do with the haunting.

Perhaps the most interesting point about the Perrault case is that the maid was generally believed to be a witch—perhaps because her parents had been accused of witchcraft. We have seen that she seemed singularly unafraid of the poltergeist—few people would try to force their way through a door when some invisible presence was trying to hold it closed. The spirit obviously liked her, and enjoyed imitating her broad *patois*. One day, when she complained that it had failed to bring her any wood, it threw down a faggot at her feet. When another maid came to the house and shared her bed, the poltergeist tormented the newcomer so relentlessly that she finally had to leave.

Modern writers on witchcraft take the view that it was a delusion due to peasant superstition. No doubt the majority of women who were burned as witches were innocent; but no one who has studied some of the best-known witch trials, like the Isobel Gowdie case in Scotland, or the notorious Chambre Ardente affair in Paris, can believe that all witchcraft is smoke without fire. In fact, this whole subject of witchcraft and magic deserves a chapter to itself.

Perhaps the best-known of all poltergeist hauntings is the case that has become known as the phantom drummer of Tedworth. It took place just half a century after the Mâcon case, and begins on a day in mid-March, 1661, when a magistrate named John Mompesson was visiting the small town of Ludgershall in east Wiltshire, and became irritated by loud drumming noises that came from the street. He inquired what these were, and was told that they were made by a vagrant named William Drury, who had been in the town for a few days. He had tried to persuade the constable to give him public assistance, on the strength of his papers, signed by various eminent magistrates; but the constable suspected they were forged.

Mompesson ordered the drummer to be brought before him, and examined his papers; just as the bailiff had suspected, they were forged. Mompesson seems to have been an officious sort of man who enjoyed exercising his authority; he ordered the drummer—a middle-aged man—to be held until the next sitting of the local Bench, and meanwhile confiscated his drum. The man seems to have tried hard to persuade Mompesson to return the drum, but without success. As soon as Mompesson's back was turned, the constable seems to have allowed Drury to escape. But the drum stayed behind.

A few weeks later, the bailiff of Ludgershall sent the drum to Mompesson's house in Tedworth. Mompesson was just on his way to London. When he came back he found the house in uproar. For three nights there had been violent knockings and raps all over the house—both inside and out. That night, when the banging started, Mompesson leapt out of bed with a pistol and rushed to the room from which the sound was coming. It moved to another room. He tried to locate it, but it now seemed to be coming from outside. When he got back into bed, he was able to distinguish drumbeats among the rapping noises.

For the next two months, it was impossible to get to sleep until the middle of the night; the racket went on for at least two hours every night. It stopped briefly when Mrs. Mompesson was in labor, and was silent for three weeks—an indication that the spirit was mischievous rather than malicious. Then the disturbances started up again, this time centering around Mompesson's children. The drumbeats would sound from around their beds, and the beds were often lifted up into the air. When the children were moved up into a loft, the drummer followed them. The servants even began to get used to it; one manservant saw a board move, and asked it to hand it to him; the board floated up to his hand, and a joking tug of war ensued for twenty minutes or so, until the master ordered them to stop. When the minister came to pray by the children, the spirit showed its disrespect by being noisier than usual, and leaving behind a disgusting sulphurous smell—presumably to imply it came from Hell. Scratching noises sounded like huge rats.

Things got worse. During the next two years lights were seen, doors slammed, unseen skirts rustled, and a Bible was burnt. The creature purred like a cat, panted like a dog, and made the coins in a man's pocket turn black. One day, Mompesson went into the stable and found his horse lying on its back with its hind hoof jammed into its mouth; it had to be pried out with a lever. The "spirit" attacked the local blacksmith with a pair of pincers, snatched a sword from a guest, and grabbed a stick from a servant woman who was trying to bar its path. The Reverend Joseph Glanvil—who wrote about the case—came to investigate, and heard the strange noises from around the children's beds. When he went down to his horse, he found it sweating with terror, and the horse died soon afterwards.

The phantom drummer seems to have developed a voice; one morning, there was a bright light in the children's room and a voice kept shouting: "A witch, a witch!"—at least a hundred times, according to Glanvil. Mompesson woke up one night to find himself looking at a vague shape with two great staring eyes, which slowly vanished. It also developed such unpleasant habits as emptying ashes and chamberpots into the children's beds.

In 1663, William Drury was arrested at Gloucester for stealing a pig. While he was in Gloucester jail, a Wiltshire man came to see him, and Drury asked what was happening in Wiltshire. When the man said "Nothing "Drury said: "What, haven't you heard about the drumming in the house at Tedworth?" The man admitted that he had, whereupon Drury declared: "I have plagued him, and he shall never be quiet until he has made me satisfaction for taking away my drum." This, according to Glanvil, led to his being tried for a witch at Salisbury and sentenced to transportation. As soon as Drury was out of the country, peace descended on the Mompesson household. But the drummer somehow managed to escape and return to England—whereupon the disturbances began all over again. Mrs. Mompesson seems to have asked it—by means of raps—whether Drury was responsible, and it replied in the affirmative.

How the disturbances ended is not clear—presumably they faded away, like most poltergeists. Certainly they had ceased by the time Glanvil published his account twenty years later.

The most interesting point about the case is Drury's admission that he caused the disturbances. This seems to fly in the face of the most popular theory of poltergeists—that they are the result of the unconscious disturbances of a child at puberty. If we regard Drury merely as the focus or medium, then we have to explain how he succeeded in causing the phenomena when he was many miles away. Few writers on the case have even bothered to quote Glanvil's remark that Drury had been a soldier under Cromwell, and learned magic from some "Gallant Books he had had of a wizard." Together with Drury's trial for witchcraft, they seem to add a disreputable air of superstition to a case that otherwise looks like a classic poltergeist haunting. To make sense of Drury's admissions, we have to suppose that (a) he knew how to practice some form of magic, and (b) that the spirit or spirits that caused the disturbances could be persuaded to help him obtain his revenge. These propositions strike a modern investigator as preposterous. Yet, as we shall see, they fit the facts rather better than modern theories about "recurrent spontaneous psychokinesis" or Fodor's sexual theory of the origin of poltergeist activity. In her book *The Night Side of Nature*—a Victorian bestseller—Catherine Crowe describes a case that occurred in Rambouillet in November, 1846, at a farm house belonging to a M. Bottel. Some peddlers came to the door and asked for bread, which they were given. Later, one of them came back and asked for more; the servant refused him, and the man went off uttering vague threats. That night, at supper, plates began to roll off the table. When the servant girl happened to stand on the spot where the peddler had stood, she was "seized with convulsions and an extraordinary rotatory motion." A carter standing beside her placed himself on the same spot, felt "suffocated" and dizzy, and fell into a pool of water outside the house. The curé was asked for help, but he was "attacked in the same manner," and his furniture began to dance about. The phenomena continued for some weeks before they stopped.

Here we can note a number of points of interest. Mrs. Crowe does not say so, but if the peddlers formed a group, then it seems probable they were gypsies, and gypsies have a strong magic tradition—in the nineteenth century it was studied by a remarkable investigator, Charles Godfrey Leland. It seems curious that the servant girl was seized with convulsions on the exact spot where the peddler had stood, and that the carter also felt dizzy and suffocated. This immediately calls to mind some of Lethbridge's comments about "ghouls." He experienced a sense of dizziness and suffocation on Ladram Beach, and his wife Mina felt the same as she stood on the clifftop at the spot where the man had committed suicide. The French dowser Barthelemy Bleton discovered his powers when he felt suffocated and dizzy over a powerful underground stream. It seems conceivable that the forces involved in this type of "magic" may involve the earth. Yet since the poltergeist also attacked the curé in his own home, we have to assume that it was an active force—in fact, one of Kardec's spirits.

Glanvil wrote his book on strange occurrences— *Saducismus Triumphatus*—just before the dawning of the eighteenth century, the age of reason. Even in the 1660s, the magistrate Mompesson was widely suspected of somehow fabricating the story of the phantom drummer, and "he suffered by it in his name, in his estate, in all his affairs . . . " A quarter of a century after its publication, Glanvil's book was regarded as an absurd relic of an age of credulity. The main reason was that the civilized world was finally—after four centuries—shaking off the belief in witchcraft. In England, there had been no mass trials of witches since the death of Matthew Hopkins, the "witchfinder general," in 1646; in America, the witch hysteria came to an end after the Salem trials in 1692. The age of science had dawned; there was no room for books like *Saducismus Triumphatus* in the age of Newton and Leibniz.

One of the most remarkable cases of the early eighteenth century was investigated by the eminent scientist Joseph Priestley who, predictably, decided that the phenomena were caused by a hoaxer. It began at the rectory of Epworth, in Lincolnshire, inhabited by the family of the Reverend Samuel Wesley, grandfather of the founder of Methodism. On December 1, 1716, the Wesleys' maidservant was in the dining-room when she heard appalling groans, like someone dying. The family made a joke of it. But a few nights later, they were awakened by loud knocking sounds, which usually seemed to come from the garret or nursery. The only person who failed to hear them was the Reverend Wesley himself, and the family decided not to tell him in case he thought it was an omen of his death. When they finally told him, he refused to believe them; that night, as if to convince him, there were nine loud knocks by his bedside.

From then on, the house was in a constant state of disturbance, with footsteps in empty rooms and up and down the stairs—often more than one set of footsteps at a time—noises like smashing bottles, and a curious sound which was compared to the "winding up of a jack" or someone planing wood. When Mrs. Wesley heard knocking noises from the nursery, she tried repeating them, and the poltergeist then made the same knocks resound from the floorboards under her feet. When she looked under the bed, an animal like a badger ran out. A manservant who saw the animal sitting by the dining-room fire said it looked like a white rabbit.

The family were at first afraid that it portended someone's death, either that of the Reverend Samuel Wesley or of his elder son (of the same name). When nothing of the sort occurred, they decided that they were dealing with witchcraft—against which the Reverend Samuel had preached. Yet they also noticed that the disturbances seemed connected with the nineteen-year-old Hetty Wesley; she often trembled in her sleep before the sounds began.

After two months, the poltergeist went away, although it is said to have made occasional brief reappearances in later years. The family came to refer to it as "Old Jeffrey." And Mrs. Wesley remained convinced that Old Jeffrey was the spirit of her brother, who worked for the East India Company, and who vanished without a trace. She could well have been right. In some respects, the poltergeist behaved like a ghost. Its activities always seemed to begin at a quarter to ten every night (few poltergeists keep to an exact timetable)—and the very first sounds heard were groans and heavy breathing, not the usual raps. Poltergeist disturbances usually—almost invariably—occur in a certain sequence. The earliest stage is usually some kind of scratching noise like rats; then raps and bangs, then flying stones or other small objects, then larger objects, then other forms of physical mischief—moving furniture, blankets pulled off beds. If voices occur, they usually occur after this stage—as, for example, in the case of the Bell Witch. It is almost unknown for phenomena to occur in a different order. So in that respect, the Wesley case is unusual, starting with what is usually one of the later developments. The chief objection to Mrs. Wesley's theory is that if the spirit of her dead brother was behind the disturbances, then why did he not try to communicate—for example, when the Reverend Samuel tried to get him to answer questions by means of raps?

One of the more obvious features of the Epworth case is that there were none of the usual physical phenomena—falling stones, dancing furniture. The explanation, presumably, is that there was not enough energy available for the poltergeist to do anything more spectacular than make noises. This is also true of the most notorious poltergeist of the eighteenth century, the "Cock Lane ghost." This began with knocking noises in the house of Richard Parsons, clerk of St. Sepulchre's church in Smithfield, London, in November, 1759. One night, a woman named Fanny Lynes, who was lodging in the house, asked ten-year-old Elizabeth Parsons, the eldest daughter, to sleep with her while her common-law husband was away on business. All went well for a few nights; then the two were kept awake one night by scratching and rapping noises from behind the wainscot. When they told Richard Parsons about it, he said it was probably the cobbler next door.

Soon afterwards, Fanny became ill with smallpox; she was six months pregnant, and her "husband" was understandably anxious. He and Fanny were unmarried only because she was his deceased wife's sister. William Kent had married Elizabeth Lynes two years earlier, but she had died in childbirth; now it looked rather as if the story was repeating itself. He moved Fanny into a house nearby, where, on February 2, 1760, she died of smallpox.

Meanwhile, the rappings in Richard Parsons' house were continuing; Parsons actually called in a carpenter to take down the wainscotting, but nothing was found. Meanwhile, the knockings got louder, and the story of the "haunted house" spread throughout the neighborhood. They seemed to be associated with Elizabeth; they came from behind her bed, and when they were about to begin, she would begin to tremble and shiver like Hetty Wesley in the Epworth case. Later that year, Elizabeth began to suffer from convulsions.

Like so many victims of poltergeist phenomena, Richard Parsons decided to call in a friend, the Reverend John Moore, assistant preacher at St. Sepulchre's. And the Reverend Moore proceeded to communicate with the "spirit," asking it to answer his questions in the usual manner—one rap for yes, two for no. (They added a scratching noise to indicate it was displeased.)

By this means the spirit told its upsetting story. It was, it declared, the ghost of Fanny Lynes, returned from the dead to denounce her late "husband," William Kent, for killing her by poison. He had, it seemed, administered red arsenic in her "purl": a mixture of herbs and beer.

Richard Parsons was not entirely displeased to

hear this story, for he was nursing a grudge against his late tenant. William Kent was a fairly rich man, having been a successful innkeeper in Norfolk, and he had lent Parsons twenty pounds, on the understanding that Parsons should repay it at a pound a month. Parsons, who seems to have been a drunkard, had failed to repay anything, possibly because he had discovered that Kent and Fanny were not married, and hoped to blackmail Kent into forgetting the loan. Kent had put the matter into the hands of his attorney.

If Parsons had been less anxious to believe the worst of his ex-tenant, he might have suspected the ghost of untruthfulness. To begin with, the knocking had begun while Fanny Lynes was still alive. And a publican named Franzen swore that he had seen a spirit in white one evening in December, 1759, when Fanny had just moved from the Cock Lane house. Parsons apparently found it easier to believe that the earlier knockings had been caused by Kent's first wife Elizabeth—who was presumably also trying to denounce him for murder.

Throughout 1761, the house in Cock Lane acquired an increasing reputation for its ghosts, and the tale about Kent's supposed murders gained wide currency in the area. Kent himself heard nothing about it until January, 1762, when he saw an item in the *Public Ledger* about a man who had brought a young lady from Norfolk and poisoned her in London. A few days later, another item about the Cock Lane ghost and its revelations led Kent to go along to see the Reverend John Moore. Moore, a respectable and well-liked man, could only advise Kent to attend a seance in Elizabeth's bedroom, and see for himself. Kent did this, taking with him the doctor and apothecary who had attended Fanny in her last illness. The small bedroom was crowded, and Elizabeth and her younger sister lay side by side in the bed. At first the "ghost" declined to manifest itself; but when the room had been emptied, Moore succeeded in persuading it, and they all trooped back. Now Kent listened with something like panic as he heard Moore asking the spirit if it was Kent's wife—one knock—if it had been murdered by him—one knock—and if anyone else was concerned in the murder plot—two knocks. Kent shouted indignantly, "Thou art a lying spirit!"

Now, suddenly, the ghost was famous all over London, and Cock Lane was crowded with carriages. In February, a clergyman named Aldrich persuaded Parsons to allow his daughter to come to his vicarage in Clerkenwell to be tested. An investigating committee, including the famous Dr. Johnson, was present. Inevitably, the ghost declined to manifest itself. Nor would the ghost rap on the coffin of Fanny Lynes in the vault of the church. Dr. Johnson concluded it was a fraud. And this was the opinion of most of London.

On the day following this fiasco, Elizabeth was staying at the house of a comb-maker in Cow Lane when the bell of Newgate Prison began to toll—a sign that someone was to be hanged. The comb-maker asked the ghost whether someone was about to be hanged and whether it was a man or woman; the ghost answered both questions correctly. Later that day, a loose curtain began to spin on its rod—the only physical manifestation in the case.

The following day, as Elizabeth lay asleep, her father heard whispering noises; he carried a candle over to her bed, but she seemed to be asleep. The whispering continued, although the child's lips were plainly closed. In fact, the poltergeist seemed to be increasing in strength. Two nights later, the noises were so violent that their host asked them to leave. (Presumably she was sleeping away from home to avoid crowds.) Elizabeth and her father moved to the house of a Mr. Missiter, near Covent Garden, and the manifestations continued, even when a maid lay in bed beside Elizabeth and held her hands and feet.

By now, the unfortunate Kent was determined to prove his innocence through the law; so the burden of proof now lay on Parsons and his daughter. Elizabeth was told that unless the ghost made itself heard that night, her father and mother would be thrown into prison. Naturally, she made sure something happened. The servants peered through a crack in the door, and saw her take a piece of board and hide it in the bed. Later, when there were people in the room, the knocking noises sounded from the bed. In fact, the listeners noticed that the knocks were coming from the bed and not, as usual, from around the room. The bed was searched and the board found. And the next day, the newspapers published the story of the "fraud."

On February 25, 1762, there appeared a pamphlet entitled: *The Mystery Revealed; Containing a Series of Transactions and Authentic Testimonials respecting the supposed Cock Lane Ghost, which have been concealed from the Public*—the author was probably Johnson's friend Oliver Goldsmith. A satirical play called *The Drummer or the Haunted House* was presented at Covent Garden. And William Kent began legal proceedings against Richard Parsons. In July, 1762, Mr. and Mrs. Parsons, and a woman called Mary Frazer—who had often acted as "questioner" to the ghost—appeared before magistrates in the Guildhall. Parsons was charged with trying to take away the life of William Kent by charging him with murder. The judges remained unconvinced by the evidence of neighbors who had heard raps resounding from all over the room, and who were certain that Elizabeth could not have made them. And finally,

Parsons was sentenced to two years in prison, and to stand three times in the pillory; his wife was sentenced to one year, and Mary Frazer to six months. The Reverend Moore and one of his associates had to pay out £588 in damages to Kent. There was universal sympathy for Parsons, and when he stood in the pillory, the mob took up a collection for him—an unusual gesture for a period when malefactors were often badly injured in the pillory. (Later in the year a man convicted of sodomy was stoned to death in the same pillory.)

For more than two centuries, the Cock Lane ghost became a synonym for an imposture. When Andrew Lang wrote about it in 1894, he began his chapter: "If one phantom is more discredited than another, it is the Cock Lane ghost." Yet for anyone studying the case today, this view seems absurd. Nothing could be more obvious than that the Cock Lane ghost was a poltergeist like the hundreds of others that have been recorded down the ages. Unfortunately, it is now too late for us to discover certain essential facts that might help to explain it. For example, what kind of a girl was Elizabeth Parsons? She was rather younger than most poltergeist-children, but she may well have been sexually mature for her age. If her father was something of a drunkard and a spendthrift—as the records indicate—then it seems fairly certain that the Parsons household was not a happy one. The father of Christine Beauchamp—Morton Prince's famous case of multiple personality—was a similar type of person, and his daughter had severe psychological problems as a consequence. We know that Christine Beauchamp became fixated on her father's closest friend William Jones, and transferred to him all her adoration. It is conceivable that Elizabeth Parsons felt the same about William Kent. In which case, sleeping in his bed while he was away must have aroused morbid emotions—especially if she was aware that Kent and Fanny were "living in sin." The convulsions that began a year after the disturbances certainly suggest she was passing through a period of emotional upheaval. But since we know so little about Elizabeth, all these things must remain a matter for speculation.

Only one thing seems fairly certain: that the spirit itself was neither that of Elizabeth Kent nor of Fanny Lynes; it was the usual mischievous poltergeist, bent on creating as much havoc and confusion as possible. It seems to confirm Chesterton's remark that the only definite thing that can be said about such spirits is that they tell lies.

The Epworth poltergeist and the Cock Lane ghost confined themselves to rappings (although the Cock Lane ghost seemed to be attempting more ambitious phenomena towards the end). A poltergeist that haunted a farm in Stockwell, London, in 1772 showed altogether less restraint. It began by throwing rows of plates off the kitchen shelf and smashing them. When the owner of the house, Mrs. Golding, fainted, the doctor bled her; the blood had only just congealed when it leapt out of the basin, and the basin smashed in pieces. When Mrs. Golding offered some of the assembled guests a drink of wine or rum, these bottles also shattered. Joints of ham leapt off their hooks on the ceiling and fell to the floor. The racket was so tremendous that they were afraid the house would fall down, and the children were sent off to the barn. The maid, Ann Robinson, went with them, and as soon as she was out of the house, the disturbances stopped. The moment she returned, they started again. The coal scuttle overturned, candlesticks flew through the air, a nine-gallon cask of beer was turned upside down, and a bucket of cold water "boiled like a pot"—as in the Amherst case of a century later. Mrs. Golding decided to sack the maid, and the uproar promptly ceased.

This case attracted little attention at the time—if Dr. Johnson heard of it, he no doubt dismissed it as another fraud. Catherine Crowe unearthed it a century later for her book *The Night Side of Nature*. And in her chapter on the poltergeist, she makes some sensible and pertinent suggestions. She discusses the case of a French girl called Angélique Cottin, who was weaving silk gloves on January 15, 1846, when the loom began to jerk violently. The other girls were terrified, and retreated to the far end of the room; then, one by one, they went back to examine the loom, which had a heavy oak frame. As soon as Angélique approached, it began to dance again.

From this time on, Angélique developed the power of giving people violent electric shocks—she was, in fact, another "human electric eel"—like those discussed in the previous chapter. Objects laid on her apron flew off violently, and the power was strong enough to raise a heavy tub with a man sitting on it. Oddly enough, metals were not affected, indicating that this form of "electricity" was not the usual kind. When Angélique was tired, the current would diminish. It also diminished when she was on a carpet, but was most powerful when she was on bare earth—another indication that the force seems to come from the earth, and is probably connected with the force that convulses some dowsers. She had to sleep on a stone covered with a cork mat. The phenomena continued for four months, and were widely studied by men of science; then they ceased.

Mrs. Crowe makes the reasonable suggestion that poltergeist phenomena may be electrical in nature, and cites a number of other cases, including a Mlle. Emmerich, sister of the professor of theology at Strasbourg, who became a human electric battery after receiving a severe fright, the nature of which is not specified. (We have already noticed that many mediums seem to develop their powers after accidents.) The interesting thing about Mlle. Emmerich was that she could give people shocks even when they were not touching her. She gave her brother a shock when he was several rooms away; when he rushed to her bedroom, she laughed and said: "Ah, you felt it, did you?"

Mrs. Crowe adds the interesting remark: "Many somnambulistic persons [she means persons under hypnosis] are capable of giving an electric shock; and I have met with one person, not somnambulistic, who informs me that he has frequently been able to do it by an effort of will."

Clearly, if someone was able to produce electric currents at will, he or she might be in a position to cause poltergeist phenomena—perhaps even at a distance, like Mlle. Emmerich; in that case, we might have some kind of explanation for the magical powers of the drummer of Tedworth. But although the theory is attractive, it could only explain the least spectacular abilities of the poltergeist—like causing raps and smashing plates. How, for example, could it account for the varieties of mischief that disrupted the domestic peace of the Reverend Eliakim Phelps in 1850?

The Reverend Phelps lived in Stratford, Connecticut, and had married a widow with four children. He was interested in clairvoyance, and attempted to treat illnesses by means of mesmerism. He was understandably excited by the news of the strange events at the home of the Fox family in 1849. And in March 1850, when he entertained a visitor from New York, the two of them arranged some kind of amateur seance, which was not particularly successful, although they managed to obtain a few raps.

A few days later, on Sunday, March 10, the family returned from church to find the front door wide open and the place in disorder. Their first assumption was that they had been burgled; but inspection showed that nothing had been taken, and a gold watch left on a table was untouched. That afternoon, the family went off to church again, but this time the Reverend Phelps stayed behind to keep watch. He may well have dozed; at all events, nothing disturbed him. But when the family returned from church, the place again showed signs of an intruder. Furniture was scattered, and in the main bedroom, a nightgown and chemise had been laid out on the bed, with the arms folded across the breast, and a pair of stockings placed to make it look like a corpse laid out for burial. In another room, clothing and cushions had been used to make various dummies, which were arranged in a tableau, "in attitudes of extreme devotion, some with their foreheads nearly touching the floor," and with open Bibles in front of them. Clearly, the poltergeist had a sense of ironic humor.

From then on, the Phelps poltergeist practiced its skill as a designer of tableaux. The astonishing thing was that these were done so quickly. One observer, a Dr. Webster, remarked that it would have taken half a dozen women several hours to construct the "dummies" that the poltergeist made within minutes. One figure was so life-like that when the three-year-old boy went into the room, he thought his mother was kneeling in prayer, and whispered "Be still . . ."

That it *was* a poltergeist became clear the following day, when objects began to fly through the air. A bucket flew downstairs, an umbrella leapt through the air, and spoons, bits of tin and keys were thrown around. A candlestick jumped off the mantelpiece, then beat the floor violently until it broke. There were loud pounding noises as if someone was trying to demolish the house with an axe, and loud screams.

The poltergeist probably derived its strength from the fact that it had two "focuses" in the house—Harry, aged twelve, and Anna, who was sixteen. Harry was persecuted by the "spirit." When he went for a drive in the carriage with his stepfather, twenty stones were flung into the carriage. On one occasion he was snatched up into the air so that his head nearly struck the ceiling; he was thrown into a cistern of water, and tied up and suspended from a tree. In front of a visiting clergyman, the legs of his trousers were violently torn open from the bottom to above the knee.

After this, the poltergeist started to break glass; it smashed seventy-one window panes and various glass articles. Another of its favorite tricks was to write on sheets of paper; when the Reverend Phelps turned his back on his writing table, he heard the scratching of the pen, and found written on the paper: "Very nice paper and nice ink for the devil." (Typically, poltergeists seem to object to being watched while they do things like this; they wait until no one is looking.)

Phelps tried communicating with the "spirit" by means of raps, and found that it would answer his questions. There seemed to be more than one spirit present; but the author of most of the mischief seemed to be a French clerk, who had handled a settlement for Mrs. Phelps, and who had since died; he now claimed to be in hell because he had cheated Mrs. Phelps. Her husband investigated this claim, and found that there *had* been a minor fraud; but it had hardly been as serious as the "spirit" seemed to believe. On another occasion the raps told Phelps to put his hand under the table; when he did this his hand was grasped by another hand, warm and human.

A well-known psychic named Andrew Jackson Davis visited the Phelps home, and put forward a theory very similar to that of Mrs. Crowe. He said that the phenomena were caused by "magnetism" and by "electricity," the magnetism attracting objects towards the boy and girl, the electricity causing them to fly in the opposite direction. But Davis—the author of a bestselling work of "spirit dictation" called *The Principles of Nature*, also agreed that there were spirits present—he claimed to have seen five of them.

The poltergeist—or poltergeists—became increasingly destructive. Pieces of paper burst into flame, although always where they could be seen; sometimes, the ashes of burnt papers were found in drawers. All kinds of objects were smashed—Phelps estimated that the poltergeist had done about two hundred dollars' worth of damage. And the poltergeist also attacked the eldest girl, Anna. A reporter was sitting with the mother and daughter when the girl shouted that someone had pinched her; they rolled up her sleeve and found a severe fresh pinch mark on her arm. On another occasion, there was a loud smacking noise, and a red mark appeared on her face.

In October 1851, more than a year after the disturbances began, the mother and children went off to Pennsylvania and stayed there until the following spring. The poltergeist did not follow them; and when they returned to Stratford, nothing more happened.

It seems fairly clear that the Reverend Phelps made a mistake in attracting the attention of spirits to his home by holding the seance; they discovered that there were two excellent mediums in the house, and the result was one of the most spectacular cases of poltergeist disturbance on record. The assertion by one of the "spirits"' that he was a French clerk, now in hell, need not be taken too seriously; another observer, the Reverend John Mitchell, also communicated with the "spirits" by means of raps, and received insulting replies in bad language. The Phelps poltergeists seem to have been the usual crowd of invisible juvenile delinquents.

FOUR

The Black Monk of Pontefract

If the Phelps haunting is the classic American poltergeist, then the classic British case is certainly the Black Monk of Pontefract. The strange thing is that this remarkable case was never officially investigated—or even recorded—and that it came so close to being forgotten. At the time it occurred—in the late 1960s—it caused much local excitement and was reported in the newspapers; but when the haunting stopped, interest faded. Almost ten years later, a young amateur historian—with a special interest in the Cluniac monks of Pontefract—heard about the case and decided to investigate. What he uncovered in the local newspapers sounded almost too good to be true: poltergeist phenomena apparently caused by the ghost of a Cluniac monk who had been hanged for rape in the time of Henry the Eighth. The historian called on the Pritchard family, who still lived in the house where the phenomena had taken place, and listened to their accounts of the haunting. He talked to relatives and friends and neighbors, and to the local vicar and the mayor and the Member of Parliament who had witnessed some of the phenomena. All this convinced him that this was more than an interesting footnote to an essay on the Priory of St. John the Evangelist. He telephoned me, outlined the story, and suggested that it might make a sensational book along the lines of *The Amityville Horror*. I drove up to Yorkshire, interviewed the witnesses, and decided that it would be pointless to dramatize it; the facts themselves are already as sensational as anything in the recorded history of poltergeist hauntings.

Pontefract is an ancient town that dates back to Roman times—the name means "broken bridge" in Latin. Although connected to Leeds and Doncaster by motorway, it still retains an air of belonging to the nineteenth century—the kind of place J. B. Priestley loves to evoke in novels like *The Good Companions*.

If you stand outside the church of All Saints, a few yards from the ruins of the old priory and the castle, you can look across to the housing estate of Chequerfields on the opposite hilltop—the hill that was once the site of the gallows. But if you try to find your way there without a map—as I did—you are likely to get lost in the maze of pleasant little tree-lined back streets with grass verges and neat front gardens. Number 30 East Drive stands on a corner, and on the top of the hill, close to the site of the old gallows. It also stands on the place where there was once a bridge over a small stream.

In August, 1966, the family at 30 East Drive consisted of Jean and Joe Pritchard, their son Phillip, aged fifteen, and their daughter Diane, twelve. During the week of the Bank Holiday, the family went on holiday to Devon, leaving Mrs. Pritchard's mother, Mrs. Sarah Scholes, in charge. Phillip had decided to stay behind; he had reached the age when holidays with the family lose their attraction.

Thursday was a sunny day, and Phillip took a book into the garden. Mrs. Scholes sat on the settee, knitting a cardigan. She was surprised that Phillip could sit in the garden; the room struck her as unusually chilly. Then, at about eleven-thirty, there was a sudden gust of wind that rattled all the windows and made the back door slam. Phillip came into the house, and Mrs. Scholes said: "Is there a wind getting up?" "No. It's quite calm out there."

He went into the kitchen to make himself a cup of coffee, and tea for his grandmother. Ten minutes later, he opened the door of the lounge, and stood staring. Mrs. Scholes was absorbed in her knitting; and all around her, floating gently down through the air, was a grey-white powder, like chalk dust. Mrs. Scholes was so absorbed in her knitting that she had not even noticed it. Then she looked up, and saw Phillip through the fine white haze. She said accusingly: "What have you been up to?"

"Nothing. I've been in the kitchen all the time. What is it?"

They both looked up at the ceiling—the obvious explanation seemed to be that its whitewash was disintegrating. In fact, the ceiling had been recently papered. And now as Phillip looked more closely, he became aware of another curious fact. The top half of the room was perfectly clear; the falling powder started on a level below his head. And when Mrs. Scholes stood up, her own head rose above the top of the falling powder like an airplane above the clouds.

Mrs. Scholes was in no way alarmed, merely baffled. There had to be some natural explanation. Perhaps it had all blown in through the window. She decided to go and consult her daughter, Marie Kelly, who lived opposite. Marie stared in astonishment as her mother came in "looking like a snowman," and crossed the road to the Pritchards' home. The powder was still falling, and it had no apparent source. It now formed a fine white layer on the furniture, and on the polished sideboard. The cup of tea which Phillip had brought in for his grandmother was covered with a white film. Mrs. Kelly stared at it for a few minutes, then said: "We'd better get it cleaned up." She went into the kitchen, and her foot skidded. There was a large pool of water on the kitchen floor. She called: "Are you sure you haven't had an accident? This place is flooded." The old lady said irritably: "I'm not senile yet.'"

Mrs. Kelly took a floorcloth from the cupboard under the sink, and mopped up the water. Then, as she squeezed out the cloth in the sink, she noticed another pool on the linoleum. She stooped and mopped it up. As she did so, she noticed another patch. It took her a few seconds to grasp that new pools of water seemed to be forming as fast as she mopped them up.

The obvious explanation was that the water was coming up through the linoleum. Mrs. Kelly took hold of a corner, and pulled it back. The floor underneath was perfectly dry.

Fortunately, no doubt, neither of the two women had the least idea that creating pools of water is one of the stranger habits of the poltergeist. No one knows quite how or why. Guy Playfair, who has investigated many cases, believes that the water is some kind of condensation of the energy used by the poltergeist, and his explanation is as plausible as any. The pools have one oddity; they have a neat outline, as if they had been poured on the floor from a jug held immediately above its surface—no splashing, and none of the bold streaks that come from pouring water from a height. You might almost suppose the poltergeist was a small animal urinating on the floor. When I went to the Pritchards' home in 1980, the first thing I asked about was the shape of the pools of water. Just as I had expected, they were rather neat little puddles.

The only peculiarity about this first manifestation in East Drive was that the poltergeist was causing a miniature snowstorm in the lounge while the pools of water formed in the kitchen next door. The East Drive poltergeist also played tricks with the water supply. When the taps were turned on, and the toilet was flushed, a greenish foam rushed out.

The next-door neighbor, Enid Pritchard (married to Joe Pritchard's brother) had heard the commotion, and came in to see if she could help. She found the stop-cock under the sink and turned it off. It made no difference. The pools of water continued to appear. So Mrs. Kelly—who had to go home to make her husband's lunch—rang the water board and explained that number 30 was having a flood. They promised to send someone around immediately after lunch.

By the time the man arrived, the powder had stopped falling in the lounge, and with the help of a duster and a dust-pan, the place had been restored to normal. But the pools of water were still appearing on the kitchen floor. The man from the water board was little more than a youth, but he seemed to know his business. He lifted the linoleum and checked that the surface of the floor was dry—this ruled out the possibility of a burst pipe under the floor. Next he examined the drains, and poked down them with a flexible metal rod, to check that there were no fractures in the pipes; again, the result was negative. Then he came back into the kitchen, surveyed the pools of water, scratched his head, and suggested that it might be some kind of condensation, due to the clammy weather. The others were too polite to say what they thought of this suggestion—that week had been exceptionally dry—and the man went off to report the problem to his superiors. And about an hour later, the pools of water stopped appearing. Mrs. Kelly and Mrs. Pritchard returned to their respective homes. And Mrs. Scholes returned to her knitting.

At about seven that evening, Mrs. Scholes was watching television when Phillip said: "Grandma, it's happening again."

The working surface at the side of the kitchen sink was covered with sugar and dry tea leaves. And, as they watched, the button of the tea dispenser above the sink went in of its own accord, and more tea showered down. And as they gaped at it, the button went gently in and out, and tea cascaded down on to the draining board. It went on until the dispenser was empty; and even then, the button continued to go in and out. When Mrs. Scholes found her voice, she shouted "Stop it!" and Phillip, who thought he was being accused, said indignantly: "I can't—it's doing it on its own!"

As he spoke, there was a crash from the hallway. They looked at one another, both pale, wondering if the intruder was about to reveal himself. Opening the door was a little like a nightmare—expecting to see something horrible. But the hall beyond was empty. As they stood staring, the hall light went on with a click, and they both jumped. They went down the corridor, to the foot of the stairs. They they saw what had made the noise. A plant that normally stood at the foot of the stairs was now halfway up them—minus its pot. The pot was on the landing above.

Another sound made them jump. It was coming from the kitchen. They found that the crockery cupboard was shaking and vibrating, as if someone was locked inside and trying to get out, Phillip went and wrenched open the door. Immediately, the vibrations stopped. At the same time, another loud banging noise started up somewhere in the house. It was not a particularly alarming noise; in fact, Mrs. Scholes had heard it a few hours earlier, and assumed that May Mountain's husband was doing a little home carpentry on the other side of the dividing wall. Now, as she observed the sudden chill in the atmosphere, she connected it with the other strange events. She said: "I'm going to get Marie." And Phillip said: "I'll come with you." He had no intention of being left there alone.

Mrs. Kelly went back with them, and as soon as she stepped into the kitchen, she knew it was not her mother's imagination. The crockery cupboard was shaking again, and the cups and plates inside were rattling. If the cupboard had been on the dividing wall, they might have assumed that the Pritchard's next door were somehow causing it. But it was on the end wall of the house—nothing beyond it but the garden.

Mrs. Scholes went next door, and asked May Mountain if she had been making banging noises. She looked at her in astonishment and said: "We thought it was *you*."

By the time Mrs. Scholes got back, the noises had stopped, and Marie Kelly had made a cup of tea. They sat and talked until nine-thirty, then Marie said she'd better get back home. She told them to come across the road if anything further happened. But they all hoped it was over for the night.

Phillip went off to bed. Mrs. Scholes decided that she needed a good night's rest, and also went upstairs. She went into Phillip's bedroom to kiss him goodnight. As she did so, she realized he was staring over her shoulder with wide eyes. The wardrobe in the corner of the room was tottering and swaying like a drunken man.

Mrs. Scholes said: "Phillip, get dressed, quick. We're going."

Half an hour later, they were tucked up in the spare beds in Mrs. Kelly's house. For them this particular poltergeist episode was at an end.

But Marie Kelly and her husband Vic had lost all desire for sleep. Vic Kelly had not bothered to go and investigate earlier, convinced that there was a natural explanation. Now he decided it was time to get professional advice; he telephoned the police station, and told his story. When the police car arrived ten minutes later,

Vic and **Marie Kelly** went out to meet them. An inspector named **Taylor** was accompanied by two uniformed constables. The five of them went into number 30, where everything seemed normal, and the policemen began a methodical search of the house. They went through every room, peered under beds, examined windows for signs of entry, and finally agreed that there was no sign of an intruder. They went back to the station, and the Kellys went back into their own home.

Vic Kelly was still not happy. As he and Marie sat discussing the events, and she again described the falling powder, the pools of water, the rattling cupboard, Vic said: "What about your friend Mr. O'Donald? He's interested in ghosts isn't he?"

It was almost midnight, but neither of them felt like sleeping. They walked up the street, and observed that Mr. O'Donald's downstairs light was still on. They knocked on his front door and explained their problem; without hesitation, Mr. O'Donald went for his coat.

From the ghost-hunter's point of view, the situation at number 30 looked promising. As they entered the house, they were met by a blast of cold air—they described it as like walking into a refrigerator. But now they were hoping for manifestations, the ghost refused to oblige. So they sat in the lounge, and Mr. O'Donald explained to them the distinction between ghosts and poltergeists—that the poltergeist was supposed to be a manifestation of someone's unconscious mind—in this case, probably Phillip's.

"In that case," said Vic Kelly, "we're wasting our time sitting here. He's in our house."

At 1:45, Mr. O'Donald yawned, and said he agreed they were wasting their time. If it *was* a poltergeist, it would no doubt signal its presence on the morrow. "They do funny things. They're very fond of tearing up photographs, I believe." He said goodnight and left. But as Marie and Vic Kelly were about to lock the door behind them, they heard a crash. They switched on the lights. On the floor of the lounge there were two small oil paintings, lying face downward. Glass was shattered, and a print in a frame—the wedding photograph of Jean and Joe Pritchard had been slashed from end to end, as if with a sharp knife. The poltergeist had apparently overheard Mr. O'Donald.

When Phillip and Mrs. Scholes returned to the house the next afternoon, all was quiet. It was still quiet when Joe and Jean Pritchard returned on Saturday afternoon. Between them, Phillip and Mrs. Scholes related the events of two days before, and Joe Pritchard listened with astonishment, and clearly suspected that they were exaggerating. "What kind of knocks?" And as if in reply, there came three loud, distinct bangs, followed by a rattling of the window frames as a cold wind blew through the house. Then there was silence again, and the temperature returned to normal. The poltergeist had said goodbye for the time being.

Two years passed. Phillip left school and went to work in his father's pet shop in the town. Diane had turned into a pretty teenager with blond hair and a good complexion. Mrs. Scholes, now seventy-two, spent most weekends with the Pritchards. Perhaps the approach of the August Bank Holiday reminded her of the events of two years ago; at all events, she began to talk again about the "haunting." Joe Pritchard found the subject tiresome, and was discouraging.

Jean Pritchard had decided to redecorate Diane's bedroom. One afternoon, she broke off to go and make tea. She and her mother drank it in the kitchen. Mrs. Scholes reverted to the topic that was obviously troubling her. "I keep hearing noises." Jean Pritchard said:

"Well I haven't, and I'm in the house practically all the time."

"Didn't you hear something then?"

"No," said Jean Pritchard, and went out into the hall. She stopped and stared. At the foot of the stairs, there was the counterpane from her bed. It had not been there ten minutes earlier, when she came down to make tea. And no one had been out into the hall. She took it back upstairs and put it on her bed. Then she went back to her decorating. A few moments later, there was a loud crash. When she looked down the stairs, she saw that another counterpane was lying in the hall, this time the one from Phillip's bed. And the crash had been made by the fall of a number of plant pots, which were upended on the carpet. There was soil everywhere. In the kitchen, Mrs. Scholes was in tears. She said: "I told you. It's starting again."

When Joe Pritchard came back, his mother-in-law had gone home. In bed, later, Jean Pritchard was unable to sleep. Even with both windows open, the room was too warm. She slipped out of bed and went on to the landing. She had moved the painting materials out from Diane's bedroom. Everything was silent. She felt in the atmosphere the typical chill that she would later come to know so well. In the half-light that came from the street lamp outside, she could see something moving in the corner of the landing, something that swayed and rustled. She switched on the landing light. As she did so, something flew past her face, missing it by a fraction of an inch; she identified it later as a paint brush. It was followed by the paste bucket which hit the opposite wall of the landing and scattered paste on the carpet. In the dim light, she could now see what was moving. It was a long strip of wallpaper, which had been lying in a roll against the wall. Now it was standing on end, and swaying like a cobra. Because there was obviously no one holding it, she took courage and made a grab for it. The paper fluttered gently to the floor. At the same moment, the carpet sweeper flew up into the air, and began to swing around as if being used as a club by an invisible giant. Too breathless to scream, Jean Pritchard fell on all fours, and scrambled back into her own bedroom. A roll of wallpaper followed her, and hit the door. At last, she managed to scream. Joe sat up in bed shouting, "What's happening?" Phillip and Diane appeared from their bedrooms in their nightclothes. As they stood there, paint brushes and other materials began to fly around. One of them missed Diane's head by a fraction of an inch. Another struck her on the shoulder. Her father shouted, "Don't stand there!" And Diane said with astonishment: "It didn't hurt." Her surprise was understandable; the brush looked as if it had been moving fast enough to knock her over; yet it had merely given her a tap.

Then they realized the invisible intruder had moved into Diane's bedroom. Phillip, staring in astonishment through the doorway, watched the wooden pelmet above the bedroom window torn out of the wall—although it was held in by two-inch screws—and fly out of the window. They heard it hit the path below. With a burst of anger Joe Pritchard slammed Diane's bedroom door. From inside the bedroom, they could hear bangs and thumps. As Diane reached out to touch the door handle, Joe Pritchard shouted: "Don't touch it." Diane withdrew her hand and, as if in response, there was a loud thump on the other side of the door.

Diane spent the night in her parent's room. They locked their doors. It was a pointless measure, but it gave them some feeling of security.

The poltergeist is basically a mad practical joker; the mentality seems to be that of an idiot child. What they seem to want is attention; but it is difficult to see why. In a few cases they have communicated—either by raps or direct voice—but as often as not their statements lack coherence.

Yet even an absurd practical joke conveys something of the essence of the personality of its perpetrator—something as indefinable yet as definite as a tone of voice. And the Pritchards soon began to develop this sense of their unseen lodger as a definite individual. No doubt this also explains why, throughout nine months of chaos, they stuck grimly to their home, and declined all suggestions that they ought to think about moving. Their sense of territoriality was outraged by this intruder, and they had no intention of leaving him in possession of the field.

So in spite of the nerve-wracking nature of the disturbances, life with the ghost—"Mr. Nobody," they called him (Jean Pritchard later christened him "Fred")—settled into a kind of routine. He seldom paid a visit during the day—possibly because Diane was at school. The racket would usually start up around bedtime—a series of loud bangs, not unlike a child beating on a big drum. Ornaments would levitate and fly across the room. The lights would go out, and when they looked in the cupboard under the stairs the main switch would be turned off. On one occasion, Mrs. Pritchard carefully taped it in the "on" position with insulating tape; half an hour later, the lights were off again, and the tape had simply vanished.

At a fairly early stage in the proceedings, Phillip made the suggestion that the spirit might be exorcised. That struck them all as an inspired idea, and Vic Kelly contacted a local vicar, the Reverend Davy. Mr. Davy explained that exorcism was not something that could be done at a moment's notice. He would need permission from the bishop. And since there had been a number of cases in which exorcists had been strongly criticized for making things worse, the bishop might well refuse. At all events, he agreed to call around on the following Thursday evening at seven o'clock. The family felt relieved; it was a comfort to think that they would be receiving professional advice, so to speak.

Jean Pritchard had prepared sandwiches and tea, and Marie and Vic Kelly had been invited over. They sat talking, describing what had been happening, and Mr. Davy told them something about the service of exorcism. Neither he nor they were aware that poltergeists cannot be exorcised—one of Allan Kardec's ghostly informants told him they treated exorcism with contempt. But at least the vicar's presence seemed to restrain Mr. Nobody. After an hour and a half, there had been no kind of disturbance, not even a rap. For the first time, Jean Pritchard began to wish the poltergeist would oblige with one of his jokes. Mr. Davy finally looked at his watch and said he ought to be getting home. Jean Pritchard said: "I'm sorry we've dragged you all this way for nothing."

And as she spoke, the house resounded to loud thumps that came from overhead. And a small brass candlestick jumped off the mantelpiece on to the floor.

"There," said Jean Pritchard.

Mr. Davy looked thoughtfully at the candlestick. "I think I know what your problem is. Subsidence."

"But subsidence," said Marie, "can only make things fall. And—"

The other candlestick rose up from the shelf, floated across in front of the vicar's nose, then dropped to the floor.

"Do you think *that's* subsidence?"

There was a tremendous crash from the next room, one of those spectacular sounds like a piece of heavy furniture falling through the ceiling. They all rushed into the lounge.

Scattered all over the carpet was every cup, saucer and plate from the china cupboard. Yet not a single one was broken, or even cracked.

Mr. Davy was convinced. He gave it as his opinion that there was "something evil" in the house, and advised them to move. Jean Pritchard said she wouldn't dream of moving—why should she be driven out of her home by a ghost? The vicar warned her that it might cause real damage—not just to property, but to people. His comment revealed an ignorance of the habits of the poltergeist: in no case on record have they been known to cause grievous bodily harm, although their bites, slaps and blows have occasionally driven their victims to despair—as in the case of John Bell.

Mr. Davy left, and the poltergeist proceeded to demonstrate that it had no intention of doing serious harm. Diane was on her way up to bed when the lights went out. She stood there in the hall, which was dimly lit by the street lamp, which shone through the frosted glass on the front door. Mr. Pritchard was looking for the torch to look in the mains cupboard. As Diane stood there, a huge shadow appeared on the wall, and the atmosphere became icy. The hall stand—a heavy piece of furniture made of oak—floated up into the air and moved toward her. She tripped and went backwards on the stairs, and the stand pressed down on her. So did an electric sewing machine that had been on it. She tried to push it away, but it was unbudgeable; it might have weighed a ton. Yet it was not pressing down on her with all its weight— merely holding her pinned to the stairs. She was too breathless to scream.

The lights came on, and Diane found her voice and yelled. The family rushed out into the hall, and her mother tried to drag the stand off her. It was impossible; it was simply being held in position by a force that was stronger than she was. Phillip and Jean Pritchard began to heave on it, but it made no difference. Diane was whimpering. Mrs. Pritchard advised her to lie still and try to relax—at least it was now clear she was not being crushed to death. And as soon as she relaxed, Diane felt a change in the force holding her down. She said: "Now try," and as they pulled, the stand came off her. So did the electric sewing machine. Yet, oddly enough, neither had bruised her.

Mrs. Pritchard helped Diane up to bed. She was shaken, but not frightened—she seemed to sense that the thing meant her no real harm. But it had not yet finished with her. As soon as her bedroom light was out, the bed-clothes were pulled off the bed, and landed in the corner of the room. The room itself had become icy cold. She had a strong sense there was someone else there with her, although the light from the landing revealed no one. Then her mattress shot into the air like a magic carpet in the Arabian Nights and she found herself on the floor, with the mattress on top of her. It all happened in about a second.

That night it happened four more times. Each time she found herself on the floor with the mattress on top of her, yet was still unhurt.

The Pontefract poltergeist seemed to be a creature of moods. It could be inventive, as when it filled the lounge with falling chalk dust. It could be destructive, as when it caused the grandmother clock to hurtle down the stairs, and shatter like a bomb in the hall. And it could be oddly seductive, as when it signaled its presence with a most delightful scent—a perfume like some heavily scented flower. But mostly it made a racket, like the phantom drummer of Tedworth. It could be heard several streets away. The Pritchards made a tape recording of it, and it sounds like someone frantically knocking for admittance; you expect to hear a voice yell, "Let me in."

In September, 1968, two young reporters came to call; they represented two local papers. I have the two press cuttings in front of me as I write. "Pontefract Poltergeist is Back" announces the *Yorkshire Evening Post* and the story begins: "Mr. Nobody" has turned up at the home of 42-year-old Mrs. Jean Pritchard, of East Drive, Pontefract, for the first time in three years (in fact, it was two). The *Pontefract and Castleford Express* announces: "Invisible hands 'Rock' family." And it goes on to describe the destruction of the grandmother clock, and how Diane was repeatedly thrown out of bed. It also mentions that when Phillip tried to record the noises, the plug was pulled out of his tape recorder. "Meanwhile," the story ends, "the Pritchards' home has become quite an attraction for amateur ghost hunters. Several people have knocked on the door and asked if they can stay the night to listen to the ghost."

The Pritchards' home had become known as "the haunted house." A neighbor heard a bus driver announcing to his passengers: "That's the haunted house," as they stopped outside. A group of students from Leeds asked permission to camp in the front garden, but Mrs. Pritchard refused. But in the warm weather, people slept on the huge, round grass verge in front of the Pritchards' home, and "Mr. Nobody" usually obliged them with his assortment of bangs and crashes. Miners on their way to work in the early hours of the morning used to stand by the fence and listen to the phantom drummer.

Not long after the disturbances began, Jean Pritchard bumped into an acquaintance named Rene Holden (Vic Kelly's sister) in the High Street. Remembering she had a reputation for being a "bit psychic," she told her what had been happening. When Mrs. Holden said she was not afraid of ghosts, Jean invited her along to see for herself.

The next day, she paid her first visit to the house. Jean Pritchard took her upstairs and showed her the chaos that "Fred" could create in a matter of minutes. The three bedrooms looked as if burglars had been through them. Bedclothes lay in heaps, drawers were pulled open and their contents lying around the rooms, and chairs were upside down. Jean explained that she'd tidied up all three rooms only half an hour before.

Jean Pritchard was glad to have somebody to talk to. The two of them took to one another immediately, and Mrs. Holden was to witness most of the events that took place over the next nine months. On that first evening, the poltergeist was on its best behavior. Jean Pritchard invited Rene to return on the following Saturday to have something to eat.

Mrs. Scholes was staying at East Drive that weekend, but she was feeling ill, and spent most of the time in her room. Joe Pritchard had gone out to the local pub with some friends. When Rene Holden arrived, Jean was making chicken sandwiches, with a bird that was still warm from the oven. Rene helped her to make the sandwiches.

As they stood there in the kitchen, the lights suddenly went out. Jean said: "It's starting." "I know," said Rene, "I can feel it." A moment later, the lights went on again. "That's odd," said Jean, "it usually makes us put them on."

The sandwiches and the teapot were placed on a tray and carried through into the lounge. Phillip and Diane were already sitting there, watching television.

Before they could start eating, the lights went out again, there was a rushing noise like a blast of wind, and objects began to fly around in the darkness. The room had suddenly gone very cold. They all noticed a pattering noise on the window, like someone gently tapping.

When they got the lights on again, the room was chaotic, with ornaments and cushions all over the floor. The sandwich plate was still on the table, but it was empty. And, at first sight the sandwiches seemed to have vanished completely. Then Jean Pritchard noticed a few of them lying behind the television. She picked one of them up. "What is it?" said Mrs. Holden, observing Jean's odd expression. "Look," said Jean, holding out the sandwich, "something's eaten it!" A huge bite had been taken out of the sandwich and there were teeth marks visible on the bread. Whoever had bitten it had enormous teeth.

Mrs. Holden asked if she could keep the sandwich as a memento. In fact, she wanted it as evidence to show anybody who thought her story sounded mad. She wrapped up the sandwich and put it in her handbag. But a few days later it had disintegrated into crumbs.

Mrs. Holden described another visit to the Pritchards' home the following weekend. The Pritchards had invited her to a local Working Mens' Club for a Ladies Night, and Mrs. Holden had had her hair set.

Afterwards, she went back to East Drive with the Pritchards for a coffee. As she sat there, the lights all went out. Things started flying around the room, and the racket was suddenly deafening. At the same time, Rene Holden felt as if her hair was swarming with tiny small creatures—perhaps ants. A cushion hit her in the face. When Joe Pritchard turned on the main switch a few moments later, everything in the room was upside down. Ornaments lay on the floor, chairs had been overturned, even the pictures had come off the walls.

Mrs. Holden made some interesting and relevant suggestions about the poltergeist. The children were both suffering from some stomach ailment, and it became worse whenever the poltergeist appeared. Diane described it as "feeling twisted up inside." Mrs. Holden was convinced that the poltergeist was drawing energy from the solar plexus of the children. She also made the interesting suggestion that it might be able to draw energy from the underground stream that flowed beneath the house.

It was Mrs. Holden who made the sensible suggestion that they should try and communicate with Mr. Nobody. Many poltergeists seem to have a definite desire to explain themselves. The Pritchards' visitant proved to be an exception. The Pritchards stood out in the hall, with their hands joined together, and tried concentrating to see if they could persuade the poltergeist to manifest itself. It did precisely that. There was a sound like a loud wind rushing down the stairs and then over the top of the banisters came a shower of objects: bedding, boxes, ornaments, mattresses, apparently every movable object in the upper part of the house.

One snowy evening, Joe Pritchard's sister Maude Peerce arrived at the house. She had decided that it was time to come and investigate the poltergeist in person. And it was clear that her attitude toward the "haunting" was skeptical. She felt there was something undignified about all the publicity. "There's got to be a logical explanation for everything—you've just got to look for it." Her idea of a logical explanation was that Phillip and Diane were having a joke at everybody's expense. Joe Pritchard became mildly annoyed and told her she didn't know what she was talking about. Phillip and Diane were indignant, but too polite to be rude.

As they sat there, the room suddenly became cold, and Jean Pritchard had the familiar sensation that the poltergeist was around. Then the lights went out. Aunt

Maude was sitting in the chair by the kitchen fire, and its red glow gave enough light to see what was happening. First of all, the refrigerator door swung open. A jug of milk floated out, sailed across the kitchen until it was poised above Aunt Maude's head, then tilted and slowly deluged her in milk. She jumped to her feet, spluttering. Jean found her way to the cupboard under the stairs, and the lights came on again. Aunt Maude pointed. "It was those kids!"

"No it wasn't," said Jean Pritchard, "they were stood by me all the time." She began to mop up the milk from the floor and the chair. Aunt Maude refused to be convinced. Why had the lights gone out before it happened? Clearly because somebody had no wish to be seen playing tricks.

Aunt Maude was very angry. Jean could understand her anger—she was soaked in milk. "Look, why don't you stay the night and see for yourself?"

"All right, I will," said Aunt Maude. She removed her hat and coat, then looked around for her gloves. She could only find one. "Don't worry," said Jean Pritchard, "it will turn up. Things always do."

They moved into the lounge. The lights went out again, and there was a violent banging sound. Aunt Maude yelled indignantly. Then the lights were turned on again, the chairs had been turned upside down and the electric fire pulled out of the fireplace. The contents of the refrigerator were strewn around the room, including a string of sausages. The children burst into shrieks of laughter, and Aunt Maude became more irritable than ever. "What keeps happening to the lights?"

"Something turns them off."

"You mean *someone* turns them off. Why don't you lock the cupboard door?"

"We do, but it doesn't make any difference."

But after this incident, the poltergeist decided to allow them to spend a quiet evening. They all retired to bed early. It was necessary to rearrange the beds—Jean, Diane and Aunt Maude moved into Phillip's bedroom, Phillip moved into Diane's, and Joe Pritchard occupied his own bed.

Jean Pritchard had only just climbed into bed when the disturbances began. The reading lamp rose into the air, sailed slowly across the room, and out through the door.

Then they saw something moving around the door—a closer look showed that it was the four small bulbs that produced the glow effect on the electric fire downstairs. Two of them were now dancing around the top of the door, and the other two near the bottom.

Then they saw the hands. For a moment, they were petrified. One enormous hand appeared over the top of the door, while the other was near the bottom of the door, about six inches from the floor. A closer look showed that they were Aunt Maude's fur gloves. Whatever—or whoever—was wearing them must have had enormous arms, since there was a stretch of well over six feet between the top glove and the lower one.

Aunt Maude, who was of an evangelical disposition—in fact, a member of the Salvation Army—pointed accusingly at the gloves and said sternly: "Get away. You're evil!" She picked up one of her boots and flung it at the door. The gloves vanished. Jean Pritchard, in spite of her nervousness, could not resist saying: "Do you still think it's the kids doing it?" Then the gloves reappeared—floating into the bedroom. One of them seemed to be beckoning to them, as if trying to persuade them to follow it. "None of us moved," said Jean Pritchard later, "we were too scared." Then the glove clenched into a fist, and shook threateningly in Aunt Maude's direction. Aunt Maude responded by bursting into "Onward Christian Soldiers." At this, the gloves began to conduct her singing, beating in time. Jean Pritchard admits that she had to smile. Then the gloves vanished again. And Aunt Maude said decisively: "You've got the devil in this house."

None of them had much sleep that night. When Aunt Maude left the next morning—saying that she wouldn't stay there again for £20,000—her gloves were nowhere to be seen. Jean Pritchard later found them in the bottom of the cupboard. She returned them to Aunt Maude, but Aunt Maude refused to touch them. She carried them into the garden with coal tongs, and burned them with paraffin on the rubbish heap.

Soon after this, the poltergeist displayed a new and interesting ability which is found only in a rare minority of cases—"interpenetration of matter." One evening, as the Pritchards were sitting in the lounge, an egg floated in through the door, poised itself very carefully in the air, then fell on the floor. As it exploded, the room filled with a delicious scent that Mrs. Pritchard compared to a garden full of flowers. (Only Phillip found it heavy and cloying.) When another egg floated into the room, Jean Pritchard rushed to the refrigerator, took out all the eggs, and put them into a wooden box. She then sat defiantly on the lid, convinced that, on this occasion at least, she'd got the better of the poltergeist. When another egg materialized in mid-air, and exploded like a scent bomb, she jumped up and looked into the box. One egg was missing. She sat down on it again; a moment later another egg exploded. It went on until all the eggs lay broken in the middle of the room, and the wooden box was empty. Yet Mrs. Pritchard had sat firmly on its lid throughout. Mr. Nobody could dematerialize solid objects—or perhaps move them into another dimension and then back into our own.

There seems to be no doubt that "Fred" possessed his own juvenile and rather destructive sense of humor. Perhaps because Mrs. Pritchard is so obviously a tidy person, the ghost seemed to take an unending delight in making messes. When Jean went to the larder one day, she found that the tea and sugar packets had been emptied, and their contents carefully mixed up together. At four o'clock one morning, after they had been kept awake for hours by the thunderous banging, she went out of the bedroom to discover that the door handles had been smeared with jam and festooned with lavatory paper. All the way down the stairs, there was a mixture of marmalade and mustard. Joe Pritchard advised her to come back to bed and deal with it in the morning. But Jean Pritchard is a typical Yorkshire housewife; she filled a bucket with hot water, and tidied up the mess before she went back to bed. It is an interesting thought that if Jean Pritchard had been an indifferent housewife who could ignore untidiness, "Fred" might have given up a great deal sooner.

Vic Kelly, who was a Catholic, continued to feel that exorcism might be the answer. So after the Pritchards had spent a particularly restless night, he decided to approach his own priest, Father Hudson. The priest seemed to be slightly better informed about mischievous sprites than his Church of England colleagues, and pointed out that exorcism was no infallible cure for poltergeists—it might even make them worse. Besides, Father Hudson would also have to approach his bishop for permission. He had, nevertheless, an alternative suggestion. There was nothing to prevent Vic Kelly from sprinkling the house with holy water and saying a few prayers as he did so. If the thing could be exorcised, a layman could probably do the job as well as a priest.

Armed with a bottle of holy water, Vic hurried to the Pritchards' house. Jean Pritchard's feelings were ambivalent; she knew the poltergeist was likely to resent an attempt to evict it. But when Vic had gone to the trouble of getting the holy water, it seemed unfair not to let him try.

Vic scattered a few drops of water in each room, starting with the kitchen, and leaving the lounge—Mr. Nobody's favorite haunt—until last. When he came downstairs, he went into the lounge, performed his rite of exorcism, and re-capped the bottle, which was now almost empty. Jean Pritchard asked: "Did Father Hudson say how long it would be before we'd know it worked?"As she spoke, an enormous crash sounded from above their heads. Jean said: "Never mind. It didn't." Then she noticed the water. It was trickling down the walls in little streams, from the level of the ceiling. It was apparently the ghost's way of indicating that he was indifferent to holy water.

That night, nobody got much sleep. The drumming went on until five in the morning. Furniture overturned, the bedclothes were snatched off repeatedly, and Diane was thrown out of bed several times. The next day they were all dizzy from lack of sleep, and Diane stayed home from school. In the early afternoon, she managed to snatch a few hours sleep on the settee.

Having allowed her to recuperate, the poltergeist proceeded to indicate that he had still not forgiven the attempt to make him feel unwelcome. As Diane stood by the kitchen fireplace, combing her hair in front of the mirror, Jean Pritchard noticed that the table drawer was gently sliding out. Then it shot across the room, and hit Diane in the small of the back, making her gasp. At the same time, she experienced the familiar sensation in her solar plexus—the "sinking feeling" that seemed to indicate that something was about to happen.

In the center of the mantelpiece there was a brass crucifix with an image of the crucified Christ. As Diane stood in the middle of the room, this suddenly leapt from the shelf, and stuck against her back. It behaved as if it were made of iron and Diane was a magnet. Diane looked in the kitchen mirror to see what had struck her, and tried to pull it off. It was impossible. She began to feel panic-stricken. "Get it off me!"

Mrs. Pritchard tugged at it, but it might have been glued on. Diane rushed into the hallway, feeling as she was wrestling with some impalpable force that surrounded her. Something fell on to the floor—not the crucifix, but the image of Jesus. At the other end of the hall, the cross also fell off against the wall. Suddenly, Diane was free. When Jean Pritchard raised the back of her blouse, they found a cross-shaped red mark between her shoulder blades; it stayed there for days before it faded.

The attempt at exorcism seems to have inspired "Fred" with a distinctly anti-Christian bias. On Easter Sunday, Jean Pritchard came downstairs and smelt the flower-like perfume that indicated that the ghost was around. On all the doors, someone had painted inverted crosses in gold. In the lounge, there were three more on the wall. It had been done with considerable precision, as if a stencil had been used, and the lack of brush marks suggested a can of spray paint. She remembered a can of gold spray paint in the outhouse, and eventually located it—Phillip had been intending to use it on his bicycle. She tried spraying it on the door, and discovered that it was impossible to reproduce the crosses; the glossy surface of the door made the paint run into globules. "Fred" had apparently encountered no such difficulty—another evidence of his peculiar power over matter.

Alarmed by this apparent evidence of a demonic intelligence, Jean Pritchard consulted the local vicar. He came—accompanied by another clergyman—and looked at the crosses, then advised her to leave them there over Easter. They promised to give further consideration to the matter and said they would be back after the holiday; in fact, neither returned.

"Fred" seemed to take delight in displaying unusual abilities, There was, for example, the curious episode of Mrs. Holden's coat. It was made of white mohair, and one day it disappeared—she had to borrow another coat to go home in. Weeks later, they found it in the coal shed, sticking out from underneath the coal. Yet when it was pulled out, it was found to be completely clean.

A friend named Alan Williams called one night, and left his car parked outside. When he went back to the car, he was surprised to find that the windscreen wipers were working. This should have been an impossibility, since the car was locked and the ignition turned off. Suspecting that there might be something wrong with the car's electrical system, Alan Williams had it checked by a garage the next day. They could find nothing wrong.

Alan Williams made another interesting observation that night. When he looked back at the Pritchards' house, he says it was surrounded by a dim glow of light. This is confirmed by a neighbor who lived opposite; she looked out of her bedroom window late at night, and observed the same phenomenon; she told Jean about it the next day. It is tempting to speculate that the effect was either electrical, or was connected in some way with earth magnetism. Poltergeists—as we have seen—appear to be able to control certain electrical forces. One of the odder features of this case is that during the period from August, 1968 until May 1969, when it vanished, the Pritchards quarterly electricity bills were only half their usual size—about £10 instead of the usual £20. Jean Pritchard was honest enough to point this out to the electricity board; they said that this was the reading on the meter, and this would therefore be all she would have to pay. It is possible, of course, that "Fred" simply turned back the electric meter to register less.

Then there was the curious mystery of the keys. One morning, as Jean Pritchard was kneeling in front of the kitchen fireplace, preparing to clean out the flue, a shower of keys descended down the chimney, some of them hitting her on the head. She counted them and found there were nineteen in all. "Fred" had collected every key in the house. But when they had been sorted out, there was still one rather old-looking key left. They never identified it, and she still has it.

And now, at this fairly late stage in the manifestations, the poltergeist began to show itself. Its first appearance seems to have been to Jean and Joe Pritchard. They were in bed one night when the door opened. Both looked across the room, and saw a dim figure in the doorway. Jean Pritchard says that it seemed to be very tall, and had a hood over its head. When they switched on the bedside light, it vanished.

The next person to see "Fred" was their next-door neighbor, Mrs. May Mountain, who occupies the other half of their semi-detached house. The ghost seems to have regarded the whole house as his domain, and made drumming noises in Mrs. Mountain's rooms. It was, admittedly, often difficult to pinpoint where the noises were coming from—one of the characteristics of poltergeist rappings—but the cracks in Mrs. Mountain's ceiling (which are still there) indicate that Fred was indifferent to the partition wall between the houses. (Cracks also appeared in the Pritchards' ceilings, but these were repaired a long time ago.)

One morning, Mrs. Mountain was at her kitchen sink when she felt someone standing behind her. She had heard no one come in, and assumed that it was her nephew, who had sneaked in to make her jump. She said something like "Oh, give over," and looked around. She found herself looking at a tall figure dressed in a black monk's habit, with a cowl over the head. Its position prevented her from seeing the face. She told me that it looked quite solid, and that—oddly enough—she felt no fear, only curiosity. Then it vanished.

During this period, it was clear that the poltergeist was becoming more powerful. Its drumming noises were now deafening. And it had added a number of other sounds to its repertoire. There were farmyard noises—the first time they heard them, the Pritchards thought a cow and some chickens had got into their bedroom; naturally, the room was empty. "Fred" also made stertorous breathing noises outside the bedroom door at night. I asked Mrs. Pritchard if she ever went out to investigate. She said: "No, we were too scared. Besides, he'd usually switched off all the lights." To counter this, she kept a large torch by her side in the evenings, but as often as not, this proved to be minus a battery or bulb when she wanted to switch it on.

Rene Holden was to see the "Monk"—or at least his lower half—at very close quarters. A local spiritualist church had invited Jean Pritchard and Rene along to talk about their experiences. They sent a car for them. Jean played them the tape, described the events that had taken place, and then answered questions. Later, the same car drove them back home. Jean Pritchard invited the driver in for a cup of tea, and to see for himself the scene of the events she had been describing. He was obviously a little nervous, but unwilling to show it openly.

As Rene Holden was crossing the lounge, on her way to sit down, the lights suddenly went out. To reassure the man—who was obviously terrified—Rene reached out and put her hand on his shoulder as he sat in the armchair. As she did so, she felt a hand on the back of her head. She glanced underneath her outstretched arm and saw in the light that still came through the curtains, a long black garment, like a dressing gown, descending to within an inch or two of the floor. Then the lights came on again, and the man in the black robe was no longer there.

The phenomena reached a kind of climax one evening when Diane had gone to the kitchen to make coffee. The lights went out, and while Jean Pritchard was groping for the torch, she head Diane scream. It was dusk, and there was, in fact, enough light to be able to see their way around the house. They found that Diane was being dragged up the stairs, and it was light enough to see that her cardigan was stretched out in front of her, as if "Fred" was tugging at it; his other hand was apparently on her throat. Phillip and Jean Pritchard rushed up the stairs and began trying to pull Diane down again; she was yelling with terror—this was the first time it had "laid hands on her," so to speak. Phillip and Jean Pritchard went tumbling backwards down the stairs with Diane. Philip has the impression that it was his thought of trying to touch the presence that caused it to let go. He made the interesting comment: "It always seemed to be ahead of you." Diane had to be given a large brandy. In the light, they saw that her throat was covered with red fingermarks.

It was at about this time that Jean Pritchard came downstairs one morning, and realized that the hall carpet was soaked with water. Then, as she looked, she saw footprints on the wet surface—huge footprints . . .

Yet "Fred's" activities were almost at an end. One day, Phillip and Diane were in the lounge, watching television when Phillip looked around, and saw the shape on the other side of the frosted glass door that led to the dining room and kitchen. Diane followed his gaze, and also saw the figure. It might, of course, have been someone who had walked in. Phillip opened the door, and saw the tall, black shape of the "monk" vanishing. He says that it seemed to disappear into the kitchen floor.

A friend of Joe Pritchard's who had just returned from Scotland told him that the crofters there hung cloves of garlic over doors and windows to keep out "spirits." The Pritchards had heard of garlic being used to repel vampires"as in the various Dracula films—but had no idea that it had a wider application. Phillip volunteered to go and buy dried garlic at the local supermarket. And this, it seems, did the trick. The house smelt strongly of garlic—fortunately, none of them minded the smell—but "Fred" disappeared. It may be that the haunting had reached its natural conclusion anyway. Or that Fred's feelings were finally hurt by this evidence of their desire to get rid of him

So the manifestations ended as abruptly as they had begun. And Jean Pritchard was at last able to settle down to redecorating her house, and assessing the damage. Fred had damaged walls and cracked ceilings, as well as smashing enough crockery to fill a tea chest. It had also destroyed the grandmother clock. Yet apart from this, it had done no real damage. Diane seemed to be the special object of its good-natured malice, yet she told me that she felt it never meant to harm her. It could certainly have done far more dangerous things than it actually did. On one occasion when Mrs. Scholes was in the kitchen, a large potato shot out of a box, flew across the room, and shattered against the wall, missing her head by a fraction of an inch. The force required to shatter a solid potato is considerable; if it had hit her it would have been like a blow from a club. Yet there seems to be some kind of law that poltergeists avoid doing severe physical damage to persons. Like the school bully, they seem to enjoy causing alarm and dismay; they would be capable of swinging a cricket bat within an inch of someone's nose after waving it threateningly. Those who can be frightened seem to be more vulnerable than those who get angry. Yet, like the school bully, the poltergeist seems to bear in mind that if he goes too far, it might come to the attention of the headmaster. There may be other explanations, but this one seems to fit.

It was about ten years after "Fred" had departed that Tom Cunniff, a young man with an interest in local history, heard of the Pontefract poltergeist, and found himself wondering whether it had any connection with the local priory, which had existed from 1090 until 1539. He went along to see the Pritchards, and wrote down their story. He was particularly excited by one piece of information. Jean Pritchard mentioned that a neighbor had found a book in the Pontefract public library which mentioned that a Cluniac monk had been hanged for the rape of a young girl in the time of Henry the Eighth (that is, not long before the destruction of the priory). A little more research showed him that the gallows had been on the top of the hill where the Pritchards' house now stood, and that their house stood on the site of an old bridge called "Priest's Bridge."

Tom's theory, which he incorporated into a typescript called *Mea Culpa*, was that the monk had committed a rape followed by murder (Mrs. Pritchard also seemed to remember that the girl had been strangled), had been executed for his crime, and now haunted the spot where he was hanged. The attack on Diane, he thought, was basically sexual in nature.

Unfortunately for this fascinating theory, there is no evidence whatever that a monk of Pontefract was ever hanged for rape. Pontefract is a small town, and there are a few local histories. They are to be found in the reference section of the library, where I spent a morning in August 1980. My search revealed that the local monks were involved in a great deal of litigation and a certain amount of violence—their virtues were war-like rather than contemplative—but there was undoubtedly no rape and murder. Perhaps the neighbor had read the story of the hanging of a vicar called George Beaumont in the time of the Civil War, when the Parliamentarians were besieging the Royalists in Pontefract Castle; he was accused of carrying on a correspondence with the Royalists. He, as far as I can see, is the only priest to have been hanged in the area.

But is it necessary to assume that the Pritchards were haunted by a Cluniac monk? We must bear in mind that the poltergeist seemed prone to take up suggestions that it heard. On its first visit, it slashed the small picture—but only after Mr. O'Donald had remarked that poltergeists often destroy photographs. The grandmother clock was destroyed one evening after a group of local councilors had been to the house and listened to the banging sounds. (Joe Pritchard's mother was Pontefract's first Lady Mayor at the time.) Before leaving, the Mayor remarked that she was surprised that the grandmother clock on the landing was still intact; half an hour later, it hurtled downstairs and shattered.

Unfortunately, Jean Pritchard kept no diary of the sequence of events. So we do not know whether the "monk's" first appearance—in their bedroom—was before or after the neighbor had borrowed the book from the library. My own guess is that it was after, and that it was inspired by what it had heard. In the same way, the upside-down crosses appeared on the walls and doors after Vic Kelly's attempt at exorcism. During the course of that evening, someone probably made a remark about evil spirits and their propensity to invert the cross.

Why was the Pritchards' home chosen? I believe that Mrs. Holden came close to the truth when she suggested that the underground stream may have some thing to do with it. If Lethbridge is correct, then the "field" of running, water—and of dampness in general—records "psychic impressions." When "Fred" first made his appearance in 1966, Phillip had just passed the age of puberty, and was therefore an ideal "focus." Poltergeists only seem to manifest in unhappy households, and in the Pritchards' home there was a certain amount of tension between Joe Pritchard and his son. Joe Pritchard had been a sporting enthusiast, and he found it incomprehensible that his son should prefer books and music. Presumably it was because of this tension between father and son that Phillip stayed at home when the rest of the family went to Devon. Tom Cunniff's theory—incorporated into his manuscript—is that "Fred's" first appearance was an unconscious expression of Phillip's resentment toward his father; but this is at odds with his view that the "ghost" was a Cluniac monk. It seems to me altogether more probable that "Fred" was simply an ordinary poltergeist—some kind of "elemental" (we shall look more closely into the meaning of that term in the next chapter)—who found the kind of energy he needed in the Pritchards home, and proceeded to make use of it. He was certainly one of the most inventive poltergeists on record; I can find nothing like him in the annals of this type of haunting. The sounds, the smells, the animal noises, the heavy breathing, the bites on sandwiches, and, finally, the appearances, make him almost unique. It is a pity that no trained investigator came on the scene while the disturbances were at their height. The Doncaster Psychical Research Group (now dissolved) became interested in the case in the spring of 1969, and their own conclusions were cautiously skeptical—as seems to be the case with such groups the world over; but most of the phenomena had become infrequent by that time. An investigator who noticed "Fred's" propensity to imitate phenomena he heard discussed might have conducted a fascinating series of experiments, trying to find out just what Fred *was* capable of. Would he, for example, have made "human dummies," like the Phelps poltergeists, if someone had mentioned this within his hearing?

I drove up to Pontefract in late August of 1980 to interview as many witnesses as possible. At this time, I was inclined to accept the usual view of poltergeists as "RSPK"—recurrent spontaneous psycho-kinesis. But on the way to Yorkshire, I spent the night at a conference in Derbyshire, and had the opportunity to meet Guy Playfair, with whom I had been corresponding for some time. We discussed the view—expressed in *The Flying Cow*— that a poltergeist is basically a mischievous disembodied spirit. I was inclined to be skeptical. Guy explained his own notion of the nature of the poltergeist: "It's a kind of football." "Football!" "A football of energy. It somehow gets exuded from disturbed teenagers at puberty. Along come two or three spirits or elementals, look through this window, and see the football lying around. And they do what any group of schoolboys would do—they go and kick it around, smashing windows and generally creating havoc. Then, as often as not, they get tired and leave it. In fact, the football usually explodes. Oddly enough, it turns into water . . . "

The more I thought about this view, the more it struck me as interesting and plausible. There are, in fact, a large number of poltergeist cases in which the phenomena occur just once. In fact, I am relatively certain that one such occurred in my own house. It was in 1960, and my family—my father, mother and thirteen-year-old sister—had moved to Cornwall to live with us. One bright, sunny morning, I was awakened by a loud, repeated banging sound. It sounded just like someone hammering on something made of metal, with slow, steady blows.

It so happened that two friends were sleeping up in the attic. My first thought was that one of their beds had collapsed, and someone was hammering at the bed-frame to try and get it apart, in order to reassemble it. I got out of bed, went to the foot of the stairs and called: "What's going on up there?" All was silence. I went upstairs, and saw both friends were fast asleep. I peeped into my sister's bedroom; she was asleep. But the sounds now seemed to be coming from outside the house—perhaps on the roof.

I went downstairs and outside. It was a very still, sunny morning—about five a.m.—and the sounds were undoubtedly coming from our house (which stands alone in the middle of a field), and not from some neighboring house. I walked all the way round the house, but could not locate the noise. It seemed to be coming from over-head. The obvious suspicion—that it was something to do with the hot water system (which sometimes "knocks" as it heats up)—was dismissed when I saw that the sounds were not coming from any of the hot water pipes.

During all this time, the sounds went on—loud, clear, metallic bangs, exactly like someone hammering on an iron bedstead with a hammer. My father was awake by this time, and we both walked around the house again. Then, as it was impossible to locate it, we went back to bed. Ten minutes later, the noise stopped. About an hour later, it started up again briefly, for per-haps a dozen bangs. Then it stopped. And we have not heard it since. I assume that the sounds were somehow connected with my sister, who was not particularly happy at being dragged away from her home town (Leicester) to live in the country.

I went to see Tom Cunniff in Pontefract, and he told me about the Doncaster Research Group. They had, apparently, fixed upon Phillip as the culprit. They had analyzed the tape recording, and decided that it could have been faked. And they had searched the house, and found in the attic a circle free of dust, which—they decided—might have been made by a loudspeaker, lying face downwards. This, then, "explained" the banging noises.

As soon as I went into the Pritchards' home, I became convinced that this theory was absurd. They had brought in a number of neighbors—like Mrs. Mountain—and Diane and Phillip were also present. They played us the tape, and then answered questions. What struck me most strongly was the spontaneity of the whole thing. They might contradict one another "No, it wasn't that day, it was the day when Alan Williams came because, you remember, he put his hat down on that chair and it disappeared . . . " but they were obviously discussing something they had all lived through. And every one of them remembered some slightly different aspect of what had taken place. No group of conspirators could have made up such a story, and then told it so convincingly. These were simply a crowd of ordinary people who had been through a strange experience, and who would never forget it.

Diane intrigued me when she told me that she had "seen things" at other times. When she was six years old, she came out of her bedroom one day, and saw an old lady dressed in grey outside her mother's bedroom door. Jean Pritchard assumed that she had been dreaming. Diane also told me how, in her teens, she was walking past the grounds of a nearby hospital, which was being partly demolished for rebuilding, and was surprised to see two women in crinolines walking among the trees. She said they seemed to be "floating" over the grass. She stood watching them for about a quarter of an hour before they vanished into the trees.

What I find even more interesting is that the whole area is permeated with stories of hauntings. At the present time, there is another house in the Chequerfields area where a "ghost" has appeared to a number of tenants. Tom Cunniff has noted a number of other stories—for example, poltergeist occurrences at a pub called the Golden Lion, kept at the time by Mrs. Pritchard's sister-in-law, Christine.

When I left the Pritchards' house that afternoon, I had become a convert to Guy Playfair's theory of the poltergeist. The first thing that struck me was Phillips' description of the water appearing on the kitchen floor on that August day in 1966. That certainly seemed to fit amazingly well with Guy's statement that the "electrical energy" used by the poltergeist turns into water. Admittedly, the "spontaneous psychokinesis" view might explain the water equally well—except that it hardly seems to make sense for the disturbed unconscious mind of a teenager to create large quantities of water on the kitchen floor. Banging and rapping noises, yes. Objects flying through the air, yes. But why circular pools of water?

But what really changed my mind about the psychokinesis theory was Diane's description of being dragged up the stairs by the entity. Nobody in the house on that evening had any doubt about her terror and confusion. It is just conceivable that Diane's unconscious mind might throw her out of bed—by way of demanding attention. But by no stretch of the imagination can I imagine it grabbing her by the throat and dragging her up the stairs.

The subsequent research for this book—the study of hundreds of accounts of poltergeist hauntings—has only strengthened my view that the RSKP theory leaves half the phenomena unexplained.

Monasteries and churches are often built on older religious sites, as we have already noted. The reason seems to be that the ground has some kind of "power," perhaps a purely magnetic force. My wife, who is an excellent dowser, said that she felt almost dizzy when she first tried dowsing on Glastonbury Tor, one of England's oldest "sacred sites." And she also obtained a powerful response when dowsing the area of Pontefract's ruined priory, and of the nearby castle. On the site of an old chapel in the castle grounds there is a stone sarcophagus that seems to date to the Roman period. When it was found in the eighteenth century, it contained the bones of a man who had been beheaded—the skull had been placed between his legs. It is believed that this is the skeleton of Thomas of Lancaster, the man who headed the opposition against Edward II, a homosexual who poured favors on his friend Piers Gaveston. In 1312, Gaveston was seized and executed in the presence of Thomas of Lancaster. The king had Thomas ambushed and beheaded. As I watched my wife walking around the stone sarcophagus, I saw the dowsing rod twisting violently in her hands—once at the foot and once at the head of the coffin. It had been placed where the altar would stand if the chapel still existed. Why should the sarcophagus be placed precisely upon this spot? Could it be to counteract some unpleasant influence associated with the sarcophagus?

I am suggesting, then, that the solution to the mystery of the Black Monk of Pontefract may lie in the ground itself. It is "haunted ground," land that retains impressions for a long time. Only a few days before I arrived in Pontefract, a nursing sister in the Pontefract Royal Infirmary—where Phillip was then working—came into the television room. There were two other members of staff there, and she noticed, as she sat down, that there was also a man in a dressing gown. Patients were not allowed in that room, and after a moment she turned her head to look at the man. He was no longer there—yet he could not have left the room without walking past her; he had been sitting in the corner.

This, then, is my own theory about the Black Monk case. The ground itself contains some peculiar force that favors "manifestations." The early haunting was triggered by Phillip and by his psychological tension. The "entity" remained in the area until Diane—who herself seems to possess undeveloped mediumistic powers—could provide the energy it needed to manifest itself. When that energy ceased to be available, it again became inactive; perhaps waiting for another provider-of-energy to offer it the chance to erupt into the space-and-time world of humanity . . .

FIVE

Fairies, Elementals and Dead Monks

Some thirty miles to the northwest of the Pritchards' home, there is another piece of "haunted ground" known as Fairy Dell. The events that took place there in July 1917 are still the subject of controversy.

On a Saturday afternoon in that month, Arthur Wright, an engineer, went into his darkroom to develop a photograph taken earlier in the day by his sixteen-year-old daughter Elsie. As the plate began to develop, Wright saw vague white shapes appearing——he took them for birds. But when the picture became clear, he was startled to see that they were fairies. The picture showed a serious-faced little girl—Elsie's cousin Frances Griffiths, aged eleven, standing behind a bush, her chin propped on her hand. And in front of her, dancing on top of the bush, were four neat little female figures with wings and diaphanous garments, one of them playing a pan-pipe. "What on earth are they?" said Arthur Wright to his daughter, who was standing behind him. "Fairies," she said, matter-of-factly.

Now working-class Yorkshiremen tend to be phlegmatic and down-to-earth. Arthur Wright did not press his daughter for explanations; he merely grunted, and awaited further developments. They came a month later, when the girls again borrowed his camera. Elsie and Frances scrambled across the deep stream—or "beck"—that ran at the bottom of the garden, and went to the old oaks in the dell beyond. And when Arthur Wright later developed the plate, it showed Elsie sitting on the grass, holding her hand out to a gnome who was apparently about to step up on to her dress.

This time, Arthur and his wife Polly looked through the bedroom of the girls, hoping to find cut-out pictures that would explain the photographs. They found nothing. Arthur Wright became mildly exasperated when both girls insisted there had been no trickery—that there really *were* fairies at the bottom of their garden. He told Elsie she couldn't use the camera again until she told him the truth.

In November 1917, Frances wrote a letter to a friend in South Africa enclosing one of the photographs, and remarking casually that it "is me with some fairies up the beck . . ."

These events took place in the village of Cottingley, in Yorkshire, on the road from Bradford to Bingley. It has long since ceased to be a separate village, and has become a part of the urban sprawl; but the Fairy Dell still exists.

In the summer of 1919, Polly Wright, Elsie's mother, went to a meeting of the Theosophical Society in Bradford. She was interested in "the occult," having had experiences of astral projection and memories of past lives. The lecture that evening was on fairies—for it is the position of the Theosophical Society that fairies are simply a type of "elemental spirit"—nature spirits—that can manifest themselves to people with second sight or "clairvoyance." Naturally, Mrs Wright could not resist mentioning her daughter's "fairy photographs" to the person sitting next to her. As a result, Arthur Wright made prints of the two photographs, and they were passed from hand to hand at the Theosophists' conference at Harrogate a few weeks later, and finally made their way to London, and into the hands of Edward Gardner, who was the president of the London branch of the Theosophical Society. Gardner was familiar with faked photographs of ghosts and spirits, and decided that these looked doubtful. He asked his correspondent if he could let him see the negatives. When these arrived a few days later, Gardner was surprised to find no evidence of double exposure or other cheating. He took the negatives to a photography expert named Snelling, who examined them carefully under a powerful lens, and announced that it was undoubtedly *not* a double exposure. Nor were the dancing fairies made of paper, or painted on to a sheet of glass. They had *moved* during the exposure. A week later, after enlarging the photographs, Snelling announced that, in his opinion, they were not faked. They were ordinary open-air shots.

It so happened that Sir Arthur Conan Doyle, the creator of Sherlock Holmes, had agreed to write an article on fairies for the Christmas number of the *Strand Magazine* (in which Holmes first appeared). When he heard about the photographs, he contacted Gardner and asked if he could see them. The two men met, and agreed that the pictures were too good to be true—the waterfall in the background (which looked like a painted backcloth), the highly appropriate toadstools . . . Gardner agreed to go to Cottingley to see the girls, and to find out whether they were hoaxers. Mr. and Mrs. Wright were startled to hear that the experts thought the photographs genuine. And Gardner was startled when he walked up the glen with Elsie, and saw the scene exactly as she had photographed it, complete with waterfall and toadstools—although without fairies.

Gardner decided to test the girls. Two cameras were bought, and the film-plates were sealed so they could not be tampered with. In due course, the negatives were returned to Gardner, and the factory that had produced them verified that they were still sealed. One showed Frances with a fairy leaping close to her face, another showed a fairy offering a flower to Elsie, while the third showed two fairies in the middle of a bush. In the center of the picture there is an object that looks rather like a bathing costume hung on a line. Elsie apparently had no idea what this was; but Gardner, with his wider knowledge of fairy lore, identified it as a "magnetic bath" which fairies weave in dull weather. (It had rained continually that August.)

Once more, the experts got to work to try to discover if the photographs had been faked; again, they concluded that they were genuine. That Christmas, Doyle's article on the fairies appeared in the *Strand Magazine* and caused a sensation. Inevitably, the majority of people thought it was a hoax; yet no expert on photography was able to say anything conclusive about how it might have been done. A reporter on the *Westminster Gazette* learned the true identities of the girls (Conan Doyle had used pseudonyms to protect them from publicity) and went to see them. He concluded that everyone seemed honest and genuine, and there was no evidence of trickery. Arthur Wright was baffled by it all, and deeply disappointed that Conan Doyle was naive enough to be taken in, "bamboozled by our Elsie, and her at the bottom of her class." Conan Doyle was himself puzzled and critical; yet he could not discount the possibility that these were real fairies, nature spirits of some kind. He contacted a well-known clairvoyant named Geoffrey Hodson, and Hodson went to Cottingley, talked to the girls, and went to the dell with them. He also saw fairy forms. (We shall have more to say about Hodson in a moment.)

By the end of 1921, most people had lost interest in the fairies. Conan Doyle was to write a book about the case, called *The Coming of the Fairies*, which came out in 1922; but there was no re-investigation.

In 1965, a *Daily Express* reporter named Peter Chambers discovered that Elsie was still alive, having spent most of her life in India, and now back in the north of England. he went to see her, and asked her straight out whether the pictures were faked. Elsie neither denied nor confirmed this; she said she would prefer to leave it "open." She made the curious statement that the fairies were "figments of her imagination." This certainly sounds like a confession; but if it is, why did she not say openly that the photographs were faked? Six years later, in 1971, the BBC's *Nationwide* program discovered that both Elsie and Frances were still alive, and interviewed both. Again, both declined to deny or confirm the genuineness of the photographs. Elsie says: "I'd rather leave that open, if you don't mind. But my father had nothing to do with it, I promise you that." Again, this sounds like a veiled admission of faking; but four years later, in 1975, Elsie gave an interview to Walter Clapham, of *Woman*, in which she stated again what both girls had maintained at the time—that they *had* seen fairies repeatedly in the dell, and had photographed them. Elsie mentioned that she was "psychic," and described a number of occasions on which she had seen ghosts. (Gardner had been convinced that both Elsie and Frances were mediums.) As to the fairy photographs, she admitted that they *had* been intended as a hoax, but not quite of the kind suspected by the non-believers. It seems that on the day they took the first photograph Frances had fallen into the stream, and had tried to get out of trouble by lying about in it. She had been soundly admonished for stretching the truth. Elsie borrowed her father's camera to comfort Frances, and when they began to discuss the lying issue, Elsie pointed out that grown-ups lie—for example, about Father Christmas. So they would get their revenge in a rather convoluted manner. They would take photographs of fairies, and show them to the grown-ups. And if the grown-ups took them seriously, they'd reply: "But you know fairies don't exist."

Their revenge fell flat, since Elsie's parents declined to believe in the fairies.

In 1976, a Yorkshire folklorist and psychical investigator, Joe Cooper, persuaded Elsie and Frances to appear on a television program. His account of what happened is contained in a book (which, at the time of writing, is still unpublished) called *The Case of the Cottingley Fairies*. I met Joe Cooper on my visit to Yorkshire in August 1980, and he told me then that his final conclusion was that Elsie and Frances are genuine; they really *did* see fairies. In his book, he records conversations with Elsie in which she makes statements such as: "Fairies and elves are tremendously interested in the doings of human beings." In the dell, she told Cooper: "Round about here the gnomes used to come," and in reply to his question about what they wore: "Russet colors—they were a bit shy." She describes the photographing of the fairies quite circumstantially, with no attempt to imply that they were pure imagination: "When it [the elf] became clear Frances pressed the trigger on the box camera." Asked why she never made a grab for the fairies, she replied: "You couldn't. It's like grabbing for a ghost or something." And to the question: "Did you in any way fabricate these photographs?" Frances replied flatly: "Of course not."

The most interesting point established by Joe Cooper is that Elsie *is* undoubtedly psychic—either that, or a liar. She told him of a lady with a dog who used to come to her bedside when she was a child of four. Elsie talked to her, but the lady never replied. On one occasion, Elsie claims, the lady brought a fox terrier, which somehow located a penny she had under her pillow, and swallowed it. When Elsie shouted, her mother rushed upstairs. The lady and the dog had vanished, but they never found the penny.

Elsie also tells of an occasion when she came downstairs one evening for a drink of water, and found a strange man in his shirtsleeves in front of the fire, reading a newspaper, and a woman with a white apron came from the kitchen with a dish of rice pudding and put it in the oven. When Elsie asked where her parents were, the man told her they were playing cards at their neighbors, the Moffs. Elsie said she wanted to see them, and the man opened the door for her—the latch was too high for her to reach. When she knocked on the door of the Moffs, her parents were highly alarmed to hear about the strangers in their house, and rushed back immediately. The house was in darkness. The only sign that anything strange had occurred was that the door was still open. And Arthur Wright had locked it when they went out.

The case of the Cottingley fairies remains unproven. For the skeptics, the strongest evidence against it is the photographs themselves. The fairies look a little too conventional. The BBC demonstrated that it is not too difficult to fake fairies; they showed their reporter surrounded by them in the studio; these fairies *were* cardboard cut-outs that moved on wire (to make them stand up). It is therefore entirely conceivable that Elsie and Frances used cutouts supported by wire. In that case, it would be perfectly understandable that they are disinclined to confess. All their defenders, from Conan Doyle to De Vere Stacpoole, would be made to look idiots, and an intriguing mystery would finally be dismissed and forgotten. Yet there is surely no reason why, in that case, they should continue to insist that they saw fairies frequently as children. Frances told Joe Cooper that she still "almost" sees them, from the corners of her eyes, but declines to have her attention drawn to them. (Cooper quotes another man who claims to have seen fairies, but only out of the corner of his eye.)

The view that was held by Gardner, Doyle and Hodson is that what the children saw were "elementals." Elementals are nature spirits, particularly of woods and streams. There are four basic elementals: gnomes, sylphs, salamanders and nereids, being respectively the spirits of earth, air, fire and water. It would be a fair assumption that in the twentieth century, only members of the lunatic fringe believe in such creatures. This is not so. Writing in his classic work *The Fairy Faith in Celtic Countries*, W. Y. Evans-Wentz writes:

> We seem ... to have arrived at a point in our long investigations where we can postulate scientifically ... the existence of such invisible intelligences as gods, genii, daemons, all kind of true fairies, and disembodied man ... The general statement may be made that there are hundreds of carefully proven cases of phenomena or apparitions precisely like many of those which the Celtic people attribute to fairies.

And by way of example, he goes on to cite poltergeists, which, he points out, sound very much like what have been called demons, fairies and elementals. He goes on to quote the famous French investigator (and astronomer) Camille Flammarion, who points out that the pranks of poltergeists are thoroughly puerile and resemble the mischief of badly behaved children. Flammarion goes on to make the important statement:

> These spirits are not necessarily the souls of the dead; for other kinds of spiritual beings may exist, and space may be full of them without our ever

knowing anything about it, except under unusual circumstance. Do we not find in different ancient literatures demons, angels, gnomes, goblins, sprites, spectres, elementals, etc? Perhaps these legends are not without some foundation in fact.

The scientist and psychic investigator Sir William Crookes came to the same conclusion, summarizing his theory in the words:

> The actions of a separate order of beings, living on this earth, but invisible and immaterial to us. Able, however, occasionally to manifest their presence. Known in almost all countries and ages as demons (not necessarily bad), gnomes, fairies, kobolds, elves, goblins, Puck etc.

Moreover, as Evans-Wentz remarks, the kind of people who claim to have seen fairies are not usually excitable, hysterical or neurotic; they tend to be very ordinary. Andrew Lang made the same observation about people who have seen ghosts—that they are usually "steady, unimaginative, unexcitable people with just one odd experience." Joe Cooper's observations bear this out: for example, a National Serviceman out having a picnic with his girlfriend in Gibraltar when the sandwich was snatched from his hand by a little man about eighteen inches high, who then ran away. The account is completely matter-of-fact: "his features were just human, they weren't distorted, a big bulbous nose or chin . . . and I noticed he had a hammer in his hand . . ."

When I was lecturing at the Edinburgh Festival in 1978, I was interviewed in the local Scottish TV studio by an interviewer named Bobbie (whose second name, regrettably, I failed to note in my journal). He was apparently a well-known interviewer on Scottish news programs, and he commuted between the Edinburgh and Glasgow studios. When, afterwards, we sat in the pub next door, he told me casually that he had seen a gnome and that it had "scared the hell out of him." He was picking up a friend outside a convent, and had seen the gnome—a very thin man—standing on the pavement outside the gate. Something about the figure had terrified him and he drove off at top speed. Most stories of "fairy" sightings are like this, oddly circumstantial and oddly pointless.

Marc Alexander tells such a story in his book, *Enchanted Britain*. He has been discussing the case of Elsie and Frances, and speculates that these strange beings are not necessarily of a definite shape and size, that would be seen by anyone who happened to be on the spot. "Mankind down the ages has interpreted visions according to his experience and metaphysical outlook— the old Christians saw angels, we see UFOs." He goes on to tell a story of a friend named Pat Andrew, whom he knew in New Zealand, and who claimed to have seen a pixie sitting on a gate when he was six. When a stage hypnotist came to town, Marc Alexander and his friend both began to experiment with hypnosis, and soon became proficient at it. One day, Marc Alexander tried regressing Pat Andrew to the age of six, to find out whether the story about the pixie was invention.

> When he reached this point he exclaimed in a wondering, high-pitched voice: "Look, a pixie." He then continued, to whatever it was that he was seeing once again on the gate, "Hello, little fellow." There was a pause, while presumably the pixie returned his greeting, then Pat said: "You're a pixie, aren't you?" Again there was a silence from the young man with closed eyes as in his memory the pixie answered his questions.

It was strange to listen to this one-sided conversation, to the questions that a child would ask a pixie such as where did it live, what did it eat, what was its name, and so on. All I could hear were the words Pat had actually used sixteen years earlier, but they left me in no doubt that as a child my friend had spoken to something sitting on top of a gate which had *replied* to him as a pixie.

What intrigued Marc Alexander was that Andrew's description of the little man made it clear that he was a traditionally English pixie with a pointed hat, not the Maori equivalent of pixies, the *turehu*—and until the hypnotic experiment he had been inclined to assume that the pixie had been a figment of his friend's imagination—not a deliberate lie, but a fantasy that had taken on reality for a small boy.

The dowser Tom Lethbridge, whom we have met in Chapter 1, was convinced that there are various types of "earth field" connected with different elements: water fields (which he called naiad fields), oread fields, associated with open spaces and mountains, and dryad fields, associated with woodland. Each field has its own kind of entity—or spirit—associated with it. But Lethbridge believes these are simply a property of the field—recordings—not real spirits. He says:

Little people are seen now and then by many races of men. They are seen in Africa, for instance, where they are just like tiny Africans. I do not for a moment doubt that they are seen, but I do doubt the interpretation placed on the seeing. We can take it as an observed fact that ordinary men and women all over the world have seen little people; but I do not believe that they really exist as such. Throughout this investigation we are assuming that people do not go out of their way to tell lies.

> When they say that they have seen a little man,
> they are not just making up a story based on tradi-
> tion. They have seen something which appeared
> to their mind as a little man.

But Lethbridge goes on to tell two stories that contradict this hypothesis. (Lethbridge evolved from book to
book, so this often happens.) In July 1922, Lethbridge
and a party of friends were visiting the Shiant Islands off
the northwestern coast of Scotland. One of them climbed
a hill, and left his waterproof coat and lunch basket there
by a marked rock. When he returned, they had vanished.
Yet the island was deserted (apart from the rest of the
party who were elsewhere); there were only seabirds,
who could hardly lift a heavy lunch basket. He was convinced that they had been stolen by the "Sith"—or
fairies—and Lethbridge acknowledged later that he felt
they were wrong to laugh at this belief.

Lethbridge himself had a supernatural experience
on the island of Skellig Michael. He was with the friend
who had lost his lunch. Lethbridge went off alone to
examine the site of a Celtic monastery, then looked over
the cliff and decided to climb down and look at the
monastery's rubbish dump. Halfway there, he had an
unpleasant sensation—what he would later call a
"ghoul"—the feeling that someone wanted to push him
down the cliff. The feeling became so strong as he went
on that he felt giddy. He decided to go back to the cliff
top. Back at the site of the Celtic church, something suddenly flung him flat on his face. There was no wind, no
animal, no other person. He later came to accept that
what had flung him down was some form of poltergeist
and, in *Ghost and Ghoul*, speculates that it may have
been associated with a shipwreck of the previous year.

But then, Lethbridge also knew that the sites of

churches are often chosen because of some "earth force," some innate "holiness" in the ground itself, and even pointed out that such churches are often named after St. Michael, because the saint became the Christian counterpart of the pagan god of light, Lugh (or Lucifer). This was the way the early Christians tried to "decontaminate" a place from its pagan origins. Unfortunately, he knew nothing about Guy Underwood's discovery of 'holy lines' around sites like Stonehenge,* and knew nothing about ley lines, which were only just being rediscovered by John Michell and others during the last years of Lethbridge's life; he might otherwise have taken the step—to which he comes so close in *Ghost and Ghoul*—of connecting some of these mysterious earth forces with the entity that stole his friend's lunch basket and knocked him flat on his face on an island named after St. Michael.

But Joe Cooper takes this step, in discussing the Cottingley fairies. He discusses a book with the off-putting title *Secrets of the Gods* by E. T. Stringer, and published in 1974. It is subtitled "An Outline of Tellurianism," and the author—who is a climatologist who teaches at Birmingham University—defines this as a philosophy based on the notion of a Telluric force (earth force, Tellus being the Roman earth goddess). This, he says, is the force made use of by dowsers and psychic investigators—that is, Lethbridge's "fields." But he adds: "The Telluric force is not a physical force, as is magnetism or gravity. It cannot be measured by any scientific instrument . . . "

From this point on, Stringer's theory departs from that of Lethbridge or Underwood. He believes that the Telluric force holds people together in a particular

---

* See Chapter 2.

place—often country areas—and that people somehow constitute the cells of a larger organism (which he calls the Oikumeos). Stringer's earth is a living creature, and human beings live in its bloodstream of Telluric force as the tiny independent creatures called mitochondria live in our bodies and assist its vital maintenance. Joe Cooper speculates that Cottingley is one of these places described by Stringer, where the Telluric force makes certain manifestations possible. Stringer, Lethbridge, Underwood and "ley hunters" like John Michell seem to have arrived independently at the same basic theory of earth forces. (Ley hunters point out that in many areas, ley lines are called "fairy paths.")

One interesting point quickly emerges from the various accounts of "fairies" or similar entities: the people who see them are almost invariably known to be "psychic." Elsie Wright saw ghosts as well as fairies. The man whose sandwich was stolen by a goblin later became a healer. The interviewer I spoke with in Edinburgh struck me as a typical Celt, and Celts seem to be more "psychic" than Saxons. Yet they may be totally unaware that they are psychic until they happen to find themselves in a place—like Ardachie Lodge near Loch Ness—where the "Telluric force" enters into a combination with their natural mediumship.

Lethbridge was also psychic—all good dowsers are (since the faculties amount to the same thing); so the sense of foreboding he experienced as he climbed down the cliff on Skellig Michael was simply a sensitivity to the force associated with the place. But if that force could knock him on his face, then presumably it was more than a tape-recording or "ghoul."

In his autobiography, *A Foot in Both Worlds*, Dr. Arthur Guirdham has also spoken of this sense of evil associated with certain places. He felt it as an Oxford undergraduate, when he spent a vacation "cramming" at an inn in Beckley, on the edge of Otmoor.

> Otmoor was strange and haunted and out of this world, a sunken plain with low hills around it . . . There was always a silence of something beautiful and evil about it . . . Even in summer, with the roses blooming, there was about it a memory of old evil.

And on the day he returned to Oxford, Guirdham experienced a peculiar fever. "My teeth chattered harshly . . . I felt deathly cold . . . Next day I felt shrunken with cold and horribly ill." Guirdham's explanation is that Otmoor was one of the last places in England to harbor malaria, and that because of this, the "yellow men of Otmoor" were traditional in the Middle Ages. But there was no malaria there for Guirdham to catch in the 1920s. He is convinced that his unconscious mind had simply picked up the memory of these sufferings of the past—what Lethbridge would call a ghoul— and begun to vibrate in tune with them, so to speak.

Guirdham describes in the same book how, as a child, he saw a demon—although he seems to feel it was the Devil.

> I lay on my bed and felt his presence. The air was crackling and electric. A wave of vibration came to me through the door of my bedroom. When the wave ebbed quickly I was drawn towards the door . . . I knew he was calling and that the minute vibrations in the atmosphere were a summons to me. I went from my bed through the air palpitating with a new cold and opened the door, and he was waiting for me . . .
>
> His face was hairy. It was covered, like his body, with a felt of blue-grey hair. He was man in his features and in his almost upright, slightly

leaning posture . . . His legs were different. I was not aware of them as human. They ended in the shaped stump of something like a hoof . . . There was a shining aura about him . . .

I do not know how I went to bed . . . After he had gone, the night was empty.

In discussing this experience, Guirdham speculates whether his visitant was the god Pan.

This experience understandably affected Guirdham's later attitude to mental illness, particularly obsessive neurosis, and in a later book, *Obsession*, he makes the bold suggestion that much mental illness may actually be due to the presence of a force of evil which the patient is sensitive (i.e., clairvoyant) enough to pick up.

Like Lethbridge, Dr. Guirdham believes that houses—particularly damp ones—can pick up negative vibrations; he has described a house in Bath, above an underground stream, in which a number of successive tenants committed suicide or became mentally ill.

But are such "vibrations" merely impressions or "tape recordings," as Lethbridge believed? Or is some more active force involved? In 1935, Admiral H. Boyle Somerville, a member of Alfred Watkins' Old Straight Track Club, accompanied Geraldine Cummins, an Irish medium who specialized in automatic writing, to some ancient stone circles in Ireland. Somerville wrote an account of the "automatic communications" that came through Geraldine Cummins. At a group of stones called the Three Fingers, near Castletownshend, County Cork, the pencil in Geraldine Cummins' hand wrote "Astor is here," and then told Somerville to touch the stones. When he rested one hand on a stone, and the other on the hand of the medium, she began to write answers to his questions. At one point the script read:

I see a picture now belonging to the second period [a period of ignorant worship and primitive practices]. A tall man, a priest, near the stones, and the figure of a bound man being dragged forward. He is a heretic, I think. He does not believe, or he is a stranger; and they sacrifice him.

It goes on to speak of a period of the Great Curse;

They called on the Spirits of the Elements to guard these stones, and any man or stranger who disturbed or removed any one of them came under the power of the Curse. I see one stone being taken away at a later period. I see a woman who lived, I suppose, in the last century, for her dress is of that period. The men are removing the stone under her orders; I see the invisible Watcher who directs upon her the force of the Curse. All the male descendants of this woman are cursed. Nothing thrives with them, and they in their souls decay. For this is the kind of a curse that assaults the soul. The men of this woman's race have come to no good in consequence, and have fallen on evil days. The curse does not seem to have fallen on the female side.

Astor goes on to speak of another man, four or five centuries earlier, who had also incurred the curse by removing stones for building. "He and all his people died violent deaths in wars." Astor went on to prophecy that the spot would one day again become a spiritual center when "old wisdom will be rediscovered."

At the Drumbeg stone circle, in County Cork, on September 23, 1935, Astor stated flatly that he did not like the place

for I see that it is specially connected with a period of Nature-worship, or rather, an offshoot of

Sun-worship, which became allied with Magic . . .
I count back three thousand years at least. The
Magic practiced here was connected with the Sun
in conjunction with the Moon. It seems that in
mid-Winter there was a very striking ceremony
performed here. Power was drawn from the earth,
that is to say, when the Sun was at its lowest, an
animal, if not a small child, was sacrificed for the
purpose of securing the blood.

After blood has been used in magical rites, "a Nature
Spirit rises like a misty shape out of the dish of blood."

Anyway, through the power of the Nature Spirits
thus evoked, these men—"Tuatha de Dananaan,"
a name I get—these men are able in the coming
year to control the tribe that occupied this region;
for the elemental beings thus summoned have the
power, when re-used and used, to inflict injury,
death or madness, as directed by their masters,
the Magician-priests who made the circle.

He goes on to describe a ceremony with dancing in
which "men and women stabbed each other in a frenzy . . .
It drew the earth-power and the lower elementals to the
controlling Masters of Magic."

Then comes the interesting comment: "Many hundreds of years later there lingered a tradition concerning
these elementals in the countryside, but they were
described as 'fairies' then, and the knowledge of their
origin in connection with this circle was lost." According
to Astor, the circles were originally built during "a
period of pure worship, when these stones were connected with the adoration of Creative Life." This first
period gave way to the second in which the original religion had become adulterated with magic.

The reason that ill-luck is attached to this place is due to its being the centre, at one time, for the evocation of the maleficent beings I have named. They set a curse upon the place . . . and the power of evil still lingers. If a stone were removed, these elemental spirits would again obtain power to strike at the human being who took the stone away.

No, I dislike this place. I feel I had better stop writing, for I can't get through to the time of a clearer, purer worship. The spirits of darkness guard this place, and keep it as their own.*

In 1944, a series of disturbances at the village of Great Leighs in Essex followed the removal of an ancient stone by the American army—it obstructed army trucks, at the crossroads, trying to get into the camp. Journalist Charles Curzon reports:

Within hours of the stone's removal, things began to happen. The bell in the church tower tolled in the small hours of the morning when nobody was near it. For several days running, the church clock struck midnight at two-thirty in the morning. Hens stopped laying. Chickens were found drowned in water butts . . . Farmer Ernest Withen of Chadwick's Farm found his newly built stacks tumbled and spread all over his yard—although it had been a windless night. And his hay waggons were all turned the wrong way round in his sheds . . . In Charlie Dickson's building yard, piles of heavy scaffolding poles, that needed a strong man to lift them, were found scattered like matchsticks . . . Thirty sheep and two horses were found dead in a field. Chickens in a run and rabbits in a hutch mysteriously changed places—and the fasteners

---

* Printed in *The Ley Hunter*, No. 90, Spring 1981.

of the hutch were found to be undisturbed . . . In the St. Anne's Castle Inn, a bedroom suddenly became haunted. The furniture was thrown all over the place—a chest of drawers tipped on its side, bedclothes were strewn across the floor, a heavy wardrobe shifted to another position. Mr. Sykes tidied it up. Next morning it was a shambles again.

A week after the disturbances started, a group of men and women recovered the Witches Stone, from where the Americans had flung it, and in a midnight ceremony, they replaced it at the crossroads, exactly where it had been for generations. The hauntings stopped from that moment. Curzon reports that the Witches Stone has since vanished completely, but the disturbances have not started again.

A huge ancient stone called the Humber Stone, near my home town, Leicester, has similar legends associated with it. It is also known as the Hell, Holy and Host stone, the last two suggesting it was once used for ritual purposes. It is believed to have been washed down the valley of the River Soar by an ice-age glacier. At the time of writing (1981) the Leicester planning authorities are thinking of building a housing estate around the site of the stone, and the Old Humberstone Historical Society has been approached about the possibility of excavating it and superintending its removal. In the *Leicester Mercury*, Mrs. J. Dailey of the Society is quoted as saying that the Society doesn't want to excavate because of what has happened to others. She speaks of a young man who placed a clock on top of the stone—and it promptly stopped; a clockmaker could find nothing mechanically wrong with it, but it still refused to start. Mrs. Bailey had an interesting suggestion about moving the stone: "Talk to it. I believe that if you told it that it would be removed to a safe place where no damage would come to it, there would be no trouble. I believe there would be disastrous results otherwise." This suggestion, which sounds preposterous in twentieth-century England, would still strike most Africans as perfectly reasonable.

The article mentions events that sound similar to the "curse" on the Irish stone circles: in the nineteenth century, William Pochin of Barkby investigated the Humber Stone, and then had an accident with a firearm in which he blew off half his hand. The farmer who owned the land allowed his plough to break off parts of the stone in the eighteenth century; legend has it that he never again prospered, and died in the workhouse. A curate who covered over the stone (it was almost totally buried in the ground in the early nineteenth century, as it is again today) was thrown from his gig shortly afterwards.

Another issue of the *Leicester Mercury** specifically suggests that the stone is associated with "supernatural" forces. A ten-year-old boy named Billingham startled his art teacher by drawing a creature with a goat's head, long curving horns, a man's body and cloven hoofs. He explained that it was a thing he often saw at the end of his bed. The house he lived in was close to the Humber Stone. The boy's mother subsequently decided to move from the house alleging it was haunted; the people who took it over also moved within two months. Mrs. Billingham said that she and her husband had once heard crying when the children were in bed; they went to investigate and found they were quietly reading. "My husband and I saw a cat which jumped on our bed. We searched for it but couldn't find it. We never owned a cat. I felt I was never alone in that house." In this case, the Humber Stone seems to affect several

---

* August 26, 1980.

houses in the area. When they told their neighbors why they were moving, the neighbors described waking up in the middle of the night and seeing a monk in an attitude of prayer in their bedroom. Two exorcisms had been carried out in nearby houses.

A few days later, the *Mercury* followed up the earlier story. Mrs. Billingham's parents still live in the area, and they contacted the reporter to report their own experience. On one occasion, they stayed in the house overnight, looking after the children while the Billinghams were away,

> On the night in question we went to bed about 11 pm and fell asleep. However, I was roughly awakened, feeling that my life was being choked out of my body. Although I couldn't see anyone in the darkness, I suffered the terrible sensation of being strangled and could actually feel someone— something—exerting a vice-like grip around my throat, so much that I was forced back into the pillow. It was not a nightmare. I was fully awake, but unable to scream. I shook my husband from what seemed a trance-like slumber. He immediately switched on the light, and although we couldn't see anyone in the room, the temperature had dropped considerably. I was unable to utter a word for several minutes . . . [I don't know] whether it was because I am slightly psychic that the presence was drawn to me. I only know that I could sense evil in that house.

Her husband, like Mrs. Billingham's, never experienced anything unusual, but "did witness the extremely disturbing effects on his wife, daughter and grandchild."

Reading this account, I was reminded of Diane Pritchard's experiences with the Black Monk. The fall in temperature, the sense of a presence in the room, all sound more like a poltergeist than a normal "haunting." I obtained Mrs. Billingham's new address from the *Leicester Mercury* and wrote to her, asking if she could tell me more about the experiences that drove her out of the house. She replied that it had all been so horrible that she had no desire to talk about it—she merely wanted to forget it.

In an article called "Gremlins at the Gates of Dawn," Paul Devereux, editor of *The Ley Hunter**, writes:

> It has been noted by earth mystery researchers from time to time that things often seem to go wrong when ancient sites are being investigated: to use a romantic notion, as if some invisible guardian of a site is making things difficult for the human investigators. Cameras inexplicably jam, accidents happen, people are taken ill. An example happened to your editor in an aircraft over Wandlebury Camp . . . an expensive, newish camera internally fell apart at the precise moment when infra-red pictures of the Gog Magog figures [first discovered by Lethbridge] were to be taken. Yet the camera had functioned perfectly before take-off.

And the article goes on to describe at length all kinds of mishaps that accompanied a trip to photograph the winter solstice sunrise at the Castle Rigg stone circle in Cumbria.

The travel writer Laurens Van der Post describes a similar incident in book *The Lost World of the Kalahari*, when his expedition, seeking the vanished bushmen of

---

* No. 84

South Africa, approached a place called the Slippery Hills. Their guide, Samutchoso, had insisted that there should be no shooting of game as they approached, or the gods would be angry. Van der Post had forgotten to tell the advance party, and they shot a wart-hog, to Samutchoso's alarm. From then on, everything went wrong. They were attacked by wild bees, and all stung. When a movie camera was focused on a rock-painting, it promptly jammed, although the magazine was new. They loaded another magazine, it jammed again. The same thing happened to a third magazine. In a natural amphitheatre, Samutchoso knelt to pray, but was pulled violently backwards, tearing both his knees. The advance party returned to camp to collect more magazines; these all jammed just as promptly. At dawn they were invaded by more bees. And as soon as they began to try to film again, the camera jammed, and continued to do so for the rest of the day. Their tape recorder simply went dead. The next day, it was the same story all over again, from the dawn attack by bees. A steel swivel of a camera—so reliable that no spare was carried—also failed.

Finally, Samutchoso offered to consult the spirits by a traditional method, in which a needle was placed along the lifeline on the palm of his hand, and he stared into it. As Van der Post and the party watched, they heard a one-way conversation, during which Samutchoso broke off periodically to listen to the spirits. Finally, Samutchos told Van der Post: "It is as I thought, the spirits of the hills are very angry with you, so angry that if they had not known your intention in coming here was pure they would long since have killed you. They are angry because you have come with blood on your hands."

Van der Post thought of an expedient to placate the spirits; he wrote a note of humble apology, made everyone sign it, and buried it in a ledge. Then Samut-

choso again consulted the spirits, and told Van der Post
that all would now be well. The spirits also warned him
that he would find bad news at the next place he went to;
in fact, he learned that his father had died.

Samutchoso's experience when trying to pray
sounds like what happened to Lethbridge on Skellig
Michael when something threw him on his face. And
this in turn suggests that what Lethbridge encountered
was not, strictly speaking, a poltergeist, but some kind of
"elemental." (This does not, of course, preclude the possibility that poltergeists *are* some kind of elemental.)

In Africa, the reality of spirits is taken for granted,
and many white men who have had experience of Africa
have also learned to accept their reality. In *Ju-ju in My
Life*, James H. Neal, former chief investigation officer for
the Government of Ghana, tells of his own first acquaintance with spirits. A port was being built at Tema, and a
small tree defied all efforts to move it—even bulldozers
were unable to tear it out of the ground. The African foreman explained that it was a fetich—was inhabited by a
spirit, and that a fetich priest would have to be called. The
priest asked for three sheep, three bottles of gin, and a
hundred pounds if he succeeded. The blood of the sheep
was sprinkled around the tree, then the gin; then the priest
went into a trance and begged the spirit to vacate it for a
more suitable home. After various rituals, the priest
announced that the spirit had agreed to leave. A small
team of men then pulled the tree out with a rope.

Another psychical researcher, Leonard Boucher
(whom we shall meet again in Chapter Seven), has a similar story about a tree in Tema, near Accra, Ghana. When
plans were drawn up for the construction of a new hotel,
it was decided that an old tree would have to be cut
down—otherwise, it would impede the view from the
lounge window. The tree had been a meeting place of ju-

ju men over centuries, and the local ju-ju man informed the builders that it would be impossible to cut it down—it was the dwelling place of the spirit of an ancient chief. The management ignored him, and told the builders to go ahead and remove it. But this proved to be more difficult than expected. Saws broke, men manning the bulldozer became ill, the ground hardened like concrete and, after all their efforts, the tree still remained intact. Finally, African workers on the site refused to make any further attempt to destroy the tree—it is still to be seen today outside the middle of the lounge picture window.

In the appendix of my book *Rasputin and the Fall of the Romanovs*, I have printed a story told to me by a friend, Martin Delany, who was managing director of a company in Nigeria. A hen flew into the saw of a Brenta band-saw and was cut to pieces, and the Nigerian workers were alarmed, declaring that the god was angry, and would have to be appeased with blood. Martin refused, because it involved the sacrifice of a puppy dog. Two days later, another hen flew into the blade. When the saw began to cut unevenly, it was stopped and the electricity turned off at the main. As soon as the manager began to examine it, the blade turned and almost severed his hand. Engineers who examined the saw said it was an impossibility. Finally, the saw blade began to "strip" when in use, and the ball of tangled metal killed the operator. At this point, Martin Delany allowed the witch doctor to make the sacrifice; and all trouble immediately ceased. From the point of view of the present chapter, the main interest of the story is the way that the saw began to turn even when switched off at the main. We have already noted that poltergeists seem to have the power to create electric currents.

But stories of curses are as common to England as to Africa. I know of a village in Cornwall where no one dares to touch a rather dangerous yew in a churchyard because there is a belief that anyone who does so will die, and this is what happened to the last man who tried to cut it down. Usually, in such cases, there is a story of a curse laid by a witch. In *The Folklore of Cornwall*, Tony Deane and Tony Shaw mention that there are two fields in Cornwall that are never tilled because they are cursed. One is at Mullion, the other at Padstow. The latter is at Lower Harlyn Farm, now farmed by a Mr. Bennett. The "curse" was laid in the nineteenth century when a cargo of pilchards was dumped in the field; the Italian buyers refused to purchase them because they were too expensive. The villagers were starving, but were refused permission to touch the pilchards. A witch named Mother Ivey cursed the field (presumably to discomfort the farmer), saying that if anyone tried to plough it, the eldest son would die. When an eldest son was thrown from his horse and killed in the field, there were no further attempts at ploughing. But during the Second World War, the Home Guard dug trenches in it. The eldest son—the present owner's father—was killed shortly afterwards. The owner, a Mr. Hellyar, has said in an article that he would need a very good reason for trying to cultivate the field. Mrs. Mary Rees, the joint owner of the field, has attempted to break the curse by burying rags in a tin—obtained from a witch—in the field; but Mr. Bennett, the tenant farmer, refuses to be convinced.

Chapter V of Conan Doyle's *Coming of the Fairies* is called "Observations of a Clairvoyant in the Cottingley Glen, August 1921." The clairvoyant was a man named Geoffrey Hodson, a member of the Theosophical Society. In their Yorkshire Television interview, Elsie and Frances indicate that they regarded him as a "phoney"; yet this is hardly borne out by his books. Still, both Elsie and Frances insist they did see fairies with Hodson, even though they exaggerated what they saw to pull his leg. (They add, interestingly, that they never saw fairies again after this.) In 1952, Hodson published a small book called *Fairies at Work and Play*, introduced by Edward Gardner, the man who "discovered" Elsie and Frances. Gardner explains the traditional "occult'" belief that man possesses an "astral body," which can leave the physical body under certain circumstances—a matter we shall discuss in a later chapter. The astral body is said to be made of matter at a higher rate of vibration than physical matter. The human aura—a kind of energy that interpenetrates the human body—also seems to belong to this realm. According to Gardner, fairies and other such elementals belong on this level. Clairvoyants are able to see or sense this realm of vibrations which, according to Gardner, explains how Elsie and Frances could see fairies. One of the purposes of fairies, or nature spirits (sometimes called devas, a Hindu word) is to aid the growth of plants and seeds, hence their association with the woodland and open countryside and their absence in built-up areas. According to Gardner:

> None of the fairies, gnomes nor higher devas, can be said to have a fixed "solid" body, as we understand the term. They may occasionally materialize, *often using as the basis of this "materialization" the thoughtforms that peasants and children have built of them.* [my italics]

The latter comment seems to explain why Marc Alexander's friend saw an English pixie in New Zealand. "The elemental life rejoices to jump into a ready-made thought-form as much as an active child delights in dressing up." He adds that the natural form of elementals seems to be a "pulsing globe of light."

Hodson's book certainly provides the skeptic with plenty of material for satirical comment: brownies who affect a medieval style of attire, gnomes of "grotesque appearance, cadaverous and lantern-jawed," and black or peat brown in color; undines—water sprites—who are beautiful nude females, about six inches long, and Manx fairies with "soft and dreamy eyes." Yet his descriptions correspond closely to dozens of others on record. His description of a "crimson nature deva" is impressive:

> After a scramble of several hundred feet up a rocky glen we turned out to one side, on to the open fell where it faces a huge crag. Immediately on reaching the open we became aware, with startling suddenness, of the presence of a great nature-deva, who appeared to be partly within the hillside.
>
> My first impression was of a huge, brilliant crimsom, bat-like thing, which fixed a pair of burning eyes upon me. The form was not concentrated into a true human shape, but was somehow spread out like a bat with a human face and eyes, and with wings outstretched over the mountainside. As soon as it felt itself to be observed, it flashed into its proper shape, as if to confront us, fixed its piercing eyes upon us, and then sank into the hillside and disappeared.

He describes "tree devas" among a group of old firs and comments: "The nature spirits do not appear to be individualized as yet, working under a group consciousness," a point that may be worth bearing in mind when considering the more traditional poltergeist. When human beings lack a sense of identity, they often do apparently pointless things, simply to give themselves a sense of existence-through-action; this could explain the apparently aimless mischief of the poltergeist.

It is to the "earth devas" that the community at Findhorn, in Scotland, attributes its astonishing success in horticulture. In 1978, after a visit to the Edinburgh Festival, I spent a few days there to gain some first-hand impressions of this unusual community. It is situated on a bare spit of land sticking out into the Moray Firth, close to the town of Forres, and at first sight looks like any holiday site, with chalets and caravans. It had been founded in the early 1960s by Peter and Eileen Caddy, after Peter Caddy had lost his job as a hotel manager. Ever since a day in Glastonbury many years earlier, Eileen Caddy had been receiving "guidance" through some kind of inner voice. This voice now led them to live in a caravan on the bleak, sandy wastes of the Forres peninsula. They had no money, and Peter Caddy decided that they ought to grow their own food. But the sandy ground seemed completely unsuitable. They used seaweed and manure from local horses as fertilizer, while Eileen's voices assured them that all would be well. And the vegetables, when they began to grow, were extraordinary—giant cabbages and marrows and lettuces.

When I was at Findhorn, there were no longer giant vegetables—they explained that the purpose of these vegetables had been to demonstrate conclusively what could be done with love and "guidance." But the gardens were certainly an astonishing sight on that windy peninsula, with their magnificent beds of flowers.

I am not "community-minded." On the few occasions in my life when I have spent some time in communities—whether monastic or just vaguely "spiritual"—I have usually felt awkward and out-of-place, totally unable to share the group-spirit. Findhorn was an interesting exception. There was a great deal of talk about love and cooperation and guidance, yet the atmosphere seemed so friendly and normal that I felt perfectly at home there. It was strange to talk to people who claimed to have had contact with—and even seen—nature devas and fairies; yet at no point did I feel that I was among cranks, or even mystics.

A book, *The Magic of Findhorn*, by Paul Hawken, speaks at length about these nature spirits. In 1966, a scholar named Robert Ogilvie Crombie—known as Roc—came to help at Findhorn. Crombie describes to Hawken how, in March 1966, he was walking in the Edinburgh Royal Botanic Gardens when he experienced a state of heightened perception, then became aware "out of the corner of his eye," of a nature spirit in the form of the god Pan. "I could see shaggy legs and cloven hooves, pointed chin and ears, and two little horns on his forehead . . . He was naked, but his legs were covered with fine hair." When Ogilvie said "Hello," the creature looked startled and asked: "Can you see me?" "Yes." "I don't believe it. Humans can't see us."

"He told me," said Crombie, "that he lived in the Garden, and that his work was to help the growth of the trees. He went on to say that the Nature Spirits had lost interest in humans, since they have been made to feel that they are neither believed in nor wanted. He thought that men were foolish to think that they could do without the Nature spirits."

Crombie's account sounds like a piece of whimsy by Sir James Barrie; yet his descriptions of his encounters with nature spirits are precise and circumstantial. He speaks of an encounter with a faun, and with some kind of nature deva. "He stepped behind me and then walked into me so that we became one and I saw the surroundings through his eyes . . . The moment he stepped into me, the woods became alive with myriads of beings— elementals, nymphs, dryads, fauns, elves, gnomes, fairies . . . The Nature Spirits love and delight in the work they do and have to express this in movement."

Crombie and Peter Caddy met in 1965, and, according to Hawken, Crombie became Caddy's "ambassador" to the world of Nature Spirits. They were together at the Faery Glen, at Rosemarkie, when Crombie claimed to have encountered elves—which were invisible to Caddy; they were highly hostile because of the damage that has been done by man to the Glen. Crombie returned to Findhorn with Caddy, and "brought with him this intimate contact with the Nature Kingdom and Pan. He sought their help and cooperation in making the gardens an example of what could be accomplished among Man, the Devas and the Nature Spirits. He was told by Pan that a 'wild area' should be established in the garden to serve as a sanctuary for the Nature Spirits . . ." All this was to be done in close cooperation with nature. When Peter Caddy cut down some gorse bushes in blossom, Crombie encountered some furious elves, and had to explain to them that man may be ignorant and tactless, but is not fundamentally wicked.

Hawken describes a conversation with two of the chief gardeners.

> I asked Mathew and Leonard about Nature Spirits, and whether in "working" with them they actually perceived them. Both said that they did not perceive them directly, but both felt that they were intuitively guided by the Nature Spirits. Leonard told the story of how he went to several deeply-rooted bushes a few days before they had to be removed and quietly told them why they had to be moved. When the day came to remove them they could easily be pulled out of the ground with one hand as if they had completely released their "hold" on life. For comparison,

> Leonard went to one of the bushes that was not to
> be taken out and pulled on it. It wouldn't budge.

While at Findhorn, I mentioned that I have endless trouble with moles in my garden, and was told that they had also had the same problem, briefly; all that had been necessary was to explain to the moles that this was now a garden, and to ask them politely if they would mind moving elsewhere. The next day, the moles had moved out to more distant fields.

All this sounds preposterous only if we happen to be unaware that reports of these elementals and nature spirits have come from all parts of the earth and all ages. It is, of course, quite possible that it is all imagination and wishful thinking. But this is largely a matter of our "common sense" prejudices. The annals of the Society for Psychical Research are full of so many thousands of well-authenticated stories of poltergeists, apparitions and "specters of the living" that we can accept that they may have some basis in fact. It seems quite conceivable that "mediums" may be able to see things that are not visible to non-mediums. But when mediums claim to have seen fairies or elves, we become skeptical. The two-volume *Encyclopedia of Occultism and Parapsychology* contains an interesting entry under "Fairy Investigation Society."

> Formed in Britain to collate information on fairy
> sightings in modern times, with membership
> from various countries. The Society used to pub-
> lish an occasional Newsletter, but this has been
> suspended in recent years. It was found that
> although reports of Unidentified Flying Objects
> received tolerant public notice, reports of fairy
> sightings encouraged press ridicule. The Society
> is at present quiescent, but is planning to reorga-

nize on a basis which will protect members from undesirable notice.

In fact, fairy sightings are just as commonplace as UFO sightings, and just as circumstantial. Joe Cooper devotes a chapter of his book to sightings that he has personally noted down—for example, the group of Bradford students who saw fairies "who were circling and dancing" and were invisible to a direct gaze but discernible "at the corners of the eye." (This is a phrase that occurs repeatedly in fairy sightings.) Cooper goes on to mention the investigations carried out in Ireland by W. B. Yeats and Lady Gregory, which they recorded in a book, *Visions and Beliefs*, in 1920. A typical example is of a Mr. and Mrs. Kelleher of Wicklow, who told Yeats: "We had one of them in the house for a while ... It was in winter and there was snow on the ground, and I saw one of them outside, and I brought him in and put him on the dresser and he stopped in the house for a while, for about a week." His wife interrupted him to say: "It was more than that, it was two or three weeks." Mr. Kelleher goes on: "He was about fifteen inches high. He was very friendly ... When the boys at the public house were full of porter, they used to come into the house to look at him, and they would laugh to see him but I never let them hurt him."

When Chesterton met Yeats, he was struck by his down-to-earth attitude to fairies.

> Imagination!" he would say with withering contempt; "There wasn't much imagination when Farmer Hogan was dragged out of bed and thrashed like a sack of potatoes—that they did, they had 'um out and thumped 'um, and that's not the sort of thing a man wants to imagine." But the concrete examples were not only a comedy; he

used one argument which was sound, and I have
never forgotten it. It is the fact that it is not abnormal men like artists but normal men like peasants,
who have borne witness a thousand times to such
things; "it is the farmers who see the fairies."

It was a meeting with Yeats, and with his friend
George Russell—the mystic "AE"—that led Evans-
Wentz to begin the studies that led to his book *The Fairy
Faith in Celtic Countries*. In this book he explains what
he calls the "psychological theory" of fairy sightings—
which is not, as might be supposed, an attempt to dismiss
them as figments of the imagination. His theory is that it
is the experience of nature in such countries as Ireland
and Scotland that "impress man and awaken in him some
unfamiliar part of himself—call it the Subconscious Self, the
Subliminal Self, the Ego, or what you will—which gives
him the unusual power to know and to feel invisible or psychical influences. What is there, for example, in London, or
Paris, or Berlin, or New York to awaken the intuitive power
of man, that subconsciousness deep-hidden in him?"

One of the most fascinating parts of his book is an
interview with "AE," under the title "An Irish Mystic's Testimony." George Russell began to have "visions" at the
time of puberty, when he was torn by sexual conflicts. He
had his first mystical vision lying on the hill of Kil-
masheogue, when "the heart of the hills opened to me, and
I knew there was no hill for those who were there, and they
were unconscious of the ponderous mountains piled above
the palaces of light."

Evans-Wentz asked him about the *sidhe* or fairies
(the same word as Lethbridge's "sith"), and Russell replied
that he divided them into two classes: those which are shining,
and those which are opalescent and seem to shine by a light
within themselves. "The shining beings appear to be lower in

the hierarchies; the opalescent beings are more rarely seen and appear to hold the position of great chief . . . " Asked under what conditions he saw fairies, Russell replied:

> I have seen them most frequently after being away from a city or town for a few days. The whole west coast of Ireland, from Donegal to Kerry, seems charged with a magical power, and I find it easiest to see when I am there. I have found it comparatively easy to see visions while at ancient monuments [i.e. stone circles and monoliths] like New Grange and Dowth because I think such places are naturally charged with psychical forces, and were for that reason made use of long ago as sacred places.

Asked about the shining beings, Russell replies:

> It is very difficult to give an intelligible description of them. The first time I saw them with great vividness I was lying on a hill-side alone in the west of Ireland, in County Sligo: I had been listening to music in the air, and to what seemed to be the sound of bells, and was trying to understand these aerial clashings in which wind seemed to break upon wind in an ever-changing musical silvery sound. Then the space before me grew luminous, and I began to see one beautiful being after another.

He describes the "opalescent beings":

> There was at first a dazzle of light, and then I saw that this came from the heart of a tall figure with a body apparently shaped out of half-translucent or opalescent air, and throughout the body ran a radiant electrical fire, to which the heart seemed to be the centre. Around the head of this being

and through its waving luminous hair, which was
blown all about the body like living strands of
gold, there appeared flaming wing-like auras.

He states that he has had many similar visions, and
"I believe they correspond in a general way to the Tuatha
De Danann or ancient Irish gods." This was the phrase
mentioned in Geraldine Cummins' automatic script at the
Drumbeg Stone Circle.

Significantly, Russell says that "among the shining orders there does not seem to be any individualized
life ... Theirs is, I think, a collective life, so unindivid-
ualized and so calm that I might have more varied
thoughts in five hours than they would have in five
years." Asked if these beings might be "inimical to
humanity," Russell says that he certainly never felt this
about the shining beings. "But the water beings, also of
the shining tribes, I always dread, because I felt whenever I come into contact with them a great drowsiness of
mind and, I often thought, an actual drawing away of
vitality." Asked if there is a resemblance between lower
Sidhe orders and elementals, Russell replies: "The lower
orders of the *Sidhe* are, I think, the nature elementals of
the medieval mystics."

What is so important about Russell's testimony is
that we know we are not dealing with a crank or a liar.
Books like *Candle of Vision* and *Song and Its Foundation*
carry their own mark of authenticity; this man is a genuine
mystic with more than a touch of literary genius. Moreover,
Russell's comments on the "power" of the earth at sacred
sites—and these comments were made about 1910, before
anyone had heard of ley lines—is independently confirmed
by Lethbridge and other sources. Like Crombie at Findhorn,
Russell was usually in a state of "heightened awareness"
when he saw his visions of the *Sidhe*.

Evans-Wentz makes the important point that the faculty to see fairies or elementals is no different in kind from the faculty to see ghosts or spirits. This is confirmed by one of the most interesting records of "clairvoyance" of the nineteenth century: the diary edited by Cyril Scott under the title *The Boy Who Saw True*. Although anonymous, the diary carries a strong air of authenticity—Scott received it from the widow of the diarist after his death. In later life the diarist commented:

> As far back as I can remember I have been clairvoyant, and could see the disembodied entities and the human aura, which I referred to as "the lights." All the same, I had never heard of clairvoyance, and imagined it was a natural faculty which everybody possessed, like the five senses.

He saw Jesus standing at the end of his bed on several occasions, and also saw dead relatives. (When he reported this to his parents they usually got very angry; they consulted an oculist and a doctor to find out what was wrong with him.) Having made up his mind to avoid a little girl who wanted to play sex-games, he told his mother:

> I didn't tell her I was cross with Marjorie because she was always begging me to take down my pantaloons. I just told her I wanted to be by myself and watch the fairies playing among the stones and seaweed on the sea shore—which was true. And then she got very vexed and said she really didn't know what she was going to do with a little boy that was so untruthful . . .

Later he writes:

> There is a lovely old tree in Uncle John's garden, and today I sat a long time watching a funny old gnome who lives inside it, like one of the gnomes in

my fairy-tale book. He has great long thin legs and wears a red cap, though the rest of him is like the colour of the trunk of the tree. Some times he comes out of his tree and goes prancing about in the grass and looking so funny that I wanted to giggle, but was afraid I might make him offended.

At Keswick, on holiday, he records: "We have been here for a week now, and I have seen crowds of fairies and elves and mannikins and gnomes, and it's simply lovely."

On holiday at Harlech, in Wales, the boy again saw his deceased grandfather in the room, and was told by him that he would find it easier to see things here because the nature forces were so strong. And when the party went on a picnic to standing stones, the boy records: "I was able to see a lot of queer looking men dressed in long clothes sort of praying and doing peculiar things . . . "

In one interesting passage toward the end of the diary, the boy describes a visit to a "fortune teller" (who seems to be a spirit medium) with his tutor. He is able to see the spirit of a Red Indian "hanging about," and when she goes into a trance, the spirit "disappears" inside her, suggesting that mediumship may be a form of "possession." Another spirit is described as trying to get inside her "but didn't seem to be able to manage it properly," and the words the spirits speak to her become jumbled and incomprehensible when she repeats them—a point worth bearing in mind when studying the seance utterances of mediums. It seems clear that the writer often finds spirits rather comic and pretentious—as in an early entry when a spirit who seems to be a clergyman delivers a "message" full of religious platitudes.

In an entry for January 24, 1887, the boy reports a "spirit" as saying that some souls who didn't want to come back to earth again (presumably in reincarnated form) can become devas, "or sort of gods or what we imagine are angels." He also states that some devas become attached to a human being and become a person on earth "so as to be close to the person they love."

> He contended that stories about fairies becoming ordinary people like we are and you meet with in fairy tales are not all flapdoodle. He then told us the queerest thing of all. He stated that ages ago, I had been a deva . . . Because I'd been a deva, I was able to see a lot of things other people couldn't see . . .

It is a pity that Scott was unable to provide better evidence of the diary's authenticity (although his own account of the diarist's later life, and quotations from his letters, are certainly convincing). It contains much that seems to support views we have encountered elsewhere. The notion of spirits reborn as devas or angels rather than as human beings sounds as if it comes straight out of Kardec. "Devas who become attached to human beings" sounds like the "higher selves" encountered in some cases of multiple personality—like Doris Fischer's "guardian angel." What the diarist has to say about "lights" can be found in many books on the "human aura," and has been made the subject of an important study by Dr. Shafica Karagulla, a brain physiologist who became convinced that many doctors have an intuitive ability to diagnose illness through the "energy field" of the patient.

From the point of view of the present chapter, one of the most interesting passages in the book is the grandfather's comments about the Harlech area, that

> this is a very old part of the world and used to be part of a huge continent called Atlantis or some such name, most of which had gone down under

the sea, and that the something or other, I've forgotten the words (probably Nature-forces) were
very strong and would help me see things.

It was John Michell's book *The View over Atlantis*
(1969) that first put forward the notion—which we have
already encountered in Stephen Jenkins—that there is a
connection between nature forces at specific places and
"supernatural" manifestations. Michell devotes special
attention to the Great Pyramid, Stonehenge and Glastonbury Tor. The last is believed to be one of the oldest
sacred sites in England, and the point of intersection of a
large number of "ley lines." And between 1908 and 1920
Glastonbury was the subject of a remarkable series of
experiments that are often cited as conclusive proof of
the existence of "supernatural intelligences."

Glastonbury Abbey was founded in the fifth century
(according to tradition, by St. Patrick) and was destroyed
under Henry the Eighth, who was anxious to acquire its
land and revenues. Within a few generations, much of the
Abbey had been used by local farmers for building, In
1907, the ruins of the Abbey were bought by the nation for
£30,000, and an architect named Frederick Bligh Bond
was appointed to take charge of the excavations.

What the Church of England—Bond's employers—did not know was that he was deeply interested in
spiritualism, having been an enthusiastic student of
Catherine Crowe's *Night Side of Nature* since his teens.
One of the chief problems in excavating the abbey was
simply to know where to start digging. Old records suggested the existence of two chapels, built in the last few
decades of the abbey's existence as a monastic order; but
no plans existed, and no one knew where to start looking.
Bond decided to ask the cooperation of a friend named
John Allen Bartlett, who was able to produce automatic

writing. On the afternoon of November 7, 1907, Bartlett and Bond sat on opposite sides of a table in Bond's Bristol office, Bartlett holding a pencil over a sheet of paper, and Bond's own hand resting very lightly on top of it. Bond asked aloud the question: "Can you tell us anything about Glastonbury?" and the hand wrote rapidly: "All knowledge is eternal and is available to mental sympathy. I was not in sympathy with the monks—I cannot find a monk yet." But soon this difficulty was overcome, and Bartlett's hand was swiftly drawing an outline plan of the abbey, with a long rectangle stuck on its eastern end. It was signed "Gulielmus Monachus"—William the Monk. Bligh Bond thought the rectangle looked too big to be the missing chapel and asked for more information. "William the Monk" insisted that this *was* correct, and made a more precise drawing. He said it was the Edgar chapel, built by Abbot Bere. Another monk who called himself Johannes Bryant, monk and lapidator (stonemason) added more details.

Some of the communications were in Latin, some in Old English. The invisible communicators claimed to include Abbot Bere (the last abbot but one), Ambrosius the Cellarer, and Peter Lightfoot the clockmaker, as well as those already mentioned. Eventually, they were to provide detailed accounts—including the exact dimensions and color of the stained glass—of two chapels, the Edgar and Loretto chapels. They also mentioned two towers that had existed in the west end of the building, underground passages, and various other items that were totally unknown.

In 1908 the money for the excavations was obtained. Bond's workmen began to dig beyond the east wall. Soon they came upon a huge and unsuspected wall running north for thirty-one feet. Bond had found the Edgar Chapel, and its dimensions turned out to be exactly those that had been given by the monks. They had told him the chapel would be ninety feet long, which seemed too large. It proved to be eighty-seven feet long, and the wall and plinth added another three feet. The windows proved to be azure-colored, as the monks had foretold. Abbot Bere said the roof had been painted in gold and crimson; fragments of arch mouldings still had gold and crimson paint on them.

Bond's employers were delighted and astounded at his success; it seemed to them incredibly good luck that he seemed to dig trenches just where they would intersect a wall. Bond, understandably, decided to keep his source of information secret. The Church of England has always been thoroughly ambivalent about Spiritualism. Although Christians believe in life after death, the Church has always declined to be convinced that the "dead" who communicate at seances are really what they claim to be (an attitude, we have seen, that is to some extent justified). As late as 1936, the Archbishop of Canterbury commissioned a study on Spiritualism which eventually came up with the finding that its claims are probably true, and that there is no contradiction between its beliefs and that of the Church; the report was promptly suppressed.

So Bond decided to keep his own council about his "communicators," who called themselves the "Company of Glastonbury" or the "Watchers from the Other Side." At times, this must have been difficult. Digging on the south side of the nave, looking for the towers (which proved to be exactly where the monks said they would be), Bond came upon a skeleton of a man almost seven feet fall. Between his legs there was another skull. It could hardly have been a case of murder, since the head of the skeleton rested on a stone cradle. Then why no coffin, and whose was the other skull in the grave, Bond asked his communicators, and they provided a prompt explanation. The skeleton—which was almost seven feet fall—was that of Radulphus Cancellarius, Ralph the Chancellor, a Norman who slew Eawulf the Saxon in fair fight. Eawulf was buried, and Ralph the Norman lived on for many years, although his bones had been broken by Eawulf's axe. It was an odd coincidence that Eawulf's skull should have turned up in the grave. Ralph asked to be buried outside the church he loved so much; Eawulf had been buried nearby, and his skull rolled into the grave . . .

The communicators said that Ralph was the treasurer in the time of Abbot Thurstan, the first Norman abbot of Glastonbury. When William the Conqueror came to England in 1066, he installed his own Benedictine abbot on the Irish order already at Glastonbury. There was trouble, and some of the Irish monks were killed by Normans. Eawulf, according to the communicator, was the Earl of Edgarley, a nearby village, who was angry about the killings, and engaged Ralph in a combat which led to his own death.

There was no historical record of an Earl of Edgarley, so Bond set out to find one. After many years, he found an entry in the *Chronicle of Fabius Ethelwerd*, dated 866 A.D. which mentioned "Eanulf," a nobleman of Somerset, who was buried at Glastonbury; that might well be an ancestor of the later Eawulf—but Eanulf is not Eawulf, and a nobleman of Somerset is not necessarily the Earl of Edgarley. But the chronicle mentioned that Eanulf had died in the same year as Bishop Ealhstan of Scireburn. Then, in a chronicle called *Annals of the Exploits of Alfred*, dated 855 A.D., Bond found a reference to Eanwulf, earl of the district of Summurton, who had died at the same time as Bishop Ealhstan of Sherburne—obviously the same person. Summerton (Somerton) is a village close to Edgarley. And Eanwulf is spelled with both the *n* and *w*. So this Eanwulf was clearly an ancestor of the one who died in fair fight with Ralph the Chancellor, and he was, like his descendant, buried at Glastonbury. Obviously, the long-dead monks were right again. Moreover, when Bond examined the skeleton of Ralph, he found the forearm had been broken, as if from the blow of an axe, and had healed again—again supporting the story of the Watchers. The communicator added that the monks of Glaston had their reward, for a Saxon again was abbot for a time. History was able to confirm this: Abbot Thurstan's excesses caused his removal by William the Conquerer, and he was succeeded by the Saxon Herlewin.

By about 1917, Bond felt that it would probably be safe enough to tell the full story—after all, his excavations had been spectacularly successful. Besides, the Watchers told him that their aim was that Glastonbury should once again be recognized as a major spiritual center, and telling the full story must have seemed to Bond the first step in that direction. So he wrote a book called *Gate of Remembrance*, in which all the communications are printed in full, together with the story of Ralph and Eawulf, and many others that are equally fascinating (for example, how the monks made their fatal mistake in inviting Henry the Eighth as guest to the abbey, hoping to gain his goodwill; they only succeeded in arousing his greed, and their downfall was assured). *Gate of Remembrance* came out in 1918. And Bond very quickly found himself out of a job. The Church of England was outraged to find that it had been—even inadvertently—involved in Spiritualism. Bond was squeezed out; by 1921 he had been reduced to cleaning and cataloguing the discoveries at £10 a month; by 1922, excavations at Glastonbury had been stopped, and he was unemployed. The Church even ordered that his books should not be sold at the abbey bookshop, an order which applies to this day.

Bond went to America, lectured widely about his experiences, and became active in psychical research. But he was never allowed to return to Glastonbury—at one point, there was even an order forbidding him to enter the grounds. He continued to receive communications about the abbey—about underground passages, buried treasure, even about King Arthur and the Holy Grail (a skeleton believed to be that of Arthur was discovered at Glastonbury in 1190, with an inscription: "Here lies the renowned Arthur in the Isle of Avalon"). In later years, a group of Americans succeeded in getting permission to dig at Glastonbury—intending to follow up this information; but as soon as it leaked out that Bond was associated with the group, the trustees withdrew permission.

Oddly enough, Bond himself did not take it for granted that the "Watchers" were dead monks; he thought that it might have been his own unconscious mind—the same part of the mind that seems to be able to locate underground water with a divining rod, or even dowse for water over a map. But this was typical of Bond. He refused to allow his remarkable success to influence his judgment as a scholar.

He died in 1945, in his eightieth year. The "communications" of his later years still await investigation; if they prove to be half as accurate as the earlier ones, the results should be very remarkable indeed. And to some extent, his faith in Glastonbury—and that of the Watchers—has been justified. Since Bond left the abbey, Glastonbury has become increasingly a center of artistic and spiritual activity. The composer Rutland Boughton tried to turn it into an English Bayreuth, and wrote a number

of huge operas on King Arthur; but Boughton's socialism incensed the conservative people of Glastonbury and
his plans collapsed. John Cowper Powys' novel, *A Glastonbury Romance*, is one of the greatest novels of the
twentieth century, and its nature mysticism catches
something of the essence of that extraordinary area that
was once King Arthur's Avalon. Margaret Murray was
living in Glastonbury when she stumbled upon the
idea—which has since become a commonplace—that
witchcraft (or "wicca") was a pagan religion of nature
worship, and that it has continued secretly down the centuries in this form. The occultist Dion Fortune—one of
the early members of the magical Order of the Golden
Dawn—moved to Glastonbury, and spent the second
part of her life studying occultism in her house at the
foot of Glastonbury Tor. Geoffrey Ashe, the author of
King Arthur's Avalon, now lives in the house; the chalet
in which Dion Fortune practiced her magical rites is
haunted by a ghost that opens and closes doors and is
occasionally seen as a shape in the darkness. We have
already noted that Eileen Caddy first heard her "voices"
in Glastonbury. And when, in 1969, John Michell's *View
Over Atlantis* described Glastonbury as one of the major
"nodal points" of ley lines, the result was the "hippy
invasion" of Glastonbury that reached a climax in the
mid-1970s.

In *The Undiscovered Country*, Stephen Jenkins
mentions that when he was studying Buddhism in Tibet,
he asked his guru about Shambhala, the legendary sacred
place of the ancient Hindus. He was told that it was
located in England, at the place now called Glastonbury.

SIX

The Black Magic Connection

Considering that poltergeists have been recorded for more than a thousand years, and that eminent scientists have been studying them for about a century, it seems a little surprising that they are still regarded as an insoluble mystery. In the past two decades, there have been three major scientific studies of the poltergeist: Dr A. R. G. Owen's *Can We Explain the Poltergeist?*, William Roll's *The Poltergeist*, and *Poltergeists* by Alan Gauld and Tony Cornell. All three raise the question of whether poltergeists could be spirits of the dead or other types of disembodied entity; all three decide that this is unlikely, and that therefore poltergeists are probably some kind of manifestation of the unconscious mind: that is, of "spontaneous psychokinesis." Owen points out that a large number of children in poltergeist cases have mental problems; Roll notes that most objects tends to move counterclockwise, and suggests that there is some kind of whirlpool or psychic vortex that drags them into motion. But no one explains why poltergeist effects are so much more powerful than the kind of psychokinesis that has been studied in the laboratory.

There is, admittedly, one case that seems to be an exception to this rule. In the early 1970s, members of the Toronto Society for Psychical Research, under the direction of A. R. G. Owen, decided to try to manufacture a ghost. For this purpose, they invented the case history of a man called Philip, a contemporary of Oliver Cromwell, who had an affair with a beautiful gypsy girl. When Philip's wife found out, she had the girl accused of witchcraft and burned at the stake; Philip committed suicide.

Having elaborated this story and created a suitable background—an ancient manor house—they set about trying to conjure up the spirit of Philip. For several months, there were no results. Then one evening, as they were relaxing and singing songs, there was a rap on the table. They used the usual code (one rap for yes, two for no), to question the "spirit," which claimed to be Philip, and repeated the story they had invented for him. At later seances, Philip made the table dance all around the room, and even made it levitate in front of TV cameras.

Owen's group rightly regarded this "creation" of a ghost as something of a triumph, making the natural assumption that Philip was a product of their unconscious minds. But this assumption is questionable. What they did, in effect, was to hold a series of seances until they got results. Philip may have been a manifestation of their collective unconscious minds. Or he may have been another of those bored and untruthful "spirits" we have already encountered, joining in the game for want of anything better to do. The Philip case cannot be regarded as a proof or disproof of the psychokinesis theory.

The trouble is that when scientists start looking for patterns, they are inclined to see what they are expecting to see. If they are good scientists, they finally notice the facts that contradict their theories, and modify the theories. But this sometimes takes a very long time; sometimes, it never happens at all.

On the whole, the scientist is better off if he collects his facts by accident, little by little, so he can study them before he tries to fit them into a jigsaw puzzle. This is how the late Tom Lethbridge came to arrive at his theories about other dimensions of reality. It is also how Guy Lyon Playfair came to develop his own theories about the nature of the poltergeist.

In 1961, Guy Playfair had been down from Cambridge for two years—he had graduated in modern languages—and was finding life in England difficult and rather boring. And when he saw an advertisement in the personal column of *The Times* saying that teachers were wanted for Rio de Janeiro at a thousand pounds a year, he applied immediately. He signed a two-year contract, and at the end of the two years, decided to stay on in Rio as a free-lance journalist. He was reasonably successful, working as a correspondent for *Time* and *The Economist*, then as a writer in the information section of the U.S. Agency for International Development. When Nixon cut the foreign budget in 1971, Guy Playfair was offered a golden handshake, and took it; as a result he was able to move into a comfortable house with a good view of the harbor.

One of his neighbors was an American film actor called Larry Carr, and it was through him that Playfair became involved in the world of Brazilian Spiritism. One day, Carr asked him casually if he would like to go and watch a healer. Just as casually—having nothing better to do—Playfair accepted. They drove out to a Spiritist center in an area full of warehouses and run-down bars—"the kind of street you end up in if you get lost on the way to an airport." The healer, a man named Edivaldo, was late, having had to drive five hundred miles from his home town; he was a school-teacher who, with his spectacles and neat mustache, looked more like a bank clerk, or possibly a bank manager. When Playfair's group entered the consulting room, Edivaldo would prod the area that was giving the trouble, write something on a prescription pad, and pass on to the next. When Playfair's turn came, Edivaldo's hand went straight to the spot on his stomach which had been giving him trouble; pills were prescribed, and Playfair was told to come back later for "a little operation." A few months later, he went back for his operation. When he went into the room, an old man was lying on the bed, and Edivaldo was bending over him. The old man's stomach had been ripped open, exposing the entrails. Playfair admits that he did not observe as well as he might because he found it all too bewildering. "He was sloshing around in blood—it was a pretty gruesome sight." He looked away for a moment, and when he looked back again, the man's stomach was "all neat and tidy," and was being covered with bandage. The man got up, and was helped out by his wife. One of the helpers told Playfair to lie down on the bed. He unbuttoned his shirt. Edivaldo came over and ran his hand over his stomach, then his hands seemed to find what they were looking for and he pressed. Playfair felt a distinct plop and the hands entered his skin and went into his stomach. "My stomach immediately felt wet all over, as if I were bleeding to death. I could feel a sort of tickling inside, but no pain at all." He seemed to smell ether. Then it was all over and he was told he could get up and go home. He felt curiously stiff as if his middle had been anaesthetized, unable to bend. (This so intrigued him that he later tried to reproduce the same effect—with the aid of a friendly doctor who gave him twenty jabs of local anaesthetic; "It wasn't the same thing at all.") When he got home, he had to take off his shoes by kicking each one off with the other foot. On his stomach there was a jagged red line where Edivaldo had pressed his thumbs, and two bright red dots nearby.

Later, after a second operation, two more red dots appeared. And Playfair's stomach complaint, though not permanently cured, was considerably eased.

Some time later, Playfair interviewed Edivaldo, and heard the remarkable story of how he had become a healer. One evening in 1962 he had been called in to sit with a neighbor who had gone temporarily insane. He became unconscious, and during this period he smashed up the room. But when he recovered consciousness the woman was cured. Soon after that, he visited a woman who had become rigid after childbirth. He suddenly became rigid himself, and the woman's rigidity disappeared. It was clear that he was somehow "taking on" the illness of other people. A psychiatrist told him he was probably a medium, and advised that he should go to a Spiritist center. The first evening he did this, he again went into a trance. When he came to, he was being driven home, and was told that he had performed several operations. Apparently he was "taken over" by various spirits who had been surgeons while alive—a Dr. Calazans, a Frenchman called Pierre, a Londoner called Johnson, and a German called Dr. Fritz, who also worked through the famous psychic surgeon Arigó.

For another year, Playfair continued to spend a great deal of time at Edivaldo's surgeries, and watched innumerable operations—on one occasion, Edivaldo (or rather, the "spirit" who was controlling him) took Playfair's hand and thrust it into the open stomach. By this time, he was convinced he had discovered the subject he wanted to write about. He began to attend Spiritist sessions (Spiritism is Brazil's version of Spiritualism, and is based on the teachings of Kardec). When he encountered Hernani Andrade, founder of the IBPP—Brazilian Institute for Psycho Biophysical Research—he decided to move from Rio de Janeiro to São Paulo, a move that struck his friends as eccentric, since it is the equivalent of moving from, let us say, the Cornish Riviera to the industrial Midlands, or from Florida to Detroit. But Andrade offered Guy Playfair full and unrestricted access to his files, as well as the insights of forty years of Spiritism. As a consequence, Playfair's interest came to extend from psychic healing to poltergeists, reincarnation, black magic and life-after-death.

In São Paulo, he began by investigating more psychic surgeons. Then he heard of a case of poltergeist haunting, and offered to help the IBPP look into it.

At the time he heard about it, in 1973, the case had been going on for about six years. The family consisted of a Portuguese mother, who had been married to a Lithuanian immigrant, and was now divorced. She had a son and daughter, both adults. There had been the usual bangs and crashes, clothing and bedding had caught fire, or had been soaked with water; and as a result of these disturbances, the family had already moved house three times. There also seemed to be some evidence of black magic involved; photographs of a girl with thread stitched through it had been found in the house. The troubles had begun after the son of the family had married a girl called Nora.

It was to their house that Guy Playfair went in October 1973, taking his tape recorder with him. He sat up into the early hours of the morning, reading Frank Podmore—one of the early psychic investigators—on the subject of poltergeists. Podmore came to the conclusion that they are invariably fakes—an example of the kind of stupidity to which members of the SPR occasionally seem to be subject—and at this stage, Playfair thought he might well be correct. Finally, just as he was on the point of dozing off to sleep, he was awakened by a series of bangs that shook the house. The poltergeist had arrived. Playfair was struck by the timing—that it began as he was drifting off to sleep; the same thing had happened to Suzuko Hashizume, the investigator who had spent the previous night in the house. Playfair subsequently came to suspect that poltergeists have an uncanny sense of timing which suggest that they are able to foretell the exact moment when the investigator will be looking the other way.

There was something odd about the bangs. They caused nothing to vibrate, as such bangs normally do, and they seemed to echo longer than they should. Kardec has noted in *The Medium's Book:*

> Spirit sounds are usually of a peculiar character; they have an intensity and a character of their own, and, notwithstanding their great variety, can hardly be mistaken, so that they are not easily confused with common noises, such as the creaking of wood, the crackling of a fire, or the ticking of a clock; spirit raps are clear and sharp, sometimes soft and light . . .

In fact, a researcher, Dr. J. L. Whitton, subjected a tape-recording of "spirit raps" to laboratory analysis, and found that they are quite different in character from normal raps. Shown on a graph, an ordinary sound has a distinctive curve, rising and falling like the slopes of a mountain; spirit raps begin and end abruptly, like cliffs. In fact, they seem to be "manufactured" noises, as if the poltergeist had a BBC sound laboratory at its disposal and had to concoct the noises electronically.

The other odd thing about these loud bangs was that they did not disturb the four dogs, which had barked themselves frantic when Guy Playfair arrived; either they failed to hear them or accepted them as perfectly normal.

These bangs were followed by more, at intervals. Later, Playfair tried to make similar bangs by thumping the end of a broom handle on the floor; it was impossible to make them as loud.

The following night, when Playfair was asleep in the downstairs room, a footstool bounced down the stairs, then a bedroom drawer full of clothes was hurled out of a window into the yard. A pillow shot out from under Nora's head and flew across the room. Again and again, Playfair noted the poltergeist's sense of timing— how things seemed to happen precisely as people were falling asleep or waking up. Bumps happened mainly at night. Outbreaks of fire could happen at any time—on one occasion, a wardrobe full of clothes caught fire, and would have burned the house down if it had not been caught in time.

At this point, the IBPP called in their poltergeist-clearance team of mediums, who went into the house, sat in the kitchen, and asked their spirit guides to persuade the poltergeist to move. After this, there was silence for two weeks; then minor disturbances began again. This time, the family decided to call in a *candomblé* specialist—*candomblé* being one of the largest of Brazil's many African-influenced cults. This man brought with him a team of helpers. He told the family that this struck him as a particularly nasty case of black magic. Rites were performed and incense burned. And at the end of it all, the poltergeist finally left the family in peace. (At least, it had not reappeared by the time Playfair wrote his book about two years later.)

Now the notion of a poltergeist being associated with black magic is one that European investigators will find bizarre and outlandish. But in Brazil, it is taken for granted. Hernani Andrade is quoted as saying:

> In every case of person-directed poltergeist activity where I have been able to study the family background, there has been evidence that somebody in the house could be the target of revenge from a spirit. It may be a former lover who committed suicide, a jealous relation, a spiteful neighbor, or even a member of the same family bearing some trivial grudge. Any Brazilian is well aware

that this country is full of backyard *terreiros* of *quimbanda* (black magic centers) where people use spirit forces for evil purposes.

You can use a knife to cut bread or to cut a man's throat, and so it is with the hidden powers of man; they can be turned to good or bad ends, though they remain the same powers. To produce a successful poltergeist, all you need is a group of bad spirits prepared to do your work for you, for a suitable reward, and a susceptible victim who is insufficiently developed spiritually to be able to resist. Black magic is a really serious social problem in Brazil, and we must find reliable ways of getting rid of it.

Playfair goes on to cite another case in a town near São Paulo, in which the poltergeist made a number of attempts to burn the baby. One day, the baby disappeared, and the mother heard stifled cries coming from a laundry basket. She rushed to it and found the baby buried inside dirty clothes, in the process of stifling to death. The poltergeist also smashed furniture and wrecked the roof by pounding on it; when the family finally left the house, it looked as if it had been hit by a bomb. All this is, of course, no proof that poltergeists can be called up by magic, but it indicates that they can, on occasion, behave with something like demonic malevolence.

In his book *The Indefinite Boundary*, Playfair devotes a chapter called "The Psi Underworld" to this problem of magic and malevolence. He cites the disturbing case of eleven-year-old Maria Jose Ferreira, who, in December 1965, became the center of violent poltergeist activity. Pieces of brick began to fall inside the house, in Jabuticabal, near São Paulo, and an attempt at exorcism made things much worse. (Poltergeists, as we have seen, seem contemptuous of attempts to exorcise them.) A neighbor who knew about Kardec took the child into his house; things got worse, with bombardments of stones and eggs. One large stone descended from the ceiling and split into two; when someone picked up the two pieces, they snapped together as if they were magnetically attracted to each other. (We have already seen that poltergeists seem to have an affinity with electricity; it is interesting to speculate whether the force that caused the stones to snap together was an example of "ley power" or what Stringer calls "Telluric force.")

For a while, the poltergeist seemed to be in an amiable mood; Maria could ask for a flower or piece of candy, and it would instantly drop at her feet. Then, quite suddenly, the poltergeist began to attack her, biting her and slapping her on the face or bottom. It tried to suffocate her while she was asleep by placing cups or glasses over her mouth and nostrils. Then it began to set her clothes on fire.

When Maria was taken to a Spiritist center, the hope of "curing" her disappeared. A spirit came and spoke through the medium, saying: "She was a witch. A lot of people suffered, and I died because of her. Now we are making her suffer too . . . " Spirits, of course, are not invariably truthful, and this one may have been inventing the tale that Maria had been a witch in a previous existence. (Kardec, it must be remembered, taught reincarnation as an integral part of Spiritism.) Special prayers and appeals to the spirits failed to stop the attacks on the girl. And, when she was thirteen, she took a dose of ant killer in a soft drink and was dead when they found her. It would be interesting to know whether Maria took the poison deliberately, or whether the poltergeist placed it there, as the "Bell Witch" dosed John Bell's medicine.

All this makes it rather difficult to follow William Roll's reasoning in this central paragraph from his book on poltergeists:

> I do not know of any evidence for the existence of the poltergeist as an incorporeal entity other than the disturbances themselves, and these can be explained more simply as PK effects from a flesh-and-blood entity who is at their center. This is not to say that we should close our minds to the possibility that some cases of RSPK might be due to incorporeal entities. But there is no reason to postulate such an entity when the incidents occur around a living person. It is easier to suppose that the central person is himself the source of the PK energy.

The source, possibly. But the whole *cause* of the phenomena? It is true that in some cases—perhaps the majority—we can interpret the disturbances as an unconscious attempt by the "focus" to draw attention to his or her problems, as an unsuccessful suicide attempt does. Esther Cox's manifestations ceased after she was put in prison. But if Maria's unconscious aggressions were causing her clothes to catch on fire and bite marks to appear all over her body, surely the despair that finally drove her to suicide would have reached through to the rebellious part of her mind and persuaded it to stop? It simply fails to make sense to believe that Maria's own unconscious aggressions drove her to kill herself.

The point is underlined by one of the most remarkable cases described by Guy Playfair, that of a girl who inadvertently incurred a "black magic curse." He calls her Marcia F. and mentions that she had a master's degree in psychology. In May 1973, when Marcia was 28, she went for a family outing to the Atlantic coast near São Paulo. As they walked along the beach, Marcia noticed something lying in the sand—a plaster statue of a woman about six inches high, with much of the paint worn off by the sea. She took it back home to her apartment, which she shared with another girl—in spite of her aunt's warning that it might bring bad luck to take a statue of the sea goddess Yemanjá, which had obviously been placed there as an offering in return for some favor. But Marcia was a good Catholic as well as a psychology graduate, and thought that the talk of bad luck was nonsense. She placed it on her mantelpiece.

Some days later she was violently ill with food poisoning after eating chocolate. Then she began to lose weight and feel rundown. Her vitality was draining away. She began to spit blood, and X-rays showed a patch on her lung. Yet a few weeks later the patch had disappeared—it would normally have taken at least a year. After a holiday at home with her parents, Marcia returned to her flat. The pressure cooker blew up and she suffered second degree burns on her arms and face. Then the oven exploded, shooting out a sheet of flame toward Marcia; an engineer found the incident unexplainable. A few days later, a friend told her that at the moment when her pressure cooker had exploded, Marcia's photograph had jumped from the wall in her parents' home.

When a friend warned her again about the statue of Yemanjá, Marcia again dismissed the idea as preposterous.

Now she began to experience suicidal impulses. Crossing the road at a traffic light, she suddenly felt a powerful desire to fling herself under the oncoming cars. Opening the window of her apartment (which was on the fifteenth floor) she seemed to hear a voice inside her urging her to throw herself out.

And at this point, the first unmistakable suggestion of witchcraft entered the case. Her bedroom seemed to be full of presences. Then they entered her bed, and she felt herself being touched all over. And one night, she felt the presence of a male body, which moved on top of her; she felt a penis entering her, and lay there while the entity had sexual intercourse. This went on happening for several nights, until Marcia, wondering if she was going insane, went again to stay with her parents. There, by chance, they were visited by a Spiritist, to whom Marcia told her story. he advised her to go to the local *umbanda* center—*umbanda* is the most popular Afro-Brazilian cult. She also took along the statue, at the insistence of her flat mate. The director of the center listened to her story, and told her that her problem was undoubtedly a case of a black magic *trabalho* (work or job) being directed at her because of her removal of the statue. It was only then that Marcia looked more closely at the statue which had only patches of paint left on it—and realized suddenly that each remaining patch corresponded to a part of her own body that had been damaged: the burn marks on her arms, neck and face matched exactly the paint on the statue, and the patch on the back was just above the "patch" that had been found in her lung. The statue still had paint on its blue eyes, which was ominous. She took the advice of the director, and returned the statue to the spot on the beach where she had found it. Immediately, the run of bad luck ceased.

This story bears too many resemblances to Van der Post's account of the spirits of the Slippery Hills for us not to feel that the same kind of "earth forces" may have been involved. Van der Post's guide Samutchoso lamented that the spirits were losing their power—that ten years earlier they would have killed him for approaching without proper respect. The implication seems to be that the spirits in Brazil are still in possession of their full powers.

Playfair personally investigated the case of Marcia, and was not surprised when she told him that, as a result of her experience, her skepticism about "bad luck" and *trabalho* had given way to a more pragmatic attitude.

Playfair's observations received strong support from those of another investigator, his friend David St. Clair, who has described his experiences of Brazil in a book called *Drum and Candle*. He speaks of walking down Copacabana Avenue with some friends on his first night in Rio, and noticing on the pavement a circle of burning candles around a clay statue of the devil. When he reached out to touch it, one of his friends pulled him back, saying: "It's *despacho*—an offering to a spirit."

"But you surely don't believe that stuff?" said St. Clair. "You're all college graduates." His friends admitted that they did not believe in it—but nevertheless would not allow him to touch the statue.

After that, St. Clair saw many such offerings. He saw offerings of cooked chicken, and the starving beggars who stared at them, then quietly went away. He even saw a dog sniff at such an offering, then back away.

St. Clair has many stories about *candomblé* and Spiritism. But the final chapter of the book describes his own experience of a *trabalho*. He had been living in Rio de Janeiro for eight years, and had a comfortable apartment with a fine view. He also had an attractive maid named Edna, a pretty, brown-colored girl. She was, he assures the reader, a maid and nothing more. Her life had been hard; deserted by the father, her family had been brought up in a shack in a slum. She was obviously delighted with the comfort and security of her job with St. Clair. She joined a folk-dance group and, after a television appearance, became something of a local celebrity. And one day, St. Clair told her that he had decided it was time for him to leave Brazil. Edna was now doing so well that he had no doubt she would easily find another job; he told her he would give her six months' wages.

Then things began to go wrong. A book he had written failed to make any headway; his typist made a mess of it, then fell ill so that it sat in her desk for weeks. A New York publisher rejected it. An inheritance he was expecting failed to materialize. His plans for moving to Greece had to be shelved. A love affair went disastrously wrong, and a friend he asked for a loan refused it. He even fell ill with malaria.

One day, he met a psychic friend in the Avenida Copacabana; she took one look at him and said: "Someone has put the evil eye on you. All your paths have been closed."' A few days later, another friend wrote to say he had been to an *umbanda* session, and a spirit had warned him that one of his friends was in grave danger due to a curse; all his paths had been closed.

An actor friend who was also a Spiritist immediately divined that it was Edna who had put the curse on him. St. Clair thought this absurd. To begin with, Edna was a Catholic, and had often expressed her disapproval of Spiritism and *umbanda*. But his actor friend told him he had attended a spiritist session where he had been assured that David St. Clair's apartment was cursed. But how could Edna do that, St. Clair wanted to know. All she had to do, his friend replied, was to go to a *quimbanda*—black magic—session and take some item of his clothing, which could be used in a ritual to put a curse on him. And now his friend mentioned it, St. Clair recalled that his socks *had* been disappearing recently. Edna had claimed the wind was blowing them off the line.

St. Clair told Edna he believed himself to be cursed; she pooh-poohed the idea. But he told her he wanted her to take him to an *umbanda* session. After much protest, she allowed herself to be forced into it.

That Saturday evening, Edna took him to a long, white house in a remote area outside Rio. On the walls were paintings of the devil, Exú. Toward midnight, drums started up, and the negroes sitting on the floor began to chant. A ritual dance began. Then the *umbanda* priestess came in like a whirlwind—a huge negress dressed in layers of lace and a white silk turban. She danced, and the other women began to jerk as if possessed. The priestess went out, and when she came in again, was dressed in red, the color of Exú/Satan. She took a swig of alcohol, then lit a cigar. After more dancing, she noticed St. Clair, and offered him a drink from a bottle whose neck was covered with her saliva. Then she spat a mouthful of the alcohol into his face. After more chanting, a medium was asked who had put the curse on him. She replied: "The person who brought him here tonight! She wants you to marry her. Either that, or to buy her a house and a piece of land . . . " The priestess ordered Edna to leave. Then she said: "Now we will get rid of the curse." There was more ritual drumming and dancing, then the priestess said: "Now you are free. The curse has been lifted, and it will now come down doubly hard upon the person who placed it on you." When he protested, he was told it was too late—it had already been done.

Three days later, St. Clair received a telegram from a magazine, asking for a story; he had suggested it to them months before but they had turned it down. Now, unexpectedly, they changed their minds, and sent him money. A week later, the inheritance came through. The book was accepted. And ten days later he received a letter asking if his broken love affair could be restarted where it had left off. Then Edna became ill. A stomach-growth was diagnosed, and she had to have an operation for which St. Clair paid. But her health continued to decline. She went to see an *umbanda* priest, who told her that the curse she had put on St. Clair had rebounded on her, and that she would suffer as long as she stayed near him. She admitted trying to get him to marry her by black magic. She declined his offer to buy her a house or an apartment, and walked out of his life.

In *The Indefinite Boundary*, Playfair goes on to discuss black magic. It seems, he says, to be based on an exchange of favors between incarnate and discarnate-man and spirit.

> Incarnate man wants a favor done; he wants a better job, to marry a certain girl, to win the state lottery, to stop somebody from running after his daughter . . . Discarnate spirits, for their part, want to enjoy the pleasures of the flesh once more; a good square meal, a drink of the best *cachaça* rum, a fine cigar, and perhaps even sexual relations with an incarnate being.
>
> The spirit has the upper hand in all this. He calls the shots. he wants his meal left in a certain place at a certain time, and the rum and the cigar had better be of good quality. Incarnate man is ready to oblige, and it is remarkable how many members of Brazil's poorest classes, who are about as poor as anyone can be, will somehow manage to lay out a magnificent banquet for a spirit who has agreed to work some magic for them . . .
>
> Who are these spirits? Orthodox Kardecists and *Umbandistas* see them as inferior discarnates living in a low astral plane, who are close to the physical world, not having evolved since physical death . . . In *Umbanda* they are known as *exús,* spirits who seem to have no morals at all, and are equally prepared to work for or against people.

Like Mafia gunmen, they do what the boss says
without asking questions.

He adds the interesting comment:

> The *exú* reminds us of the traditional spirits of the
> four elements; the gnomes of earth, the mermaids
> of water, the sylphs of air, and the salamanders of
> fire. These creatures are traditionally thought of
> as part human and part "elemental," integral
> forces of nature that can act upon human beings
> subject to certain conditions. There is an enor-
> mous number of *exús*, each with his own special-
> ity. To catch one and persuade him to work for
> you, it is necessary to bribe him outright with
> food, drink and general flattery. An *exú* is a vain
> and temperamental entity, and despite his total
> lack of morals he is very fussy about observing
> the rituals properly.

All this sounds so much like the poltergeist that it
is tempting to feel that we have finally pinned down his
true nature and character.

Studying the background of the Ipiranga case—
already described—Playfair found strong evidence that
the poltergeist had been unleashed on the family by
black magic. In 1968 an "offering" of bottles, candles
and cigars had appeared in their garden, indicating that
someone was working a *trabalho* against the family.
Playfair lists the suspects. A former boyfriend of Iracy,
the daughter, had committed suicide; then there was an
elderly aunt who had died abandoned by the rest of the
family, and may have borne a grudge. Then Iracy had
had a love affair with a man who was (unknown to her)
already married; the man's wife could have organized
the *trabalho*. Or it could possibly have been some for-

mer disgruntled lover of Nora, the girl who married the son of the family; photographs of Nora's husband were frequently disfigured, and they found many notes claiming that she was having an affair with another man.

Playfair mentions that at the time he was investigating the Ipiranga case, Andrade was studying one in the town of Osasco where there was definite evidence that a poltergeist was caused by black magic. Two neighboring families were having a lengthy dispute about boundaries, and one of the families ordered a curse against the other. The result was that the other family was haunted by a poltergeist that caused stones to fall on the roof, loud rapping noises, and spontaneous fires. One original feature of this case was that when the family went to ladle a meal out of a saucepan—which had been covered with a lid—they found that the food had been spoiled by a large cigar.

Candomblé—one of the bigger Afro-Brazilian cults—seems to have originated among freed negro slaves in the 1830s, and it has the same origin as voodoo, which began in Haiti when the first slaves arrived early in the seventeenth century. This, in turn, originated in Africa as ju-ju. Europeans are naturally inclined to dismiss this as the outcome of ignorance and stupidity; but few who have had direct experience of it maintain that skeptical attitude. James H. Neal—whose anecdote about the immovable tree has already been cited—describes his own experience in *Ju-Ju in My Life*. When, as chief investigations officer for the Government of Ghana, Neal caused the arrest of a man who had been extorting bribes, he found that he was the target for a ju-ju attack. It began with the disappearance of small personal items of clothing as in the case of David St. Clair. One day he found the seat of his car scattered with a black powder; his chauffeur carefully brushed it off, and urinated in it to destroy its power. Then, one night, Neal became feverish, and experienced pains from head to foot. He felt he was going to die. Suddenly, he found himself outside his body, looking down at himself on the bed. He passed through the bedroom wall, and seemed to be traveling at great speed, when suddenly he seemed to receive a message that it was not yet his time to die; he passed back into his room, and into his body. After this he spent three weeks in a hospital suffering from an illness that the doctors were unable to diagnose. An African police inspector told him he was being subjected to a ju-ju attack. More black powder was scattered in his car. One night, lying in bed, he felt invisible creatures with long snouts attacking his solar plexus and draining his vitality. A witch-doctor who was called in described in detail two men who were responsible for the attacks—giving an accurate description of two men involved in the bribery case. Finally, after a ceremony performed by a Muslim holy man—who surrounded the house with a wall of protection—Neal slowly recovered. The white doctor who tended him agreed that he had been the victim of a ju-ju attack.

He also describes how, not long after the "exorcism" ritual, his servant killed a cobra outside his bungalow. As they were exulting about the death of the snake, Neal noticed another snake—this time a small grey one—slithering toward them. When he drew the servant's attention to it, the man went pale. This, the man said, was a "bad snake"—meaning a snake created artificially by witch-doctors; a man bitten by such a snake has no chance of recovery. Neal was understandably skeptical. Then he saw the snake—which was still slithering at a great speed toward them—come to a halt as if against an invisible wall. It had encountered the "wall of protection" put there by the holy man. With a single stroke, the servant chopped off its head with a cutlass. No blood came out. Soon after this, Neal began to itch all over. Two perfectly healthy trees just beyond the "wall of protection" split down the middle with a loud crash. Consultation with another skilled sorcerer elicited the information that both Neal and his servant were victims of a new ju-ju attack, but that because of the protection, Neal could not be seriously harmed; the itch was the worst the magician could do.

This kind of witchcraft can be found in primitive societies all over the world. In a book called *Mitsinari*, a Catholic priest, Father André Dupreyat, describes his years in Papua, New Guinea. When he clashed with local sorcerers, he was also placed under a "snake curse." One day, walking toward a village, he was surprised to see a silvery-colored snake wriggling toward him. The villagers all scattered. Knowing it would have to lower its head to come closer, Dupreyat waited until it was no longer in a position to strike, and killed it with his stick. The next day, when he was lying in a hut, a snake lowered itself from the roof-beam and dropped on to his chest. He lay perfectly still until it slid down to the floor, when he was able to kill it with a stick. A few days later, as he lay in a hammock, a native warned him that two black snakes had writhed up the support of the hammock, and were close enough to bite him. They cautiously handed him a knife and told him when to strike; he succeeded in killing both snakes.

Dupreyat also has a remarkable account of a local sorcerer named Isidoro who was able to turn himself into a cassowary (a kind of ostrich). One evening as they all sat talking of Isidoro, they heard the distinctive sound of a cassowary running, and Isidoro came into the hut. He talked with them for a while, then said he would be staying in a house in the village overnight, and went out.

They again heard the sound of a cassowary running. Dupreyat checked, and found that Isidoro was not in the house where he had claimed he would be staying. The next day, he visited Isidoro's village—five hours away on the other side of the mountain. There he was greeted by Isidoro. Villagers assured him that Isidoro had spent the early part of the previous evening in the communal hut, then gone away at seven o'clock. By nine o'clock he had been with Dupreyat, a five-hour journey away on the other side of the mountain. And at dawn, he had been observed in his own village again. Yet in the dark, it was at least an eight-hour journey away.

James Neal's own experiences of witchcraft in Ghana ended disastrously. Leaving his home in a hurry, on a morning when he intended to go to the Accra races—to capture a race-course gang—he left behind a protecting amulet that had been given him by the holy man. From an almost empty grandstand he watched the men being arrested by his own officers. Then, walking down from the grandstand, with no one within twenty yards of him, he was pushed violently, and fell. The multiple fractures he sustained kept him in hospital for months; and when he recovered, his broken bones prevented him from continuing his police work and he was forced to resign. The holy man, who came to see him in hospital, told him that he had been pushed by an "astral entity." Neal insists that, as he was pushed, he twisted round to see who was responsible, and that there was no one there.

On the evening of September 9, 1977, Guy Playfair attended a lecture on poltergeists at the Society for Psychical Research, and found himself sitting next to a man named Maurice Grosse. After the lecture, Grosse announced that he was in the middle of a case, and would be glad of some help. No one volunteered. A few days later, Playfair heard a broadcast on BBC Radio 4 in which Maurice Grosse described some of the amazing things that were happening in the house of the Harper family down at Enfield. Reluctantly—because he had just finished a book and was looking forward to a holiday—Playfair decided to offer some help.

The Enfield poltergeist had put in its first appearance on the evening of August 30, 1977. There were four children in the house: Rose, thirteen, Janet, eleven, Pete, ten and Jimmy, seven; their mother was separated from her husband. Pete and Janet shared a bedroom. That evening, just after Pete and Janet had gone to bed, their beds began to shake in an odd way. They called their mother, but the shaking had stopped. She assumed they were "larking about" and told them to get to sleep. The next evening, the children heard a shuffling noise, like a chair moving. Mrs. Harper came in and asked them to be quiet. The room all seemed to be perfectly normal. But when she switched off the light, she also heard the shuffling noise. It sounded like someone shuffling across the room in slippers. Then there were four loud, clear knocks. And when Mrs. Harper put the light on again, she saw the heavy chest of drawers moving on its own. It slid a distance of about eighteen inches across the floor. She pushed it back. It slid back again. She tried to push it back, but it wouldn't budge—it was as if someone was standing on the other side, preventing it from moving. Mrs. Harper began to shake with fear. "All right, downstairs everybody . . . " She went next door and asked the help of their neighbors. Vic Nottingham and his son went back to the Harpers' house, and searched it from top to bottom. Then the knocking started. Vic Nottingham rushed outside, to see if it was some practical joker on the other side of the wall. There was no one there.

They sent for the police. When the lights were switched off, the knocking started. Then, in the light from the kitchen, everyone saw a chair that was wobbling into motion. It slid toward the kitchen for three or four feet.

The police could do nothing about ghosts, so they left. And the Harper family slept in the living-room.

The next day, all was quiet until evening. Then the poltergeist began throwing things. Marbles and Lego bricks came zinging through the air as if shot from a catapult. When someone picked up one of the marbles, it was found to be burning hot.

Wondering what to do, Mrs. Harper allowed her neighbor to phone the *Daily Mirror*. A reporter and photographer arrived, but saw nothing. They decided to go in the early hours of the morning. As soon as they were outside, the Lego bombardment began again. Mrs. Harper rushed out and told them. As the photographer came in, his camera raised, a Lego brick flew across the room and hit him over the right eye. It caused quite a bruise—one of the few examples of a poltergeist actually hurting someone. Yet the photograph showed no Lego brick flying towards him—it must have been just beyond the range of the camera. It was later to occur to Guy Playfair that the poltergeist seemed to go to great trouble not to be *seen* doing things.

The *Daily Mirror* contacted the Society for Psychical Research, and the SPR contacted Maurice Grosse, a recent member who was looking for a case to investigate. A few days later, Guy Playfair made his way down to the house in Enfield. It was the beginning of a two-year involvement.

Playfair was inclined to suspect Janet, an extremely lively little girl. He asked Mrs. Harper to keep a special watch on her, adding: "Even if Janet is playing tricks, it may not be her fault." For he had come across a curious discovery made by earlier researchers like Nandor Fodor and William Roll: that the "focus" of a poltergeist case may throw things—in the ordinary way—without being aware of it. Through a one-way mirror Roll saw one of his "suspects" throwing things; yet a lie detector test showed the suspect was telling the truth when he denied throwing anything. The implication seems to be that a poltergeist can get *inside* someone and "make them do things."

While Playfair and a *Mirror* photographer waited in the dark in Janet's bedroom, a marble landed with a bang on the floor. The odd thing was it did not roll, as a marble normally would. It stayed put; Playfair tried hard to duplicate this, but found it impossible; unless dropped from very close to the floor, a marble will roll, particularly on smooth linoleum.

When the photographer tried taking a test picture, all three flash-guns on all three cameras failed to work. When he examined the guns, he found that they had all been drained of power—although he had charged them a few minutes before trying to take the photograph.

Playfair tried tying the leg of Janet's bedside chair to the leg of her bed. He used wire. Within minutes, the chair had fallen over; the wire had been snapped. He bound it with several twists of wire. Not long after, the chair fell over again—the wire had snapped. A big armchair tipped over, then the bed shot across the room. A book flew off the shelf, hit the door, proceeded on at right angles, and landed upright on the floor; it was called *Fun and Games for Children*. As they looked at one of the pillows on a bed, an indentation appeared on it, as if an invisible head was resting there. The head seemed to be a small one, which led Mrs. Harper to voice her suspicion that this was the ghost of a four-year-old girl who had been suffocated by her father in a nearby house; some of the furniture from the house had found its way into the Harper home, and Mrs. Harper had already thrown it out, suspecting it might be the cause of the trouble. Clearly, she was mistaken.

There came a point when Guy Playfair began to feel that the "entity" wanted to communicate—it kept up its knocking on one occasion for two hours and a half. A medium named Annie Shaw came to the house with her husband George. Annie went into a trance, then suddenly screamed, "Go away," and began to cackle. When her husband spoke to her, she spat at him. She moaned: "Gozer, Gozer, help me. Elvie, come here." George spoke firmly to the "entity" that had taken over her body, advising it to go away and leave the Harper family alone. When Annie returned to normal, she stated that the haunting centered around Janet, and that there were several entities behind it, including an old woman. George added: "This Gozer is a nasty piece of work, a sort of Black Magic chap. The other one, Elvie, is an elemental." Annie explained that the auric field around Janet and her mother was "leaking," and that when this happens, poltergeists can use the energy for their manifestations. The Shaws "cleaned" their auras by a well-known technique—moving their hands from head to foot around the contours of the body, about six inches away. The trouble, said the Shaws, was due to the negative atmosphere in the house—and Mrs. Harper admitted that she *did* feel bitter about her ex-husband, and had been keeping the feeling bottled up for years. One way of preventing a poltergeist from manifesting itself, said Annie Shaw, was to learn to control one's energies, so they stop "leaking."

For a few weeks after this healing session, the manifestations almost ceased. Then, in late October, they started up again—furniture flung around, beds shaking, blankets ripped off beds—Playfair and Grosse recorded about four hundred incidents in a brief space. Pools of water also began to appear on the kitchen floor—pools with very distinct outlines, as if made by pouring water from a jug immediately onto the linoleum. One puddle was shaped like a human figure.

The entity began doing things that could have caused serious damage. One evening, an iron grille from the bottom of a fireplace sailed across the room and landed on Jimmy's pillow—a little closer, and it could have killed him. The next evening, the heavy gas fire was ripped out of the wall—it had been cemented into the brickwork. (Poltergeists can display frightening strength; in *The Flying Cow*, Playfair records a poltergeist that lifted a Jeep forty yards through the air.)

On the advice of the veteran researcher E. J. Dingwall, Playfair tried communicating with the "entity." When it rapped, he rapped back. When he asked it to use the usual code—one rap for yes, two for no—there followed a volley of loud raps. Playfair asked: "Don't you realize *you are dead*?" which seemed to infuriate it. Crashes came from a bedroom, and when they rushed up, the room was in chaos, with objects scattered all over. Evidently "Gozer" was not anxious to make polite conversation.

Maurice Grosse was more successful a few weeks later. "Did you die in this house?" The rap-code indicated "Yes." "Will you go away?" A loud thud said "No." The entity indicated that it had lived in the house for a long time—more than thirty years. It had left fifty-three years ago. When the raps seemed to become non-sensical, Grosse asked: "Are you having a game with me?" A cardboard box containing cushions flew across the room and struck Grosse on the forehead. Guy Playfair, who was outside the door with his tape recorder (the poltergeist had taken a dislike to him), recorded all this on tape; the box made an odd, swishing noise. Yet no one actually saw the box flying across the room. It was as if it had vanished from its old position, and rematerialized as it struck Maurice Grosse on the head.

Like most poltergeists, this one was getting into its stride as it became more skilled. The children began to see shadowy figures, and seven-year-old Jimmy was terrified when he looked toward the wall, and saw a disembodied face—an old man's face with big white teeth—staring at him. In front of Grosse and several other witnesses, it threw Janet off her chair, across the room, a distance of eight feet. As Rose, the eldest girl, went upstairs, the ghost literally pulled her leg—the investigators found her standing on one leg, the other stretched out behind her, unable to move. She was only able to walk when Grosse twisted her sideways.

They decided to ask the ghost to write out a message, and left a pencil and paper. A few minutes later, they found that someone had written: *"I will stay in this house. Do not show this to anyone else or I will retaliate."* Another message read: *"Can I have a tea bag."* Mrs. Harper placed one on the table and, a few moments later, a second tea bag appeared beside it.

When Mrs. Harper's husband came to call to pay his maintenance money, he expressed disbelief in all this, and Mrs. Harper showed him the message—forgetting that it had ordered her not to. She said out loud: "I'm sorry, I forgot." Another piece of paper appeared on the table: *"A misunderstanding. Don't do it again."*

A few days after this, the Society for Psychical Research sent a team of investigators to look at the place. They had evidently decided that the poltergeist activity was all due to the girls. Balloons full of water were placed under the beds for some reason; and, when they burst, water dripped through the ceiling. When the team had left, Grosse and Playfair—who had been present—had some irritable things to say about the SPR's obsession with fraud.

By now it was very clear that Janet was the poltergeist's main target. She was often thrown out of bed seven or eight times before she succeeded in getting to sleep. When she fell asleep, she twitched and moaned; Playfair began to feel increasingly that she was "possessed." He recalled the case of Maria Ferreira, the South American girl who had been driven to suicide by a poltergeist, and felt some misgiving. On one occasion, with a photographer in the bedroom, Janet was hurled out of bed—the event was photographed—and then, as the photographer and Maurice Grosse tried to hold her, she went into convulsions, screamed hysterically, and bit Grosse. When finally put back into bed, she fell asleep. Later, there was a crash, and they found her lying on top of the radio set, still fast asleep.

The following night, Janet had more convulsions, and wandered around, talking aloud. "Where's Gober. He'll kill you."

Two of Playfair's friends from Brazil, who happened to be in London, called at the Enfield house, and succeeded in bringing Janet out of one of her trance-like states. Their view was that Janet was a powerful medium and ought to be trained to use her powers. One of the two Brazilian mediums wrote on a sheet of paper: "I see this child, Janet, in the Middle Ages, a cruel and wanton woman who caused suffering to families of yeomen—some of these seem to have now to get even with the family." Soon after this, Janet began producing drawings, in a state of semi-trance; one of them showed a woman with blood pouring out of her throat, with the name "Watson" written underneath. Other drawings continued this theme of blood, knives and death. When Playfair asked Mrs. Harper if she knew of a Watson, she replied that it was the name of the previous tenants of the house. Mrs. Watson had died of a tumor of the throat.

Playfair asked Janet if she could bend a spoon like Uri Geller. He glanced away for a moment, as Mrs. Harper spoke to him; when he looked back, the spoon was bent in the middle—it was lying in the center of the table. Janet said she had experienced a sudden feeling of headache as the spoon bent.

In December 1977, the poltergeist began making noises—whistling and barking sounds. Maurice Grosse decided to try asking it to speak. "Call out my name, Maurice Grosse." he went out of the room, and a strange voice said: *"Maurice . . . O . . . "* Grosse asked it to say its own name. *"Joe Watson."* When Guy Playfair asked: "Do you know you are dead?" the voice said angrily: *"Shut up!"* And to further requests that it go away, it replied: *"Fuck off."* Joe seemed to be incapable of polite conversation. When another researcher, Anita Gregory, asked it questions she was told to bugger off.

The investigators wondered whether Janet could be simulating this voice, although it seemed unlikely; it was a masculine growl, and had an odd quality, as if electronically produced. (I have one of Guy Playfair's tape recordings of the voice, and it reminds me strongly of a record I have of an electronic brain singing "Daisy, Daisy.") The voice would not speak if the investigators were in the room. But their attempts were rewarded with long sentences. The voice now identified itself as Bill, and said it had a dog called Gober the Ghost. Asked why it kept shaking Janet's bed it replied: *"I was sleeping here."* "Then why do you keep on shaking it?" *"Get Janet out."* Rose asked: "Why do you use bad language?" *"Fuck off you,"* replied Bill. And when Janet asked why it played games with them it replied: *"I like annoying you."* "Where do you come from?" *"From the graveyard."* It even named the graveyard—Durant's Park, which is in the area.

At Guy Playfair's suggestion, Rose asked why it didn't go away. *"I don't believe in that."* "Why? What's so different about being up there?" asked Rose, and received the wistful reply: *"I'm not a heaven man."* It went on to say in a jerky manner: *"I am Bill Haylock and I come from Durant's Park and I am seventy-two years old and I have come here to see my family but they are not here now."*

On the tape, the words come out one by one, as if the speaker is so breathless that he can only get out one at a time. (The voice is so obviously that of an old man that the notion of Janet producing it by ventriloquism is absurd.) Rose's next question is interrupted by a furious outburst: *"You fucking old bitch, shut up. I want some jazz music. Now go and get me some, else I'll go barmy."*

Maurice Grosse's son Richard paid a visit to the house and succeeded in holding a lengthy conversation with the voice. When he asked it what it had done with thirty pence that had vanished it said it had hidden the money in the radio—which is where it was found. Asked how he had died, "Bill" replied that he went blind and had a hemorrhage—he fell asleep and died in a chair downstairs.

Richard Grosse found that if he looked at Janet's face while the voice was speaking, it would stop. If he *thought* of looking around, the voice would also stop, as if reading his mind.

Another researcher named David Robertson had no difficulty getting the voice to talk, although the main thing it wanted to discuss was girls' periods. Then the ghost was asked to levitate Janet, and then draw a line round the light on the ceiling. Robertson withdrew outside, and heard Janet being bounced up and down on the bed. Suddenly there was a gasp and silence. He tried to open the door and found that it was jammed tight. When it opened again, Janet was on the bed and there was a red line around the light. Janet claimed that she had floated through the wall, into the bedroom of the next house—belonging to Peggy Nottingham (who was with David Robertson at the time). She described it as "all white"— a fairly accurate description of the light wallpaper. Peggy asked her to try doing it again. and went next door to see what happened. Janet was not there. But on the floor, there was the book *Fun and Games for Children*, which had been on the mantelpiece in Janet's bedroom a few minutes earlier.

Robertson handed a red plastic cushion to Janet and said: "See what you can do with that." *"All right, David boy,"* said the invisible entity—which seemed to like Robertson—*"I'll make it disappear."* Robertson went out of the room, and there was a cry from Janet. When he went back, the cushion had vanished; the window was tightly shut. But a neighbor who was passing the house at that moment suddenly saw a red cushion appear on the roof. Another neighbor later testified that she had also seen the cushion as she walked past. And looking at Janet's bedroom window, she had seen books and cushions striking the window, and Janet rising into the air—in a horizontal position—and descending again, as if being bounced on a trampoline. "She was definitely lying horizontal, coming up and down." Guy Playfair tried bouncing on Janet's bed, and found that no matter how hard he bounced, it was impossible to get up into the air.

Playfair was struck by Janet's comment that when she had floated through the wall into Peggy's bedroom, it was "all white" and there were no colors. He arrived at the conclusion that what had happened was that Janet had had an "out of the body" experience—other astral travellers have observed the lack of color during "OOBs." But this fails to explain how the book also passed through the wall.

Was there, Playfair asked himself at this point, any more the poltergeist could do to demonstrate its versatility? In fact, it went on to produce a whole variety of new phenomena. It became rather more violent with Janet, making an attempt to suffocate her with the curtains, and making a knife follow her around in the air. (The voice claimed that this was the doing of another entity called Tommy.) It produced a biscuit out of nowhere and stuck it into Janet's mouth. It put butter and cheese on a piece of bread. (When Guy Playfair tried to touch it the voice rasped, *"Leave it alone."*) It smeared ordure around the place. It began causing fires in closed drawers—fires which, fortunately, extinguished themselves. It produced some appalling stinks, like rotten cabbages. After a visit from the psychic Matthew Manning, it began scrawling obscene messages on the kitchen walls. When the two pet goldfish died, the "voice" claimed it had electrocuted them by accident (which, if true, seems to confirm that poltergeists use some form of electrical energy).

A medium called Gerry Sherrick told the Harpers that they had all been together in a previous existence and that the girls had dabbled in witchcraft. He also told them he felt that a nasty old woman was connected with the "haunting" and that she had lived near Spitalfields market. Had there been any smells like rotten vegetables? After this, he went into a trance and an old woman's voice announced: "I come here when I like . . . I'm not bleedin' dead and I'm not going to go away." Sherrick performed "psychic healing" on the family—to heal the "leaks" that were causing the trouble. After his visit, the Enfield house became quiet for several weeks, as it had after the two previous visits by mediums.

The case was beginning to create something more like a normal haunting. Mrs. Harper saw an apparition of a pair of legs in blue trousers going upstairs and also saw a child. The children continued to see old men. A neighbor who was looking after the house when the Harpers went to the seaside saw a man in his shirtsleeves sitting at the table. Another neighbor knocked on the front door, and through the window saw Maurice Grosse in the hall, then watched him go upstairs. When finally admitted, she discovered that Maurice Grosse had been in the upper part of the house for the past half hour or so. The poltergeist was "imitating" him.

In mid-1978, Janet went into the Maudsley Hospital for observation and testing. Playfair expected the disturbances in Enfield to cease while she was away; in fact they continued, although on a smaller scale. And Janet claimed that a number of small poltergeist incidents happened to her while in hospital. But Janet's spell in the Maudsley—which made her healthier and stronger—was the beginning of the end of the Enfield case.

The haunting seems to have been brought to an end by a Dutch clairvoyant named Dono Gmelig-Meyling, who was brought to the house by a Dutch journalist who wanted to study the case. The day before their first visit had been eventful—overturned furniture. knocks. footsteps. sounds of breathing and excrement smeared on the floor. Dono spent some time in the house, then returned to his hotel. There, he later told Playfair, he went on an "astral trip," and met a twenty-four-year-old girl who was somehow involved with the case. This was an interesting new departure. Later, Dono met Maurice Grosse, and again had a strong sense that he was somehow connected with the haunting—and not purely as an investigator. When Grosse mentioned that his own daughter had been killed in a motorcycle accident two years before—she would have been twenty-four if still alive—Dono said: "Well that's it. It's your daughter . . . " There was no suggestion that she was responsible for any of the poltergeist activity, only that she was somehow connected. In the final chapter of his account of the Enfield case, *This House is Haunted*, Playfair tries to draw together his speculations about the disturbances. His suggestion is that Maurice Grosse's daughter—whose name was also Janet—was involved indirectly. It was she who had drawn her father's attention to the case. Janet had died after a motorcycle crash in 1976—and Grosse had been impressed by a series of odd events and coincidences. A birthday card she had sent to her brother just before the accident showed someone with her head swathed in bandages, and an inscription about falling on it. Janet had died of head injuries. Grosse found himself wondering if Janet was somehow still alive, and thought that a suitable sign would be some rain—there had been a drought for months. The next morning, the kitchen roof below Janet's bedroom window was wet, although everywhere else was dry. It had been because of Janet's death that Grosse had thought about engaging in active psychical research, and his first case had been the Enfield haunting.

Playfair speculates that it was Janet who had somehow put it into the neighbor's head to ring the *Daily Mirror*, and who put it into the journalist's head to ring the SPR. So her father became involved in investigating a case that centered around another Janet. (Kardec claims that spirits often influence our thoughts.)

As to how the poltergeist haunting came about in the first place, Playfair's speculation is as follows:

When Mr. and Mrs. Harper were divorced, an atmosphere of tension built up among the children and their mother, just at the time when the two girls were approaching physical maturity. They were a very energetic pair to start with, both of them school sports champions, but even they could not use up the tremendous energy they were generating. So a number of entities came in and helped themselves to it.

As to the identity of the "entities": "it looks as if we had half the local graveyard at one time or another." These included Joe Watson, husband of the woman who had died of a cancer of the throat and Bill Haylock, later identified as a former local resident. There could well have been a dozen entities altogether, and they were able to take energy from practically everyone in the house. (Mrs. Harper experienced premonitory headaches before things happened, and while Janet was in hospital, the youngest boy, Jimmy, began having trances.) The Dutch clairvoyant Dono Gmelig-Meyling stated confidently that he would be able to put an end to the haunting, (by some kind of intervention "on the astral plane"), and it is a fact that his visits marked the end of the Enfield case.

And why did so many entities invade the Harper residence? The answer, Playfair believes, may be provided by Kardec, who states that many dead people are quite unaware that they are dead. In *The Flying Cow* he cites the interesting Ruytemberg Rocha case in support of this view. In November, 1961, a spiritist group in São Paulo found themselves listening to a voice—coming through the medium—which identified itself as Ruytemberg Rocha, a pupil in the second year of the Officers' School of the São Paulo State Police. The voice gave details of its family and date of birth, and added that it was wounded by shrapnel in the revolution in 1932.

When Dr. Carvalho—in charge of the session—said that this was now 1961 the spirit was astonished, and said that that was impossible. Carvalho assured him that he was dead, and that they would do all they could to help him.

It was an excellent case for verification, since the spirit had given so many details about himself and his family. A little research revealed that it all checked out—the family, the officer school, the battle in which he had died. One minor discrepancy was that Rocha had been killed by a bullet through the head, while the spirit spoke only about a shrapnel wound in the chest. But a bullet in the brain *could* have stimulated the chest area, giving him the impression that this is where he was wounded. According to Kardec, the state of confusion happens mostly in cases of sudden death, and may last for anything from hours to years. In the Enfield case, we have seen how angry the "entity" became when Playfair declared that it was dead, and how the quarrelsome old woman asserted "I'm *not* bleedin' dead."

Yet, as usual in poltergeist cases, it is practically impossible to get at the truth. The spirits themselves seldom seem to have any interest in the truth. In the present case, there are intriguing hints about a man called Gozer or Gober who practiced black magic, and about the involvement of Janet and Rose in witchcraft in a previous existence. There was a former resident in the house called Joe Watson, who did die in the house much as described by Janet's bass voice and whose wife did die of throat cancer, and there was a former neighbor called Bill Haylock. All of which adds at least a semblance of logic and reason to one of the best-authenticated poltergeist cases on record.

Perhaps the last word should go to a medium—and police commissioner—called Dr. Rafael Ranieri, quoted by Playfair in *The Flying Cow*:

A medium is an open door to the invisible world. What comes through that door depends to a large extent upon the personality of the medium, and it is quite wrong to suppose that the spirit world consists entirely of angelic beings devoted to our welfare. There are plenty of evil spirits around, also others who seem to have nothing better to do than fool about and amuse themselves at our expense by such elementary ... parlor tricks as lifting up tables and throwing things around the room. This would seem to be the level of spirit most often to be found at some of the widely publicized seances, and those who find spirit communications trivial, as many are, should blame the mediums, not the spirits.

If Janet and other members of the Harper family are unconscious mediums, perhaps it is hardly surprising that the entities who make use of their energies should belong to a fairly low level of the spirit hierarchy.

SEVEN

Ghost Hunters and Ghost Seers

If the history of ghost-hunting has to have a starting point, then the year 1829 is probably as good as any. It saw the publication of a book called *The Seeress of Prevorst*, which became one of the bestsellers of the nineteenth century, and familiarized the general public with the idea that we may be surrounded by invisible spirits. It was written by Dr. Justinus A. C. Kerner, a rich and eccentric doctor who was also a well-known poet and songwriter. In 1826, the forty-year-old Kerner was practicing in Weinsberg, near Heilbronn, when he was consulted by the relatives of a woman called Friederike Hauffe, who was dying of a wasting disease. She had lost all her teeth and looked like a walking skeleton.

It seemed that marriage was responsible for her sad condition. Ever since childhood she had fallen into trances, seen visions, and conversed with invisible spirits. She could also accurately predict the future. When she was nineteen, she had married a cousin, and gone into depression; at twenty, her first child was born, and she began to develop hysterical symptoms. Every evening, she fell into a trance in which she saw spirits of the dead.

Kerner was at first inclined to be skeptical about her visions and spirits—he put them down to hysteria. Yet he found Friederike Hauffe a fascinating case for study. She claimed to be able to see into the human body, and certainly had a remarkably precise knowledge of the nervous system. She could read with her stomach-

Kerner tested her by making her lie down with her eyes closed, and laid documents on her bare midriff; she read them perfectly. She could make geometrical drawings at great speed, even in the dark, and could draw perfect circles that looked as if they had been drawn by compasses. She claimed that her spirit often left her body and hovered above it.

Kerner tried ordinary medicines on her, but they had no effect. Friederike told him that if he placed her in a "magnetic trance" the spirits would instruct him on how to treat her, but he was reluctant to accept this advice. Eventually, he decided that he might as well try the effects of mesmerism.

This, it should be explained, is not another name for hypnotism. Franz Anton Mesmer believed that the human body is permeated with a vital fluid, which needs to move around freely if we are to remain healthy. If this fluid becomes "blocked," the result is illness. (Modern acupuncture holds roughly the same belief.) According to Mesmer, this vital fluid could be moved around the body by stroking it with magnets—a technique that sometimes produced the "magnetic trance." (It was his pupil, the Marquis de Puysegur, who accidentally discovered the parallel technique of hypnosis.)

Friederike reacted well to "magnetism," passing easily into a trance. But Kerner remained skeptical about the things she said in this condition. Then, one day, a remarkable experience changed his mind. Friederike declared that she was being haunted by an unpleasant man with a squint. From her description, Kerner recognized him as a man who had died a few years earlier. It seemed, according to Friederike, that the man was suffering from a guilty conscience. He had been involved in embezzlement and, after his death, another man had been blamed. Now he wanted to clear the man's name, for the sake of his widow. This could be done by means of a certain document, which would be found in a chest. The spirit "showed" Friederike the room where the document was to be found, and a man who was working there. Her description was so good that Kerner was able to identify him as a certain Judge Heyd. In her "vision," Friederike had seen Judge Heyd sitting in a certain place in this room, and the chest containing the document on the table. The document was apparently not in its proper numerical order, which is why it had not been found.

When Kerner told him about his patient's vision, Judge Heyd was astounded; he *had* been sitting in the position described on that particular day (Christmas Day), and the chest, contrary to regulations, had been left open on the table. When they searched, the document turned up where Friederike had said it would. The widow of the man who had been wrongly accused was able to obtain redress.

From now on, Kerner believed in Friederike's supernatural powers, and took whatever she said seriously. She told him that we are surrounded by spirits all the time, and that she was able to see them. These spirits often try to attract our attention in various ways: knocking, movement of objects, throwing of sand. And by way of convincing him, Friederike persuaded one of the spirits to make rapping noises, to make gravel and ash fall from the air, and to make a stool float up into the air. Kerner watched with amazement as the stool rose gently, then floated down again.

Friederike provided him with further proof of the accuracy of her visions when she succeeded in putting an end to a haunting. Kerner heard about a house where the ghost of an old man was frightening the inhabitants. He brought one of them, a woman, along to see Friederike; the seeress went into a trance and explained that the ghost was that of a man called Bellon, who was an "earth-bound spirit" as a result of defrauding two orphans. Kerner made inquiries, but no one had ever heard of a man called Bellon. But since the ghost claimed that he had been Burgomeister, it seemed probable that some record existed. He claimed he had been Burgomeister in the year 1700, and had died at the age of seventy-nine. Armed with this information, Kerner asked the present mayor to check the legal documents; they soon found that in the year 1700, a man called Bellon had been Burgomeister and director of the local orphanage. He had died in 1740 at the age of seventy-nine. After "confessing," the spirit took its departure.

While Friederike was in Kerner's house, there were constant poltergeist phenomena: knocks and raps, noises like the rattling of chains, gravel thrown through the window, and a knitting needle that flew through the air and landed in a glass of water. When Friederike was visited by a spirit one night her sister heard her say: "Open it yourself," then saw a book on the table open itself. A poltergeist tugged her boots off her feet as she lay on the bed, and threw a lampshade across the room. In the Kerners' bedroom, a table was thrown across the room. The poltergeist threw a stool at a maidservant who went into Friederike's room while she lay asleep. It extinguished a night light and made a candle glow.

Friederike also produced what would later be called "spirit teachings," an amazingly complex system of philosophy in which man is described as consisting of body, soul and spirit, and of being surrounded by a nerve aura which carries on the vital processes. She spoke about various cycles in human existence—life cycles (or circles) and sun circles, corresponding to various spiritual conditions. She also described a remarkable universal language from ancient times, said to be "the language of the inner life." (A mystical sect was founded to expound those doctrines after her death.)

All these mediumistic activities made Friederike more and more feeble, and she died in 1829 at the age of twenty-eight. Kerner's book *The Seeress of Prevorst* (the name of the Swabian village where she was born) created a sensation, and was equally successful when it was translated into English in 1845 by Catherine Crowe, whose own book, *The Night Side of Nature*, created an equal sensation four years later. It is arguable that *The Seeress of Prevorst* and *The Night Side of Nature* were two of the most influential books of the nineteenth century.

In the second half of the nineteenth century, as the scientific reaction against spiritualism increased, *The Seeress of Prevorst* ceased to be taken seriously by those engaged in psychical research, and by the twentieth century it had been virtually forgotten. Writing about it in his *Modern Spiritualism* (1902), the skeptical Frank Podmore—who believed that all poltergeists are due to naughty children—dismisses most of the evidence as second-hand, while another eminent researcher, E. J. Dingwall (writing in *Abnormal Hypnotic Phenomena*) seems to feel that Kerner was stupid to take her claims seriously, and that if he had remained skeptical and treated her simply as a case of hysteria, she would have lived longer. But reading Kerner's own account, it is difficult to see how he would have remained skeptical without being downright dishonest or blind; on one occasion, he saw a cloudy figure hovering in front of her, and although it had vanished when he came back with a lamp, Friederike continued to stare at the spot as though listening to it.

In fact, we can see that the case of the seeress of Prevorst is a thoroughly typical case of poltergeist phenomena caused by a medium. In detail after detail, it sounds like any number of other cases of "haunting." If anyone killed Friederike Hauffe, it was the spirits themselves, who must have been using her energy to manifest themselves. No doubt the poltergeist phenomena were unspectacular because Friederike was weak from the moment Kerner set eyes on her. (In a case cited by the novelist William de Morgan, a maidservant who was able to cause rapping noises gradually lost her powers as she became weaker from tuberculosis.)

In another of his books, Kerner describes another remarkable case with some of the characteristics of poltergeist haunting. He was asked to treat a "possessed" peasant girl in Orlach, near Stuttgart. For some reason which is not clear, she was persecuted by "spirits" from the age of twenty, and there were the usual bangs and crashes, movements of furniture, and even outbreaks of fire. Then, after five months of this, she saw two ghosts, one of a nun dressed in white, the other of a monk dressed in black. The nun asserted that she had been smuggled into the monastery disguised as a cook, and had had two children by the black monk, both of whom he had killed at birth. He also murdered three monks during the four-year period she was with him; and, when he suspected she was about to betray him, he killed her too. The black monk also spoke to the possessed girl, saying that he was the son of a nobleman from nearby Geislingen, and that as the Superior at the monastery of Orlach, he had seduced a number of nuns and killed the children they bore. He also confessed to killing monks. The bodies, he said, he threw into a hole in a wall.

The white nun told the girl that her sufferings would cease only if her parents agreed to allow their cottage to be demolished. By this time they were so desperate that they agreed. On March 5, 1833 the house was finally demolished. Most of the walls were made of mud, but one corner was constructed of limestone, obviously part of a far older building. When this was pulled down, they found underneath it an empty well containing a number of human bones, including those of children. The girl's possession ceased from the moment the wall collapsed.

The story sounds like a typical invention of a German romantic novelist; but Kerner devotes a whole book to it, describing it in the same detail as his investigation of Friederike Hauffe. In spite of this, modern investigators are inclined not to take it seriously. Yet readers who are impressed by the clarity and detail of Kerner's reporting may feel that this case of the possessed girl of Orlach is one of the most convincing arguments for the close connection between poltergeists and spirits of the dead.

Ten years after publication of *The Seeress of Prevorst*, another doctor—this time of philosophy—produced an equally remarkable account of a case of possession, this time benevolent. In *Die Schutzgeister* (*The Guardian Spirit*, 1839), Heinrich Werner identifies his eighteen-year-old subject only as "R.O." Like Friederike, she had been subject to all kinds of illnesses; then, at a certain point, found herself haunted by spirits. One day the girl fell into a trance; and from then on she was able to do so at will, and to supply Werner with all kinds of information obtained "clairvoyantly." She had a guardian spirit called Albert, who seems to have acted rather like the "spirit guide"' of later mediums. And the spirit who caused her so much trouble was—again—a wicked monk. One day when the girl claimed that the wicked monk was present in the room, Werner was puzzled to hear an odd sound coming from a small table—like a cup rattling on a saucer. This occurred a number of times, becoming steadily louder (a typical characteristic of poltergeist noises); R.O. said that the monk was pro-

ducing the noise, and was delighted at Werner's astonishment—which also sounds typical of a poltergeist.

One day, Werner was startled to hear a loud crash
from an empty room; he rushed in to find that two large
flowerpots, which had stood on the window sill, had
been hurled to the floor so violently that there was earth
all over the room. The blind was closed and there was no
breeze. One of the curtains had also been twisted around
a birdcage. Later that day, Werner went to call on R.O.,
who went into a trance, and then told Werner that the
black monk had been responsible for smashing the flowerpots (Werner had not mentioned this to her). Albert
apparently had ejected him from the house.

Werner was greatly impressed by his patient's
clairvoyant powers. She demonstrated these one day
when she woke up from a trance and told him that she
had seen herself driving in a green-lacquered chaise.
Now Werner had, at the time, made some enquiries
about a chaise that was for sale in a town some fifteen
hours away, and he expected to get an answer in about a
week. R.O. told him he would hear much sooner than
that—in fact, the following afternoon; she also went on
to describe the chaise, in some detail. The following
afternoon, Werner received a message about the chaise,
and discovered that the girl was right in every detail.

Her most dramatic piece of clairvoyance concerned her younger sister. One day, in a trance, she cried
out "Albert, help me! Emilie is falling down into the
street." Then, after a short period, she said: "Thank God,
help has already come!"

Asked what had happened, she explained that her
little sister had been leaning out of a top-story window,
trying to grab a rope suspended from a winch above the
window; she had been on the point of falling when her
father had entered the room and pulled her back.

Werner contacted the father to ask if anything remarkable had happened on that particular day, and received a reply which Werner printed in his book; it said that the father had been sitting in his office when he had felt uneasy. He went home, and went upstairs, in time to find his daughter had leaned too far out of the window to catch the rope, and could not get back into the room; he grabbed her dress and hauled her back in. R.O. said that it was Albert, the guardian spirit, who had made her father feel uneasy.

Again, writers like Podmore and Dingwall express strong skepticism about Werner's book—Dingwall says that when the flowerpots were smashed, Werner should have checked on the key (or keys) to the room and whether anyone could have got in past the Venetian blind. In a case like this, such pedantic hairsplitting is irrelevant. After all, Werner *might* have invented the whole case. In a book like this: the basic question is of Werner's honesty, and whether he reported the case to the best of his ability. If he did, then the real question is not whether he could have spent more time double-checking on everything that happened, but whether we can accept his own interpretation of the things he witnessed. As "tough-minded" psychical researchers, Podmore and Dingwall naturally reject the whole notion of a guardian spirit, as well as of malevolent dead monks; therefore, they are inclined to question the whole story. In fact, there is nothing in Werner's account that is inconsistent with the behavior of poltergeists as explored and described in this book, and a great deal that fits very convincingly And whether we interpret Albert as a spirit guide, or simply as a higher level of R.O's personality, he also seems to deserve rather more serious treatment than Podmore seems willing to grant.

The cases described by Justinus Kerner and Heinrich Werner excited widespread interest in Europe, and led to much serious discussion. A similar case that occurred in America in 1844 received almost no publicity, and led to a persecution of the two principals that seemed to prove that the spirit of the Salem witchcraft trials was still alive. The case is documented in Emma Hardinge's *Modern American Spiritualism* (1870).

Dr. Lyman B. Larkin was a physician of Wrentham, Mass., whose servant girl, Mary Jane, suffered from fits. Larkin was another practitioner of "magnetism," and he began trying to cure Mary Jane by this method—probably stroking her with large bar magnets. Mary Jane was soon falling into hypnotic sleep, during which she became clairvoyant. (The same thing was to happen to another American in the 1890s; Edgar Cayce was put to sleep by a hypnotist in an attempt to cure the loss of his voice; he was not only able to prescribe for his own ailment, but for other people's. Cayce went on to become one of the most famous "psychics" of his time.) Mary Jane could instantly diagnose the illnesses of any of the doctor's patients, and often suggest the correct prescription.

Mary Jane told Larkin that when she went into her trance states, she saw a beautiful "fairy" called Katy, and it was she who performed the diagnoses. There were also other "fairies," who all came from Germany.

At this point, Mary Jane began to attract less benevolent entities. There were loud rapping noises from various articles of furniture as soon as she fell into trance. Mary Jane began to speak in a strange voice, uttering awful obscenities. Then the furniture began to move about. One day, as the whole family sat in the room, with Mary Jane asleep on the couch, a flat iron suddenly appeared in the room—it had last been seen in the kitchen. When Mrs. Larkin requested the spirit to take it away, the iron vanished, and was later found in the kitchen. (It is a pity that Larkin failed to record whether anyone was looking at it at the time; as we have seen, poltergeists seem to prefer to perform their tricks when no one is watching.) The mischievous spirit, according to Mary Jane, was the ghost of a sailor boy.

It seems probable that Larkin was himself an unconscious medium, for some of the manifestations followed him on his rounds; in one house, loud knockings terrified the family, who were convinced they were a premonitory warning of disaster.

Like Werner's patient R.O., Mary Jane was able to describe to the doctor exactly what he had been doing during the day—an ability known to researchers as travelling clairvoyance. On one occasion, she even told him about some irritations he had suffered at supper on the previous evening, due to the salmon being underdone, and the roast pig eaten up before the doctor had helped himself.

The sailor boy now became more violent, and began to cause powerful convulsions of Mary Jane's body, in the course of which her joints were dislocated. Although these dislocations were painless they caused a great deal of inconvenience. The poltergeist claimed it could not set them right, and other doctors and helpers had to be called in. On one occasion, a doctor who had just attended to a dislocation was in a hurry to get away, and said he hoped he wouldn't be needed again; the sailor boy then cursed him with foul language, and dislocated another joint on the spot.

This had been going on for almost three years when a delegation from the local church—of which Larkin was a faithful and enthusiastic member—called on him to ask about the strange rumors. Larkin explained quite openly, and was upset when the committee seemed to feel he had been guilty of "scandalous behavior," possibly suspecting his motives in plunging Mary Jane into hypnotic sleep. Larkin defended himself, and offered to allow members of the committee to live in the house and observe the phenomena. They turned down this offer, but began to behave like inquisitors, calling at all hours of the day and night, and interrogating Mary Jane, obviously hoping to find something incriminating. Finally, Larkin lost his temper and told them that they must conduct an orderly investigation, or let him alone. So a Reverend Mr. Thatcher and his wife moved into the Larkin household for a week. He saw Mary Jane go into trances, and on one occasion was much impressed by the prayers she offered up in this state. Mr. Thatcher wrote a report that was circulated to all the ministers concerned, asserting his "entire conviction of the supra-mundane character of the events he had witnessed." No one, he said, was attempting any kind of fraud or deception.

But the ministers were far from satisfied. Larkin's chief enemy, the Reverend Horace James, won over three magistrates to his side, and they ordered Larkin to appear in front of them. Mary Jane was seized and accused of "necromancy." She was put on trial and sentenced to sixty days in solitary confinement in the Dedham jail. Not long after being released, she died.

Larkin himself was found not guilty, but the ministers told him he was excommunicated from the church until he "made full confession of his crimes." Larkin protested that he believed "in the communion of spirits; did realize that they could and had through the organism of Mary Jane again and again communicated with him." The Reverend James found this thoroughly unsatisfying, and demanded a full recantation; because he wanted to return to the church, Larkin signed a paper agreeing that his statements about communication "were the biggest lie ever written." Larkin, who later told the whole story to Emma Hardinge, said that he was ashamed of himself for denying the phenomena, but it was the only way he could again be accepted into the church. Two years after these events, the whole country was talking about the strange goings-on in the home of the Fox sisters and, within another two years, Spiritualism had swept across America. If the Larkin case had occurred in the mid 1850s instead of the mid 1840s, there seems no doubt that it would have aroused widespread interest and sympathetic study; as it was, Larkin and Mary Jane were the victims of the witch-hunting mentality.

In retrospect, one of the oddest things about this whole period is that there were so many "spirit manifestations" appearing simultaneously, with no possibility of influencing one another. It looks almost as if the "spirits" had decided to make a concerted effort to make human beings aware of their existence. An alternative possibility is that the discovery of mesmerism and hypnotism meant that far more doctors were placing their patients in a trance. And there seems good reason to believe that "spirits" can make use of the bodies of certain people when they are in trance.

At the same time that Larkin was "magnetizing" Mary Jane, a twenty-one-year-old shoemaker named Andrew Jackson Davis was conducting experiments in hypnotism. He had been fascinated by a lecture on animal magnetism, and persuaded a local tailor to try and hypnotize him. It worked, and Davis, like Mary Jane, began to diagnose illnesses with the aid of the "spirits." In 1844, on a country walk, he encountered two men who said they were the physician Galen and the mystic Swedenborg, and who told him that he was destined to become an important teacher. In the following year,

Davis encountered two men who decided to work with him in carrying out his mission: a Dr. Lyon, of Bridgeport, Conn., and the Reverend William Fishbough. Dr. Lyon would hypnotize him, and then the Reverend Fishbough would write down the revelations that came from him in a trance state. These amounted to a remarkable and sizable volume which appeared in 1847 under the title of *The Principles of Nature, Her Divine Revelation, and a Voice to Mankind*. Podmore quotes long extracts from this work in his *Modern Spiritualism*, and it seems to be rather more interesting than he gives it credit for. He describes the beginning of the universe as being an "unimaginable ocean of liquid fire," and adds that "particles did not exist, but the whole was as one Particle"— a view that most astrophysicists would now endorse. When he speaks about the origin of life, Davis makes the odd assertion that water is condensed light, but goes on to make some interesting observations about the influence of light on water which sound like an anticipation of photosynthesis; it sounds even more like the heterodox views of Wilhelm Reich on the creation of life through "orgone energy." Davis also predicts the existence of an eighth planet in the solar system—this was written about six months before the discovery of the planet Neptune. A third part of Davis's book deals with his own plan (or that of the spirits) for the reorganization of society—a kind of Christian socialism.

The Principles of Nature became something of a bestseller, and the story of its composition undoubtedly prepared the American public for the revelations that were to come from Hydesville in 1849. Davis was, as we have seen, one of the witnesses of the Phelps poltergeist case (see Chapter 3), and made the interesting comment that the raps were due to "discharges of vital electricity" from the organisms of the children concerned; but he also said that the disturbances were caused by spirits—five in number.

This same epoch also saw the emergence of the most remarkable of all spirit mediums—Daniel Dunglas Home, whose experience of "spirits" began in 1846, when he was thirteen (that is to say, three years before the Hydesville rappings). Home was a Scottish highlander—a race with a reputation for "second sight"—and claimed to be the grandson of the Earl of Home (pronounced Hume) by a natural son. At the age of nine, he traveled to America to live with his aunt, a Mrs. Cook. And in 1846 he had a vision of a friend named Edwin, who stood at the foot of his bed and made three circles in the air; Home took this to mean he had died three days earlier, and this later proved to be correct. In 1850, Home's mother died, and the Cooks were alarmed by various poltergeist effects in their home—furniture sliding around, strange bangs and raps, which led his aunt to accuse him of bringing the devil into her house. When the local minister began praying for Daniel's soul, loud raps sounded from his chair. When the news of these events spread around the area, neighbors began calling at the house to ask about long-lost relatives or mislaid jewelry. At the end of the week, Mrs. Cook threw him out, and threw his best suit after him.

Home was lucky; he could hardly have timed his debut more perfectly. Leading Spiritualists invited him to their homes, and he had no trouble making a name for himself as a medium. And his powers were certainly extraordinary. He had no objection to performing in a well-lit room and, within minutes, the table was usually resounding to loud knocks and floating free of the ground. Shocks would make the floor vibrate like artillery fire. Spirits of the dead spoke from his mouth, and his body would often float into the air—a phenomenon which had once been regarded as a sure sign of demoniacal possession

Home was a good-looking young man with pleasing manners and a tenor voice; he became the favorite of any society he moved into, and a number of affectionate elderly people wanted to adopt him as a son. But, like many spirit mediums, he seems to have been in many ways a rather weak and neurotic character. (A modern psychic, Robert Cracknell, has pointed out that a large number of mediums have had disturbed childhoods, and that many are homosexual; a certain emotional instability seems essential to clairvoyance.) He was something of a snob, and was fond of society. In 1856, the spirits became so exasperated with him that they told him he would lose his powers for one year. It happened as they predicted, and his powers returned precisely one year later to the day.

Throughout his life, Home performed spectacular feats. It was nothing for a heavy table to rise into the air when he was in trance, and float up to the ceiling. At seances, trumpets sounded, tambourines played, raps sounded from all over the room, birds sang, ducks squawked, water splashed and spirit voices sang and spoke. Heavy articles of furniture—like grand pianos—floated around like thistledown. Meanwhile, Home sat in full view of everybody, separated from the main circle, often tied hand and foot to his chair. Hundreds of unimpeachable witnesses testified to these phenomena. In the 1860s he became a friend of a young man called Lord Adare, an Irish peer with no interest in spiritualism, and Adare subsequently wrote a book about the phenomena he saw during this period of friendship. Dead people materialized in the room and held conversations, looking as solid as the living. Home would take live coals from the fireplace, blow them to red heat, and hand them to other people who would find them quite cold—so long as they held them. On one occasion, he floated out of a third-story window which was open only about a foot— and floated in by another. When Adare asked him to repeat it, Home floated off the floor, became horizontal, and popped in and out of the open window like a shuttle. Standing against a wall, his legs and waist tightly held, he could increase his height by eight inches.

Home was responsible for the "conversion" of a young physicist, William Crookes, to an interest in psychic phenomena. Crookes investigated Home, expecting to discover fraud, and was amazed by what he witnessed. Fellow scientists were scandalized and contemptuous when Crookes published his reports on Home, and Darwin said he could not disbelieve Crookes's statements or believe his results. Crookes was one of the many scientists—Sir William Barrett and Sir Oliver Lodge were others—who studied "spirit" phenomena objectively, and arrived at the conclusion that there was no basic deception. Home made an admirable subject for such study. There was never the slightest breath of suspicion of fraud (Browning's poem "Mr. Sludge the Medium"— about Home—was an outright slander), and the phenomena were all so amazing and clear-cut that there could be little dispute about interpretation. In fact, anyone who reads Crookes's papers on Home* will find it incomprehensible how any scientific researcher can still regard the basic facts of "spirit manifestation" as unproved; either Crookes was lying, or they are proved as unambiguously as the existence of the planets. In Home's case, it may be the sheer variety of the phenomena that caused a kind of bewilderment.

---

* Published in *Crookes and the Spirit World,* edited by R. G. Medhurst. London and New York, 1972.

Studying Home's life—he retired at the age of thirty-nine, and died fourteen years later—also makes it clear that most of the "telepathic" and "psychokinetic" explanations of the phenomena are simply inadequate. Home himself had no doubt whatsoever that everything he did was due to Spirits who "used" him. His first experience was the vision of his dead friend Edwin. His second was sudden knowledge of his mother's death; and from then on, "spirits of the dead" played a constant part in his career. When Home attended a lecture on Cagliostro, the great charlatan himself materialized in his bedroom later, and sat on the bed talking to Home and his wife Sacha. After Sacha's death, she materialized in the room when Adare was present, looking quite solid and kissed Home. When the famous actress Adah Mencken died, she took possession of Home, and had a long talk with Adare (who had known her). At Adare Manor, Home saw a ghost wandering around and went and engaged it in conversation; his companions could see both Home and the ghost quite clearly in the moonlight. When Home left the ghost, he floated toward them at a height of two feet from the ground. In an Italian villa in Florence, Home raised the spirit of an Italian monk named Giannana, who had committed murder; the old man had been wandering restlessly around the house ever since his death, and Home persuaded him to go away. The monk's hands were materialized for inspection; they had skinny yellow fingers and were cold to the touch. In another villa, rented by Mr. and Mrs. Hiram Powers, there were poltergeist disturbances, and a spirit explained that these were caused by no less than twenty-seven dead monks "who must have been very improper persons in their lifetime, judging by the indecorousness of their behavior." They tugged Mrs. Powers's skirt hard enough to break the cotton where it held "gathers." These monks also agreed to leave quietly after making the sign of the cross "in a way that conveyed the sense of something devilish and spiteful"—a fair description of most poltergeists. (It is interesting to speculate why so many monks are involved in hauntings; possibly the general unsatisfactoriness of their lives, and the frustration of sexual energies may provide the basis for an explanation.)

In short, Home himself never had the slightest doubt that his powers came from spirits; there was no question of unconscious psychokinesis; and reading the many detailed accounts of his manifestations it is hard to reject his explanation.

When the Society for Psychical Research was formed in 1882—by men like Sir William Barrett, F. W. H. Myers, Henry Sidgwick and Edmund Gurney—its founders entertained a hope that now strikes us as absurdly optimistic. They felt that psychic science was now about to take its place among the respectable sciences and that, within a decade or so, man would know as much about the soul and life after death as he knows about stars and atoms. The phenomena seemed real enough, which meant that the "facts" behind them must be equally real and solid; so it was simply a matter of discovering these facts and verifying them by scientific testing.

And why did this hope come to nothing? The answer that has suggested itself throughout the course of this book is that studying spirits is not quite as straightforward as studying, say, Australian or African aborigines. Kardec seems to have been lucky in his choice of mediums, and to have obtained sensible and consistent answers to his questions. His "system" remains the most impressive that has so far emerged in the history of spiritualism. But even Kardec came to realize that many spirits—apparently the majority who hang around the earth—have no desire whatever to cooperate with human beings in discovering the truth about "the other side." In short, as Chesterton says, spirits tell lies. They also do their best to confuse the earnest investigator. They seldom manifest themselves when expected to, and when they *do* choose to make their presence felt, their aim often seems to be to create confusion and bewilderment. To judge by poltergeist phenomena, most of the accessible spirit world seems to be made up of bloody-minded anarchists with a slightly sadistic sense of humor.

Where the early ghost-hunters were concerned, these problems were sometimes accentuated by a certain naivete of approach. Robert Dale Owen, son of the famous socialist pioneer Robert Owen, began as a determined skeptic who deplored his father's conversion to Spiritualism; but when he became American Charge d'Affaires in Naples, he encountered Daniel Dunglas Home, and—understandably—became totally convinced. Owen made a vow that he would not rest until he had proved survival after death either a certainty or a delusion. His conclusions appeared in a work called *Footfalls on the Boundary of Another World*, which appeared in 1860. It is an admirable work, full of interesting stories, and it became immensely popular. In his second "inquiry," *The Debatable Land Between this World and the Next* (1874), Owen shows his hand: "In the following pages I seek to show that Religion, such as Christ taught, though sure to prevail in the end, is yet, for the time, hard pressed." And accordingly, the Spirit World is to be called to its defense. But why should life after death prove the truth of religion, any more than life before death does? It may "prove" that man is a spirit, but even an agnostic can believe that by deciding that he is more than a mere machine.

In short, by mixing up their psychical investigations with their religious convictions, men like Owen brought the "spirit world" into disrepute with the scientists. Catherine Crowe—author of *The Night Side of Nature*—kept her religion and her "facts" in separate compartments; few later writers show the same restraint. This is a pity, for what they have to say is often important. In 1924, an American doctor named Carl Wickland brought out a book called *Thirty Years Among the Dead,* describing his wife's experiences of mediumship. A series of spirits speak through the medium, and are instructed and sermonized by Dr. Wickland. On June 6, 1907, the spirit was a criminal called Charles the Fighter, who seems to be under the influence of drink, and threatens to have everybody shot. When told that he is using the body of a medium, and ordered to look at her hands, he shrinks in terror, and explains that he once cut off a woman's hand to get her diamond ring. He looks around and gasps: "Have I killed all those people? Have they all come to accuse me?" And finally, he tells his life story, his "hideous career of crime," how he stole to buy whiskey and drank to drown his conscience. Killed in a brawl in 1870, he did not even realize he was dead, and went on trying to commit crimes—when he hit a policeman, he was puzzled that the club went through his head. After being lectured on the "law of cause and effect," Charles the Fighter sees his mother standing beside him, and

> the hardened criminal cowered in his seat and wept piteously ... Crushed by guilt and remorse he cried abjectly: "I cannot go with you! Dear mother, don't ask me to go with you! You must go back to heaven, and I must go to hell, where I belong ... " But maternal love prevailed and the spirit, humble and penitent, followed his mother.

But immediately after this scene from a Victorian melodrama, there is an account of a seance with a man called Harry Hayward, who had his girlfriend murdered and was himself hanged in 1894; it carries the ring of truth. A female invalid with psychic abilities began to develop a craving for ice cream, but felt herself choking when she tried to eat it. She flung open a window and ordered any "spirit entities" to leave the place. That evening, at Wickland's seance, a spirit identified itself as Harry Hayward, and said that he had a craving for ice cream, and had tried to get some earlier that day, but had been "chased away by a woman." He talked about his trial and execution, mentioning a guard with whom he spent a great deal of time playing cards. Wickland said he thought this man was dead; the spirit replied "No, he's not dead. I see him playing cards at his son's home in Minneapolis." This, says Wickland, later proved to be true.

What Hayward says about his craving for ice cream brings to mind Guy Playfair's comment that earth-bound spirits long for the things they enjoyed while alive. And the experience of the invalid lady—the sudden desire for ice cream, and the choking sensation when she tried to eat it—would be explained by Kardec as an example of the type of minor "possession" that occurs all the time. Kardec, it will be recalled, said that our thoughts and actions are constantly influenced by spirits. People who can be fully "possessed" are called mediums; most of us, fortunately, have only feeble mediumistic powers. But spirits can still wander in and out of our bodies at will. So the Spiritist explanation of what happened to the invalid is that she was a natural medium—the text makes it clear that she was aware of this—and Hayward managed to "possess" her to the extent of making her long for ice cream. But in order to enjoy the ice cream vicariously, he had to "take over" her body. As he tried to do this, the lady began to choke—presumably because Hayward had been hanged—and she realized what was happening and threw him out.

Anita Gregory, an eminent psychical investigator, discusses Wickland's *Thirty Years Among the Dead* in her introduction to Oesterreich's book on possession. and dismisses it as an example of self-deception. The cases cited above suggest that it is not as simple as this. Mrs. Wickland was a genuine medium, and no doubt most of the phenomena were genuine. But Wickland is simply *imposing his own preconceptions* on every thing he witnesses. And seances are fairly easy to influence in this way. In *The Occult*, I have quoted the case of Louis Singer, who deliberately experimented with suggestion and telepathy at a seance.

> One of the sitters announced she could see lights, I too giving my consent as I was too polite to disagree. Another said she could feel a wind. Again agreement, to which I assented. Then for a while, nothing. At last I felt it was my turn, so I remarked it was getting lighter. This met with concurrence. Indeed, one went so far as to remark upon the beautiful lights that played around me. I then suggested I felt a wind. So did everybody present. Later the trumpet miraculously floated into the air, the voice recognized by one sitter as a relative spoke. They were all certain it was not the medium's voice, and not too cleverly disguised.

So Singer decided to try to influence the seance by telepathy. A dog basket made him think of a coracle, and he visualized one. By accident, one chair too many had been put in the circle, and the medium suggested that they leave it for a spirit to occupy.

Sure enough, a spirit invisible to us occupied it. It was, the medium said, a drowned sailor. After this, I tried on more than one occasion to dictate what spirit should come through, using the method of visual projection. I was largely successful . . .

All this seems to suggest that seances are entirely a matter of self-deception: that is, of some unexplored power of the human mind, directed by our own preconceptions. But in that case, how did the trumpet float into the air? How did Daniel Dunglas Home make tables float up to the ceiling? We have to fall back on the idea of "spontaneous psychokinesis," and we have already seen that this is simply inadequate to cover the facts of poltergeist hauntings. So the sensible position would seem to be somewhere midway between the two: that is, that spirits do exist, but that the phenomena they cause is very easily influenced by the human mind. We have seen that poltergeists are frequently influenced by what people say; in the Enfield case, one investigator visiting the house mentioned that he had just come from a case where the poltergeist caused fires; the Enfield poltergeist immediately acted upon the suggestion. The Dagg poltergeist did not seem to be sure whether it was supposed to be a devil or an angel; it seemed quite prepared to be whatever people wanted it to be. And this is the basic cause of the failure of psychical research. If we know as little about "the spirit world"' now as we did a century ago, it is because we keep on imposing our own preconceptions and prejudices, and the "facts" become hopelessly muddled with our interpretation of them. The early investigators insisted on mixing religion with psychical research; the result, predictably, was that Spiritualism seemed to confirm the Christian faith.

But within twenty years of the founding of Spiritualism (around 1850) there was already a strong reaction against this tendency. In Ireland, a professor of physics called William Barrett used to stay with a friend in the country, and became interested in his friends experiments in mesmerism with the village children. One little girl became strongly telepathic as soon as she was placed in a trance. If the experimenter held his hand over a lighted lamp, the girl—who was facing the other way—instantly snatched her own hand away as if it was burnt. If he tasted sugar, she looked pleased, while salt made her grimace. In France, the psychologist Pierre Janet investigated a case in which a peasant woman could be put into a hypnotic trance when the hypnotist simply *thought* about it—even at a distance. Another investigator, Dr. Julian Ochorowicz, studied a "somnambule" called Madame Lucille, who, when in a trance, was able to tell him what he was doing behind her back. A boy investigated by Ochorowicz could even repeat aloud the words that Ochorowicz was reading in a book. All this seemed to prove beyond all doubt that the human mind has some curious unknown power to influence other minds. Janet pointed out that if his hypnotist tried to hypnotize the peasant woman without concentrating on what he was doing, she remained unhypnotized. Yet when he concentrated hard, he could even hypnotize her at a distance. Obviously, the mind itself has some peculiar power, a kind of radar beam of will. (In *Mysteries*, I have described a simple experiment by which any group of people can verify this; it was first shown to me by the theater historian John Kennedy Melling. Two or three people stand around the person who has been selected as the subject, and the subject closes his eyes. The others then press their fingertips lightly against the subject's body, at shoulder level, then withdraw them so they are a few inches away. The whole group now concentrates on forcing the subject to sway in a definite direction, chosen at random by one of the group. When I first tried the experiment, acting as subject, I was astonished to feel a curious force pushing me in a certain direction—the direction chosen by those standing around me. If the subject tries to resist, the result is usually a feeling of dizziness. An interesting extension of this experiment is to try to move a paper roundabout, balanced on a needle, by will-power. The roundabout is made by taking a small square of paper, about an inch square, folding it four times—like the crosses on a Union Jack—and then pinching the four folds to make a paper dart, which is then balanced on a needle stuck in a cork. The hands should then be gently cupped around the "roundabout." Most people will try making tremendous efforts of will and produce no effect—as I did myself the first time I tried it. The trick seems to be visualizing the roundabout turning one way or the other as you exert the will. With a little practice, most people can make the roundabout turn clockwise, then stop, then turn counter-clockwise.)

It was these experiments in will-power and hypnosis that convinced Barrett that an unknown human faculty was waiting to be investigated; and, together with a spiritualist called Edmund Dawson Rogers, he decided to found a Society for Psychical Research. It came into being in 1882, and one of its chief tasks was to study examples of "paranormal occurrences," and take evidence from as many witnesses as possible. They soon began to accumulate a considerable body of evidence on one particular subject: the so-called "phantasms of the living"—when the "ghost" of a living person is seen at some distance from his physical body. A typical example concerns the poet Goethe who was walking home one day after a heavy shower when he saw a friend named

Friedrich walking in front of him; what surprised him was that Friedrich was wearing his—Goethe's—dressing-gown. When he got home, he found Friedrich in front of the fire, wearing the dressing-gown—he had been caught in the shower, taken off his wet coat, and borrowed Goethe's dressing-gown. The SPR collected hundreds of similar cases. Many of these were concerned with "crisis apparitions"—people seeing a relative who was seriously ill or on the point of death. The immense work *Phantasms of the Living* (1886) by Gurney, Myers and Podmore contains hundreds of such cases. And what it seems to demonstrate beyond all doubt is that human beings have the ability to project an image of themselves—a quite solid-looking image—to distant places.

What is odder still is that, in most cases, the "projector" has no idea that he is being seen elsewhere, and no particular reason for wanting to be seen elsewhere. There is, for example, the curious case of Canon Bourne, cited by G. N. M. Tyrrell in *Apparitions*. Canon Bourne was out hunting with his two daughters when the girls decided to return home. On their way home, the girls saw their father, looking dirty and dishevelled, waving to them from the other side of the valley. When they reached the place, there was no sign of him. They searched the area, then went home. Their father arrived home soon afterwards—quite unhurt. He could not explain why he had "appeared" to his daughters, and neither could they. One odd point is that one of the girls noticed the maker's name inside their father's hat as he waved it to them—which would obviously have been impossible at such a distance. This seems to suggest that it was their minds rather than their eyes that were seeing him. Yet both girls *and* the coachman saw the figure clearly.

Now cases like these may be quite bewildering, but they seem to make one thing perfectly clear: that there is far more to human beings than meets the eye. In fact, they seem to suggest that we are making a false distinction when we talk about "ghosts" as if they were quite distinct from living people. It would probably be more accurate to say that human beings *are* ghosts—ghosts with bodies.

Faced with such a mass of evidence, this conclusion—or something very like it—slowly forced itself upon even the most skeptical members of the SPR. So by the beginning of the twentieth century, a new theory of Spiritualism had developed, according to which there is no need to suppose that the world is full of invisible "spirits." Man himself could be the invisible spirit who causes tables to rise into the air and trumpets to play themselves. And if poltergeists seem to require a disturbed child or teenager at the center of the disturbances, then perhaps the child is the poltergeist? This, as we have seen, is the view that still prevails today. One of the aims of this book is to demonstrate that it is unsatisfactory.

By the time Lombroso died, in 1909, psychical research was marking time. Spiritualism continued to flourish; but as scientific investigation, it had come to a halt. The reason can be seen by anyone who reads Owen's *Footfalls on the Boundary of Another World* and then turns to Lombroso's *After Death—What?* The books were published fifty years apart; yet they might both have been written at exactly the same time. Lombroso offers some "scientific evidence," by way of a few experiments in telepathy; otherwise, he presents just the same kind of evidence that Robert Dale Owen had presented. There was plenty of evidence for ghosts, for poltergeists, for telepathy, for precognition, for "out of the body experiences," and a dozen other varieties of "paranormal" experience. But the evidence seemed to lead nowhere. One remarkable case had even proved life after death, to the satisfaction of most open-minded inquirers. This was the celebrated "cross-correspondences." By 1904 three of the chief founders of the SPR—Henry Sidgwick. Frederick Myers and Edmund Gurney—were dead, and it seemed logical to hope that if they were still alive in another world, they would try to communicate through mediums. In the previous year, a psychic named Mrs. Holland, the sister of Rudyard Kipling, began receiving written messages—through automatic writing—that seemed far more intelligent and thoughtful than the majority of such scripts. And in 1904, another psychic; Mrs. Verrall, the wife of a Cambridge don, also received some messages, one of which included the words "Record the bits, and when fitted they will make the whole."

And it slowly became clear that the "senders" claimed to be the spirits of Sidgwick, Myers and Gurney, and that what they were attempting was a "proof" of such complexity that there could be no possibility of fraud. In effect, they seemed to be using a large number of mediums—others included Mrs. Flemming, Mrs. Forbes, and the famous American medium Mrs. Piper—to produce a complex jigsaw puzzle or conundrum, giving each woman only part of the puzzle, so that there could be no possible doubt that there was no collusion between them. Unfortunately, the conundrums were so complex that it would take a short book even to give a simple outline. A typical one is as follows:

In 1906, Mrs. Flemming produced a script containing the words Dawn, Evening, and Morning, a reference to bay leaves, and the name Laurence. Six weeks later, Mrs. Verrall wrote out a message mentioning "laurel" and a library. Mrs. Piper came out of a trance speaking of laurel, "nigger," and a phrase that sounded like "more head." Mrs. Flemming produced more scripts referring to Night and Day, Evening and Morning, and also a reference to Alexander's tomb with laurel leaves. And eventually, all these clues pointed to the tomb of the Medicis in the Church of San Lorenzo in Florence. It had been designed by Michelangelo, and contained his sculpture of Night and Day, Evening and Morning. Lorenzo de Medici's emblem was the laurel, and near the tombs is the Laurentian Library. Alexander (or Alessandro) de Medici was half negro; after his murder, his body was hidden in the tomb of Giuliano. "More head" was actually "Moor head"—the head of a negro. This conundrum was solved only four years after the first "clue," and there could be no question of telepathy between the mediums, since they did not understand what it was all about. Altogether, the case of the cross-correspondences is one of the most impressive—perhaps the most impressive—in the history of psychical research. It is true that the various "clues" are so complicated that few people have ever taken the trouble to study the case. Yet the sheer complexity of the code at least indicates that it originated on a far higher level of intelligence than most spirit messages. In addition to which, it effectively disposes of the objection that spirits never have anything interesting to say.

If the "spirits" of Myers, Gurney and Sidgwick failed to convince the world of the reality of the afterlife, a far more skillful and flamboyant publicist was now preparing to launch himself into the project.

Harry Price, ghost-hunter extraordinary, claimed that he was born in Shrewsbury, son of a wealthy paper manufacturer. A brilliant critical biography by Trevor Hall, *The Search for Harry Price*, reveals that he was, in fact, the son of an unsuccessful grocer, and that he was born in London in 1881. From then until he was about forty, he seems to have supported himself by a variety of jobs, including commercial traveling, manufacturing patent medicines, journalism and giving gramophone concerts. What is certain is that his lifelong interest in stage magic began at the age of eight, when he saw an itinerant magician and patent medicine salesman, the Great Sequah, giving a public performance. Price began collecting books on magic, and became an expert magician. It may have been the interest in magic that led him to join the Society for Psychical Research in 1920—the SPR was then, as now, much concerned with trying to detect fraud in mediums. E. J. Dingwall, who was then Research Officer for the Society, asked Price if he would care to come with him to Munich, to attend some seances of a remarkable German medium, Willi Schneider—one of two brothers. The man who arranged the seances was the German investigator, Baron von Schrenk-Notzing, a friend of Lombroso's, and the author of a sensationally successful book called *Materialization Phenomena*, which had aroused widespread skepticism in Germany when it appeared in 1914. Schrenk-Notzing himself was something of a flamboyant publicist, and Trevor Hall suggests that Harry Price took his example to heart, and decided that this was the way to achieve the fame he craved. (He admitted frankly that he had always wanted to get his name in *Who's Who*.)

The Schneider brothers, Willi and Rudi, the most psychic members of a psychic family, were born at Braunau-am-Inn and, according to one friend of the family, the phenomena began after they had spent an evening playing with a ouija board. Willi had then reached the age of puberty—in 1916—and the family was disturbed by loud knocking noises. Then objects began moving around, and Willi saw a ghost in the sitting room. Neighbors became so alarmed about the racket that the family were on the point of vacating the flat. By means of the ouija board, they tried questioning the "spirit," which identified itself as a girl named Olga Lindtner, who claimed to be a reincarnation of the notorious Lola Montez. In due course, Willi went into a trance, and Olga spoke through him. In spite of doubts later raised by Harry Price—after he had quarreled with the brothers—there can be no doubt that the phenomena were genuine. The novelist Thomas Mann attended one seance, and has recorded how, as he pressed Willi's knees tightly between his own, and two other people held his hands, a handkerchief floated into the air, a bell began to ring and then floated into the air, a music box played, and the keys of a typewriter were struck. Mann was convinced that deception was impossible.

Harry Price and E. J. Dingwall witnessed similar occurrences, and also saw a white hand which materialized in front of them; they had no doubt whatever of the genuineness of the phenomena, and said as much at a lecture to the SPR. But by way of keeping his options open, Price helped to edit and publish a book called *Revelations of a Spirit Medium*, in which a fake medium described the tricks of the trade.

In 1923, Price got into conversation with a young nurse on a train; her name was Stella Cranshawe. He was fascinated to hear that mild poltergeist phenomena occurred around her—a feeling like a breeze, movement of small objects, rapping noises, and flashes of light. By this time, Price knew enough about psychical research to realize that the girl was probably, without knowing it, a medium. He persuaded her to allow herself to be investigated. And at the first seance, a heavy table levitated and moved across the room on two legs, raps sounded, lights flashed, and the temperature in the room dropped considerably. (At later sittings it became very low indeed.) At another seance, the table hit Harry Price under the chin, then three of its legs snapped off, the top broke into two pieces, then the whole table crumbled into matchwood. Stella herself found all these phenomena rather boring and, after she married in 1928, refused to take any part in further experiments. It is possible, in any case, that her powers would have vanished with marriage; many investigators have noted that there is a connection between sexual frustration and "poltergeist effects," and that such effects cease when the "focus" leads a normal sex life. (She may also have felt that seances were bad for her health—they often leave the medium exhausted.)

In 1926, Price came upon one of the most remarkable poltergeist cases of all time. In February 1925, a thirteen-year-old Rumanian peasant girl called Eleonora Zugun went to visit her grandmother at the village of Buhai, and on the way found some money by the roadside, which she spent on sweets. Her grandmother, who was 105 years old, and had a reputation as a witch, told Eleonora that the money had been left by the devil, and that she would now be possessed by the devil. The next day, stones rained down on the house, smashing windows and small objects near Eleonora rose up in the air. Eleonora was quickly sent home to Talpa, and the phenomena continued there. A jug full of water rose slowly in the air and floated several feet. A trunk rocked up and down. A porridge bowl hit a visitor on the head and made a nasty wound. Eleonora was sent to a nearby monastery, then shut in a lunatic asylum. A psychical researcher managed to get her removed and taken back to the monastery. There he witnessed all kinds of things flying through the air. The "spirit" also began slapping the girl. Then a countess with an interest in psychical research—Zöe Wassilko-Serecki—heard about Eleonora, went to see her, and brought her back with her to Vienna. Eleonora was delighted with her new life in the countess' flat, and began training as a hairdresser. And the poltergeist phenomena continued—indicating perhaps that a poltergeist does not need a psychologically "disturbed" teenager for its manifestations. The countess observed what most other researchers into poltergeist activity have noted: that the poltergeist seems to dislike anyone actually seeing it move objects; the countess noted that various small items would fall from the air without being seen to move from their original place. The poltergeist—or *dracu* (demon) as Eleonora called it—communicated by automatic writing, even spoke a few sentences in a "breathy and toneless voice." But what it had to say indicated that its level of intelligence was extremely low.

The *dracu* also punched and slapped Eleonora, threw her out of bed, pulled her hair, filled her shoes with water (the poltergeist seems to be able to create water, as we have seen), and stole her favorite possessions. In March 1926, it began scratching and biting her, as well as sticking needles into her. The bite marks were often damp with saliva.

Price came to Vienna at the end of April 1926, and was soon convinced that this was a genuine poltergeist. He took her back to London, where she was subjected to laboratory tests. The movement of objects was less violent than in Vienna, but the bites and scratches continued to appear. One day, when she was tying up a parcel in front of several witnesses, she gave a gasp, and teeth marks appeared on her wrist, then scratches appeared on her forearm, cheeks and forehead.

Back in Vienna, the movement of objects ceased, but the scratches and bites continued, now often accompanied by quantities of an unpleasant spittle. Subjected to chemical analysis, this was found to be swarming with micro-organisms (whereas Eleonora's own saliva was relatively free from them). When she went to Berlin to be studied by Schrenk-Notzing, a researcher named Hans Rosenbusch accused her of cheating—with the co-operation of the countess; but this seems to be typical of the extreme skepticism of certain investigators. Finally, in 1927, the "spirit" got tired of tormenting her, and went away. She moved to Czernowitz, in Rumania, and ran a successful hairdressing business.

The countess was convinced that Eleonora herself—or rather, her unconscious mind—was responsible for the attacks: she believed that Eleonora had powerfully developed sexual urges, and that these were fixated on her father (it sounds as if she had been impressed by Freud); so the "attacks" were a form of self-punishment. Harry Price was inclined to agree, likening the bites to the "stigmata" that appear on the hands of saints and religious fanatics. Yet as we read the account of Eleanor's sufferings at the hands of the *dracu* (there is an excellent account in Alan Gauld's *Poltergeists*), these explanations seem more and more preposterous. A girl does not go on scratching and biting herself for two years because she feels guilty about her sexual desires, particularly if she finds herself transformed, like Cinderella, into the protégée of a wealthy countess. Then what exactly happened?

Clearly, the grandmother was in some way responsible for "triggering" the attacks. Eleonora had reached the age—thirteen—at which such things happen; she was not particularly happy in her present surroundings in Talpa, so there was an underlying sense of frustration. Peasants are superstitious, and when her grandmother told her that from now on she would belong to the devil and never get rid of him, the effect must have been traumatic. Eleonora's energies began to "leak." And some delinquent entity saw its chance, and made use of them. It may or may not be relevant that her grandmother had a reputation as a witch. If magic—and presumably witchcraft—makes use of "spirits," as Playfair suggests, then her grandmother's house may have been the worst possible place for a frustrated adolescent like Eleonora. (This matter of witchcraft is a subject to which we shall return in the final chapter.)

As to Harry Price, he continued his triumphant career as the chief Public Relations Officer of the spirit world. He investigated fire walking and the Indian rope trick, organized seances, was photographed in "haunted beds" (with "Professor" Joad), and staged an experiment on the summit of the Brocken to try to change a goat into a young man. (This was a failure.) Price loved publicity, and lost no opportunity to be photographed by journalists. He was delighted that so many correspondents seemed to think that his name was Sir Harry Price. Yet he also made the general public conscious of psychical research in a way it had never been before. Because Price emphasized that he was a skeptic and a scientist, not a Spiritualist, people took him more seriously than they did a "believer" like Conan Doyle or Sir Oliver Lodge. When he announced in 1933 that he now felt that Rudi Schneider might be a fake, and produced a photograph that seemed to show him cheating during a seance, people felt that he was showing unflinching honesty. (In fact, the photograph was later shown to be a fake; Price's motive was almost certainly desire to get his own back on Rudi for, as he saw it, "deserting" him for another investigator, Lord Charles Hope, whose findings Price denounced.)

Yet in spite of his craving for publicity and his desire to get into *Who's Who*, Price did much important and valuable work during these years. In a sense, his motivation is irrelevant; he was a genuine enthusiast for psychical research. The majority of his investigations were not spectacular: just the plodding, day-to-day work of a patient researcher, sitting with mediums, psychometrists, healers, miracle workers. And, if anything, Price was inclined to be over-critical. In Norway, he visited the home of Judge Ludwig Dahl, and had a sitting with the judge's daughter Ingeborg, whose "controls" were her two dead brothers. While not regarding her as a downright fake, Price was unimpressed. Yet one of the dead brothers prophesied that their father would die on August 8, 1934, seven years later, and this was precisely the day on which he did die from a stroke during a swim.

A case which certainly deserves mention in any account of Price's career is the curious affair of the talking mongoose of Cashen's Gap. It was far from being one of Price's successes; yet it remains an intriguing mystery.

In 1932, Price heard about a farmer called Irving, at Cashen's Gap on the Isle of Man, who had made friends with a mongoose that could speak several languages. It could also read minds and sing hymns. Price could not find time to go to the Isle of Man, but a friend of his, a Captain M. H. Macdonald, offered to go.

It seemed that the Irving family—who (significantly) had a thirteen-year-old daughter named Voirrey—had been disturbed by noises from behind the panels of the house: barking, spitting and blowing noises. The farmer lay in wait with a gun, without success, and tried putting down poison; the creature eluded him. So the farmer tried communicating with it, making various animal noises; to his astonishment, it seemed to be able to imitate them. Voirrey tried nursery rhymes, and it began to repeat these. Finally, it showed itself—a small, bushy-tailed creature that claimed to be a mongoose. They called it Gef. And Gef told them he was from India. Mr. Irving seldom saw Gef, except in glimpses, as he ran along a beam, but Voirrey and Mrs. Irving often saw him face to face.

Macdonald arrived at the farm on February 26, 1932, and saw nothing; when he left to go to his hotel a shrill voice screamed: "Go away! Who is that man?" The farmer said this was Gef. The next day, as Macdonald was having tea with the Irvings, a large needle bounced off the teapot; and Irving remarked that Gef was always throwing things. Later, he heard the shrill voice upstairs talking with Voirrey and Mrs. Irving; when he called to ask if the mongoose would come down, the voice screamed: "No, I don't like you." He tried sneaking upstairs, but the mongoose heard a stair creak, and shrieked: "He's coming!" And from then on, Macdonald saw and heard no more of Gef.

According to Irving, who kept a diary, Gef talked in a language he claimed to be Russian, sang in Spanish and recited a poem in Welsh. He killed rabbits for them—by strangling them—and left them outside. He claimed to have made visits to the nearest town, and told the Irvings what various people had been doing; Irving checked and found this was correct. He was able to tell Irving what was happening ten miles away without leaving the farm. And when he was asked if he was a spirit, Gef replied: "I am an earth-bound spirit."

In March 1935 Gef told Irving that he had plucked some hairs from his tail and left them on the mantelpiece; these were forwarded to Price, who had them examined. They proved to be dog hairs—probably from the collie dog on the farm.

When Harry Price was mentioned, Gef said he didn't like him because he "had his doubting cap on." And when Price finally visited Cashen's Gap, the visit was a waste of time. Gef only came back to the farm after Price had left. And this, virtually, was the end of the story—although Macdonald paid a second visit to the farm and again heard the mongoose talking in its shrill voice.

It is possible, of course, that the Irvings were hoaxers. But they struck the investigators as honest. And it is difficult to see why, if they wanted attention, they should invent anything as bizarre as a talking mongoose. Why should Irving have invited Price to stay if he was simply a hoaxer?

What seems rather more probable is that Gef was a poltergeist—an "earth-bound spirit," as he himself claimed. Voirrey was a lonely girl who had just reached puberty. The disturbances started like most poltergeist disturbances, with noises in the woodwork, scratchings and other sounds. Later small objects flew through the air, and Gef was assumed to have "thrown" them. But he also seemed to be able to cause "action at a distance"; when a saucepan of water turned over on the stove and soaked Irving's shoes, he assumed this was Gef. The clairvoyance also sounds like a poltergeist, and the knowledge of other people's affairs. And it seems odd that the rabbits were strangled—not a mongoose's normal method of killing. In fact, the Gef case seems to belong on the borderland between the straightforward poltergeist and the elemental or hobgoblin. (In the mid-nineteenth century, as Robert Dale Owen points out, the word poltergeist was usually translated hobgoblin.)

Trevor Hall is of the opinion that the poltergeist case which Price claimed to be his first experience of "ghost hunting" was pure invention, and he could be right—Price says that it took place when he was fifteen, at a village which he calls Parton Magna; but since the rest of the details concern his wealthy relatives and his return to a public school, we are probably safe in assuming it never took place. But with Price, one can never be sure. In *Confessions of a Ghost Hunter* (1936), he has a chapter called "The Strange Exploits of a London Poltergeist," in which he states that he is forced to disguise the names and the location because it occurred so recently. But the case which he goes on to describe is thoroughly well authenticated, and is, in fact, one of the most remarkable of this century.

It actually took place in Number 8 Eland Road, Battersea, and began on November, 29, 1927, when lumps of coal, chunks of washing soda, and copper coins began to rain down on the conservatory roof. The house was occupied by an eighty-six-year-old invalid, Henry Robinson, his son Frederick (twenty-seven), his three daughters, and a grandson of fourteen, Peter. When some of the falling objects smashed the glass, they sent for the police. As the constable stood in the back garden, a lump of coal knocked off his helmet. He rushed to the garden wall and pulled himself up—but there was no one around.

The Robinsons' washerwoman was terrified when she went into the wash-house and found the place full of smoke, and a pile of red hot cinders on the floor; she gave notice.

Then the poltergeist began to get into its stride—and it was an exceptionally destructive spirit. Ornaments smashed against walls, articles of furniture overturned, windows were broken. When they moved the old man out of his bedroom, a huge chest of drawers toppled over; a few minutes later the hall stand began to move, and broke in two when Frederick tried to hold it.

In January, an out-of-work journalist named Jane Cunningham was passing the house when she heard an almighty crash. A young man in shirtsleeves ran out. Jane grabbed her notebook and went in to investigate. This time, the poltergeist had smashed the whole conservatory just as if it had placed a bomb in it—all over the garden there were glass, lumps of coal and washing soda—and pennies. Her report on the occurrence led to widespread press interest in the case.

Price went to see the house, and the poltergeist threw a gas-lighter past him; otherwise, nothing much happened. Soon afterwards, Frederick had a mental breakdown and had to be sent to a hospital. Chairs marched down the hallway in single file. When Mrs Perkins—the mother of the boy Peter—tried to lay the table, chairs kept scattering all the crockery.

Price assumed that Peter was the "focus" and suggested he should be sent away; he went to stay with relatives in the country. But the poltergeist remained. Objects continued to be thrown around. The old man had to be removed to a hospital, and one of the daughters fell ill. The police could only advise the family to vacate the house for the time being, which they did, staying with friends.

A medium held a seance in the house, and began to shiver. But she was unsuccessful in identifying the "spirit." Price paid another visit, with a newspaperman, and more objects were thrown—although not when anyone was watching. Finally, Frederick Robinson came home from the mental home where he had been confined, and quickly moved the whole family elsewhere. This was virtually the end of the story.

Yet there was a postscript. Price had heard that small slips of paper with writing on them had fluttered from the air. Frederick, sick of the whole business, declined to comment. But many years later, in 1941, he broke silence in the Spiritualist newspaper *Two Worlds*, stating that slips of paper *had* fallen from the air, and that some of them contained writing made by tiny pinholes. (The Seeress of Prevorst also produced sheets of paper with geometrical drawings made by the same method.) One of these messages read: "I am having a bad time here. I cannot rest. I was born during the reign of William the Conqueror." It was signed "Tom Blood." Other messages were signed "Jessie Blood."

The Battersea poltergeist seems to be in every way typical of the species. Whether or not it was genuinely an earthbound spirit from the days of William the Conqueror must remain in doubt; poltergeists are not necessarily truthful. (But, as the Rochenberg-Rocha case shows, the dead have no sense of passing time.) The chief mystery of the case is where it obtained the energy to continue the "haunting" after the boy Peter left—for it seems reasonable to assume he was the "focus." The answer may be provided by Price's observation that at the back of the house there was a mental home. Price actually suggested that some ex-servicemen patients in this home might have thrown lumps of coal (but this is probably an example of his desire to be regarded as a hard-headed skeptic). The mentally disturbed are often the "focuses" of poltergeist activity, so it seems possible that the "spirit" found a convenient reservoir of surplus energy just over the garden wall.

The case with which Price's name has become most widely associated is, of course, that of Borley Rectory. And in spite of the "debunking" that has taken place since Price's death in 1948, it remains one of the most interesting hauntings of the twentieth century. After Price's death, a whole volume of the *Proceedings of the Society for Psychical Research* was devoted to "The Haunting of Borley Rectory, A Critical Survey of the Evidence," by Dingwall, Trevor Hall and Kate Goldney. They allege that Price probably produced some of the "poltergeist" phenomena himself by tossing pebbles—which, from our knowledge of Price, must be admitted as possible. Their overall conclusion is that there are so many doubts that it would probably be simplest to regard the haunting of Borley as a fairy story. But this is to ignore the fact that stories of hauntings were common long before Price came on the scene, and have continued since he left it. Anyone who feels that the SPR survey proves that Price was a liar should read the long account of Borley in Peter Underwood's *Gazetteer of British Ghosts*, with Underwood's own first-hand reports from interviews with witnesses.

Borley Rectory was built in 1863 on the site of Borley Manor House, which in turn seems to have been built on the site of a Benedictine abbey. It was built by the Reverend H. D. E. Bull. It is difficult to pin down the earliest known "sightings," but it is clear that during Henry Bull's tenancy, a number of people saw the apparition of a nun. Henry Bull himself knew of the legend that a nun and a Benedictine monk had tried to elope, been caught, and had both been killed, the nun being bricked up alive. Bull's daughter Ethel confirmed in a letter to Trevor Hall in 1953 that she had awakened to find a strange man standing beside her bed, and had felt someone sitting down on the bed on several occasions; she also told Peter Underwood how, on July 28, 1900, she and her two sisters all saw a nun-like figure gliding along "Nun's Walk," apparently telling her beads. The other sister, Elsie, saw the nun, who looked quite solid, and went to ask her what she wanted; the nun vanished.

After the Reverend Henry Bull's death, his son, the Reverend Harry Bull, took over the rectory. He was interested in psychical research, and claimed that he saw many ghosts. His daughter told Price that he had seen a legendary phantom coach (in which the lovers were supposed to have fled) and that, one day in the garden, the retriever had howled with terror, looking toward some legs visible under a fruit tree. Bull, thinking this was a poacher, followed the legs as they walked toward a postern gate; at which point he realized that the "poacher" was somehow incomplete. The legs disappeared through the gate without opening it.

Harry Bull died in 1927, and the rectory was empty until 1928, when the Reverend Guy Smith and his wife moved in.

One stormy night, there was a furious ringing of the doorbell; when Smith arrived there, he found no one. It happened again later—a peal so prolonged that Smith was able to get to the door before it stopped; again, there was no one. After that, all the keys of all the rooms fell out of the locks overnight; later, they vanished. Then they began hearing slippered footsteps. Stones were thrown—small pebbles. Lights were switched on. One day, Mrs. Smith thought she saw a horse-drawn coach in the drive. Mr. Smith thought he heard someone whisper,"Don't, Carlos, don't," as he was walking into the chapel. The Smiths decided to contact the *Daily Mirror*, who asked Harry Price if he would be willing to go along with an investigator. They told Price their story, and gave him every facility to investigate. But within nine months, they had had enough of the place—perhaps because its plumbing left much to be desired—and moved to Norfolk. According to the SPR report, the Smiths only called the *Daily Mirror* because they were concerned about all the stories that the house was haunted, and wanted to reassure their parishioners by getting the place a clean bill of health. This story sounds, on the face of it, absurd. Moreover, there exists a letter from Mr. Smith to Harry Price stating: "Borley is undoubtedly haunted." (It is true that Mrs. Smith wrote a letter to the *Church Times* in 1929, saying she did not believe the house to be haunted, but this seems to have been a belated attempt to stem the flood of sensational publicity that followed the *Daily Mirror* story.)

In October 1930, the rectory was taken over by the Reverend L. A. Foyster, and his much younger wife Marianne. Foyster, oddly enough, had lived near Amherst at the time of the Esther Cox case, and the SPR survey makes much of this coincidence; however, it seems doubtful that the vicar would attempt to fake disturbances on the model of his earlier experience. Certainly, the Foyster incumbency saw the most spectacular exhibitions of the Borley poltergeist. Foyster kept a diary of the disturbances. Bells were rung, bricks thrown, footsteps heard and water out of a jug poured over the couple when in bed. Foyster was even awakened by a violent blow on the head from his own hairbrush. They saw a number of apparitions, including the nun and a clergyman who was identified as the Reverend Henry Bull, the builder of the rectory. Writing appeared on the walls, asking for a mass to be said, and asking for "Light."

There is much independent confirmation of all these events. A Justice of the Peace named Guy L'Estrange visited Borley at the invitation of the Foysters, and wrote a lengthy account of it. As soon as he arrived, he saw a dim figure near the porch, which vanished as soon as he approached. Mrs. Foyster had a bruise on her forehead—something "like a man's fist" had struck her the previous evening. The Foysters were telling L'Estrange about mysterious fires that kept breaking out in locked rooms when there was a loud crash in the hall; they found it littered with broken crockery. Then bottles began flying about. L'Estrange notes that they seemed to appear suddenly in mid-air. The bottles were coming from a locked storage shed outside. All the bells began to ring, making a deafening clamor—but all the bell wires had been cut. L'Estrange shouted: "If some invisible person is present, please stop ringing for a moment." Instantly, the bells stopped—stopped dead, as if each clapper had been grabbed by an unseen hand. Later, sitting alone in front of the fire, L'Estrange heard footsteps behind him; he turned, but the room was empty. The footsteps had come from a part of the wall where there had once been a door. In bed, L'Estrange felt the room become icy cold, and saw a kind of shape materializing from a patch of luminosity; he walked toward it, and had a feeling of something trying to push him back. He spoke to it, and it slowly vanished. He was luckier than another visitor who thought that the ghostly figure was someone playing a joke, and tried to grab it; he was given a hard blow in the eye.

The rector and others tried praying in the chapel, taking with them a relic of the Curé of Ars, and then went around the house making signs of the cross. Finally, they all spent the night in the Blue Room, where Henry Bull (and others) had died; they asked that the entity should stop troubling the inmates of the house; a black shadow began to form against the wall, then dissolved. But after this, temporary peace descended on Borley Rectory.

In 1935, the Foysters decided they had had enough, and moved. Price rented the rectory in 1937, and arranged for a team of investigators to go in. But the major phenomena were over. Even so, the chief investigator, Sidney Glanville, a retired engineer, became completely convinced of the reality of the haunting.

In March 1938, the team were experimenting with a planchette, which wrote the message that Borley would be destroyed by fire. This happened in February 1939, when the house mysteriously burned down. Yet the phenomena continued; a Cambridge team investigating the ruins heard footsteps, saw patches of light, and recorded sudden sharp drops in temperature.

In August 1943, Price decided to try digging in the cellars at Borley, which he had been advised to do by a planchette message which claimed to come from "Glanville"—the same Glanville who wrote the account of the Tedworth drummer. They found a cream jug, which had also been referred to by the planchette, and some fragments of a human skull. The jawbone showed signs of a deep-seated abscess—Peter Underwood speculates that this is why the phantom nun always looked miserable.

The SPR survey on Borley, which appeared eight years after Price's death, had the effect of seriously undermining his credit. Trevor Hall's *Search for Harry Price* (1978) completed the work of destroying his reputation. Yet although this leaves no doubt that Price lied about his origins—perhaps romanced would be a better word—and hungered for fame, it produces no evidence that Price was not exactly what he always claimed to be: an enthusiastic scientific investigator of paranormal phenomena. To assume that, because Price wanted to be thought a "gentleman," he was also dishonest as a paranormal researcher, is surely poor psychology. Price was one of those ambitious men who crave an outlet for their energies. He was forty years old before he found the opportunity he was looking for—a long time for a man of Price's impatient temperament. It came when Dingwall invited him to Munich to study the Schneider brothers. From then on, Price had discovered his vocation; at last, he had found the outlet he needed for his explosive energy and romanticism. And when a man as energetic and romantic as Harry Price finally finds what he is looking for, he does not risk spoiling everything with a little cheap skulduggery. It only takes one scandal to destroy a scientist's reputation. But to put it this way is to imply that Price disciplined his natural dishonesty solely to maintain his reputation and this is to miss the real point; that once a man has found his vocation, he pours into it all that is best about himself. Bernard Shaw has left an interesting description of the socialist Edward Aveling, who was Eleanor Marx's common-law husband; he was an inveterate seducer, and a borrower who never paid his debts, yet where socialism was concerned, he was fiercely sincere. Everything we know about Price reveals that, where psychical research was concerned, he was totally dedicated—although not above grabbing publicity wherever he could find it.

In short it would be of no advantage to him to pretend the Borley phenomena were genuine when they were not. His reputation was based on his skepticism as much as on his support of the reality of psychic phenomena. Possibly—like most of us—he was capable of stretching a fact when it appealed to his romanticism. But in the case of Borley, there was no need to stretch facts. The haunting of Borley does not rest on Price's evidence alone; there are dozens of other witnesses, such as Guy L'Estrange—or Dom Richard Whitehouse, cited by Underwood, who witnessed just as many incredible occurrences: flying objects, ringing of bells, writing on walls, outbreaks of fire, materialization of bottles.

And is there evidence that Price *did* stretch the facts? The SPR survey cites as an example of his dishonesty the episode of the pair of legs that Harry Bull saw walking through the postern gate. Price says, admittedly, that when the man emerged from behind the fruit trees, he was headless. But the report then goes on to cite Price's original notes, which read: "Rev. Harry Price saw coach, Juvenal, retriever, terrified and growled. Saw man's legs rest hid by fruit trees, thought poacher, followed with Juvenal, gate shut, but saw legs disappear through gate." Clearly, what Bull saw disappearing through the gate was not a complete man, or Price would not refer only to the legs. It sounds as if the upper half of his body was missing—in which case, headless is a fair description.

What seems clear from all accounts of the case is that the "ground" itself is haunted, and continues to be so. Like Ardachie Lodge, Borley is a "place of power," the kind of place that *would* be chosen for a monastery, and that probably held some pagan site of worship long before that. In the Rectory's early days, Harry Bull himself—son of the Reverend Henry Bull—was probably the unconscious focus or medium; Paul Tabori says that he was probably psychic. This is borne out by the fact that young Bull saw so many of the "ghosts," including the coach and the nun. It is important to realize that not all people can see ghosts. The "ghost hunter" Andrew Green describes, in *Our Haunted Kingdom*, a visit that he and other members of the Ealing Psychical Research Society paid to Borley in 1951.

> One of the Society members grabbed my arm and, although obviously terrified, proceeded to describe a phantom that he could see some thirty feet in front of him, standing at the end of the "Nun's Walk." It was of a Woman in a long white gown, and moved slowly towards the end of the neglected garden . . . the witness was perspiring profusely with fear and later with annoyance that I had failed to see the ghost.

Green had only heard the rustle of trees and bushes, as if something was walking through the undergrowth. We may assume, then, that if Green had been a tenant of Borley before its destruction, he would probably have seen no ghosts. Bull was, it seems, enough of a "medium" to see the ghosts. And Marianne Foyster was a far more powerful medium who changed the character of the haunting into poltergeist activity. (Most of the messages scrawled on walls were addressed to her.) The reason that the subsequent investigation of Borley (during Price's tenancy) was so unsuccessful was that there was no medium present to provide the energy.

Asked about the "ley system" of the Borley area, the ley expert Stephen Jenkins replied as follows: "Norfolk and Suffolk are a spider-web of alignments, many of which are linked to curious manifestations. Borley church stands at a node where four lines cross, one going from Asher church to Sproughton church . . . " After giving further details of the ley system, he goes on:

> My wife photographed me as I was standing with my back to the south wall of Borley churchyard, at ten o'clock on the morning of Saturday the 1st of September, 1979. Recently, this was borrowed for a magazine article, and the editor kindly sent me an enlargement. No less than three people, not one of them known to the others, have on separate occasions noted in the enlargement some odd— and not very prepossessing—faces among the trees close to the church. The same identifications have been made without possibility of collusion.
>
> More dramatic than unexpected faces in a photograph, which can always be explained away as "simulacra," or something wrong with the emulsion, is an incident of Sunday the 28th of August, 1977, on the road north of Belchamp Walter Hall. The time was precisely 12:52 p.m., and we were driving southwest along the minor road which marks the north end of the Hall grounds, when on the road in front, in the act of turning left into the hedge (I mean our left, across the path of the car), *instantaneously* appeared four men in black—I thought them hooded and cloaked—carrying a black, old-fashioned coffin, ornately trimmed with silver. The impression made on both of us was one of absolute *physical* presence, of complete material reality. Thelma

and I at once agreed to make separate notes without comparing impressions. We did so, and the descriptions tallied exactly, except that she noted the near left bearer turn his face towards her. I did not see this as I was abruptly braking at the time.

What I had seen as a hood, she described as a soft tall hat, with a kind of scarf falling to the left shoulder, thrown across the cloaked body to the right. The face was that of a skull. The enclosed sketch [below] gives a fair idea of what she saw.

The next day we returned to the precise spot at exactly the same time and took a picture. It is a Kodak colour slide. In the hedge near the gap where the "funeral party" vanished (there is a path there leading to Belchamp Walter churchyard) is a short figure, apparently cloaked, its face lowered with a skull-like dome to the head. A year later I returned searching the area where it had apparently stood. There was nothing, no post or stump that might have provided such an image, nor was there the slightest sign of the ground having been disturbed by the removal of anything that might have been rooted in it. The image is simply there on the film——we saw nothing wrong with the eye.

That minor road alongside the north edge of the Belchamp Walter Estate precisely coincides with a line passing through the node in the water west of Heaven Wood. That node itself linked with the node at Borley.

He adds a postscript: "I hazard a guess that the dress of the coffin-bearer is that of the late fourteenth century. There seems to be no local legend of a phantom funeral."

If Price invented the ghosts of Borley, he must have been in collusion with a remarkable number of people.

I did not like [Harry Price] because he was a difficult man to like. He was intensely selfish, jealous, and intent on his own glory at all costs, but these weaknesses of his character do not detract from his investigation as an honest investigator and ruthless exposer of frauds. This was the shining feature of his life.

These words were written by another man who deserves to be remembered as one of the prominent ghost-hunters of the twentieth century. Unlike Price, Nandor Fodor seems to have had no great compulsion to achieve personal glory; the result is that, since his death in 1964, his name has been largely forgotten, and most of his books are out of print. Yet at least one of his books—his account of the Thornton Heath poltergeist case—deserves the status of a classic.

Fodor was born in Hungary in 1895, studied law, then became a journalist, and visited America. In 1926, he interviewed two remarkable men: Hereward Carrington, the psychical researcher, and Sandor Ferenczi, one of Freud's most prominent disciples. Fodor became simultaneously fascinated by psychoanalysis and psychical research and, in due course, became himself a psychoanalyst. Predictably, therefore, his analysis of poltergeist cases is dominated by the conviction that they have a sexual origin. But since—as we have seen—there is a large element of truth in this view, Fodor's psychoanalytical beliefs distorted his outlook rather less than is often the case with Freudians.

Fodor attended his first seance at the house of a well-known American medium, Arthur Ford, in October 1927 and what he heard there left him in no doubt that the dead can communicate. In the semi-darkness, a trumpet sailed up into the air, then a voice began to speak. Various relatives of people who were present then came and (apparently) talked through the medium. Fodor then asked if the "control" could bring someone who spoke Hungarian. It was, perhaps, an unreasonable request, but an excellent test for the medium. And after a few moments, a voice spoke from the air saying: "Fodor, journalist," using the German pronunciation of the word—just as Fodor's father did. Then the entity proceeded to speak to Fodor in Hungarian. The voice identified itself as Fodor's father, and mentioned various relatives; it named his oldest brother by his pet name. The "spirit" was having great difficulty communicating because, explained the control; it was the first time he had tried to speak. The control helped out by telling Fodor that his father died on January 16. The "spirit" ended by saying "Isten áldjon meg. Éides fiam"—"God bless you, my dear son." After this another Hungarian came through—the deceased brother of Fodor's wife, who was present. It mentioned that "poor Uncle Vilmos" was ill and would go blind. And, in due course, this is exactly what happened to Uncle Vilmos.

It emerged later that the medium—a man called Cartheuser—could speak Hungarian. Yet this scarcely helps to explain his knowledge of Fodor's father, and the prophecy about Uncle Vilmos. Cartheuser also had a speech impediment, due to a hare lip; the voices had no such impediment.

Fodor came to England to work for Lord North-cliffe—owner of the *Daily Mail*—and, in his spare time, compiled an *Encyclopedia of Psychic Science*, which is still one of the best available (a new edition combines it with a similar work by Lewis Spence). After publishing the book, in 1934, Fodor had first-hand experience of the ambiguous nature of "psychic phenomena." He heard of a remarkable Hungarian medium called Lajos Pap, a carpenter, whose specialty was causing "apports" of live birds, animals and beetles to appear at seances. In June 1933, Fodor attended such a seance in Budapest. Pap was undressed and searched, then dressed again in a robe of luminous cloth, so that his movements in the dark could be clearly seen. Two men held Pap's wrists during the seance, although he could move his hands with their hands on him. In an hour-long seance, Pap groped into the air and produced thirty live beetles, many of them an inch long. He also produced a cactus plant with soil on the roots and a rose bush. On other occasions, Pap had produced birds, caterpillars, dragonflies, snakes, and a live goldfish. His "control," the Rabbi Isaac (who claimed to have lived six hundred years earlier in Galicia) had a sense of humor. At one seance, a toy pistol arrived, and a number of explosive caps were fired; the Rabbi claimed to have shot dead twenty-one crickets and, after the seance, dead crickets were found in the room.

On another occasion, nine lumps of dirty snow arrived during the seance, and proved to be mixed with horse manure and straw. The temperature in the room was 72 degrees Fahrenheit, so it would have been difficult to keep the snow unmelted for long if it had been concealed under the medium's robe.

Fodor arranged for Lajos Pap to be brought to London. At a seance there a dead snake, more than two feet long, appeared. Fodor was impressed; but he nevertheless insisted that Pap should have an X-ray examination to find out whether he could have anything secreted in his body. To Fodor's surprise and dismay, Pap proved to be wearing a belt of linen and whalebone under his robe. He said it was a kind of rupture truss, because he had a dropped kidney; but Fodor decided regretfully that this is where the dead snake had been hidden, and that it had been worked out through the neck of the robe. Accordingly, in his subsequent report, "The Lajos Pap Experiments," Fodor concluded that Pap's psychic powers should be regarded as "not proven." Yet he adds:

> Nor would I be willing to declare him a fraud and nothing but a fraud. Too long has psychical research been the victim of the fatal delusion that a medium is either genuine or fraudulent. It is a minimal assumption that mediumship means a dissociation of personality. There was plenty of evidence that Lajos Pap was suffering from such a dissociation.

In fact, Pap is still regarded as a non-fraudulent medium, and accounts of his seances at which live birds and insects appeared seem to indicate that his powers *were* remarkable.

Fodor had been appointed Research Officer of the International Institute for Psychical Research. In November 1936, he was asked to investigate a case of poltergeist haunting at Aldborough Manor in Yorkshire. The bells for summoning servants had rung almost non-stop for five days, doors had opened and closed of their own accord, and two maids had seen a ghost above an ancient cradle. Lady Lawson-Tancred, who lived in the house, was afraid she would have to move out if the haunting continued. But when Fodor arrived, it was already over. One of the two maids had had a nervous breakdown and left. The bells had rung during the night she left and the following morning, then stopped. To Fodor, therefore, it was clear that the maid was the "focus" of the disturbance. Her nervous breakdown was probably caused by the "drain" upon her energies caused by the poltergeist. The other maid, a very pretty girl, also had a strange power over animals; birds would settle on her shoulders, and mice run into her hands. Lady Lawson-Tancred thought that she might also be connected with the disturbances, and dismissed her. (Fodor seems to have explained to her the difference between a poltergeist and a real "haunting," where the house itself seems to concentrate the negative forces, as at Borley.) After this, Aldborough Manor became peaceful.

The same solution was found in the case of a Chelsea poltergeist that disturbed a house with its knockings. Fodor went to the house, in Elm Park Gardens, and heard the rappings himself—he said they were like hammer blows. Fodor looked around for the focus, and soon found it: a seventeen-year-old servant girl named Florrie. He engaged her in conversation, and she told him that this was not her first experience of mysterious knockings—the same thing had happened at home four years before, when she was thirteen. The children were all sent away, and when they returned, the knocking had stopped. Clearly, Florrie was quite unaware that she had been the "cause" of the knockings.

Fodor told the house's owner, Dr. Aidan Redmond, that Florrie was probably the unconscious medium. That night, the raps were like machine-gun fire. Dr. Redmond regretfully sacked Florrie. And silence descended on the house.

In July 1936, Fodor investigated a case in which the distinction between ghost and poltergeist becomes blurred; this was at Ash Manor, in Sussex, and he disguises the family under the name of Keel. It is among the most remarkable ghost stories ever recorded.

The house was bought by the family in June 1934; when they said they could not pay the price demanded, the owner dropped his demand so surprisingly that the Keels decided there must be something wrong with the place, probably the sanitation. But the wife soon began to get extremely unpleasant feelings in a bedroom that had been used for servants. (The previous owner said they had run away.)

The first manifestations were stamping noises from the attic. But this room had no floorboards—only the bare joists. In November 1934, Mr. Keel was awakened by three violent bangs on his door. He went to his wife's room down the corridor—she had also heard them. This happened at 3 a.m. The next night, there were two thumps on the door at the same time, and the following night, one loud thump. Keel went away on business for a few days, and when he returned, decided to stay awake until 3 a.m. to see if anything happened. Nothing did, and he fell asleep. Then a violent bang woke him up. Although the room was dark, he could see quite clearly a small, oldish man dressed in a green smock, with muddy breeches and a handkerchief around his neck. He looked so solid and normal that Keel was convinced this was an intruder and, when he got no reply, jumped out of bed and tried to grab him: His hand went through him, and Keel fainted. When he came to, he ran to his wife's bedroom, babbling incoherently, and his wife rushed out to get some brandy. Outside her husband's room she saw the feet and leggings of a man, then looked up and saw the same little old man. She was also able to see him quite clearly in the dark, although he did not seem to be shining. She observed that he was wearing a pudding basin hat, that his face was very red, "the eyes malevolent and horrid," and that his mouth was dribbling. She also asked him who he was and what he wanted. When he made no reply, she tried to hit him. Her fist went through him, and she hurt her knuckles on the doorpost. Her husband was in a faint in her room at the time, so he had not had an opportunity to describe the man he saw; it was only later that they realized both had seen the same ghost.

After this, they continued to see the little old man in green several times a week. They also heard footsteps and knocking. The old man usually walked across Keel's bedroom, appearing from the chimney on the landing, and vanished into a cupboard which had once been a priest hole. After a while, the family ceased to be afraid of him. The wife discovered that she could make him vanish by extending a finger and trying to touch him. The third time she saw him, the old man raised his head, and Mrs. Keel could see that his throat was cut and his windpipe was sticking out. One day she heard heavy footsteps approaching along the corridor, and thought it was her husband. Her bedroom door, which was locked, flew open and invisible footsteps crashed across the room (although the floor was carpeted), then the footsteps went upward toward the ceiling, as if they were mounting a staircase. A trapdoor in the ceiling flew open, and the footsteps continued in the attic—again, sounding as if they were on floorboards, although these had been removed. A dog in the room was terrified. Mrs. Keel's sixteen-year-old daughter Pat was sleeping in her mother's room, and witnessed the whole episode. The man who sold them the house told them that there *had* been a staircase in the room, which he had had removed to replace it with the fireplace.

Two psychical investigators who were called in declared that the house had been built on the site of a Druid stone circle, and that this explained why it was haunted. The ghost, they said, was a man called Henry Knowles, who had cut his throat in 1819 when a milk-maid had jilted him.

As the Research Officer for the International Institute, Fodor was called in to investigate; he had with him Mrs. Maude ffoulkes, who also published the story of the manor house in her book, *True Ghost Stories,* later that year (thus providing independent corroboration of the story). An amateur photographer had succeeded in taking a picture of a dim shape on the haunted landing, so Fodor took his own photographic equipment.

Fodor now had enough experience of hauntings to look for unhappiness in the house. The daughter, Pat, struck him as nervous and very jealous of any attention given to her mother, and admitted to suffering from temper tantrums. On the first night, nothing happened. The next time, Fodor slept in the "haunted room," but, apart from awful nightmares, had nothing to record. He decided to ask the help of the famous American medium, Eileen Garrett, who happened to be in England. In late July Mrs. Garrett came to the house and immediately had strong psychic impressions. The ghost, she said, was a man who had been imprisoned nearby. There had been a king's palace nearby, and the man had been tortured. He had something to do with a king called Edward. Her further observations suggested that the "ghost" she saw was not the same old man, for she described him as sharp-featured, with blond hair, and said he had taken part in a rebellion against his half-brother, the king. (In fact, there were two royal castles in the area, Farnham and Guildford.)

Mrs. Garrett went into a trance, and was taken over by her trance personality, Uvani, an Arabian. Uvani made the interesting comment that hauntings take place only when there is someone in a "bad emotional state" who can revivify old unhappy memories. There were bad emotional states in this house, said Uvani. "Life cannot die," said Uvani, "you can explode its dynamism, but you cannot dissipate its energy. If you suffered where life suffered, the essence that once filled the frame will take from you something to dramatize and live again." About five hundred yards to the west of this house, said Uvani, there had been a jail in the early part of the fifteenth century, and many unfortunate men and women had died there. "There are dozens of unhappy souls about." (The early fifteenth century was the period of the battle of Agincourt, Joan of Arc, and many revolts and rebellions. The plot against Edward the Fourth by his brother, the Duke of Clarence, was in 1470.)

"According to this," says Fodor,* "our ghost was a spectral automaton, living on life borrowed from human wrecks—a fascinating conception which was very different from ordinary spiritualistic conceptions and very damning for the owners of the house.

Uvani then said that he would allow the ghost to take possession of Mrs. Garrett's body. The medium grew stiff and her breathing became labored. She seemed to be trying to speak, but was unable. The "spirit" pointed to its lips, tapped them as if to signal it was dumb, then

---

* *The Haunted Mind*, Chapter 8.

felt its throat gingerly. He beckoned to Fodor, then seized his hand in such a powerful grip that Fodor howled with pain. Although another person present tried to help him free his hand, it was impossible. Fodor's hand went numb, and was useless for days after the seance.

The "man" threw himself on his knees in front of Fodor, seemed to be pleading, and clicked his tongue as if trying to speak. Then it called "Eleison, eleison," pleading for mercy in the words of the mass. Aware that the ghost was taking him for its jailer, Fodor tried to reassure it, and said they were trying to help him. Finally, the man seemed reassured, and sat down. He began to speak in an odd, medieval English (unfortunately, tape recorders did not exist in those days—it would have been fascinating to have an authentic example of the English of Chaucer's period), and spoke about the Earl of Huntingdon, calling him ungrateful. It asked Fodor to help him find his wife, then raged about the Duke of Buckingham, (perhaps the one who led a rebellion against Richard III in the late fifteenth century). It seemed that the Duke of Buckingham had offered the man "broad acres and ducats" in exchange for his wife, then betrayed him. The spirit identified itself as Charles Edward Henley, son of Lord Henley. On a sheet of paper, it wrote its name, then "Lord Huntingdon," and the word "esse," which was the medieval name for the village near the manor house. It made the curious statement that Buckingham, the friend of his childhood, had "forced her eyes," "her" being his wife Dorothy. He added: "Malgré her father lies buried in Esse," and went on: "You being friend, you proved yourself a brother, do not leave me, but help me to attain my vengeance."

Remembering that, according to the teachings of Spiritualism, it is remorse or desire for vengeance that often keeps spirits bound to earth, Fodor and another sitter, a Dr. Lindsay, tried hard to persuade the spirit to abandon its hatred. Finally, it seemed to agree, then cried out, "Hold me, hold me, I cannot stay, I am slipping . . ." Then it was gone, and Mrs. Garrett woke up.

During this seance, the Keels had been present. Mrs. Keel peered closely at the medium's face while "Henley" was speaking through her, and was horrified to see that it now looked like the old man she had seen.

But *had* the ghost been laid? Apparently not. Some time later, Keel rang Fodor to tell him that the old man was back again, standing in the doorway and trying to speak.

Dr. Lindsay, who had been present at the seance, had also had a remarkable experience. At the College of Psychic Science, he had been involved in a seance with another medium when the ghost of "Henley" came through. It complained that Fodor had promised to stand by him, but that when he had come back the following night, there was no one there. The old man said he had seen his son, for whom he had been searching, but not his wife.

They had another session with Mrs. Garrett that afternoon. Again, the ghost came through, and made more pleas for help, as well as saying a little more about his background. It was not particularly informative; but the control, Uvani, had some interesting things to say. He asserted that the Keels had been "using" the ghost to "embarrass" each other. What was being suggested was that the ghost-laying ceremony *would* have worked if the Keels had not wanted to cling on to the ghost as a device for somehow "getting at" one another.

Following this hint, Fodor talked to Mrs. Keel. She then admitted that Uvani was right about the unhappiness in the household. Her husband was homosexual, so their sex lives left much to be desired. And the daughter was jealous of her mother—Fodor hints that it was a classic Oedipus complex. Mrs. Keel was keeping up her spirits with drugs.

Soon after this, the case began to reach a kind of climax. Mr. Keel himself was becoming "possessed" by the spirit, talking in his sleep and saying things about "Henley" and his life. Fodor sent him a transcription of the things Uvani had said about the desire of the Keels to "hold on" to the ghost; as a result, Keel rang him to admit he felt it was true.

This confession had the effect that Fodor's "ghost-laying ceremony" had failed to achieve; the ghost of Ash Manor disappeared and did not return.

This is undoubtedly one of the most interesting cases of haunting on record, for a number of reasons. First, the corroboration is impressive: the story was also written up by Maude ffoulkes and published in 1936,* and the participation of Eileen Garrett rules out any suggestion that Fodor might simply have invented the whole story—a suggestion that *has* been made about one of Harry Price's most impressive cases, "Rosalie."† Second, the behavior of the ghost seems to show that the "tape recording" theory of Lethbridge and Sir Oliver Lodge does not cover all hauntings; "Henley" was clearly more than a "recording." And third, it demonstrates very clearly that there is no clear dividing line between a ghost and a poltergeist. This case started with bangings and rappings, and then developed into a haunting. And, if we can accept Uvani's statements as any kind of evidence, it also suggests that there are such things as "earth-bound" spirits, probably in dismaying abundance. The other implications—about the nature of such spirits—must be left until the final chapter.

---

* It is also described in *Unbidden Guests* by William O. Stevens, 1945.
† See *The Occult*, Part 3, Chapter 2.

If Fodor had possessed Price's flair for publicity, the "Henley" case might have made him as famous as Borley made Price. But he made no attempt to publicize it. Neither did he attempt to make capital out of a visit to study the talking mongoose of Cashen's Gap (except for a single chapter in a book), although his investigation was rather more painstaking—if hardly more successful—than Price's. (Fodor concluded that the mongoose was probably genuine, but denied that it was a poltergeist on the dubious grounds that poltergeists are always invisible; we have seen that "elementals" are rather less easy to classify than this implies.) In fact, Fodor's only flash of notoriety occurred almost accidentally as a result of a libel action he brought against *Psychic News*. He was asked whether it was true that he wanted to take a medium, Mrs. Fielding, to the Tower of London to steal the Crown Jewels by psychic means, and he admitted that this was true, and that he had been willing to go to prison if the experiment had been successful. However, it had been forbidden by the other members of the International Institute. From then on, Fodor was known as the man who wanted to "spirit away" the Crown Jewels.

Mrs. Fielding was, in fact, the "focus" of the most interesting and complex poltergeist case he ever investigated. Mrs. Fielding (Fodor calls her Mrs. Forbes in his book *On the Trail of the Poltergeist*) was a thirty-five-year-old London housewife, living at Thornton Heath, an attractive woman with a seventeen-year-old son. The disturbances began on Friday, February 19, 1938, as the Fieldings were in bed, and on the point of sleep. A glass shattered on the floor, and when they put on the light, another glass flew past their heads. They put off the light, and the eiderdown flew up in their faces. They tried to switch on the light again, but the bulb had been removed.

A pot of face cream was thrown at their son when he came in to see what was happening. The next day, cups, saucers and ornaments flew through the air. They notified the *Sunday Pictorial*, and two reporters came. The poltergeist obliged with an impressive display. A cup and saucer in Mrs. Fielding's hand shattered and cut her badly, a huge piece of coal struck the wall with such force that it left a big hole, an egg cup shattered in the hand of one reporter, and Mrs. Fielding was thrown out of her chair by some force. As Mr. Fielding went upstairs, a vase flew through the air and struck him with a crash—yet although he looked dazed, his head was not bruised. Within three days of the coming of the poltergeist, it had broken thirty-six tumblers, twenty-four wine glasses, fifteen egg cups and a long list of other articles.

When Fodor arrived a few days later, the poltergeist did not disappoint. Fodor records twenty-nine poltergeist incidents during that first visit. Again and again, he had his eyes on Mrs. Fielding when things happened—glasses flew off tables, a saucer smashed against the wall, glasses were snatched from her hands and broke on the floor. It was soon clear that Mrs. Fielding, and not her seventeen-year-old son, was the focus and "cause" of the disturbances. One glass flew out of her hand and split in mid-air with a loud ping, as if it had been hit by a hammer.

Fodor asked Mrs. Fielding to come to the headquarters of the Institute, Walton House, for tests. She was dressed in a one-piece garment after being searched (a precaution he may have learned from the Lajos Pap case) and they went into the seance room. While Mrs. Fielding was standing in full view, with three witnesses around her, there was a clatter, and a brass-bound hair brush appeared on the floor. It was warm, as "apports" usually are (the theory being that

they are "dematerialized" and then re-materialized).
Mrs. Fielding identified it as her own, and said she had
left it in her bedroom at home. The poltergeist then
obliged with several more apports, and also made
saucers fly out of Mrs. Fielding's hands and split with
a ping in mid-air. Strong men found that they could not
break them in their hands.

The idea of stealing the Crown Jewels probably
came to Fodor when he and Mrs. Fielding went into a
gift shop and she decided against buying a small elephant; as they were getting into the car, a box in Mrs
Fielding's hand rattled, and they found the elephant in it;
they had committed "psychic shop-lifting."

At a later "sitting," Mrs. Fielding produced some
impressive results. On one occasion she sat with her
hands tightly clenched while someone held them. The
person holding them felt one hand convulse "as if something was being born," and when Mrs. Fielding opened
her hand, there was a tortoiseshell cross in it.

She also began to experience "psychic projec-
tions," finding herself in other places in her trance states.
In the seance room, in a semi-trance, she projected herself back to her home. They telephoned her husband,
who said she was there, and even handed her the telephone; at that moment, they were cut off. Mrs. Fielding's
"double" handed her husband a recipe that she had written in the seance room; he read it back to them over the
telephone, and it was identical with the one they had in
front of them. He also handed the "double" a compass,
which then reappeared in the seance room, ten miles
away. The "double" had walked out of the front door
with the compass.

A full account of Mrs. Fielding's phenomena
would occupy a whole chapter. She produced some
ancient artifacts like Roman lamps and pottery labeled

"Carthage," white mice and a bird, and a spray of violet perfume around her body (as well as violets which fell from the air.) Under increasing strain, she started to show signs of breakdown. She began going hysterically blind, burn marks appeared on her neck, and she claimed she was being clawed by an invisible tiger (producing an unpleasant "zoo" odor). When her husband said jokingly that he would like an elephant, there was a crash and an elephant's tooth appeared in the hall. She also had a phantom pregnancy.

At a seance, a spirit that claimed to be her grandfather declared that he was responsible for the apports. Asked to prove its identity by bringing something of its own, it materialized a silver matchbox—which Mrs. Fielding said had belonged to her grandfather—in her clasped hands.

And at this point, the story took a bewildering turn. Mrs. Forbes [Fielding] apparently began cheating. Fodor saw her producing a "breeze" during a seance by blowing on the back of someone's neck. Fodor became convinced that she was producing small "apports" from under her clothes, and an X-ray photograph showed a brooch hidden beneath her left breast. Later, she produced this brooch as an apport. When being undressed, a small square of linen fell from between her legs, stained with vaginal secretion; it looked as if she was also using her vagina to hide apports.

Two days after this, she claimed to have been attacked by a vampire. There were two small puncture marks on her neck, and she looked listless and pale.

One of the oddest incidents occurred when Fodor was walking with her into the Institute. With no attempt at concealment, she opened her handbag, took something out, and threw a stone over her shoulder. When Fodor asked her about this, she indignantly denied it.

In his account of the case in *The Haunted Mind*, Fodor makes the statement: "This discovery eliminated any remaining suspicion that a spirit or psychic force was still at work." But the "still" implies that he felt there had been genuine psychic forces at work at an earlier stage. Reading his full account of the case, this seems self-evident. It would have been impossible for Mrs. Fielding to have faked the poltergeist occurrences in her home, and later in the Institute.

Fodor's own analysis is as follows:

As a child, Mrs. Fielding was both accident- and illness-prone. At the age of six, recovering from tonsillitis, she thought that a muscular black arm tried to strangle her in bed; it vanished when her mother ran in. She was bitten by a mad dog, and attacked (and scarred) by a parrot. She lived in a house with a reputation for being haunted, and Fodor states as a fact that neither the windows nor mirrors ever needed cleaning—they were cleaned by invisible hands during the night.

At sixteen, she had "visions" of a ghost; a cupboard in her room opened and a man stepped out, then vanished. Subsequently she saw him several times. On one occasion he left a piece of paper with sooty scrawls on it beside her, but her mother burned it. A bicycle accident at this time led to a kidney abscess, which later necessitated many operations. At seventeen she made a runaway marriage, had her first baby at eighteen, her second at twenty-one. (This died of meningitis.) At twenty she contracted anthrax poisoning, and tried to stab her husband with a carving knife. She ran into the street in her nightdress screaming "Murder, fire," and recovered after having twenty-eight teeth extracted.

At twenty-four she had a vision of her father, trying to pull her away from her husband. He made the sign of the cross over her left breast. When she woke from her trance, this was bleeding. At the hospital they discovered she had a breast cancer, and the breast was amputated. At twenty-six she had an attack of hysterical blindness which lasted for six weeks and, at twenty-seven, was in an accident on a steamer which was smashed against Margate pier. At twenty-eight she aborted twins after being terrified when she found a dead rat in among her washing. At thirty she had a kidney operation, and at thirty-two, pleurisy. Altogether, it can be seen, Mrs. Fielding was a thoroughly unlucky woman.

Fodor then proceeds to interpret the evidence from the Freudian point of view. He is convinced that the basic truth is that Mrs. Fielding was attacked and raped, probably in a churchyard, by a man in round glasses, before she was five years old. Everything else, he thinks springs from this trauma. On two occasions, when lying awake at night, she felt a shape like a man—but as cold as a corpse—get into bed with her; then it "behaved like a man" (i.e., had sexual intercourse). One day, on her way to the Institute, Mrs. Fielding was attacked by a man on the train. Fodor does not doubt that she was attacked—she arrived in an upset condition—but thinks that the man's round glasses may have aroused in her a mixture of loathing and desire which was wrongly interpreted by the man as an invitation. Fodor goes on to suggest that her husband became somehow identified in her mind with her attacker, so that the poltergeist attacks were due to her unconscious aggressions against him.

There are times when Fodor's Freudian interpretations verge on the comic. For example, he is convinced that her apports are a cipher "in which her tragic life story is hidden." On one evening, the apports were: elephant's tooth, tiger claw, Carthage pottery, a tropical nutshell and a piece of coral. These, says Fodor, symbolize the hugeness of the man who assaulted her (an elephant), his savagery and beastliness, his scaliness (the nutshell), while the pottery symbolizes the breaking of her hymen. The coral stands for music from the church nearby. (Organ music always made Mrs Fielding cry, and Fodor surmises that the coral was organ-pipe coral.)

There is, of course, one basic objection to the whole theory. Mrs. Fielding did not tell Fodor she had been raped, and apparently had no such memory. Fodor naturally thinks it was suppressed. But do memories of that type become so suppressed that they vanish completely? It seems highly unlikely.

Fodor was never able to bring the case to a satisfactory conclusion. When he began explaining his rape theories to the Institute for Psychical Research, they objected so strongly that he felt obliged to drop the case. At least it enabled him to believe that Mrs. Fielding was getting closer and closer to remembering her rape experience, and would one day have confirmed all his theories. It will be recalled that, in the case of the Bell Witch, Fodor believed that Betsy had been sexually attacked by her father, and that this produced the poltergeist, "tearing loose part of the mental system and letting it float free like a disembodied entity." As a good Freudian, he felt bound to seek a sexual explanation in the Thornton Heath case. Yet, like so many of the "primal scenes" that Freud believed caused lifelong illness, the one posited by Fodor is completely inverifiable.

It would be a pity to leave this case without at least an attempt at an alternative explanation. And the simplest and most obvious is that Mrs. Fielding was a born medium. Her many illnesses turned her into what nineteenth-century investigators liked to call a "sick sensitive." Her vision of the black arm that tried to strangle her in bed may not have been a dream or hallucination, as Fodor thinks. If she lived in a haunted house, then it seems likely that spirit entities drew energy from her, increasing her tendency to illness. And later in life, she actually developed into a medium. During the investigation, she often went into trances, and a "control" called Bremba spoke through her. Sitting near a pub—and a church—in Coulsdon, she had a vision of an evil, leering face, which she continued to see for ten minutes. "Bremba" later stated at a seance that the man she saw had belonged to the church, and had been hanged for interfering with small children. "She was probably sitting on the spot where one of the outrages took place." When Mrs. Fielding came out of her trance, she could not speak or even whisper, then, as they all watched, strangulation marks appeared on her throat. When she could speak she said: "I feel as if I am being pulled up"—as if she was suffering from the man's hanging. Later, when she was telling friends about it, the noose marks again appeared on her throat. Fodor uses this as a support for his theory about the early rape; but it could, in fact be ordinary mediumship. Bremba could have been telling the truth about the man hanged for sexual offenses against children.

Then why did Mrs. Fielding begin to cheat? There are two possible explanations. One is that she was enjoying her new position as a subject of investigation. She was a bored housewife, and, as Fodor says, the phenomena meant "a new interest, a new life for her." This could be true; but *if* Mrs. Fielding was developing genuine powers as a medium, then she had no need to cheat in order to keep them. It sounds as if they had been latent since childhood; all she had to do was to allow them to develop.

The other explanation is that she was unconscious that she was cheating—which would explain the stone thrown in front of Fodor, with no attempt at concealment, and her subsequent denial. I have mentioned the case cited by Roll in which a man being investigated was seen, through a two way mirror, to throw an object—yet a lie detector test supported his denial that he had done it. We have seen that there is considerable evidence that poltergeists can enter the mind and influence people-mediums more than others.

To anyone who reads straight through Fodor's *On the Trail of the Poltergeist*, it seems obvious that Guy Playfair's "spirit entity" theory fits better than most. Both the Fieldings had been ill for some time before the first outbreak. So Mrs. Fielding may have been in a suitably "low" condition to enable the entity to begin using her energy. From then on, it used her continually, and accordingly she began to suffer from nervous exhaustion. Yet her attitude toward all this must have been ambiguous, for it brought new interest into her life; this could have enabled the entity—or entities—to manipulate her to cheat. And why should they? Because, for some reason, poltergeists seem to delight in producing bewilderment and confusion.

The one point that emerges above all others is that Mrs. Fielding was not just the focus of the poltergeist disturbances; she was a *medium*, and soon began to develop her ability, with apports, travelling clairvoyance, projection of the "double," and so on. In short, Mrs. Fielding was a potential Daniel Dunglas Home or Eusapia Palladino. And this, it seems probable, is true for all the people who became "focuses" for poltergeist phenomena. With her illnesses, her early marriage, even the loss of her teeth, Mrs. Fielding calls to mind another medium, the "Seeress of Prevorst," whose history forms the starting point of this chapter. Nandor Fodor, like Justinus Kerner, was a medical man. Yet it cannot be said that his study of Mrs. Fielding is as penetrating or as suggestive as Kerner's study of Friederike Hauffe. To read *On the Trail of the Poltergeist* after *The Seeress of Prevorst* is a depressing experience. It is to realize that a century of psychical research has brought very few advances—that, on the contrary, an unimaginative and over-cautious approach to the phenomena has only made them less comprehensible than ever.

Discussions and Conclusions

EIGHT

Speculations and Conclusions

The more we attempt to study the poltergeist, the clearer it becomes that it has no intention of cooperating.

This was borne in upon me in October 1975, when I received a letter from a man who claimed that he knew the identity of the criminal known as the Black Panther. Earlier that year the Panther had kidnapped an heiress named Lesley Whittle, and in March her body had been found down an underground tunnel in Bathpool Park, near Kidsgrove. The Panther was also wanted for a number of burglaries in post offices, during which he had killed three sub-postmasters. So, in October 1975, he was the most wanted criminal in England. Understandably, I was intrigued by the letter claiming to know his identity.

It had come from a village not far from St. Ives, in Cornwall, and on October 16, 1975, I drove down to see the writer, taking with me a guest who happened to be staying with us. Enroute, we called in to see Dora Russell, widow of Bertrand Russell, with the result that we arrived at the village in the late afternoon.

The writer of the letter was the village postman, and he was young, bearded, and had an appearance of sturdy common sense. It was his wife, he explained, who was psychic, and who had discovered the Panther's identity. His wife was a slim, pale girl who looked distinctly "delicate." Their cottage was freezing—he explained that it had to be kept at that temperature to prevent his wife from becoming feverish.

During the next hour, the two of them told us an incredible story. But they began by asking us if we could stay until eight o'clock. We asked why. "Because that's when the knockings begin." Every evening, they said, at eight o'clock some entity beat a regular tattoo on their bedroom wall. It sometimes made such a racket that it sounded like the drums of the Scots Guards. This had now been going on for several months. They were disappointed when we said that we had to be back in St. Austell by eight o'clock to take some friends out to dinner.

The story had begun a few months earlier, when his wife had had a series of vivid dreams and trance communications. She was Irish, and apparently this kind of thing had been happening all her adult life. Then, one evening, the rapping noises had started on their bedroom wall. It was clearly a "spirit," so they tried to communicate with it by the usual code, one rap for yes, two for no. They learned it was a girl, that she was recently dead, and that she had been murdered. Lesley Whittle's body had only recently been found in Bathpool Park, and when asked: "Are you Lesley Whittle?" the entity set a tremendous triumphant tattoo, as if to say "You've got it."

Odd coincidences began to occur, obviously engineered by the "spirit." The wife had a number of vivid dreams or visions of a certain set of park gates with an inscription on them. Her husband happened to open a *Reader's Digest Guide to Britain*, and saw gates that sounded like the description; his wife instantly recognized them. The entity told them by means of raps that the Black Panther had buried his gun under a stone in this park, and the wife saw the spot—in a vision—so clearly that she was able to make a sketch map of the whereabouts of the stone. Her husband finally rang the police who were hunting the Panther, and, after some difficulty, persuaded them to go to the park and look underneath the stone. Astonishingly, the stone was there, and the description of the immediate vicinity proved to be accurate; but a metal detector found nothing under the stone . . .

They had tried ringing the post office in the village near the park, and had concluded that the people who ran it knew the identity of the Panther, and were shielding him. They had made the mistake of giving their own telephone number. And now, they were absolutely convinced, the Panther was "on to them." A strange car had been parked in the lay-by opposite their house for night after night in August, with a gypsy-like man and woman in it, and someone had prowled around their house trying to break in . . . The car had followed them around, but on one occasion, when they pulled into a beach car park, and the other car turned in a few minutes later, a police car happened to enter the car park, whereupon the other car drove off "like a bat out of hell."

Their story was extremely long, extremely circumstantial. The "spirit of Lesley Whittle" had told them that the Panther had escaped through the underground tunnel in a boat, and gone straight to the park, where he hid his gun under the stone. He lived in a caravan in the garden of a cottage. When I asked the name of the Panther, they gave it without hesitation: it was W. E. Jones, and his caravan was in the village of Baynhall, Worcestershire.

As my guest and I drove away, at about seven o'clock (frozen to the bone), we agreed that it had been an impressive story, and that the husband seemed completely balanced and down to earth, even if the wife seemed a little "fey." Accordingly, the next morning, I sat down and dictated a long letter to the Commissioner of Police, Sir Robert Mark, with whom I was acquainted. I told him I agreed it all sounded preposterous, but that the couple struck me as genuine, and it was surely worth checking up on the stone in the park—digging, instead of using a metal detector—and on Mr. W. E. Jones—if he existed—of Baynhall, Worcestershire. He wrote back, promising to pass it all on to the officer in charge of the case. And, a couple of weeks later, he wrote again to say that both the stone, and Mr. Jones of Baynhall, had proved negative.

On December 11, 1975, two policemen at Mansfield Woodhouse saw a man carrying a hold-all, and stopped their police car to ask a few routine questions; he pointed a shotgun at them, climbed into the car and made them drive on. One of the policemen tackled him; two men in a fish and chip queue joined in, and the man was handcuffed to the railings. Two "Panther" hoods in his bag revealed that he was the man the police had been looking for. And when the news of his arrest was broadcast on the television news, I crossed my fingers that this name would turn out to be Jones. It was not. It was Donald Nielsen, and he lived in Bradford, not Baynhall. In due course, he was sentenced to life imprisonment for the murder of Lesley Whittle and three postmasters.

Oddly enough, the psychic and her husband refused to accept that their poltergeist had been mistaken, and wrote to me asking if I could find out whether Donald Nielsen had paid a visit to Cornwall during August 1975. I checked with the police officer in charge of the case, and was told that he was pretty certain Nielsen had not been that far south. The couple declined to believe it. They had found the "communications" circumstantial and convincing. My own conclusion was that the "spirit" had simply been a circumstantial and convincing liar.

While I was still collecting material on poltergeists, I was asked if I would write the text of an illustrated book about witchcraft; and since it was a subject on which I have written a great deal—and which would therefore require a minimum of research—I agreed. It proved to be an excellent preparation for writing a book about poltergeists. It is possible to believe you know a subject fairly thoroughly, and then to discover, as you write about it, that you have overlooked its very essence. And as I plunged into the history of witchcraft, it struck me that not only had I failed to understand it, but that the twentieth-century mind had lost the key to the whole phenomenon. This applies as much to modern witches and "occultists" as to scientists and skeptics. When we look into a work like Francis Barrett's *The Magus* (1801), with its pictures of the heads of demons, we feel a kind of irritation that anyone could have been so stupid as to take them seriously. We can accept the idea of the strange powers of the unconscious mind, even of psychokinesis; but the assumptions that have formed the basis of witchcraft for the past three or four thousand years strike us as absurd superstitions. Margaret Murray convinced a whole generation that witchcraft was an ancient pagan religion called *wicca*, which was basically a form of nature worship, the cult of the Moon Goddess and the Earth Mother, and that the witches who were burned at the stake were simply carrying on the old practices. As far as she went, she was probably correct. But Margaret Murray was a modern rationalist, for whom "magic" was an absurdity. And *all* witchcraft has been based on the idea of magic: that the witch or magician can make use of spirit entities to carry out her will. (These are known as "familiars.")

The earliest literary record of a witch is the story of the witch of Endor in the Bible, and it makes clear that the chief business of a witch in those days (about 1000 B.C.) was *raising the dead*. And later tales of witches—in Horace, Apuleius and Lucan—make it clear that this was still true a thousand years later on. After the beginning of the Christian era (whose own major contribution was the idea of the Devil), the witch also became the invoker of demons. The most famous picture of John Dee, the Elizabethan magician, shows him in a graveyard with the spirit of a dead man he has just raised. "Necromancy"— the raising of the dead—was a synonym for magic. We may infer, therefore, that although the ancients knew nothing about Spiritualism, they had stumbled upon the same discovery as the Fox sisters and Daniel Dunglas Home: that it is, apparently, possible to communicate with the "dead," as well as with other invisible entities. In his notorious *History of Witchcraft*, the Reverend Montague Summers denounces modern Spiritualism as a revival of witchcraft. He may simply have meant to be uncomplimentary about Spiritualism; but, as it happens, he was historically correct. The kind of spiritualism initiated by the Fox sisters was the nearest approach to what Lucan's Erichtho, or Dame Alice Kyteler, would have understood by witchcraft. It begins and ends with the idea that we are surrounded by invisible spirits, including those of the dead, and that these can be used for magical purposes. Accordingly, magicians like Paracelsus, Cornelius Agrippa and John Dee took care to protect themselves in magic circles—or pentagrams—when they conjured "demons," and to perform the rituals with pedantic exactitude (which, according to Guy Playfair, is essential, the spirits being sticklers for detail).

Some cases, like that of Isobel Gowdie and the Auldearne witches, are incomprehensible unless we recognize that witchcraft is about "spirits"—the kind of spirits we have been discussing in this book. In 1662, Isobel Gowdie, an attractive, red-headed farmer's wife, shocked the elders of the local kirk (in Morayshire, Scotland) when she announced that she had been a practicing witch for the past fifteen years, had attended Sabbats, and had sexual intercourse with the Devil (whose semen was "as cold as spring water"). The notion that she was insane or simply hysterical is contradicted by the fact that several of the witches she named made full confession, without torture, and corroborated her statements in detail. Isobel claims that she encountered the Devil, a man in grey, when travelling between two farms. and that she agreed to meet him in the church at Auldearne, where he made her renounce Jesus. He came to her in bed a few days later and copulated with her; she found his penis thick and long and his semen "abundant and as cold as ice." Elsewhere in this book we have encountered women who had a similar experience—for example, Mrs. Fielding, and Playfair's Marcia. And from the drop in temperature that usually occurs during spirit manifestations, we might also expect his semen to be cold. Isobel Gowdie also mentions various acts of black magic, by which people are killed, and (significantly) a visit to fairyland, where she encountered the Queen of the Faery.

Again, the case of the Salem witches suddenly becomes more comprehensible when we consider it in this light. In 1692, the daughter and niece of the Reverend Samuel Parris began having convulsions like the possessed nuns of Loudun—and a doctor gave his opinion that they were bewitched. Parris had come from Barbados, and had brought with him a number of black servants, including a woman called Tituba, who knew a great deal about magic or voodoo. The girls had apparently been trying out some of these magical ceremonies at a remote spot in the countryside. When a magistrate questioned the girls about their convulsions, they screamed and claimed that they were being bitten and pinched. At the trial Tituba fully admitted practicing witchcraft and having dealings with the Devil. The affair was blown up by local hysteria until over a hundred people were accused, and twenty-two executed (not including Tituba). Montague Summers argues convincingly that there *was* a witches' "coven" in the area (although its members had nothing to do with "bewitching" the children). But if Tituba was genuinely skilled in voodoo, and the children tried practicing it, then the result may well have been poltergeist manifestations, complete with scratches and bites, and "demoniacal possession" producing convulsions. Anne Putnam, the oldest of the girls, was of the right age—twelve—and was physically mature.

Magic prescribes certain rituals and precautions to protect the would-be sorcerer from unfriendly spirits. When these are not observed, the results can be alarming. Even a simple seance can be dangerous if the participants are inexperienced. In *Mysteries*, I have described the experience of Bill Slater, former head of BBC television drama, who made facetious remarks at a seance with a ouija board, and woke up in the middle of the night convinced that some invisible entity was trying to take over his body. He says that it was "massing itself on my chest, making every effort to take over my mind and body." It took twenty minutes of intense struggle before he could "push it away."

The psychical investigator, Leonard Boucher—quoted in an earlier chapter—has described how, after an improvised seance (in an attempt to contact the recently departed husband of his hostess), he and his wife spent a highly disturbed night at the House of Knock, near Stranraer.

> After retiring and switching off the light, the room seemed to take on a chilly atmosphere, although it was summer time and the air outside was very warm. A few minutes later there came from under the bed a loud scratching noise as if an extra-large

cat had been trapped underneath . . . Investigation proved that there was not a single cat anywhere around. Getting back into bed and again turning off the light, we were startled to feel the bed-clothes suddenly pulled off the bed. This unpleasant operation was repeated several times over the next hour or so, and throughout the whole night we heard bumps and thuds coming from various parts of the room. Probably looking rather weary and worn, I explained the next morning to our hostess that we had not slept too well; she then remarked that she too had a restless night owing to scratchings and bangings in her room.

In spite of which, Leonard Boucher states his conviction that the poltergeist is a manifestation of the unconscious mind— explain his experience in the House of Knock.

What this seems to suggest, then, if that almost anybody can "summon up" a spirit, especially if they happen to have mediumistic powers. Witches and shamans summon them deliberately; and in that case, their main problem is controlling them. Much depends, of course, on the *intention*. People who play around with ouija boards to pass an idle hour are likely to attract some passing vagabond of a spirit, and the results may then be unpredictable. Mediums seem to attract "controls" who then act as policemen and keep out the undesirables. But even they are not always successful. John Dee, for example, was always being told that the information he received the previous day was all useless because it came from a mischievous intruder . . . But serious intentions are likely to produce the best results, whether or not the "magician" has any previous experience. This is illustrated by a case recounted to me by a Filipino girl, Mimitan Wigan, of the Besao tribe of the Wester Bontoc. The

Besao are a breakaway group from the Bontoc (part of the Igarot tribes), who are war-like head hunters. The Besao are peaceable, and have concentrated on developing their natural psychic powers; they are, for example, skilled in healing and rain-making.

Mimitan's Aunt Kadmali lived (and still lives at the time of writing) in the mountain village of Dandanak, on Luzon; she is now in her eighties. When she reached the age of thirteen, she inherited an orchard or plantation that grew pineapples, oranges, lemons and other fruits. But the orchard was mysteriously being plundered. One night, the girl sat outside the house, and prayed and chanted until dawn; she was praying for the nature spirit to reveal to her the identity of the thief. At dawn, she went into the orchard, and, to her astonishment, found a man with his arm uplifted to pick fruit, standing as if paralyzed. Seeing that he was unable to move, Kadmali rushed off to her neighbors and brought them to witness the thief's discomfiture. The man was able to speak, and was asked how he intended to make reparation for his thefts; he said that he would work for the girl for a year without wages. As soon as he had said this, he was able to move.

Aunt Kadmali has since become well-known for her psychic powers; but her first experience of them was on this occasion. They are not regarded as in any way unusual among the Besao, who—although Christian—take it for granted that human beings can commune with spirits. She is not regarded as a "witch" as she would be in the West—because the Besao recognize that all human beings possess similar powers, to a greater or lesser extent.

All this throws a new light on the concept of witchcraft in Western civilization. There must have been a time when our ancestors took "shamanistic" powers for granted, as the Besao do. But this was when people lived close to nature. As soon as cities began to develop, attitudes toward these powers began to change. H. G. Wells remarks that it was only ten thousand generations ago that human beings "were brought together into a closeness of contact for which their past had not prepared them." And he points out that these cities were not communities, but "jostling crowds in which quite unprecedented reactions were possible." People were living more closely together than ever before, yet were separated by a new hostility, a sense of mutual isolation. Crime became the rule instead of the exception. And the city dwellers created their own exaggerated mental image of witchcraft and magic. Now they were no longer in daily contact with the real thing, they invented stories of magic and malevolence, witches with sagging breasts and pointed nails who desecrate the dead and summon demons. Lucan's Erichtho, the foul and evil hag who digs up graves and destroys crops, is a symbol of horror, like Dracula or Frankenstein's monster; there is nothing real about her.

It is tempting to jump to the conclusion that we have simply lost contact with nature and with the hidden powers of the unconscious mind, and that the solution may be to turn a suspicious eye on the idea of technological progress—like the inhabitants of the village of Sagada, on Luzon, who have simply ignored the electricity that has been brought to their homes, and continue to use oil lamps and cooking fires. But this would be an oversimplification. The members of a primitive tribe may have a deeper understanding of nature than do city dwellers; but this does not necessarily mean a deeper understanding of themselves. An animal's attitude to nature is passive; it simply adjusts itself, and chooses the path of least resistance. Primitive peoples are inclined to do the same. The hardship of city life caused people to take a more active attitude towards their own existence. Witchcraft continued to exist; but it took on a darker coloring, since, as far as the city-dweller was concerned, magic was simply a short cut to power and wealth, or an instrument of revenge. The magician ceased to be the shaman, who lived in conformity with nature and conversed with spirits, and became the sorcerer, the person of power who could "summon up spirits from the vasty deep." There is a sense in which the magician—from Simon Magus to John Dee or Aleister Crowley—is a new human archetype. These suspect that they have far more power than human beings generally take for granted. And they are undoubtedly correct. The spirit of Cornelius Agrippa and Faust has created modern civilization and modern science. So although this new relation to nature may be in some ways a bad one—full of aggression and alienation and *hubris*—it is still an important advance beyond the primitive attitude of passivity in the face of nature. It would be absurd for members of Western civilization to think of exchanging hard-won knowledge for the ancient simplicity. What is needed is to *rediscover the things we have long forgotten*, the truths that the Besao take for granted.

And if a primitive shaman were asked to state the most basic of these forgotten truths, he would reply: We are not alone on this planet; we are surrounded all the time by unseen spirits. Western men and women find this idea disturbing and disquieting because it seems to be a return to the superstition that made our ancestors cross themselves against the evil eye. Such misgivings may be justified. Nevertheless, we have seen that an objective examination of the facts about the poltergeist points to the conclusion that it is some form of earth-bound spirit. I have to admit that I reached this conclusion with extreme reluctance; from the scientific point of view it would be far more acceptable if we could agree with William Roll that poltergeist phenomena originate in the unconscious mind. But the facts point in another direction.

How, for example, can the RSPK theory explain the curious events which are still—as I write these words—going on in the pub in Croydon called the King's Cellars? In the autumn of 1980, shortly after I had returned from interviewing the Pritchard family in Pontefract, Guy Playfair told me something of the Croydon poltergeist, which he and Maurice Grosse had been studying for the past year. It apparently caused the usual phenomena—bottles and glasses floating off shelves or simply smashing on the floor, sudden chills, inexplicable malfunctions of tills. As Guy and I were walking along Oxford Street, talking about the case, we encountered a friend of Guy's from the SPR, who had been in contact with the pub earlier in the day, and who said that several tills had jammed at the same time, although the firm that supplied them could find nothing wrong with them. This piece of synchronicity decided me, and I phoned the pub's manager—Mike Delaney—to ask if I could come down and see for myself. I asked an old friend, the psychic Robert Cracknell, if he would like to go with me.

The King's Cellars proved to be less of a public house than a kind of continental bar, with a cellar which is also a restaurant. The downstairs bar has been decorated to look "ancient," with imitation masonry. The manager, Mike, had been there for only a few months; the previous manager and his wife had left abruptly, after deciding to separate. This, Mike told us, seemed to be one of the unfortunate characteristics of the place: in the twelve years it had been open, it had wrecked the marriages of about a dozen couples.

He had been sent there by the brewery to act as a stop-gap until another manager could be found—he was the brewery's "trouble-shooter," who went to pubs that were having problems. When he arrived, he knew nothing about the place, and certainly did not believe in ghosts or poltergeists. On the fifth night, he stayed late to examine and balance the books. And, since it was a lock-up pub, he decided to stay there overnight in a sleeping bag. After working at the books, he lay down in the sleeping bag on a padded seat. The place seemed unusually cold—far colder than it should have been. And as he closed his eyes, he heard the sound—a rattle of glasses. He sat up, then went over to the bar. All the glasses on the top shelf were vibrating, as if a juggernaut lorry was going past. But there was no juggernaut; all was silent. The place was now so icy that he decided to go upstairs and sleep in the office. The next morning he went back to the hotel where he was staying for a shower, locking the pub behind him. When he returned to the downstairs bar, he was surprised to find it covered in broken glass. The row of glasses that had been vibrating had been swept all over the floor. To do this, three dozen glasses had had to cross the bar.

Then the tills began to go wrong. They were new electronic tills, and were supposed to be foolproof. One night, one of the tills was apparently more than £26,000 short. It was absurd. When a member of staff was approaching a till—together with a stocktaker—it suddenly rang up £999. The suppliers sent an engineer, who could find nothing whatever wrong. The telephones would also begin to malfunction, for no obvious reason; again, engineers could trace no fault. One morning, all the ashtrays—which had been left, full, on the top of the bar—had been neatly emptied on to the floor, making a long, continuous line of ash; but they had been on the bar when Mike had locked up the pub the night before.

Another problem was the lavatories. These would flood for no obvious reason—even when there was no one in them. When this happened, they went icy cold. On one occasion, a stream of water shot up out of the urinal, flooding the place. But this should have been impossible, for the urinal was simply a metal trough, at thigh level, with a pipe descending from it into the floor-level gutter; water could flood into the trough from the tank above, but this was shooting up from the trough itself. Plumbers could find nothing wrong with the water system in the lavatories.

Oddly enough, Mike was not unduly disturbed about all this; neither was his wife, Shirley. She had been there only six weeks, and had seen nothing. She told me she thought she was "ESP-thick." Mike now had no doubt that the place was "haunted," but it did not bother him unduly. He said. "I love this place, and I intend to stay." After years of moving from pub to pub, he had found one he liked. A poltergeist was a nuisance, but it did no real harm—except scaring the staff. It had swept a whole row of beer bottles off the upstairs bar one day, smashing them all. One warm evening, it had made the downstairs bar so cold that two huge fan heaters had no effect, and Mike was forced to close it down. When Maurice Grosse arrived one day with a television crew, it had made a smell so disgusting, accompanied by the usual freezing cold—that they all felt sick. One day, with customers in the bar, flames suddenly crept up the wall-with an oddly bright light—and across the ceiling; then they extinguished themselves. The likeliest explanation seemed some odd electrical fault; but neither the fire-prevention officer nor the electricity board could find anything wrong. Stella, the catering supervisor—who had been there longest—had watched a bottle of wine sail across the room, to shatter itself against a wall.

Maurice Grosse came while Bob Cracknell and I were eating lunch in the downstairs bar, and we talked about the case. He agreed that the most puzzling thing about it was the lack of a "focus." The disturbances had been going on for years. They had not worked themselves up to a climax, as in most cases. And there seemed to be no single person who might provide the entity—if that was what it was—with energy

As we were speaking, someone shouted: "It's happening again." We all rushed down to the ladies' lavatory. It felt icy cold, and the floor was covered in water, which had gushed out of the lavatory pan.

When I left the place at midafternoon, I had reached only one conclusion: This was obviously a thoroughly non-typical case. A female member of the staff was reported to have seen a ghost—a woman—in an annex of the downstairs bar, but I was unable to speak to her. A girl had committed suicide by throwing herself from the Nestlé building opposite the pub, landing on the roof, and Mike seemed to think that this could have been the cause of the "haunting." One of the managers had fallen downstairs late at night, and had been found dead in the morning. But no one seemed certain exactly when this had occurred.

I kept in touch with Maurice Grosse, who said he would let me know if there were any interesting developments. A few weeks later, Bob Cracknell rang me, to tell me that Shirley had walked out. She had been alone in the downstairs bar late at night, and had apparently seen something. She had refused to say what it was—had simply walked out and refused to go back. (I have her voice on tape saying how much she liked the pub, and that she had no intention of going away.) Mike himself, said Bob, also looked as if he was beginning to feel the strain; but he still said he had no intention of leaving.

A few weeks later, Bob rang me again. Mike had quite suddenly decided he could take no more, and he too had walked out. He had found himself some kind of job in Africa, and intended to go in mid-January. Meanwhile, he badly needed a rest; could he come down and stay with us in Cornwall? I said he would be welcome and, in early January, Bob drove down with Mike, and left him with us. We could both see that Mike was under severe strain; he seemed exhausted and distracted. He admitted that he had been drinking very heavily, and said that this was because he had begun to feel permanently exhausted. Day after day, as he opened the pub and went down to the cellar, he encountered the same wall of cold at the foot of the stairs. Without Shirley, he had begun to feel the strain. One day, he suddenly felt that if he stayed there any longer, it would drive him into a nervous breakdown. He said that, late one night, he went down to the cellar, and said aloud: "All right, you've beaten me, I'm going." Instantly, the place became freezing cold . . .

Mike spent only a week with us, then decided to commit himself voluntarily to the local mental home at Bodmin. A few days in St. Lawrence's Hospital worked wonders; among people who were severely ill, his natural vitality and dominance reasserted themselves. He discharged himself in less than a week, spent a few more days with us—now drinking moderately again—and finally left for Africa. I have a cassette on which he talks for two hours about his experiences in the King's Cellars, and there is a great deal that I have left out of this account. As a poltergeist, the Croydon spirit was not particularly inventive; only incredibly persistent.

Bob Cracknell rang me a few weeks later to say that he had interviewed the latest manager, who told him that he did not believe in ghosts. About a month later, he phoned again to say the manager had just left.

My only other contact in the Croydon area was Stephen Jenkins, the author of *The Undiscovered Country*; I asked him if he would try and find out anything he could about the pub. His reply begins: "My researches into the supposed manifestations in the King's Cellars, Park Street, Croydon, have come into the expected 'no thoroughfare,' as I rather foresaw . . . " He goes on:

> Two things are clear, however, which suggest strongly that we are dealing with an area in which unusual phenomena might be expected, in view of what your inquiries (and mine) elsewhere in this island have shown.
>
> First, an enormously long alignment passes quite close to the north-west end of the cellars. The alignment starts at the church in the moated site of Jericho Priory in Essex and goes to the centre of an earthwork at Valdoe. This is northeast of Chichester, and inside the great system of concentric circular alignments that center on the old Roman forum. This great Essex/West Sussex line passes through some important-seeming nodal points, some of which are (supposedly) the sites of curious manifestation . . .

He goes on to say that a map of Croydon for 1847 shows a house in its own park close to the site of the present King's Cellars. He concludes:

> All that I can offer is the observation that long experience has led me to *expect* odd occurrences to be situated on or very near alignments, especially at the nodes. Further, houses or the sites of buildings on or adjacent to leys are more likely to be the haunts of phenomena. I must not omit to

note that the vanished house on the plan of 1874 touches—or is on—the long Jericho Priory to Valdoe earthwork alignment . . .

In the Croydon case, then, the "human focus" theory seems to be untable. A straightforward haunting remains a possibility, and here we have at least two "suspects"—the landlord who died at the foot of the stairs, and the girl who committed suicide from the Nestlé building. Before the King's Cellars became a pub, it was a fire station, and this may also have been associated with some tragedy. Yet the disturbances are clearly of the poltergeist-type, if we ignore the dubious sighting of a female ghost in the annex. The likeliest theory, then, is that we are here dealing with some mischievous entity of the elemental type, which draws some of its energy from human beings, and some from the site itself.

This, of course, begs the question of what *is* an "elemental"? In his book *Operation Trojan Horse*, which deals with the mystery of UFOs, John Keel has a chapter which discusses the problem.

> Throughout history occultists have called these [mysterious visitors] elementals. There are several kinds of elementals in psychic lore. One type is supposedly conjured up by secret magical rites and can assume any form ranging from that of a beautiful woman to hideous, indescribable monsters. Once a witch or a warlock has whipped up such a critter, it will mindlessly repeat the same actions century after century in the same place until another occultist comes along and performs the rite necessary to dissolve it.

Keel points out that these "thought forms" can be encountered in traditional magic from Tibet to Ireland.

In Tibet they are called *tulpas,* and Alexandra David-Heel's book on Tibet contains a great deal of information about them. She claims to have created an imaginative "projection" of a monk that looked so solid that a herdsman took him for a real lama. This thought-form eventually began to get beyond her control and become hostile, and she claims that it took six months of hard work to "dematerialize" him. Otherwise he might have continued to haunt her, or, more likely, have remained behind in the area where he was created, and been seen by people as a ghost. George Owen's Toronto team seem to have created a kind of *tulpa* in Philip, the manufactured ghost. In *Psychic Self Defence,* the occultist Dion Fortune has a story of how she involuntarily created an "elemental" when she was thinking negative thoughts about someone who had done her an injury. In a semi-dozing state, she thought of Fenris, the Nordic wolf-god—probably (although she does not say so) fantasizing on how satisfactory it would be to set it on her enemy.

> Immediately I felt a curious drawing-out sensation from my solar plexus, and there materialized beside me on the bed a large wolf . . . I knew nothing of the art of making elementals at that time, but had accidentally stumbled upon the right method—the brooding highly charged with emotion, the invocation of the appropriate natural force, and the condition between sleeping and waking in which the etheric double readily extrudes.

She ordered the creature out of the room and it went. But when people in the house began to dream of wolves and imagine yellow eyes shining out of the darkness, she decided to "re-absorb" it, and succeeded in summoning it and then turning it into a "shapeless grey mist."

So, according to this fragment of magical lore, an elemental is not a spirit entity but a "thought form" which has somehow acquired a kind of life of its own. This view certainly offers a better explanation of fairies and similar creatures than Conan Doyle's suggestion that they are a separate line of evolution. It suggests that "fairies" exist where people believe in them, and that you would expect to find a "ju-ju spirit" in Africa where generations have directed their thoughts at a particular tree as the home of an ancestral spirit, and "sidhe" in Ireland.

This theory goes a long way toward explaining many traditional hauntings; for example, the old man of Ash Manor could conceivably have been a "thought form," projected by some previous owner—perhaps accidentally, like Dion Fortune's wolf—and revitalized by the atmosphere of hostility and neurosis in the family of the latest occupants. But why do so many such "ghosts" seem capable of poltergeist activity? The Cornish historian Harold Phelps has described his own encounter with a "ghost" in his old family home in a Berkshire village; the house had been built in the time of Elizabeth the First by Sir John Phelps, executed in 1660. In the early 1920s, Harold Phelps was visiting the aunt who then lived in the house, and when she mentioned a haunted room, asked if he could sleep in it. He was then in his mid-teens and, as a science student, was firmly convinced of the unreality of the paranormal.

> For a considerable time . . . I lay as still as I could listening for the least sound. As absolutely nothing happened, I must have fallen into a deep sleep . . . At some moment in the night I was woken up very suddenly by a most frightful racket in the room. I reached for my torch, half-sitting up in bed, and even before I could switch on the torch I received a stinging slap across my

left cheek. At the same instant I got the light on, and the room was obviously empty . . . The two cane chairs were overturned . . . and my money, keys and small effects had been knocked off the dressing-table and scattered all over the room.

Here the deciding factor may have been that the teenage boy was an unconscious medium. But whatever was present in the "haunted room" was presumably there before he arrived. So again, we have the puzzling phenomenon of an entity that declines to fit any of the normal categories of psychical researches.

Could it be, perhaps, that our preconceptions are simply too rigid, and that this is creating divisions and dichotomies where there are none? We are inclined to make a simple and sharp distinction: between living creatures (or spirits) and "illusions" or tape recordings, which—to some extent—owe their existence to the human mind. So, in a case like the one cited above, we ask: was there really a ghost present in the haunted room, or was it a delusion (or some form of projection) of Harold Phelps's mind? Yet the two categories may not really be mutually exclusive. In the previous chapter, Eileen Garrett's "control" Uvani declared: "Life cannot die. You can explode its dynamism, but you cannot dissipate its energy. If you suffered where life suffered, the essence that once filled the frame will take from you something to dramatize and live again." To our normal way of thinking, this hardly seems to make sense. The "ghost" of the old man sounds like a "person," not a revivified memory (i.e., a "recording"). But this is because we have the idea of a person so deeply embedded in our own way of thinking. We forget that it is connected largely with the physical body: a person looks solid and real so he must be an "individual." Yet most

people have experienced mental states—for example, in
high fever—when the personality seems to have disintegrated. As absurd as it sounds, "I" am still there, but that
"I" is not "me." It is a kind of disembodied being without a "self." People who have seen someone they know
well lose their faculties—through illness or senility—
have this same eery sensation: that the body of the person remains, yet the "person" is no longer in it. In other
words, our concept of a "personality" may contain certain fundamental errors. For example, if, in a high fever,
"I" exist without my "personality," then I could imagine
my personality going elsewhere, and manifesting itself
independent of "me." And this seems to be getting close
to what Uvani is talking about. Perhaps we shall not be
in a position to understand ghosts and poltergeists until
we have eliminated the errors from our thinking.

The Glastonbury Scripts hint at this same concept
of personality. The monk Johannes asked, at one point:

> Why cling I to that which is not? It is I, and it is
> not I, but parte of me which dwelleth in the past
> and is bound to that whych my carnal soul loved
> and called "home" these many years. Yet I,
> Johannes, amm of many partes, and ye better
> parte doeth other things *Laus, Laus Deo!* [praise
> be to God]—only that part which remembereth
> clingeth like memory to what it seeth yet.

Here there are many suggestive hints "It is I, and it
is not I"—"part of me which dwelleth in the past" and
"which remembereth [and] clingeth like memory to what
it seeth yet." And this presumably means that if some
"sensitive" at Glastonbury saw the "ghost" of Johannes,
it would be seeing this part of him that clings to the past,
not "ye better parte." All of which suggests that our sim-

plistic notion of a "soul" inside a body may be too crude to explain the facts of psychic phenomena. It totally fails, for example, to explain what happens in the "projection of the double"—as when Mrs. Fielding made her double visit her husband in their home while her body sat in the laboratory. We have also seen that in many cases, people are unaware that they are projecting their "double"—like Canon Bourne; which implies that the everyday "I" which knows what we are doing is quite ignorant of a great deal that goes on inside us. In occult philosophy, the double—or doppelganger—is also known as the "etheric double."

There also seems to be a part of us that could be called the "mental double." This is illustrated in another classic case, that of Gordon Davis, recorded by the well-known investigator Dr. S. G. Soal. At the turn of the century, Dr. Soal was at school with a boy called Gordon Davis, and in 1920, he heard that Davis had been killed in the Great War. Soal began attending seances with Mrs. Blanche Cooper in 1921, and at one of these seances, the "spirit" of Gordon Davis spoke through the medium. It declared that its only worry now were the wife and children. Davis asked Soal if he remembered their last conversation, and reminded him that it had been a chance meeting on a train. At a subsequent seance, Davis tried to describe the house where his wife lived. There were six steps—or rather, five and a half. It was not in a street but in "half a street." Opposite the house there was "something like a veranda." There was a kind of dark tunnel nearby. In the house there was a big mirror and various pictures of landscapes, as well as some large vases. Downstairs, a room with brass candlesticks on the shelf. A woman and a little boy lived in the house . . .

Three years later, Soal learned by chance that the house was in Southend-on-Sea, and he went to investigate. Everything was exactly as the "spirits" had described it. The house was on the esplanade facing the sea—therefore on "half a street." Opposite the house was a bus-shelter—a kind of "veranda." There were six steps, one of which was very thin. There was a dark tunnel next to the house leading to the back gardens of the block. Inside the house there was a large mirror, various land-scapes, big vases, and brass candlesticks in the down-stairs dining room. And Gordon Davis himself was in the house, alive and well, together with his wife and five-year-old son. Davis had no knowledge whatever about the "spirit" that had given all this information at the seance.

It is conceivable, of course, that this was another earth-bound spirit playing games. But if not, then it was a fragment of Davis's personality that was wandering around—unknown to its owner.

A book called *Journeys Out of the Body* seems to support this latter view. The author, Robert Monroe, is an American businessman who one day, to his astonish-ment, found that he could leave his body—the ability known as "astral projection." In August 1963, he de-cided to "visit" a female business acquaintance whom he calls R.W. He found himself in her kitchen, sitting in a chair and drinking from a glass; two girls were also with her. He asked R.W. if she knew he was there, and she replied (mentally), "Oh yes." He asked her if she would remember, and she said she would. Monroe said he would pinch her to make sure, and did so; she gave a loud shout of pain. Later, Monroe asked her what had happened. She had no memory whatever of seeing or conversing (mentally) with Monroe. But she was in the kitchen with two girls; she suddenly felt a pinch, and jumped up in alarm. She showed Monroe the bruise produced by the pinch (which seems to demonstrate, beyond all doubt, that the "astral body" *can* produce physical effects). On another occasion, Monroe visited the researcher Andrija Puharich in his study, and held a mental conversation with him. Puharich later agreed that he *had* been in the study and that everything Monroe said about it was correct; but he had no memory of a conversation.

In his book *The Romeo Error*, Lyall Watson reviews the evidence for "astral travel," and makes the suggestion that human beings may have no less than seven "bodies" or levels upon which they exist, the first three being the physical body, the "etheric" level (the level of the "aura" which is supposed to surround the human body), and the astral level. The Spiritualist philosophy asserts that when we die, we move on to the "astral plane," shedding the physical body like a garment; but there are various planes *beyond* this. This suggests the interesting notion that if human beings possess an "astral body," they may also possess "bodies" belonging to the various other planes. And we have already seen that some such notion seems to be suggested by the whole problem of multiple personality. It is as if human beings contain a whole series of "selves," arranged in the form of a ladder (a concept I have developed at length in a book called *Mysteries*).

Monroe's experiences "outside the body" seem to be in many ways consistent with notions explored in this book. For example, in a chapter called "Intelligent Animals," he writes: "Throughout man's history, the reports have been consistent. There are demons, spirits, goblins, gremlins and assorted sub-human entities always hanging around humanity to make life miserable." And he, goes on to describe a number of disturbing experiences in his "OOB" states. A kind of child climbed on to his back, and forced him to "retreat" back into his body. The next time he "left the body," the same entity climbed on to his back; when he tugged at the leg, it stretched like rubber. Two of the rubbery beings—which now seemed shapeless—proceeded to "attack"' him, although it was with a casual persistence rather than malice. Finally, a "man" came along, picked up the two entities, and seemed to cause them to deflate. On another occasion, Monroe was threatened—or attacked—by three humanoid figures who seemed to be hooligans of the astral plane. He also describes an attack from some sort of invisible animal that seemed to be determined to "take" vitality from him—a struggle he terminated by returning to his physical body, which lay in bed.

These entities begin to sound very much like the beings we encounter in cases of "possession." But even here, there is ambiguity. In his book on possession, Oesterreich cites one of the best known cases in the literature, that of Janet's patient "Achille." Achille was a businessman who had been brought up in a religious family; returning from a business trip in 1890, he sank into depression, then went dumb. After waking from a two-day coma, he became convinced that he was in hell, then declared that the Devil was inside him. He screamed and uttered horrible blasphemies. Finally, he was confined in the Salpêtrière. Janet was fascinated by the case. Achille would curse God in a deep voice, then protest in his own voice that the Devil had made him do it. Like Father Surin of Loudun, he evidently felt that the Devil was making use of his body, "making him" do things.

Janet made the interesting discovery that he could communicate with the "Devil" without Achille noticing—by placing a pencil on Achille's fingers, then asking the "Devil" questions in a low voice. The "Devil" would write replies.

Janet asked who he was. "The Devil," came the reply. Achille asked if he could make Achille raise his arm, and Achille's arm rose. When Janet pointed this out to Achille, he was astonished. "That demon has played another trick on me." After a number of similar experiments, Janet asked if the Devil could put Achille to sleep. Earlier attempts to hypnotize Achille had failed, but he now fell asleep, and when Janet asked him questions, he replied without opening his eyes. Janet now discovered the cause of Achille's illness; on his last business trip he had committed a "grave misdeed"—probably going to bed with a prostitute. On his return home he brooded on his guilt, and was afraid he would blurt it out to his wife—hence the psychosomatic dumbness. Things had quickly gone from bad to worse until Achille fell into a coma, and woke up convinced he was possessed.

Janet arranged for Achille's wife to visit him in hospital and to pronounce forgiveness; Achille immediately began to recover. Although he still dreamed of hellish torments at night, he laughed at his superstitions during the day, until the fears and hallucinations vanished.

Janet cites the case as an example of multiple personality: Achille's own terrors convinced him he was possessed, his anxiety produced a state of tension in which he was in a permanent state of hysteria—trapped in the left brain, as it were—and his subconscious mind proceeded to play tricks. But the possession-hypothesis fits just as well. Achille came back from his business trip in a state of neurotic worry, and allowed himself to become more and more anxious—so becoming increasingly weak and passive. He fell into a coma, which allowed a mischievous "elemental" to take over. Fortunately; like most elementals, it was stupid, and allowed itself to be persuaded to place Achille in a trance. As soon as Janet knew what was troubling Achille, she possessed the means of persuading Achille to "fight back." And slowly, the more responsible and mature part of Achille gained control . . .

We may either take our choice of these two views, or we may decide that they are not mutually exclusive. If "spirits" can pass in and out of our bodies at will, as Kardec says, then perhaps many of the feelings and emotions we assume to be "our own" are caused by the intruder. Perhaps our belief that we are "individuals" is a mistake, and we are a whole assemblage of people, with one of them more-or-less "in charge." According to Gurdjieff, we do not possess one "self" but dozens; this is why we are so changeable, and find it so difficult to complete things we set out to do. Gurdjieff's comment seems to be only "a manner of speaking" since our changeableness is really a lack of self-discipline. But perhaps he intended it as more than a manner of speaking. Perhaps the first step to understanding these mysteries would be to think of ourselves as a "conglomerate" rather than as individuals, as a mass of personalities and sub-personalities and personality fragments.

Such notions as these are thoroughly foreign to our Western modes of thought; yet they can be found in many other cultures. For example, the notion of man's "seven bodies" is to be found in Hindu and Egyptian occultism, and is discussed in the books of Madame Blavatsky and Annie Besant, as well as in works like A. E. Powell's *The Astral Body* and *The Etheric Double*. And the concept of multiple personality has been used by Max Freedom Long to buttress a system of ideas originating in Africa and now represented mainly in the Kahuna culture of Polynesia. Long's book *The Secret Science Behind Miracles* contains a great deal that is relevant to this investigation of the poltergeist.

Long arrived in Hawaii in 1917 and became intrigued by references to native magicians, kahunas or "keepers of the secret." All his attempts to find out more about them encountered a brick wall. The kahunas, apparently, had been outlawed by the Christians, but their practices continued to survive. Long heard about a local minister who had challenged a kahuna to a contest of prayers; the kahuna declared that he would pray the minister's congregation to death. Long actually saw the diary of this minister, reporting death after death in his congregation. Finally, the minister persuaded someone to teach him the magic involved in the death prayer, and tried a counter attack. The kahuna magician died within three days. The missionary seceded from the church, and built his own small chapel, over which he continued to preside.

At this point, Long met a doctor, William Tufts Brigham, who had been studying the kahunas for years. He was able to give Long certain vital clues. And later, in America, Long studied the Hawaiian language, and gradually began to crack the "code." One of his first discoveries was that the kahunas seem to accept that man has at least two "selves." (He later discovered that there is a third.)

> The Kahuna idea of the conscious and subconscious seems to be, judging from the root meaning of the names given to them, a pair of spirits closely joined in a body which is controlled by the subconscious and used to cover and hide them both. The conscious spirit is more human and possesses the ability to talk. The grieving subconscious weeps tears, dribbles water and otherwise handles the vital force of the body. It does its work with secrecy and silent care, but it is stubborn and disposed to refuse to obey. It refuses to do things when it fears the gods (holds a complex

or fixation of ideas), and it intermingles or tinc-
tures the conscious spirit to give the impression
of being one with it.

A number of important points are stated here. The
"subconscious" spirit intermingles so closely with its
partner that we do not realize that it has a separate identity. But this spirit is rebellious and highly emotional. It
refuses to obey. Long is here speaking of what Poe
meant by the "imp of the perverse," which has been
mentioned elsewhere in this book: that curious tendency
of the human mind to turn against itself. There is part of
us that seems to be little better than an immature child,
howling with misery and defeat when confronted by
problems it regards as "unfair." This part of us is dangerous because we fail to recognize it is a separate entity,
and may be unaware of its existence until it has betrayed
us into some act of stupidity. We have all met people
who seem to be balanced, strong, self-possessed, and
who, when confronted by some sudden frustration or
injury to their self-esteem, become mean, petty and often
violent; we stand aghast at this sudden revelation of their
immaturity. Until we can recognize this element in ourselves, we are unable to take the measures that might
bring it under control.

In addition to these two "souls," we also "possess"
(or "are"?) a higher self, a superconscious being who
might be regarded as the guardian angel, and—this is
perhaps the most interesting suggestion—controls our
future. It does so according to the desires and suggestions of the "middle self—the conscious ego—and most
of us have such messy lives because our suggestions are
so muddled and contradictory.

These three souls use three kinds of vital force, or
mana, each with a different "voltage," so to speak. The

form used by the higher self is symbolized in religions by the sun. Long adds the interesting comment that *mana* can be stored up in wood and in water—a remark that would have excited Tom Lethbridge.

By way of illustrating this vital force on its lowest level, Long cites Nandor Fodor's *Encyclopaedia of Psychic Science*, and Lombroso's case of the poltergeist in the tavern. For the poltergeist, according to Long, *is* a spirit—"lower soul" which has somehow, in death, become separated from the middle and higher selves. According to Long, the lower self possesses memory, and the middle self does not. So a disembodied lower self is an earthbound spirit of the type that causes poltergeist disturbances. The disembodied middle self, separated from the other selves, is a wandering wraith without memory—in fact, what we would generally regard as a ghost. According to Long, then, the old man who haunted Ash Manor would be a disembodied "middle self."

The death prayer, and other forms of black magic, are, according to Long, performed by means of low spirits, who obey the magician. On this point he is totally in agreement with the view put forward by Andrade and Playfair. These low spirits lack intelligence, and (like the low self) are highly suggestive to hypnotic suggestion. Long tells a typical story of his master, Dr. Brigham. Brigham had hired a party of Hawaiian natives to climb a mountain, and one of them (a fifteen-year-old boy) became ill. His feet had become numb, and the numbness was slowly rising up his body—a sign that someone had practiced the death prayer on him. Brigham questioned the boy, who then remembered that before he left his native village, the local kahuna—witch doctor (who hated the influence of white men)—had declared that any villager who worked for the whites would become a victim of the death prayer. The boy had, in fact, worked with Hawaiians until Long offered him a job in his party, and the boy had accepted it without thinking of the consequences.

Because of his study of the Huna religion, Brigham was regarded by the natives as a powerful kahuna—an idea he encouraged—so they now asked him if he would direct the death prayer back at the magician who had sent it. With some trepidation, Brigham decided to try. Standing above the boy, he spoke aloud to the spirits, praising and flattering them, then argued warmly that the boy was an innocent victim, and that it was the kahuna who sent them who ought to be destroyed. He then directed them to return and leave the boy alone. For another hour, he kept his mind concentrated on this idea until quite suddenly, he said, the tension seemed to vanish, and the boy declared that he could feel his legs again. Soon after, the boy was quite well. In order to verify if the "magic" had worked, Brigham got the boy to take him to his own village, where the villagers fled at the sight of the white magician. It seemed that, on the night Brigham had redirected the prayer, the magician had come suddenly out of his hut where he had been sleeping, told the people that the white magician had redirected his prayer, and that he had omitted to take any ritual precautions against such redirection because he believed he was in no danger. By morning, the kahuna was dead.

How did the kahuna know that the boy was working for a white man? The "spirits" told him. The same clairvoyance should have protected him from Brigham's attack; Brigham thinks that this attack was successful because the kahuna had gone to sleep early, and woke up to find himself already under attack.

The death prayer, Long says, depends on these "subconscious spirits," which a kahuna might inherit from another kahuna, or find for himself if he happens to be sufficiently psychic. Long adds the disturbing comment that in the early days in Hawaii, prisoners of war were sometimes given potent hypnotic suggestion to cause the subconscious spirit to separate from the "middle self" after death. We must return to this matter of hypnosis in a moment.

When the low spirits reach the victim, they have to await the chance to enter his body, and they can do this because they have been given a surcharge of *mana*, or vital force, by their master. Normally, says Long, the unconscious mind can protect itself against invading spirits, because its vitality is greater than theirs. The spirits of the death prayer have to enter by brute force, as it were. They then proceed to drain the victim of vital force, which would cause the feet to grow numb, then the rest of the body. Having killed the victim, the spirits are now supercharged with energy.

"In the event of a successful mission," says Long, "the kahuna ordered his spirit slaves to play until they used up the vital force they had taken ... Their play usually took the form of what we would call 'poltergeist activities.' They would throw objects, make loud noises, and create a bedlam of some proportions. Dr. Brigham once heard a great commotion in the hut of a kahuna at night, and was later told that spirits were at play in this manner."

According to Long, this same *mana* can be transferred to a stick, which is then used in war; when it strikes the victim, he receives a kind of paralyzing shock. He speaks of a Reo Indian medicine man who could knock a brave unconscious by merely placing his finger against his chest.

In order to offer further demonstration of his theory of the three spirits, Long turns to cases of multiple personality, citing Mary Reynolds and Christine Beauchamp—already discussed in Chapter 2. He then mentions an unusual case that he heard from a Dr. Leap-sley in Honolulu. The daughter of a prominent California attorney had been a dual personality since she was a child, and the two alternated every four years. At the age of four, the girl had gone into a deep sleep, and had apparently reverted to babyhood when she woke up. This baby learned very quickly—as Mary Reynolds did—and quickly developed into a person completely unlike the original girl. "Miss First" was studious, shy and retiring, "Miss Second" was a noisy tomboy. At the age of eight, Miss First came back, unaware that she had been absent. At twelve, Miss Second returned one afternoon. At six-teen, Miss Second fell asleep and woke up as Miss First, asking her mother to go on reading a book she had been reading when Miss Second took over four years earlier.

When the girl reached the age of twenty-eight, the parents consulted medical men, who decided to try to make the secondary personality go away through hypnosis, or to cause the two to amalgamate. Under hypnosis, each personality appeared, and the doctors learned that each was aware of the actions of the other by "reading" the other's memory. Then the order to "blend" was given. It had no effect. More hypnosis was tried, and the two personalities were asked why they had not blended; Miss First said she had been unable to carry out the instructions.

More hypnosis led to the "hypnotic syncope"—the body seemed to become dead. Then, suddenly, the lips moved, and a completely new personality spoke through them. This spoke in a firm voice, and seemed to be older and wiser than the other two. It was the voice of an old man. It explained that it had the two girls under its guardianship, and that what the doctors were trying to do was wrong: the girls had to go on sharing the same body. When one of the doctors threatened to keep the girl hypnotized indefinitely the "guardian" replied firmly that in that case it would withdraw, and leave them with a corpse. It spoke with such quiet conviction that the doctors decided not to put this to the test.

This, says Long, is an example of the "higher self." But what about the two girls? According to Long, multiple personality is simply a case of a body being invaded by a spirit—sometimes a low self, sometimes a middle self, sometimes a combination of the two. Long accepts without question the idea of "possession," declaring that some "low selves" may prey on the living, draining their vital energy, or taking up residence in their bodies and rendering them insane. Like Arthur Guirdham, Long is convinced that much mental illness is a kind of "haunting" by spirits. But he points out that most people have very powerful resistance to invading entities—even those sent by kahunas. Only people suffering from deep-seated guilt feelings are fairly easy prey.

Notions such as these will strike most people as absurd. Yet they seem to explain some of the mysteries we have examined in this book more convincingly than the "scientific" theories of psychologists and psychical researchers. It seems curious that so many cases of multiple personality involve the same pattern—a repressed, well-behaved young woman, like Christine Beauchamp, Doris Fischer, Mary Reynolds, sinking into a state of misery and low vitality, then being "taken over" by a mischievous tomboy. In many such cases, the "takeover" occurs after some well-meaning psychiatrist has placed the girl unde hypnosis, making her defenseless. In most cases, the invading entity is lacking in intelligence, and in no case has the secondary personality been more intelligent than the primary one. (In the case of Doris Fischer, a number of less intelligent entities seem to have taken over, each one more stupid than the last.)

Long's picture of the world of "low spirits" is a depressing one: he even has a chapter discussing "horrid things of darkness."

> The world of invisible spirits is much like our solid earth in as much as it has its jungles and wild animals so to speak. If in this world a man should go into wild country and meet lions, tigers and gorillas, he would have to defend himself. The same applies over there in the world of disembodied things living in their shadowy bodies. Fortunately for us, the contact with the shadowy world is slight. Only now and then do the dangerous or actively evil things break through to us and endanger our lives or sanity.

Now it has to be admitted that a passage like this—with its suggestion of H. P. Lovecraft—arouses an automatic reflex of rejection, which in turn leads on to question the whole system of ideas of the kahunas. Some of Long's stories certainly sound like traveller's tales. We find it difficult to accept the notion of a jilted girl making her ex-lover seriously ill by asking the spirit of her dead grandmother for vengeance. Yet everything Long says about poltergeists is consistent with the tentative conclusions reached elsewhere in this book. They *do* behave like half-witted spirits; they *do* seem to have a certain limited power of "possession"; they *do* seem to be easily influenced by remarks and suggestions thrown off by human beings; they *do* seem to be capable of draining the physical energies of their victims. At the same time they are not fundamentally evil; their malice has often an almost jovial quality, and—like the fairies of legend—they even seem to enjoy performing small services for people they like. (Jean Pritchard tells how she arrived home one day and found that the "black monk" had laid the table for tea.) Attempts to question them about their motives usually fail because they lack the ability to reason. All these characteristics sound very much like the "lower spirits" of Freedom Long, and hardly at all like the rebellious unconscious posited by William Roll, George Owen and Alan Gauld.

It is, of course, this notion of hostile magic that the Western intellect finds most difficult to accept. Yet Nandor Fodor himself, in spite of his support for the "unconscious" theory, accepts both the idea of black magic and the death wish. He speaks of a woman he knew in London who claimed to be skilled in the black arts, and who told him how she had conjured up the Devil by hypnotizing a boy and sending him to summon the Devil. Fodor, in his role as psychoanalyst, says that he has no doubt that she tried to conjure up the Devil, but that he could not believe that he had appeared to her. What probably happened, he says, is that the boy's unconscious "rose to the occasion" and summoned up visual auditory hallucinations. Having said which, he tells how, when the woman lost some silver spoons, she pronounced a curse against the thief, and how the woman's discharged cook dropped dead at the moment the curse was pronounced. He goes on to tell a story of a spy of his acquaintance who successfully willed an accomplice to commit suicide. He goes on: "This man was a weird creature. He was convinced that he had a familiar spirit always ready to do his bidding . . . Fodor later tells a story about G. R. S. Mead—an eminent student of the occult—in which Mead describes how he himself survived an "astral attack":

> I woke from a troubled sleep, but remained in a twilight state, as if under a spell. There was a growing chill in the air, or in my mind. I saw a soft

> glow and a menacing shape which boded evil and which I thought I recognized. I knew I was in danger, but the peril was not on the physical plane.

Mead claims to have used his own knowledge to counter-attack effectively.*

Cases like these are easier to explain with reference to Long's Huna concepts than to Fodor's Freudian theories. The same is true of the puzzling case of the Barbados tomb, discussed by Father Thurston and many other writers on poltergeist hauntings. The vault, hewn partly out of solid rock, was opened in 1812—only five years after it had been used for the first time—and two coffins were found standing on end. Four years later, the coffins had again been scattered when the tomb was opened. When it happened for a third time, in 1819, the floor was scattered with fine sand; the following year, when the tomb was opened again, the sand was undisturbed, but the coffins had again been thrown around in the vault. The case seems completely non-typical of poltergeist haunting; not only was there no disturbed teenager to act as "focus," there was no human being of any kind from whom the entity could have "borrowed" the energy. But the island of Barbados has its voodoo practices, and the Huna explanation would be that some enemy of the family had sent spirits to discharge their excess *mana* in this way.

The *mana* theory is, in a sense, the essence of Long's spirit theory, and the aspect that would probably be the easiest to investigate scientifically. Long points out: "Modern studies of the vital electricity have been made by attaching wires to the skin of the body and of

---

* Fodor: *The Haunted Mind*, Chapters 7 and 9.

the scalp, then using very sensitive instruments to measure the electrical discharges." In fact, the experiments of Harold Burr in measuring the "life field" of trees and animals are now well known. Long adds:

> *Life* magazine files show in the issue of October 18, 1937, some pictures of tests with charts and graphs. Two voltages of electricity have been found, a low voltage in the body tissue and a higher voltage in the brain.

And as an example of the use of *mana* he cites the "lifting experiment" that has always been popular at parties. The subject sits in a chair, and four people attempt to lift him with a single finger placed beneath his knees and armpits; it is, of course, impossible. All four now place their hands on the subject's head in an alternating "pile" (that is, so that no person's two hands are together) and concentrate for a moment. Then they remove their hands and quickly attempt the lifting again; the subject can usually be raised without difficulty. ("Professor" Joad was much intrigued by this phenomenon, and described how he had often seen heavy men sailing up toward the ceiling in one case, with a small child as one of the lifters.) According to Long, this is a simple demonstration of the human ability to concentrate *mana*. And, if Long is correct, this is also the energy used by the poltergeist. (Elsewhere in the book, he mentions the case of the Cottingley fairies, and implies that they are also "thought forms" created by *mana*.)

Yet although the "spirit" theory seems, on the whole, to explain the phenomena rather more convincingly than the "unconscious" theory, it would be a mistake to go to the opposite extreme and dismiss the latter as a scientific rationalization. This would be throwing out the baby with the bath water. To grasp the real importance of the unconscious theory, we have to go back to the origins of organized psychical research, and to the first attempt by an investigator to create a comprehensive theory—*Human Personality and Its Survival of Bodily Death* (1903) by F. W. H. Myers, one of the founders of the SPR. Myers is, in fact, less concerned with "life after death" than with the mysterious powers of the human mind. There are chapters on multiple personlity, on genius, on hypnosis, and on specters of the living and the dead. Myers is fascinated, for example, by "calculating prodigies," children (often of less than average intelligence) who can do immense calculations in their heads within seconds. Myers ends by concluding that "discarnate spirits" exist; but his conclusions are otherwise disappointingly tentative.

Writing at about the same time as Myers, and from the same starting point, the American Thomson Jay Hudson reached far more interesting conclusions. *The Law of Psychic Phenomena* (1892) begins by considering the mystery of hypnosis, in which the powers of the hypnotic subject seem to be enormously increased. People in hypnotic trances have spoken foreign languages they have never studied (although it is usually found that they had unconsciously "absorbed" them in childhood) and have exercised powers of clairvoyance and telepathy. (We may recall Barrett's hypnotized girl who winced when he held his hand over a candle flame, or the boy who could speak aloud the words in a book from which Ochorowitz was reading.)

Hudson then advances an important thesis: that we all contain "two selves" or minds. He calls these the objective mind and the subjective mind. The objective mind is the conscious ego, whose business is to "cope" with the physical world. The subjective mind seems to be more concerned with our internal functions, and it works through intuition. The subjective mind is far more powerful than the objective mind, which is why hypnotic subjects are capable of feats that they could never perform through conscious effort. What excites Hudson is that this subjective mind—or unconscious—is the servant of the objective mind, and will obey its commands. So, in theory we are all capable of becoming clairvoyant, or of curing our own illnesses (and those of other people) at will. (Hudson convinced himself of the soundness of these theories by performing some remarkable experiments in "absent healing.")

But because he is so impressed by the amazing powers of the subjective mind, Hudson concludes that it is responsible for all the phenomena of spiritualism—for example, automatic writing and "spirit voices." He has, of course, no difficulty in explaining multiple personality in terms of the subjective mind. He is even convinced that it explains the miracles of the New Testament. Only one major psychic manifestation is absent from his remarkable book: the poltergeist. And this is obviously because he feels he would be stretching things too far to explain the violent movement of objects in terms of the subjective mind. (It was J. B. Rhine's studies in psychokinesis in the 1930s that opened the way for the RSPK theory of poltergeist phenomena.)

In the 1960s, an American doctor named Howard Miller took up the theory of the "two minds" where Hudson left off. Miller became fascinated by hypnosis when he saw a dentist extract a tooth after hypnotizing the patient and telling her that she would not bleed; to Miller's astonishment, there was no bleeding. Bleeding is, of course, controlled by the involuntary nervous system, and cannot, in the normal course of things, be affected by thinking. Yet here was evidence that the dentist's "thought" could stop bleeding. Miller began to try hypnosis on various ailments—including cancer—and was astonished by its effectiveness. He concluded that our major "control system" lies in the cerebral cortex: the thinking part of us. In effect, Miller had rediscovered the subjective and objective minds.

Miller carried his thinking an important step beyond Hudson. If the cerebral cortex, the conscious ego, has the power to control the automatic nervous system, why do we fail to recognize this power? What stops us from curing our own illnesses, whether headaches or cancer? Obviously, the main reason is that we never make the attempt. This is because we feel that consciousness counts for so little compared to the forces of the unconscious mind-the power of the emotions and the body. And this is not simply because Freud and D. H. Lawrence have taught us to distrust the conscious ego. It is because our own experience seems to support the notion that thought is helpless when compared to the forces of the unconscious.

The problem, says Miller, is that the conscious mind is *unaware* that it is supposed to be in control. The brain is like an enormous computer, overflowing with activity that seems to be independent of the will. This is particularly obvious during sleep, when all kinds of strange phantasmagoria swarm into consciousness. It is equally obvious if I get a tune stuck in my head and cannot get it out, or if I find myself thinking obsessively about something I would prefer to forget. The brain physiologist Wilder Penfield discovered that if he touched an area in the temporal cortex—the seat of memory—with an electric probe, the patient would relive experiences from his past life in cinematic detail. The brain is a vast library. No wonder the conscious self feels like a visitor with only limited right of access.

Yet this is a mistake, as we discover every time a crisis produces a flood of concentration and vitality, or when ecstasy brings a sense of control and power. In such moments, we suddenly realize that it is the "I" that is in control, not "it."

The "I" only achieves this recognition when galvanized by intensified consciousness. Yet if it *is* a recognition, and not an illusion, then we should be able to use this insight to reach unprecedented levels of self-control. Miller compares our situation to a man sitting idly in a cinema, watching a jumbled phantasmagoria on the screen, and wondering what has happened to the projectionist. He is unaware that he is the projectionist. It takes a sudden crisis to wake him up, and make him realize that his proper place is in the projection room, not yawning in the "audience."

What Miller is saying is that we must come to terms with this recognition that the "controlling ego" (which he calls "the unit of pure thought") is intended to be the director of both the conscious and the unconscious minds. *As a species,* we have slipped into the habit of regarding consciousness as somehow subservient to the body and the emotions. So that if I feel sick, or feel convulsed with jealousy, it seems self-evident that my ability to think is of no particular use; on the contrary, it seems to make things worse by looking on detachedly and telling me I oughtn't to be such an idiot.

Yet the moment I feel the need to *turn my thought into action*, the moment I determinedly search for solutions, I experience a sense of control, a surge of power and insight. The sensation is not unlike the surge of power and purpose produced by the orgasm. And the more I become accustomed to these efforts of control, instead of lying down and surrendering to my emotions, the more I learn that "I" am not a cork tossed about on a sea of feelings and sensations; I am the *director*. In fact, if I study my perceptions—which seem to occur without my volition—I realize that even they depend on a form of unconscious effort (which the philosopher Husserl called "intentionality"). If I look at my watch without paying attention, I fail to grasp the time; my mind has to make an effort, like a hand grasping an object.

It can be seen that the two minds of Hudson correspond to the two hemispheres of the brain—discussed in Chapter 1—with the left brain as the objective mind, the right as the intuitive, subjective mind. So it would seem a reasonable assumption that they also correspond to the Huna notion of the "lower self" and the "middle self"— the unconscious and conscious minds. Yet this proves to be inaccurate. In Enid Hoffman's *Huna: A Beginner's Guide*, a chapter is devoted to the split brain, and, as expected, the "middle self" is placed in the left cerebral cortex. But the "lower self," according to the kahunas, is located in the solar plexus.

This is less surprising than it sounds; after all, D. H. Lawrence identified the solar plexus as the center of intuition and emotion. And this is confirmed by self-observation. If some unpleasant thought enters my head—the left brain—I experience a "sinking feeling"— a leak—in the area of the solar plexus.

And what of the right brain? This, according to Dr. Hoffman, is the seat of the "higher self." And this, again, is supported by self-observation. In moods of serenity produced by music or poetry—both of which make their appeal through the right brain—we experience a sense of *expanding identity*, or contact with powerful vital forces. It is the right brain that is involved in mystical ecstasy, in the feeling that G. K. Chesterton calls "absurd good news."

So Huna philosophy has removed another of the puzzling contradictions of modern psychology: the notion that the unconscious mind is the source of our best and worst impulses, of inspiration and anarchic violence. It anticipates Aldous Huxley's suggestion that if the mind has an unconscious "basement," full of repressions and neuroses, it must also have a superconscious "attic."

The kahunas go considerably further than Howard Miller in defining the role of the "controlling ego." The higher self, says Long, has control over the future, so that it is possible for us to direct the future, if we go about it in the right way. Long describes his own experience of visiting an old kahuna woman during the Depression, when his camera shop in Honolulu was on the point of bankruptcy.

> The healer told me that in her experience most people sent to the High Self a continuous jumble of conflicting wishes, plans, fears and hopes. Each day and hour they changed their minds about what they wished to do or have happen. As the High Self makes for us our futures from our averaged thoughts which it contacts during our sleep, our futures have become a hit-and-miss jumble of events and contrary events, of accidents and good and bad luck. Only the person who decides what he wants and holds to his decision doggedly, working always in that direction, can present to the High Self the proper thought forms from which to build the future.

The High Self, says Long, must be contacted through the intermediary of the low self; the middle self cannot do it directly.

Long claims that as a result of the kahuna's advice—which she arrived at through "scrying" with a glass of water—she was able to tell him: "Your path is not badly blocked," and to give him precisely detailed instructions which showed an accurate foreknowledge of the future, and which saved him from bankruptcy.

All of which raises an obvious question: if the High Self knows the future, and is the "guardian angel," why does it not do a better job of shaping our destinies? The answer is to be found in Howard Miller. Because the middle self is the director, the controller, it is *its* job to contact the high self, not vice versa. It must do this by using its power of choice and rational analysis, by trying to grasp the insights of "moments of vision" and intensity, and living by these, instead of by the impulses of the low self, which is still close to the animal world. The kahunas say that only the middle self can sin, for it has the power of choice.

It all sounds depressingly difficult. In fact, it is not; for we are always receiving flashes of insight, "glimpses." Every time a spring morning brings a surge of "absurd good news," every time we experience a sense of interest and absorption that arouses a glow of sheer affirmation, we *see* the solution, and see that it is astonishingly simple. (This is why every mystic has expressed a feeling that can only be translated: "Of *course!*") The problem is that the low self fails to grasp it, so that half an hour later we can no longer remember what it was. The romantics of the nineteenth century died off like flies because they suspected the "moments of vision" were an illusion, and the basic truth is that life is dull, brutish and short (Tennyson's *In Memoriam* is a classic expression of this anguish). Trained in kahuna teaching, they would have recognized that this is a purely technical problem of communication between the "selves," and that despair is due to an absurd misunderstanding.

According to Long, Huna teachings originated in ancient Egypt and the Sahara, in the days when the

Sahara was still fertile. This original Huna people left in an exodus and spread in many directions; Long produces strong evidence that the Berber tribes of the Atlas mountains, in north Africa, spring from the same people. We may, of course, reject the whole notion that Huna is a secret knowledge system (Huna means secret), and regard it simply as a form of intuitive psychology mixed with ancient superstition, in which the low, middle and high selves are simply aspects of the human psyche (corresponding roughly to Freud's unconscious, conscious and superego). What must be acknowledged is that, as a psychological system, it has a depth that is lacking in most modern psychologies.

Our concern in this book is with the poltergeist and its mysteries; and here the kahuna explanation seems to fit the facts rather better than most. As Guy Playfair points out, the kahunas seem to have explanations for most "psi'" phenomena. Before considering some of these explanations, let us look once more at the "facts."

It is Playfair's contention that, after fifteen hundred years of poltergeist observation, and a century of psychical research, it is no longer true to say that our position is one of complete ignorance. "If it were the mating habits of cockroaches, there'd be quite enough evidence for someone to produce a definitive paper in *Nature*." In *This House is Haunted* he lists the nineteen or so "symptoms" of what he calls "the poltergeist syndrome," beginning with raps and ending with equipment failure of cameras, tape recorders and so on. He points out that in some cases, only half a dozen of these appear—let us say raps, overturning furniture, apports, "possession" and outbreaks of fire.

You always get them in the same order. You don't get puddles of water before stone throwing, you don't get fires before raps. So that there is a predictable behavior pattern. They appear to be random to us, but they're obeying some sort of rules that they understand even if we don't.*

What can we say about these rules?

We can say there is a source of energy. There has to be, because physical work is being carried out, and since it's being carried out in our space and our dimension, then it has to obey at least some of the laws of mechanics.

And he goes on to suggest that this energy source (the poltergeist) could be compared to a crowd of mischievous children who find a football in a field (some form of energy extruded from a "leaking" human being) and proceed to kick it around, smashing a few windows in the process.

The Brazilian novelist Chico Xavier, who claims that his novels come through "dictation" from "spirits," states in one of his books (quoted by Playfair in *The Indefinite Boundary*) that the source of this "energy plasma" is the pineal gland. This gland, a tiny grey mass like a slightly flattened pea, lies roughly in the center of the brain, and seems to be a vestigial eye. In some creatures, like the Tuatera lizard of New Zealand, it is still a non-functioning eye. One of its chief purposes is the inhibiting of the sexual hormones—people with a damaged pineal show abnormal sexual development. There is some evidence that it also plays some role in the evolution of our higher functions; when the brain cells are deprived of the chemical messenger serotonin (secreted

---

* These comments come from a tape I recorded in conversation with Playfair.

by the pineal gland) we become incapable of rational thought. At puberty, according to Xavier, it ceases to be purely a controlling mechanism, and becomes a fountain of energy, an escape valve. It secretes "psychic hormones" that generate creative energy. These energies represent our "spiritual potential"; unfortunately, most of us are inclined to misuse them for purely animal sensations. (De Sade would probably be a good example of extreme misuse.) When a child suddenly acquires this new force, at the age of puberty, there is a need for a channel or outlet—perhaps vigorous sporting or sexual activity. If this outlet is lacking, Playfair suggests, the energy will be available for "marauding entities to steal and put to their own purposes." "Perhaps if Brazilian girls played hockey or lacrosse there would be fewer poltergeists in São Paulo."

The vital force involved seems to have some resemblance to electricity or magnetism. This is what the Hunas call *mana*. And since the earth is covered with living creatures and organism—it may even be regarded as a living organism in itself—then it also, presumably, has a permanent supply of this force (what Stringer calls Tellurian force). This force may be said to have been discovered, as far as Europeans are concerned, by Mesmer, who also made the interesting discovery since forgotten by Western science—that it can be influenced by magnets and by various metals. Half a century later, it was rediscovered by Baron Reichenbach, who called it "odic force." According to the kahunas, this is the force used by poltergeists. (It may even be involved in that still-unexplained phenomenon, spontaneous combustion, which seems to be largely confined to the old in the way that poltergeist phenomena are largely confined to the young.) The poltergeist uses *mana* to solidify its own "shadowy body," and so can act upon objects.

Clearly, there is a great deal of this energy available: not just in children at puberty, but in sexually frustrated adults, and even in the earth itself, where it seems to be concentrated at certain points. (Presumably ancient peoples chose such points as sacred sites because they attracted spirits.) Mediums also seem to produce large quantities of this force—perhaps secreting it as a cow comes to secrete milk. Under the controlled conditions of a seance, this force seems to return to its origin, like an electrical circuit; but mediums who are awakened violently seem to be drained of vitality, and often stunned, as if by an electric shock. (It is another odd fact that very many successful mediums become physically large, as if to compensate for this draining effect; those who—like Home—remain thin often seem to die young.)

According to Long, each of man's three "selves" possesses its own astral (or "shadowy") body. He says: "[Mana] is electrical in its nature and shows strong magnetic qualities. The invisible substance through which the vital force acts is called aka, or "shadowy body stuff." When Long considered the Huna word for the lower self, unihipili, he was puzzled that it contained the root pili, meaning sticky. What was sticky, he later concluded, was the "shadowy body," which sticks to anything we contact or see, like the glue on fly paper. This explains how psychometry works: the "stickiness" transfers itself through touch, and can be "read" by a "paragnost." This stickiness can be drawn out into long, fine threads, like spiderweb; and, according to the kahunas, these filaments are the conductors of psychic force. Telepathy operates by means of these telephone wires of aka; people who have "out of the body" experiences remained connected to the physical body by a cord of this substance.

The "electrical" nature of mana also explains why so many poltergeists seem to be associated with electrical forces. The clergyman in the Esther Cox case was convinced that her powers were basically electrical. And in the case of the Rosenheim poltergeist, which occurred in a small town near Munich in the mid-1960s, all the early manifestations were electrical; strip lights exploded, electrical apparatus failed to function, and even a one and a half volt battery registered three volts. The telephone registered enormous numbers of calls to the "speaking clock"—far more per minute than could actually be dialed—and the investigator Hans Bender, realized that the poltergeist must be getting through direct to the relays. (This need not imply that the poltergeist understood the telephone system; bursts of electrical energy could trip the relays.*)

It is also worth noting that one of the commonest delusions of mental patients is that they are being subjected to persecution by electric shocks—which could be explained as an excess of unused *mana*.

How does the poltergeist use this energy? Here again, scientific observation has produced a great deal of data. Objects are not thrown in the normal way, for they can change direction in mid-air; they seem to be "carried" by the poltergeist. (Diane Pritchard described to me her sensation of being somehow enveloped in the energy as the poltergeist dragged her upstairs.) Why this should be so is another of those "laws" of poltergeist phenomena which we can observe, but for which we have no explanation. It may be that the poltergeist cannot convert this energy into the ordinary kinetic energy necessary for throwing. And this, in turn, underlines Guy Playfair's point that poltergeists do not seem to live in our "dimension." This may explain how they can cause "interpenetration of matter"—like the Borley ghost, which caused

---

* There is a full account of the case in my book *Mysteries*.

bottles from a shed to hurtle into the hall through locked doors, or the "black monk" who emptied eggs from a box when Jean Pritchard was sitting on the lid. This whole phenomenon is again connected with oddities for which we have no explanation. "Apports" are usually warm, and in many cases, objects that have been thrown are heavier than before they were thrown.

Another oddity is that poltergeist noises do not seem to be normal sounds; when analyzed on a graph they show a "ramp function" which is unlike the "gradual curve" of a normal sound of knuckles rapping on wood. They are like noises manufactured in an electronics lab. Yet there seems to be an "interface," a point of connection, between the "dimension" of the poltergeist and "our world"; when Bill Haylock spoke—in the Enfield case—he somehow used Janet's vocal cords.

We have also noted, in the course of this book, that poltergeists seem—to a limited extent—to be capable of "possessing" human beings. In a book called *The Supernatural in Cornwall*, Michael Williams has described a case that took place at St. Issey in 1941, when poltergeist disturbances began in a small cottage immediately after the death of a baby girl. A nine-year-old boy—brother of the dead child—was suspected of causing some of the effects. The boy admitted this was so, but said that he had been somehow forced to get up from the settee and lift a table. A witness spied on the boy when he was alone in the living room, and saw him throw a tin can across the room—whereupon the tin rose of its own accord and flew back. But the local vicar was unconvinced, and accused the boy of causing all the phenomena. Convinced of his innocence, the boy's mother tied his hands behind his back with a belt and sent him into the scullery; and, as they watched through the door, they saw pots, pans and chairs dancing round the room. When the boy was sent away, the phenomena ceased. Here it seems clear that the shock of his sister's death caused the kind of "energy leak" that gave the poltergeist its energy. But it was also able to force the boy to throw things. This should be borne in mind in considering Podmore's comment that poltergeists are usually children throwing things. No doubt this is often true; and in some of the cases, the child is unable to help it.

This, then, seems to be the sum of what we know, and what we can deduce, about the poltergeist. It is not, perhaps, a great deal; yet it is surely enough for us to assert that the poltergeist, like the duck-billed platypus, really exists, and that some of its habits have now been positively established.

One interesting question still clamors for an answer. Why does the malice of the poltergeist seem to be so distinctly limited? They could quite easily kill; yet there is no recorded case in which they have done so. Heavy wardrobes miss people by a fraction of an inch; fires break out in locked cupboards and drawers a few minutes before they are "accidentally" discovered. Is there some psychic "law" that prevents poltergeists from being more destructive? Or does the answer lie—as the kahunas declare—in the nature of the poltergeist itself? They assert that a poltergeist is a "low spirit" that has somehow become separated from its proper middle and high spirit. Unlike the middle spirit, it possesses memory; but it has only the most rudimentary powers of reason. It may be mischievous, but it is not evil. Only the middle spirit is capable of evil—of directed, murderous malice. So, according to the kahunas, the poltergeist is only capable of such malice when it is directed by a human magician.

As usual, the conclusion seems to be that, where evil is concerned, human beings have a monopoly.

BIBLIOGRAPHY

Alexander, Marc. *Haunted Inns*. London: Frederick Muller, Ltd., 1973.

Bennett, Sir Ernest. *Apparitions and Haunted Houses. A Survey of Evidence*. London: Faber & Faber, Ltd., 1939.

Bond, Frederick Bligh. *The Gate of Remembrance*. Oxford: Basil Blackwell, 1921.

Buchanan, Joseph Rodes. *Manual of Psychometry. The Dawn of a New Civilization*. Boston: Published by author, 1885.

Burton, Jean. *Heyday of a Wizard*. London: George Harrap & Co., 1948.

Charters, Daphne. *A True Fairy Tale* (Privately printed).

Crowe, Catherine. *The Night Side of Nature or Ghosts and Ghosts Seers*. London: George Routledge and Sons, Ltd.

Dingwall, Eric J. *Abnormal Hypnotic Phenomena*, Vols. 1-4. London: J. & A. Churchill, Ltd., 1967-8.

_____. *Very Peculiar People. Portrait Studies in the Queer, the Abnormal and the Uncanny*. London: Rider & Company.

Douglas, Alfred. *Extra-Sensory Powers*. London: Victor Gollancz, Ltd., 1976.

Doyle, Arthur Conan, *The Coming of the Fairies*. New York: Samuel Weiser, 1921.

Dupreyat, André. *Mitsinari. Twenty-One Years Among the Papuans*. London and New York: Staples Press, Inc., 1954.

Ebon, Martin. *Exorcism: Fact Not Fiction*. New York: New American Library, 1974.

Fodor, Nandor. *Haunted People. The Poltergeist Down the Ages*. New York: Dutton, 1951.

_____. *On the Trail of the Poltergeist*. New York: The Citadel Press, 1958.

_____. *The Haunted Mind. A Psychoanalyst Looks at the Supernatural*. New York: Garrett Publications, 1959.

Fortune, Dion. *Psychic Self Defence. A Study in Occult Pathology and Criminality*. London: The Aquarian Press, 1930.

Gardner, Edward L. *Fairies. The Cottingley Photographs and their sequel*. London: The Theosophical Publishing House, Ltd., 1966 (First pub. 1945).

Gauld, Alan and Cornell, A. D. *Poltergeists*. London: Routledge & Kegan Paul, 1979.

Goss, Michael. *Poltergeists: An Annotated Bibliography of Works in English, circa 1880-1975*. Metuchen, NJ & London: The Scarecrow Press, Inc., 1979.

Grant, Douglas. *The Cock Lane Ghost*. London, Toronto & New York: Macmillan & Co., Ltd., 1965.

Graves, Tom and Hoult, Janet. *The Essential T. C. Lethbridge*. London: Routledge & Kegan Paul, 1980.

Halifax, Lord. *Ghost Book*. London: Geoffrey Bles, 1936.

Hall, Trevor H. *Search for Harry Price*. London: Gerald Duckworth & Co., Ltd., 1978.

Haynes, Renée. *The Hidden Springs. An Enquiry into Extra-Sensory Perception*. London: Hutchinson & Co., Ltd., 1973. (First pub. Hollis & Carter, 1961.)

Head, Joseph and Cranston, S. L. *Reincarnation*. New York: The Julian Press, Inc., 1967.

Hodson, Geoffrey. *Fairies at Work and at Play*. London: The Theosophical Publishing House, Ltd., 1925.

Hoffman, Enid. *Huna: A Beginner's Guide*. Massachusetts: Para Research, Inc., 1976.

Inglis, Brian. *Natural and Supernatural. A History of the Paranormal*. London: Hodder & Stoughton, 1977 .

Jenkins, Stephen. *The Undiscovered Country. Adventures into Other Dimensions*. Suffolk: Neville Spearman, 1977.

Kardec, Allan. *The Spirits' Book containing The Principles of Spiritist Doctrine*. São Paulo: Lake—Livraria Allan Kardec Editora Ltda, 1972.

_____. *The Medium's Book* (Being the sequel to *The Spirits' Book*). London: Psychic Press, Ltd., 1971.

Knight, David C. *The ESP Reader*. New York: Grosset & Dunlap, Inc., 1969.

Lang, Andrew. *Cock Lane and Common-Sense*. London and New York: Longmans, Green & Co., 1894.

Lombroso, Cesare. *After Death—What? Spiritistic Phenomena and their Interpretation.* London: T. Fisher Unwin, 1909.

Long, Max Freedom. *The Secret Science Behind Miracles.* California: Huna Research Publications, 1948.

_____. *The Huna Code in Religions.* California: DeVorss & Co., 1965.

MacKenzie, Andrew. *Apparitions and Ghosts. A Modern Study.* London: Arthur Barker Ltd., 1971.

Manning, Matthew. *The Strangers.* London: W. H. Allen, 1978.

Monroe, Robert A. *Journeys Out of the Body.* London: Souvenir Press, 1972.

Myers, F. W. H. *Human Personality and its Survival of Bodily Death.* New York: University Books, Inc., 1961.

Neal, James H. *Ju-ju in My Life.* London: George G. Harrap & Co., Ltd., 1966.

Oesterreich, T. K. *Possession. Demoniacal and Other among Primitive Races, in Antiquity, the Middle Ages, and Modern Times.* London: Kegan Paul, Trench, Trübner & Co., Ltd., 1930.

Owen, Robert Dale. *Footfalls on the Boundary of Another World.* London: Trübner & Co., 1860.

_____. *The Debatable Land between This World and the Next.* London: Trübner & Co., 1874.

Owen, A. R. G. *Can We Explain the Poltergeist?* New York: Garrett Publications, 1964.

Playfair, Guy Lyon, *The Flying Cow. Research into Paranormal Phenomena in the World's Most Psychic Country*. London: Souvenir Press, 1975.

_____. *The Indefinite Boundary. An Investigation into the Relationship between Matter and Spirit*. London: Souvenir Press, 1976.

_____. *This House is Haunted. An Investigation of the Enfield Poltergeist*. London: Souvenir Press, 1980.

_____. and Scott Hill, *The Cycles of Heaven. Cosmic Forces and What they are Doing to You*. London: Souvenir Press, 1978.

Powell, Arthur E. *The Etheric Double and Allied Phenomena*. USA: The Theosophical Publishing House, 1925; reprinted in 1969.

_____. *The Astral Body and other astral phenomena*. USA: The Theosophical Publishing House, 1927; reprinted to 1972.

Price, Harry. *Confessions of a Ghost-Hunter*. London: Putnam, 1936.

_____. *Fifty Years of Psychical Research. A Critical Survey*. London: Longmans, Green & Co., 1939.

_____. *The Most Haunted House in England*. London: Longmans, Green & Co., 1940.

_____. *Poltergeist Over England. Three Centuries of Mischievous Ghosts*. London: Country Life, Ltd., 1945.

_____. *The End of Borley Rectory*. London: George G. Harrap & Co., Ltd., 1946.

Prince, Morton. *The Dissociation of A Personality. A Biographical Study in Abnormal Psychology.* London: Longmans, Green & Co.; and USA: University Press, 1905.

_____. *Contributions to Psychology. The Doris Case of Quintuple Personality and others.* Boston: Richard G. Badger, 1916.

Richet, Charles. *Thirty Years of Psychical Research. Being A Treatise on Metapsychics.* London: W. Collins Sons & Co., Ltd., 1923.

Roll, William G. *The Poltergeist.* New York: New American Library, 1972.

Scott, Cyril, introduced by. *The Boy Who Saw True: anonymous.* London: Neville Spearman, 1953.

Shepard, Leslie, *Encyclopedia of Occultism & Parapsychology,* vols. 1-2. Detroit: Gale Research Company, 1978. (Compiled from Lewis Spence, *Encyclopaedia of the Occult.* London: 1920; and Nandor Fodor, *Encyclopaedia of Psychic Science.* London: 1934, with additional material ed. by Leslie Shepard.)

Smith, Susy, *The Enigma of Out-of-Body Travel.* New York: New American Library, 1965.

St. Clair, David, *Drum and Candle. First-hand experiences and accounts of voodoo and spiritism.* London: Macdonald, 1971.

Tabori, Paul. *Harry Price. The Biography of a Ghost-Hunter.* London: The Athenaeum Press, 1950 and Sphere Books, 1974.

Thurston, Herbert. *Ghosts and Poltergeists*. London: Burns Oates and Washbourne, Ltd., 1953.

Tyrrell, G. N. M. *Science and Psychical Phenomena and Apparitions*. New York:, University Books, 1961.

Wickland, Carl A. *Thirty Years Among The Dead*. California: National Psychological Institute, 1924.

Wilson, Colin. *The Occult*. London: Hodder & Stoughton, 1971.

_____. *Mysteries*. London: Hodder & Stoughton, 1978.

Wolman, Benjamin B. *Handbook of Parapsychology*. USA: Litton Educational Publishing, Inc., 1977.

INDEX

STAY IN TOUCH

On the following pages you will find books on related subjects. Your book dealer stocks most of these and will stock new Llewellyn titles as they become available. We urge your patronage.

You may also request our bimonthly catalog, *Llewellyn's New Worlds of Mind and Spirit*. A sample copy is free, and it will continue coming to you at no cost as long as you are an active mail customer. Or you may subscribe for just $7.00 in the U.S.A. and Canada ($20.00 overseas, first class mail). Many bookstores also have *New Worlds* available to their customers. Ask for it.

Llewellyn's New Worlds of Mind and Spirit
P.O. Box 64383-883, St. Paul, MN 55164-0383, U.S.A.
* * *

TO ORDER BOOKS AND TAPES

You may order books directly from the publisher by sending full price in U.S. funds, plus $3.00 for postage and handling for orders *under* $10.00; $4.00 for orders *over* $10.00. There are no postage and handling charges for orders over $50.00. Postage and handling rates are subject to change. We ship UPS whenever possible. Delivery guaranteed. Provide your street address as UPS does not deliver to P.O. Boxes. Allow 4-6 weeks for delivery. UPS to Canada requires a $50.00 minimum order. Orders outside the U.S.A. and Canada: Airmail—add retail price of book; add $5.00 for each non-book item (tapes, etc.); add $1.00 per item for surface mail. For customer service, call 1-612-291-1970.

FOR GROUP STUDY AND PURCHASE

Our special quantity price for a minimum order of five copies of *Poltergeist* is $17.85 cash-with-order. This price includes postage and handling within the United States. Minnesota residents must add 6.5% sales tax. For additional quantities, please order in multiples of five. For Canadian and foreign orders, add postage and handling charges as above. Mail orders to:

LLEWELLYN PUBLICATIONS
P.O. Box 64383-883, St. Paul, MN 55164-0383, U.S.A.

EXTRA-TERRESTRIALS AMONG US
by George C. Andrews

According to a law already on the books, which may be activated whenever the government wishes to enforce it, anyone found guilty of E.T. contact is to be quarantined indefinitely under armed guard. Does that sound like the government doesn't take Extra-Terrestrials seriously? This book blows the lid off the government's cover-up about UFOs and their occupants, setting the stage for a "Cosmic Watergate."

Author George Andrews researched the evidence concerning E.T. intervention in human affairs for more than a decade before presenting his startling conclusions. *Extra-Terrestrials Among Us* is an exciting challenge to "orthodox" thinking and will certainly broaden your perception of the world we live in.

This well-written book presents fascinating and documented case histories of cattle mutilations, lights in the sky, circular flying machines, strange disappearances, objects falling from the sky and spontaneous combustion. You are given direct information as to why E.Ts are here, case history descriptions of the varying appearances, and what they are trying to accomplish. You will also learn how to determine whether an alien contact is beneficial or harmful.

Here also is the story of CIA involvement, Nazi contacts, Martian landings, and much more. If you believe in E.T.s, or if you're not really sure, *Extra-Terrestrials Among Us* will open your eyes to new worlds—some existing right here on earth! Actual photos included.

0-87542-001-X, 304 pgs., mass market, illus. $4.95

COMPANY OF PROPHETS:
African American Psychics, Healers & Visionaries
by Joyce Elaine Noll

This is a unique and significant collection of supernatural and ethnic materials never before arranged in one volume! *Company of Prophets* describes African Americans born in the United States who have extrasensory perception, psychic abilities and spiritual gifts, in a time frame from the 17th century to the present.

This book adds to the historical data not previously available on African Americans, unearthed through recent nationwide interviews and research. It features people from all ages and walks of life, including contemporary and historical leaders in education, business, theology and the arts. They share their experiences with astral projection, soul travel, levitation, healing, past lives, channeling and divination. In their own words, gifted subjects provide practical advice and workable techniques to assist readers in increasing their own psychic awareness.

Discover how Harriet Tubman used her ESP to bring slaves safely North to freedom; how an internationally known sculptor astral projects to perfect his work; how a child learned to gather, cook and use herbs from disembodied Indian spirits. These are just a few of the amazing reports in *Company of Prophets*. With photos!

0-87542-583-6, 272 pgs., 6 x 9, softcover $12.95

EXPLORING THE FOURTH DIMENSION:
Secrets of the Paranormal
by John Ralphs

Just when you thought you'd read everything about paranormal phenomena, John Ralphs offers new theoretical concepts for research and consideration into the nature of poltergeists, out-of-body experiences, telepathy and UFOs.

Whether you are a believer or skeptic, Ralphs' theory of the "fourth" dimension as a logical explanation for paranormal activity is certain to open your mind, stimulate discussion— even alter your concept of reality.

Ralphs suggests that the universe and all material things exist in four dimensions and have a shape in a fourth dimension. So far, no one has proven that a fourth dimension cannot exist—and it can even be calculated mathematically.

The fourth dimension theory can explain a vast array of phenomena including spirit communication, movements of objects through space and time, automatic writing, deja vu, clairvoyance, and dowsing.

Even the human mind has the ability to operate in four dimensions. With this book, you can learn to train your mind to break the boundaries of normal perception and access the fourth and other dimensions, tapping into the infinite body of universal knowledge available to you.
0-87542-655-7, 256 pgs., 6 x 9, illus., softcover $9.95

HOW TO MEET & WORK WITH SPIRIT GUIDES
by Ted Andrews

We often experience spirit contact in our lives but fail to recognize it for what it is. Now you can learn to access and attune to beings such as guardian angels, nature spirits and elementals, spirit totems, archangels, gods and goddesses—as well as family and friends after their physical death.

Contact with higher soul energies strengthens the will and enlightens the mind. Through a series of simple exercises, you can safely and gradually increase your awareness of spirits and your ability to identify them. You will learn to develop an intentional and directed contact with any number of spirit beings. Discover meditations to open up your subconscious. Learn which acupressure points effectively stimulate your intuitive faculties. Find out how to form a group for spirit work, use crystal balls, perform automatic writing, attune your aura for spirit contact, use sigils to contact the great archangels and much more! Read *How to Meet and Work with Spirit Guides* and take your first steps through the corridors of life beyond the physical.

0-87542-008-7, 192 pgs., mass market, illus. $3.95

THE LLEWELLYN PRACTICAL GUIDE
TO ASTRAL PROJECTION
The Out-of-Body Experience
by Denning & Phillips

Yes, your consciousness can be sent forth, out of the body, with full awareness and return with full memory. You can travel through time and space, converse with nonphysical entities, obtain knowledge by nonmaterial means, and experience higher dimensions.

Is there life after death? Are we forever shackled by time and space? The ability to go forth by means of the Astral Body, or Body of Light, gives the personal assurance of consciousness (and life) beyond the limitations of the physical body. No other answer to these ageless questions is as meaningful as experienced reality.

The reader is led through the essential stages for the inner growth and development that will culminate in fully conscious projection and return. Not only are the requisite practices set forth in step-by-step procedures, augmented with photographs and visualization aids, but the vital reasons for undertaking them are clearly explained. Beyond this, the great benefits from the various practices themselves are demonstrated in renewed physical and emotional health, mental discipline, spiritual attainment, and the development of extra faculties.

Guidance is also given to the Astral World itself: what to expect, what can be done—including the ecstatic experience of Astral Sex between two people who project together into this higher world where true union is consummated free of the barriers of physical bodies.

0-87542-181-4, 266 pgs., 5-1/4 x 8, illus. $8.95

THE LLEWELLYN PRACTICAL GUIDE TO THE DEVELOPMENT OF PSYCHIC POWERS
by Denning & Phillips

You may not realize it, but you already have the ability to use ESP, Astral Vision and Clairvoyance, Divination, Dowsing, Prophecy, and Communication with Spirits.

Written by two of the most knowledgeable experts in the world of psychic development, this book is a complete course—teaching you, step-by-step, how to develop these powers that actually have been yours since birth. Using the techniques, you will soon be able to move objects at a distance, see into the future, know the thoughts and feelings of another person, find lost objects and locate water using your no-longer latent talents.

Psychic powers are as much a natural ability as any other talent. You'll learn to play with these new skills, working with groups of friends to accomplish things you never would have believed possible before reading this book. The text shows you how to make the equipment you can use, the exercises you can do—many of them at any time, anywhere—and how to use your abilities to change your life and the lives of those close to you. Many of the exercises are presented in forms that can be adapted as games for pleasure and fun, as well as development.

0-87542-191-1, 272 pgs., 5-1/4 x 8, illus. $8.95

THE LLEWELLYN PRACTICAL GUIDE TO PSYCHIC SELF-DEFENSE AND WELL-BEING
by Denning & Phillips

Psychic well-being and psychic self-defense are two sides of the same coin, just as are physical health and resistance to disease. Each person (and every living thing) is surrounded by an electromagnetic force field, or AURA, that can provide the means to psychic self-defense and to dynamic well-being. This book explores the world of very real "psychic warfare" of which we are all victims.

Every person in our modern world is subjected to psychic stress and psychological bombardment: advertising promotions that play upon primitive emotions, political and religious appeals that work on feelings of insecurity and guilt, noise, threats of violence and war, news of crime and disaster, etc.

This book shows the nature of genuine psychic attacks—ranging from actual acts of black magic to bitter jealousy and hate—and the reality of psychic stress, the structure of the psyche and its interrelationship with the physical body. It shows how each person must develop his weakened aura into a powerful defense-shield, thereby gaining both physical protection and energetic well-being that can extend to protection from physical violence, accidents . . . even ill health.

0-87542-190-3, 306 pgs., 5-1/4 x 8, illus. $8.95

BEYOND HYPNOSIS
A Program for Developing Your Psychic
& Healing Powers
by William Hewitt
This book contains a complete system for using hypnosis
to enter a beneficial altered state of consciousness in order
to develop your psychic abilities. Here is a 30-day program
(just 10 to 20 minutes per day is all it takes!) to release
your psychic awareness and then hone it to a fine skill
through a series of mental exercises that anyone can do!

Beyond Hypnosis lets you make positive changes in your
life. You will find yourself doing things that you only
dreamed about in the past, including easy and safe out-
of-body travel and communication with spiritual, nonphysical entities. Speed up your learning and reading
abilities and retain more of the information you study. A
must for students of all kinds! *Beyond Hypnosis* shows
you how to create your own reality, how to reshape your
own life and the lives of others—and ultimately how to
reshape the world and beyond what we call this world!
This book will introduce you to a beneficial altered state
of consciousness which is achieved by using your own
natural abilities to control your mind. It is in this state
where you will learn to expand your psychic abilities
beyond belief!
0-87542-305-1, 240 pgs., 5-1/4 x 8, softcover $7.95

1/18

GHOSTS, HAUNTINGS & POSSESSIONS
The Best of Hans Holzer, Book I
Edited by Raymond Buckland
The best stories from best-selling author and psychic investigator, Hans Holzer—in mass market format!

- A psychic visited with the spirit of Thomas Jefferson at Monticello. What scandals surrounded his life that history books don't tell us?
- The exact transcript of a seance confrontation with Elvis Presley—almost a year after his death!
- Ordinary people had premonitions about the murders of John and Robert Kennedy. Here are their stories.
- Abraham Lindoln's prophetic dream of his own funeral. Does his ghost still roam the White House?

0-87542-367-1, 288 pgs., mass market **$4.95**

ESP, WITCHES & UFOS:
The Best of Hans Holzer, Book II
Edited by Raymond Buckland
Best-selling author and psychic investigator Hans Holzer explores true accounts of the strange and unknown: telepathy, psychic and reincarnation dreams, survival after death, psycho-ecstasy, unorthodox healings, Pagans, Witches, and Ufonauts. Reports include:

- How you can use four simple "wish-fulfillment" steps to achieve psycho-ecstasy.
- Several true accounts of miraculous healings achieved by unorthodox medical practitioners.
- The reasons why more and more people are turning to Witchcraft and Paganism as a way of life.
- When UFOs land: physical evidence vs. cultists.

These reports and many more will entertain and enlighten all readers intrigued by the mysteries of life!

0-87542-368-X, 304 pgs., mass market **$4.95**